THE
LANGUAGE
OF
RESPECT

The Right of
  Each
  Student to
  Participate in an
  Environment of
  Communicative
  Thoughtfulness

Ellyn Arwood and Edmund Young

Lightning Print, Inc. is a division of Ingram Book Group and Nashville-based Ingram Industries, Inc.

The Language of Respect:
The Right of Each Student to Participate in an Environment of Communicative Thoughtfulness

Lightning Print, Inc. is a division of Ingram Book Group
Paperback edition, April 2000

For information contact:
Lightning Print, Inc., a division of Ingram Book Group
www.ingrambook.com
or
Apricot, Inc., PO Box 18191, Portland, OR 97218
www.spiritone.com/~apricot

ISBN 0-9679720-0-0

Lightning Print, Inc. is a division of Ingram Book Group and Nashville-based Ingram Industries, Inc.

Printed in the United States of America

To our families

CONTENTS

Preface

Who is a great teacher? Is it someone who has knowledge about "what works" in a classroom? Is a great teacher someone who has been a good student? Is a great teacher a living model of how to learn? Whatever the reader's personal answer, ancient history signals the "great teacher" as a philosopher, mentor, coach, leader...*a person to be respected and to respect.* For example, Aristotle, Plato, St. Thomas Aquinas are often referred to as "The Teacher" not to mention that Socrates has present day teaching methodologies named after him (Socratic Method). More current history points to great teachers as personal idols of belief, commitment, and leadership...Mahatma Ghandi, Martin Luther King, and Susan B. Anthony to name a few. These great men and women are regarded in history as philosophers as well as teachers because they ask themselves questions about their universe and they seek to add knowledge to the answers of such questions. And, though each of these great teachers challenged the beliefs and knowledge of many, they **respect**ed the rights of others to be challenged. They could use what they learned to advance not only their own needs, but to advance the needs of others through their language. These "great teachers" advocated for the **respect** of humankind. It was through their willingness to communicate such **respect** that others were challenged.

Today, most educators don't expect to be another Ghandi or Socrates, but they may have the makings of such a great person just waiting to fulfill their potential within the classroom. Today, teachers have the awesome task of creating an environment where the next Socrates could flourish while promoting the human wholeness and well being of all class members. Today, teacher education programs often ask preservice teachers to write or reflect about a great teacher that they experienced. Most write about how this person inspired them to learn, challenged them to create, and most of all treated them with thoughtful acts of **respect**. When students are asked to describe what they would change about the schools today, they often talk about getting rid of mean teachers, teachers who don't care because they don't treat the students with **respect,** teachers who name call, teachers who can't stay focused or organized to assist all students. In addition to changing the way students are treated by teachers, students ask that their basic needs such as their food, environment, and school interactions reflect what most of us expect at home, a safe and healthy environment.

But, to create a school environment where students feel treated the way we want to be treated means that a personal philosophy as well as theoretical basis for education must be individually developed by teachers. Most teachers cannot describe their own personal philosophy for the classroom while also addressing how methods and practices adhere to that philosophy for maximum learning. Furthermore, educators are not trained to use language to promote maximum learning. When students don't meet teachers' expectations, then the teaching process becomes even more objectified by teachers trying to emphasize products, not the learners. **Respect** for the learner as an individual contributing to the whole is lost.   **Respect** for the teachers' colleagues is lost to controlling the environment.   And, most importantly, the individual's learning needs are lost to the mediocrity of a group being more important than the individual. **Language** tools, such as the ability to read, write or speak also deteriorate.

The purpose of this text is to provide preservice and inservice educators, specialists, as well as parents and administrators with knowledge about a classroom atmosphere where language is used as a tool to foster **RESPECT,** the cornerstone to creating an environment that is safe for all learners. **RESPECT is defined as the *Right of Each Student to Participate in an Environment of Communicative Thoughtfulness*. And, language is defined as the neurobiological tool used to communicate, develop, and learn "respect."**

These authors have 55 years of combined educational experience. Their values, beliefs and techniques have been positive for parents and students and for each of these authors' own children. What is unique for these authors is that their experiences necessitate a cultural paradigm shift from an *authoritarian* approach to education and parenting to an *authoritative* approach. This latter approach affords learners the opportunity to feel included, to feel successful, and to develop life long language skills for social and cognitive responsibility, **respect,** and interdependence.

Philosophically, the authors find the following beliefs to be central to creating an effective daily reality that reflects the paradigm shift:
- respect is central to human interaction
- respect is part of *learned* communicative thoughtfulness
- all students can learn
- all students have strengths that can be used for social and cognitive growth or maximum learning as a responsive citizen
- all students create the classroom parameters (the quality, the excitement factor, fun factor) through safe communication in a positive learning environment
- all students can be experts within a safe environment that respects the individual as well as the group process
- all students can learn to read, write, and use a marketable level of oral language through respecting the students' communicative learning needs
- all students deserve the right to be nurtured, supported, and protected in a healthy environment of communicative thoughtfulness much like a healthy pseudo-family
- all people including children appreciate and feel comfortable when permitted to interact within healthy boundaries and consistent limits
- language is the tool for assigning meaning and for generating learning necessary for the aforementioned beliefs
- language originates from an interactive social and cognitive neurobiological process

In addition to their years of experience, these authors have a theoretical background in learning. Dr. Arwood's expertise is in language and its relationship to how learning occurs. She has been the director of an effective model school (TEACUP*) which provided students with positive change and she is the author of three previous textbooks and one monograph on how language affects learning. Mr. Young's expertise is in his ability to assist students in becoming citizens by creating a responsive classroom that models a healthy pseudo-family. Prior to retiring this past year, professionals from all over the world visited his unique classroom, a room safe for all learners. Visitors often left saying, "The students are so positive and empowered."

Both authors currently consult. Dr. Arwood provides training and workshops on "language based learning" through the philosophy of "pragmaticism." This term was coined by Charles Sanders Peirce in the 1800's to mean that the "whole is greater than the parts." It is from this philosophy that Dr. Arwood believes that expending the energy to create a classroom benefiting all participants offers greater life long lessons than just teaching the content or skills to students. Mr. Young continues to apply his philosophy and teaching principles to other educational ventures. Both authors have a cultural background in western and eastern philosophical training coupled with the aforementioned learning/language theory that allows for a different perspective about education, its culture, and its outcomes. So, the integration of theory and philosophy is not by accident. Mr. Young's classroom experiences are supported by Dr. Arwood's theoretical and clinical background. The combination of these two authors' ideas offers the reader a unique experience, learning about usable language methods and activities while also learning why the methods or activities will work to create a responsive learning environment for all students.

This book will describe the philosophical tenets of a safe learning environment based on the language of respect. In addition to philosophy, the theoretical basis for how different children learn followed by language-based techniques for developing the whole

---

* TEACUP. Teacher Education: A Clinical University Program. Funded by US Dept. of Education, Office of Special Education, 1991.

learner--the cognitive as well as social aspects of skills and concepts will be offered. All examples of students and teachers are "real;" but names, dates, ages and any other identifying information have been changed to protect the learners' identities. The book is also designed to challenge its readers to rethink old practices, philosophies, or even developmental levels as an educator or parent.

Learning requires a challenge of past information. So, each chapter is organized to assist the reader in refining past information about how to educate. First, a visual flowchart of the overall set of ideas is offered for those readers who learn best by seeing the whole before the parts in order to learn the concepts in focus. And, at the beginning of each chapter, a summary of principles and learner outcomes is offered in words for those who learn best by using sound based words. Activity questions are provided at the end of each section so that the reader may use the activity questions to check learning.

At the conclusion of a chapter, the reader is given the learner outcomes in the form of questions. These questions summarize the main concepts with words and the words are also given as a visually organized graphic. Throughout each chapter important principles are bolded, defined concepts are italicized, and all points are restated within each chapter and overlapped into other chapters.

The expected outcome of this book is to help educators develop the same, effective environment that Mr. Young created for years with a theoretical explanation supplied by Dr. Arwood to explain why tasks or activities work or don't work. Both authors have often been given the opportunity to work with students that other educators refused or felt they could not reach. Educators have been asking these two authors to team up for years to describe through example how to create a respectful classroom while promoting maximum learning for all individual students. Language is the glue between the philosophy and theory for the **Language of RESPECT:** *the Right of Each Student to Participate in an Environment of Communicative Thoughtfulness.*

Acknowledgments

We would like to thank the many professional colleagues, friends, and family members who have encouraged us to finalize this work. Without your support, we would not have finished the task. Your respect for us and our work is appreciated.

Chapter One

Learner Outcomes

Upon completion of this chapter, the reader will be able to do the following:

1. Define his or her own level of developmental readiness for a classroom based on the language of *respect*.
2. Assess his or her own use of self-esteem in communicating *respect* through language.
3. Recognize judgmental language as not *respect*ful.
4. Define the "who" constituents which show *respect* for one's "self."
5. Recognize the self-constituents of others in order to *respect* the needs of others.
6. Recognize language that emphasizes the listener's "who" as *respectful*.
7. Give examples of communication assumptions that interfere with the language of *respect*.
8. Give examples of communication strategies that promote the language of *respect*.
9. Give examples of communication fallacies that interfere with the language of *respect*.
10. Define the acronym "**RESPECT**."

CHAPTER ONE

Developmental Awareness of the Language of RESPECT

Are we developmentally ready to respect others?

We gaze into the fog,
Little is clear, but all is apparent.
We know not why we gaze,
But we know what we expect.
We see all--but nothing is there.

The differences in a classroom based on **"the Language of RESPECT"** are noticeable from the time the students enter. The following scenario is from the first day of a classroom based on the language of respect. The purpose of the scenario is to begin to paint a picture of what makes this type of classroom unique from most other classrooms. From this scenario, a beginning definition of *"the language of respect"* follows. The tools for developing *cognitive and social respect* regardless of age, sex, gender, race, economic background are found in the use of *language*. This chapter defines these language tools and subsequent chapters offer theoretical as well as philosophical underpinnings of the *"language of respect."* Upon completion of Chapter One, the reader will be provided with the opportunity to determine his or her own level of readiness for using the **"Language of RESPECT."** Upon completion of the *last* chapter, the reader is offered two more first day scenarios from the same teacher with different classrooms and with different student backgrounds for the reader to connect the *"Right of Each Student to Participate in an Environment of Communicative Thoughtfulness"* with the **"Language of RESPECT."**

Scenario

The fifth-grade students enter the classroom and all seem to notice something is not the same as they have experienced on other "first days of school." One student asks, "Where are the pictures?" Mr. Smith, the teacher, calls the attention of the class and points out that a *member of the class has made a very important observation.* He asks everyone to take a seat and he asks the student, Mr. Flanders, to repeat his question, "Where's all the pictures?" Mr. Smith asks Mr. Flanders to stand up so that everyone in the class will know to whom to *give their complete attention. The students are learning that their ideas are important.*

Mr. Flanders stands up while busily looking around to see what the other students are doing. He repeats his question while standing, "Where are all the pictures?" A few students begin to shout out answers or possibilities. Mr. Smith then asks the class, "To whom should we pay attention? There are *several people with good ideas*." Several voices blurt out their thoughts while a few voices die out. Mr. Smith smiles and says, "Thank you to those of you who *chose to listen* instead of shouting-out your answers. I can see that this going to be a great class!" *The students are learning that behavior which facilitates the group's functioning is personally rewarding.*

Mr. Smith then asks, "Who can remember the basic rule of this class?" One young lady raises her hand immediately and replies, "We have to raise our hands first if we want to talk." Mr. Smith replies, "Great answer, Miss Sommers. Miss Sommers, do you have any ideas about our bare walls?" *The students are learning that the way a person shares ideas is as important as the idea.*

Miss Sommers stands in response to a *hand prompt* by Mr. Smith. She suggests, "You were too busy to do the pictures." Mr. Smith *validates* her, "That is very true, but I honestly did have some time left over. I *chose* to work on some ideas for our first school assembly. The truth is that the walls belong to you, too. This is *your classroom* isn't it?" Heads nod. Mr. Smith continues, "We will all be here in this very classroom for nine months. Don't you think that *you deserve* to have some ideas as to what pictures go up on the walls?" Several hands go up. *The students are learning that Mr. Smith believes that they are capable of making choices and determining what is appropriate for their space.*

Mr. Smith points to Mr. Taylor, another student. Mr. Taylor stands up and says, "I think we can bring some posters from home. I have a picture of Michael Jordan making a basket." Mr. Smith thanks Mr. Taylor and writes Mr. Taylor's name on the chalkboard next to a *stick figure and the words,* "Michael Jordan poster." *The students are learning that all individuals have something to contribute.*

Hands are flying up all over the classroom. Within minutes, there are *promises* to bring posters, pictures of vacations, charts of what "little girls and boys are made of," a map of Disneyland, and more. Mr. Smith *records all ideas* on the board and *accepts* all possibilities. *The students are learning that all ideas given in earnest are respected.*

As the morning proceeds, the students have their *chosen seats* with the thought that they may keep those seats unless "the seat causes a problem." At that time, Mr. Smith has the right to choose another seat for the student. It's a deal! *The students are learning that their choices have consequences.*

Introductions are now the next item of business, despite the fact that the *first* bell has rung during their *discussion* of how the classroom should be decorated. Mr. Smith leads off by telling them his full name, but out of *respect* he would prefer to be called Mr. Smith. He tells the students about his birthplace, his family members, his leisure time activities, his teaching experiences, and some of his dreams (to own a sports car, to go on an African safari, to visit as much of the world as possible, and to win a photo contest). *Students are learning about themselves as well as about their classmates.*

Mr. Smith then writes the words: Name, favorite color, favorite TV show, favorite sport, favorite food on the chalkboard. Since this is a 5th grade classroom, Mr. Smith *expects* the students to be able to read what he has said and written. As he finishes *writing and saying* each of the ideas, a flurry of hands stretches toward the ceiling. Mr. Smith suggests that the class simply starts introductions from the first row and goes around the classroom "so that there is a *system.*" *The students are learning that a systematic or organized approach to a task respects the needs of many.*

As each student recites, Mr. Smith takes down the student responses on his laptop computer. At the end of the activity, he asks, "Would you like to see if I have it all correct?" Nods are seen and a few "yes's" are heard. Mr. Smith *thanks* those who nodded and did not blurt out their answers. With that he *prints* out the record of introductions. The students beam and some hang their heads in bashful poses as they hear their own responses read by the teacher from the printed list. *The students are learning that an adult thinks their ideas are so important that their ideas are written and shared.*

From this reading, several students want to add activities or comments to the list. Mr. Smith points to the schedule written on the chalkboard under "Today's Schedule." He points out that he is 12 minutes off schedule, but *if he could, he would like to transfer* the responses to the computer that sits next to the door. He then tells the students that any *student who wishes to add or change* something to the introductions file may do so. *The students are learning to ask for what they need and Mr. Smith will listen.*

This is a perfect lead to the next activity, "computer skills check." Many of the students are old hands at working the computer, but two students who have transferred in from elsewhere, do not raise their hands when Mr. Smith asks the class who can "boot" a computer and find a file? Mr. Smith *notes this information* in his grade book and the class goes on to the next activity.

Mr. Smith *asks the students* why the reference books are stored on three different shelves in different parts of the room. *Students learn, again, that speakers are chosen when they raise their hands and that they are expected to stand when they answer. The students learn that "convenience" to all class members is a form of respect.* Mr. Smith *explains* that if the encyclopedias were all stored by the windows, then the students at desks farthest from the windows would have long walks to the reference books. Furthermore, the students closest to the reference books would have a better chance of getting books that they wanted when there were research activities. *Convenience for everyone* in the classroom **is** appropriate. *Using language to decide what is convenient is also appropriate.* Everyone agrees. **The students are learning that conventional language tools are used for negotiating, sharing, agreeing, discussing, explaining, learning, etc.** *Students are also learning that others' needs are equally important as their own needs.*

With the *discussion* about the reference books complete, *questions* come up pertaining to their seat selections. "Would there be a chance to rotate their seats so that they could sit next to the door?" Mr. Smith does not answer but defers the question to the class by asking, "What do you think, class; how about rotating seats so that we are not left with the same seats all year long?"

A *discussion* follows. Mr. Smith nods his approval for all *objective comments*. He is silent when comments seem to favor only one person or a small group of students. In time, *the students would become experts at spotting these verbal "clues" and other body language or nonverbal signals as part of their curriculum based on the language of respect. The students are learning that the group is as strong as the individuals who make up the group. They are also learning that the group is better supported by individuals' supportive comments.*

Finally, Mr. Smith calls a halt to the activity and suggests that they *save some of their ideas* until tomorrow. Since it is the first day of school, the classes are out earlier than usual and they will be going home in 20 minutes. Mr. Smith points out that there is a stack of 3 X 5 cards on his desk. He asks who would like to pass them out to the first desk of each row? He *chooses* the first hand to fly up. *The students are learning that Mr. Smith is consistent in the way he interacts with students.*

As the students rise to get the cards, Mr. Smith *compliments* the class for *being so quiet and prepared* for the next activity. With their *order and cooperation,* he will be able to let them out right on schedule. *The students are learning that they are capable of choosing behavior that results in positive outcomes.*

As the cards are passed out, Mr. Smith *points to a drawing* on the chalkboard that has a name in the upper right hand corner of the card. It is Mr. Smith's own name. He *asks* the students to use their titles and full names, too. The silence is obvious as the class complies. *Students are learning that their quiet presence is respected as well as their spoken ideas. They are learning that the group functions for the betterment of the individuals and that each individual's learning system is to be respected by the group.*

Mr. Smith then *thanks* those who have finished their names for looking up at him. He tells them that he uses their looking as a *signal* that they are finished and are ready for the next task. *The students are learning about how individuals learn, how others' perceive them, and how to interpret others' behaviors.* Several stares intensify as if to assure Mr. Smith that they are anxious to comply. *The students are learning that Mr. Smith shows appreciation for their efforts.*

Mr. Smith rubs his chin and *asks* the class, "What is your own definition of the word '*respect*'?" He then directs, "Write or draw your own definition of the word "*respect*" without checking your dictionaries." As each student finishes writing on his or her card, Mr. Smith *uses body posturing and hand movements to quietly signal* them to bring the cards to him. He gives each student a colored tack. He does not check the definition of *respect* for content or spelling errors nor does he check the drawings for content. He simply asks the students to post their cards in a neat pattern on the bulletin board decorated with colored paper and titled with the letters, **RESPECT.** *The students are learning that any product is initially accepted as a valuable contribution.*

Mr. Smith *assures* the students that tomorrow they will have time to *refine* their definitions and that he will check for their ideas, spelling, and handwriting. Time will be given to them to check their dictionaries and even to work in small groups. He tells them that working in small groups does not mean that they are cheating. He assures them that the people who know a lot about schools and learning know that we all *feel* more comfortable working in small groups sometimes. Yet, there will be special times when working alone is the best thing. They will have that *discussion* tomorrow. *The students are learning that all products may be refined or improved and that the process for such learning is sometimes a group effort and always an individual effort.*

There are smiles of anticipation as Mr. Smith *thanks* the students for a great start on the school year and he excuses the girls first. The girls pick up their coats and form a line by the door. The boys frown at that decision. As the boys saunter over to the coats, Mr. Smith points out that gentlemen often prefer that ladies get their coats first. Yet, if that is a problem, they could have a class meeting tomorrow before recess and they could set up some class rules about who should get their coats first. *The students are learning that negotiation is always possible in this classroom.* Smiles spread across the room. The first day ends on a very positive and happy note. *The students leave the classroom believing that the relationship between the students and Mr. Smith is safe for learning.*

Mr. Smith spent the first day of class using *language* to set up the tone of *respect* for individuals, themselves, their peers, their quality of work, their ideas, their teacher's needs, and their environment. Attention is given to individual needs to *socialize* as well as to the development of a *culture of group respect.* Nonverbal as well as verbal ways to assign meaning to each person's individual needs as well as to the group needs through discussions, active listening, and *language strategies of respect* are developed. This type of classroom is unique because it appears so "simple," and yet, most educators find it difficult to create. The *language of respect* is different from most educators' past personal experiences and/or educational training. In truth, most educators do not hear the difference in the language between Mr. Smith's room and their room. But, the results are amazingly different! The students in Mr. Smith's room want to come to school. Their background does not dictate their success in Mr. Smith's room and their love for learning doesn't end when they leave his classroom. These students learn life long lessons about how to be a citizen. In order to begin to recognize the uniqueness in this classroom, the next section defines the *"language of respect"* followed by strategies and examples.

Activity

1. **List some language tools used the first day of class to set the learning tone (italics have been used to mark some of the examples).**
2. **Explain one way that Mr. Smith defined *respect* on the first day of class.**

Defining the Language of RESPECT

Respect seems simple. Most adults typically think that they know what **"respect"** means. And most adults are sure that they are *respectful*. *But, "respect" is a concept that is defined by multiple meanings that cannot be readily shown with individual pictures or simple words.* The purpose of this chapter is to help the reader to determine whether or not his or her *"language"* is developmentally ready to create "RESPECT."

Language develops from concepts that function as cognitive tools. A concept such as "RESPECT" is developmentally learned or acquired as part of the language system. The tone of the classroom is based on the teacher's language of *respect* for himself or herself as well as for the *respect* of others. However, to "teach" *respect*, the teacher creates multiple language opportunities throughout the year to provide the students with ways to communicate and to demonstrate acts of *respect*. With multiple opportunities to use the language of *respect*, the learners also acquire a higher developmental understanding of the concept of *"respect."* Likewise, the teacher will need to maintain lots of "self-respect" to continue that first-day enthusiasm of providing the language of **RESPECT**.

By dictionary definition, **respect** *has something to do with honoring another or one's own esteem* (American Heritage, 1987). But, if an adult is to foster *respect* in a student, then the adult most also know how to *respect* oneself, that is to know one's SELF. The "self" is made of many parts including, but not limited to, self-esteem, self-concept, and self-awareness. These parts are formed from "constituents." Chapter One examines how to know one's "self" through defining the "constituents" and how to know others as the first step of defining **the language of RESPECT.** *Language refers to a system of signs and symbols to communicate thoughts, feelings, and ideas.* Therefore, **the language of RESPECT refers to the way a person communicates with another person to show "honor" or "respect" for the other person as well as a positive value for one's "self."**

Activity

1. **Define respect.**
2. **Define language.**

Knowing One's "Self "

Each person's SELF consists of his or her own passions, interests, desires, thoughts, feelings, past cognitive experiences, a unique socialization process, a specific learning system, and so forth. *These components of "self" are the constituents.* The more of these constituents that a person knows, the better the person knows himself or herself. So, one indicator that reveals how well a person "knows" these pieces is to have the person self introduce. "Tell us about yourself." Most adults respond with titles, possessions, family connections, roles and responsibilities. Their language represents these roles, possessions, etc. For example, "I am Suchette Johnson. I am a social worker for Child's Only Center, a mother of two children, a wife, and the family cook."

These introductions consisting of names, roles, responsibilities, family connections, etc., are really about "what" a person does, not about "who" a person is. Suchette's introduction about "who" she is might be, "I really like to climb the Cascade Mountains on the weekends, but during the week I stay busy helping families find ways to better interact with each other. One of my most favorite things to do is to spend time with Garrett, my two-year-old, who loves to climb, run and play outdoors. I like to chase him and have him tag me and chase me back. He gets such a kick out of this event. He giggles all the way to his toes just like I do, but I guess son like Mother fits here." Suchette's second introduction is more about "who" she is.

The average healthy adult should be able to quickly self-list 10 things about their "who." These self constituents include passions (e.g., painting landscapes); interests (e.g., volunteering for the crisis line); desires (e.g., I would really like to see the real Mona Lisa); thoughts (e.g., riding in a hot air balloon); feelings (e.g., I feel sad when I think about the death of Butch, my very first dog); cognitive experiences (I think best when I read and then write about the ideas); socialization processes (e.g., I like to go to the movie theater with other people); learning system skills (e.g., I can only spell when I can clearly see the letters as a word in my head); and, so on.

These constituent categories define the "person" in terms of the **language of RESPECT**. This is why Mr. Smith asks the students to introduce themselves using constituent categories. As the year progresses, the students will refine their initial introductions to fit with what they learn about themselves. Early childhood teachers as well as elementary and middle school teachers should also be able to describe themselves using these constituents, positively describe colleagues, and provide such constituent information for each of their students. Some teachers make home visits. Some teachers send home a form letter asking parents to describe their child in terms of strengths, ambitions, interests, victories, fears, concerns, and anything else the parents want to say. The parents are "experts" about their children and they give insights that might take a teacher most of the school year to gain. High school teachers may have too many students to know many of the students' constituents, but even knowing their names and being able to assess their interests the first day by collecting a writing sample will prove beneficial in relating to the students throughout the class. The students will tell about themselves, if the adults are listening!

Teachers and parents assign constituent meaning to students and children based on the teachers' or parents' past communication experiences. These past experiences become part of what a person thinks about him or herself. *Without conscious effort to change communication strategies, many adults choose language based on these past experiences.* For example, an adult may have been told as a student that she couldn't spell. As an adult, the person, who is now a teacher, still believes she can't spell. Being defined as a non-speller has become one of her constituents. So, when a child asks this teacher about a spelling task, the teacher says, "Don't worry about the task, I can't spell either." The teacher doesn't really know herself; she knows what others have said about her. Through past experiences, the teacher learned to believe that she "can't spell." The teacher also doesn't know the child. The child likes to spell, and thinks, at least before this comment, that he is a good speller. But, the teacher's use of language assigns value to the child as a poor speller. Learning *about oneself requires recognizing past communicative experiences that have affected personal beliefs, passions, interests, desires, learning system effectiveness, etc.*

Once these aspects of one's "self" are recognized then the adult is able to think differently than past experiences dictate. For example, the classroom is busy. The teacher is tired. She grew up believing that adults are always right and children are to do only what the teacher or adult instructs. Rachael, a student, asks the teacher, "Can I take my booklet home?" The teacher automatically resorts to communication similar to her past experiences of childhood language. The teacher says, "Rachael, you weren't listening. I told you to put your booklet into the basket on my desk." Rachael is feeling embarrassed so she says, " I was listening. I want...." The teacher interrupts with the feeling of past experiences of adults telling the teacher, as a child, that she must not talk back. "Rachael, do not talk back. You are to stay in during last recess." The teacher's language devalues Rachael. Rachael puts her head down on her desk. For the next twenty minutes, Rachael does no work. She is waiting to spend her recess in punishment. Rachael spends her time in recess and sulks as she slowly walks home. At home she is angry and sassy to her mom. Rachael has spent a lot of time thinking about the communication. Rachael thinks that the teacher doesn't care about her and she feels that school "hurts." Chances are that Rachael may not volunteer, risk, or share in future classes or grade levels; being put down by a person in authority was too hurtful an experience.

Rachael just wanted to take her booklet home *after* she turned it into the teacher, but the teacher responded to Rachael's voice *before* she could hear what Rachael was asking. The teacher responded to the "what" of the situation, not the child's needs. In other words, *this teacher's language represented what others said the teacher did as a child, not what Rachael wanted.* As a result of the teacher reliving her own childhood experiences through Rachael, this teacher did not choose to respond to Rachael as an independent person with different constituents than the teacher. This teacher was meeting her own child-like needs. The teacher mixed up her own ability to control Rachael's behavior with knowing who the teacher is as a person. For this teacher, positive language tools can only be developed once the teacher knows that she is okay as a person and once she knows who she is separate from who Rachael and her students are.

A teacher who uses past ways to communicate may want to spend personal time to find out about these experiences so as to develop a clearer self-image about oneself. Some adults prefer to do this exploration with professional counselors. Some adults are able to hear the difference between utterances that communicate about the person's past behaviors or "what's" and utterances that communicate about the present person's constituents or "who." For example, this same teacher could have used positive language strategies, "Rachael, you want to take your booklet home?" Rachael probably would have said, "Yes." The teacher could then say, "Yes, after you turn the booklet into me so I can see it, I will pass it back to you. When I pass it back to you, then you may take it home. Okay?" This gives Rachael a chance to ask for clarification. *The shift in communication from emphasis on the teacher's needs to emphasis on the student's needs results in a **respectful** atmosphere that honors the thinking of both the student and the teacher. The teacher communicates **respect** for the child by listening to what the child thinks. The language shifts from being about the teacher's needs to a more natural, positive interpersonal form of communication between the child and the adult. These opportunities for personal chats build "bonds" and insights. Short 2-3 sentence chats create wonderful "moments of thoughtfulness" between teacher and student. Insights about the teacher and the student are shared during these moments.*

Knowing one's "self" means knowing the personal constituents in terms of desires, interests, ideas, beliefs, feelings, past cognitive or communication experiences as well as knowing how one thinks or learns. Most adults **assume that one's mental ideas or thinking uses the same properties as spoken, oral language.** Since most US classrooms use English as the form of language to communicate ideas, then most teachers assume that students or children think or understand communication by hearing the spoken characteristics of the English language. More research (Lucas, 1980; Arwood, 1991; Arwood 1999) is available today suggesting that speakers of English may actually be able to think or to listen with properties of language that are not mentally heard as spoken language (Chapter Four describes these properties).

Unless the adult recognizes the personal thinking needs of a learner, then there may be a lack of *respect* for the child's personal way to think or learn. For example, Temple Grandin, an adult with autism, has provided numerous (1995) accounts of how she uses pictures to understand other people's communication. Honoring her needs requires a listener to also understand how Dr. Grandin thinks. Chapter Two describes how thinking corresponds to acquired language properties and how mental linguistic properties may differ from the spoken linguistic properties. *For communication to be thoughtful so as to respect the learning process, the way a child acquires language for communicating and the way the child thinks during communication must also be understood as part of one's "self."*

The assumption that a child thinks like the child talks results in many gaps in learning. *A child's learning system is part of the child's constituents as a person.* Therefore, *RESPECT for the child necessitates a respect for the child's differences in learning.* For example, a seven-year-old child struggles with saying the sounds to the print on the page. Special support services are given to the child for many years. Teachers become frustrated and begin to blame the parents for the child's inability to read, even though the parents avidly read to the child. The parents begin to pay for all types of support services outside the school from equestrian therapy to acupuncture to reading programs given on a one-to-one basis. As a 12 year-old, this child may still not read *aloud* very well. But, the same child is observed looking at above grade level science fiction books and then is able to talk about what he understood from looking at the books. So, what is the problem?

Past communication experiences create the assumption that oral reading defines "reading." Furthermore, most teachers learned to read by saying the patterns of the words aloud. So the assumption is that the 12 year-old child also mentally thinks in the sound patterns of saying the words. Instead of sounds and letters, the 12 year-old child sees the written patterns as mental pictures. By listening to what the child needs, by understanding that the child is not the same person as the adult or educator, and by using positive interpersonal communication strategies, **the educators and parents may be able to** *respect* **this child's learning system (part of the child's who).** First, they assign positive meaning to how the child reads by telling the child to emphasize silent reading, not oral reading (based on listening to the child talk about his learning system). Then they ask the child to tell them how he thinks when he reads. By listening to the child tell how he reads silently, the adults use the child's information to teach the child strategies (Chapters Two, Four, Five, and Six provide more ideas on strategies) for dealing with requests to orally read.

If, the educator or parent continues to assume the child thinks the same way as the adult, then the child's attempts to be successful and to develop wholly will be ignored. *Respect for the person comes from listening and communicating about the person...the person's thoughts, beliefs, desires, interests, past cognitive and communicative experiences, and even the learning system* (see Chapters Two, Three, and Four).

If the adult is able to separate his or her own past experiences and communication from the child's needs, then the adult will respond to requests for meeting the child's needs. In other words, when a child says, "I can't read" the child's utterance is validated, "Oh, you can't read?! Okay. Let's see if we can figure out another way to take meaning off this page." The child told the adult about him or herself. Now, it is the adult's responsibility to meet the needs of the child's feelings as well as to set the goals of how to help the child be successful at reading. *Respect* for how the child learns is as important as *respecting* the child for what the child believes about him or her "self." **To *respect* the child's constituent needs, the adult must be able to separate his or her own needs based on past experiences from the child's current needs.** *Such a separation of needs allows past assumptions to be challenged and conscious language strategies to be used by the adult to foster* **RESPECT:** *the Right of Each Student to Participate in an Environment of Communicative Thoughtfulness.* Being able to use language to honor or know one's "self" *respects the development of others.*

The wonderful thing is that the students, even adult students, take great pride with being recognized through activities such as self-introductions, writing about each other, talking about each other's needs, etc. They enjoy compliments and unsolicited praises and recognition. Within a few, short weeks, improved posture, voice modulation and eye contact become very apparent as daily language continues to refer to the constituent lists. The use of introductions lead to the students learning about themselves, the teacher appropriately self-disclosing about him or herself, and the students learning about classroom peers. Communicating *respect* within a classroom begins with multiple interpersonal *language* interactions to *know* the members of the room as well as to *know oneself* as others see one's "self."

Activity

1. **Define the constituents of "self."**
2. **Give examples of the constituents of your "self."**

Knowing Others

The *language of* **RESPECT** begins in knowing one's "self" as a parent or teacher as well as knowing the constituents of the students. Constituents are personal aspects of the "self." However, in teacher education, the emphasis is often on "what" can be accomplished or "what" can be completed with a student or a classroom rather than on the student as an independent learner. Educators perpetuate the emphasis on the products by often saying, "Just tell me 'what' to do and how to do it." Although efficient and sometimes timely, the emphasis on classroom products or on student products usually results in a narrowed focus.

The narrow focus is on the content and the skills, but *not* the student. For example, in a summer model program, TEACUP (Arwood, 1991-93), the teachers were all volunteers and post master's degree veterans who had completed additional training on how students learn best and on how to provide opportunities for special needs students within a classroom. The first summer was painful for the directors and many teachers. Teachers were talking about "what" other teachers were doing or not doing, complaining about other teachers who were not doing things the "right way," crying about not having the "what" (skills, methods, etc.) to do the class activities like some other teacher did, etc.

All of these teachers had the necessary academic preparation and professional experience, but only a few of the teachers *knew* themselves. Only a few teachers understood their **constituents, what makes up "who" they are as people.** In other words, only a few teachers had the **passion, interest, desire, thoughts, feelings, cognitive experiences, socialization, and learning systems** to try an open ended model that did not tell them what to do and how to do it. Only a few teachers had the **language of RESPECT** tools to interpersonally relate with their colleagues about the classroom activities.

During this first summer of TEACUP, debriefing times had to be spent on the teachers' needs of understanding themselves and how to communicate their needs to others before the students' learning needs were addressed. The model program lasted three years. By the third summer of the model program, debriefing time was spent on the learning needs of students. The TEACUP third-year teachers had sufficient developmental awareness of their own personal *constituents* to *respect* or honor the differences of other teachers as well as themselves.

Teachers, who were not "ready" to use the **language of RESPECT** to participate in this type of program because they did not know themselves well enough or did not have the language tools, either self-selected themselves out of the program or were not included by other teachers as part of the necessary faculty. The third-year emphasis of the model program was on assisting all students with learning. Experience with TEACUP showed many professionals how important it is for teachers to know themselves before trying to help students learn. The formal preparation, in this case, did not determine student or program success. The teachers' understanding of themselves and their ability to use **language of RESPECT** for themselves as well as others coupled with formal preparation were the determining factors.

Similarly, school districts are using more personality inventories as part of hiring practices, since specific "types" of teachers are desired. However, filling out an inventory may only provide a personality profile. Such inventories may not give information about the person's **language**

of RESPECT. From an interpersonal communication perspective, individuals with healthy, *respectful* communication about oneself and about others are typically the most desirable teachers. However, *knowing what healthy communication sounds like and being able to hear oneself produce healthy communication may not be the same.* An adult may be able to use healthy constituent language with colleagues that is supportive of interests, desires, passions, feelings, learning system difference, socialization background, and desires, but **not** with students in the classroom. For example, in the faculty lounge, Mr. A. says, "Are you going to the game tonight?" to one of his colleagues. But, in the classroom when the student says, "Are you going to the game, Mr. A.?" He says, "That is none of your business. Get to work. You are always off task. What is your problem? Do I need to call your mom again?"

Learning when to ask a personal question is part of the socialization process (see Chapter Three), but being devalued when the question is asked does not show **language of RESPECT** for another person's socialization process. In this example, the teacher's language actually devalues the student! Such responses do not show that the teacher is ready for *respecting* the students in the classroom the same way he *respects* his colleagues in the faculty lounge. And, the student loses out on important socialization lessons of how to use *language* with others.

Each person who wants to maximize his or her effectiveness in parenting or working with students *needs to know oneself and to honor the diversity of others' constituents; their passions, interests, desires, learning systems, socialization, past experiences, etc.* An educator may say that he or she honors and *respects* others, but, without the communication skills or language tools to show such *respect,* the educator's thoughts may not match his or her actions. Mr. A. will say he *respects* his students, but until he can respond to a student's needs without devaluation, he does not show *respect.* *The primary tool for fostering respectful behavior is language, used as an interpersonal tool of thoughtful communication.*

Activity

1. **Explain why is it important to know oneself before trying to respect the needs of others.**
2. **Explain how language is a tool of respect.**

Communicating with the Language of RESPECT

All people communicate. How does communication foster more than academic content and social skills? How does the development of *language* tools create more conceptualization of *respect*? How does a teacher or parent communicate *respect*? This section provides an overview of the components of communicating with the **language of RESPECT**. Communicating with the **language of RESPECT** requires awareness of six interpersonal language components: 1) how complex concepts such as respect develop; 2) how to develop active listening; 3) how to use positive interpersonal language strategies; 4) how to remove personal barriers to positive communication based on faulty assumptions; 5) how to remove communication fallacies of thinking; and 6) how to develop an understanding of shared, thoughtful ways to communicate.

Developing Complex Concepts

The concept of "respect" is like other complex concepts such as "responsibility" and "independence." *These complex or formal concepts are learned through language that communicates or assigns meaning over time.* These acts of communication provide the learner with experiences that are both cognitive and physical in nature. *In other words, formal concepts like "respect" are learned by how another person communicates such concepts and by how a learner is cognitively able to integrate meanings.* Therefore, knowing how to use *language* to communicate is an essential element of establishing a classroom that is based on *respect. The language of the classroom will determine whether or not there is "respect."* Respectful language is *felt* as well as *heard.* It *is verified through multiple experiences of respect over time.* Chapter Four will provide an in-depth explanation of the various levels of concept development.

Activity

1. **Describe "respect" as a complex concept.**
2. **Give a simple explanation of developing a complex, formal concept.**

Active Listening

Communication requires a dyadic process of both the speaker and the listener. With *each spoken utterance, a teacher or parent commits a communicative act that creates a physical sensory experience that is interpreted cognitively by the receiver through the lenses of whom the person is.* So, the listener's constituents (passions, desires, interests, learning system, socialization, and past experiences) contribute to "what" the listener is actually able to receive. For example, when Mr. A. responded to the student with the utterance, "That's none of your business" the student filters the meaning of this utterance through his personal constituents. What is the teacher's "real message?" Is the teacher having a bad day or is this a "mean" teacher?" Mr. A. may just be having a "personally bad day," but the student may not know Mr. A.'s underlying intent. Mr. A. is also a listener of his own utterance. He also hears the utterance in relationship to his personal constituents. So, both Mr. A. and the student bring their passions, desires, interests, experiences, and learning systems to the communication. Since Mr. A.'s intent is to separate his personal life from the work setting, he responds, "That's none of your business." However, the student does not have the same past experiences. The student or listener hears the utterance only in relationship to the present situation. Since Mr. A. does not explain his reason for not responding to the student's question, the student assumes that Mr. A. does not care about him or any other student. Mr. A. needs to become a listener of his own utterances as well as others' utterances. *Being an active listener is an important component of being an effective communicator with* **language of "RESPECT."**

To produce respectful language, one has to be able to listen and to hear respectful language. *Listening to one's own language develops the listener's ability to match intent with the communication act.* In other words, when Mr. A. is able to hear that his language communicates a form of devaluation, then he will be able to change his language.

Being able to hear one's own utterances or another speaker's utterances requires training. One strategy, for learning to listen, is to videotape or audiotape the spoken communication interactions between speakers and listeners. After recording these interactions, the listener writes the speakers' exact utterances from reviewing the tapes. Most educators need training beyond teacher education to be able to hear exactly what a student says. *Assuming what a speaker means or assuming what the speaker intends creates a communication gap.* These gaps negatively affect the speaker and listener's communication. For example, a teacher asks an eight-year-old, "What did you do over the holidays?" The young boy says, "dirt bike." The teacher says, "Oh, you went dirt bike riding?" The child says, "Mother, Dad, Aunt Sue, James." The teacher says, "Oh you went with your mom and dad, Aunt Sue and James. That's nice." The teacher assumes meaning for the child without necessarily hearing the child's intent. The child begins to tantrum to communicate emphatically. When the child becomes upset, a support specialist observing in the classroom asks the child to draw about the dirt bike in order to find out what the child is meaning to say. The drawn pictures show that the child is trying to say, "I wanted to go ride my dirt bike, but my bike was broken. And, my mom and Dad invited Aunt Sue over to the house and James, my baby brother, got sick."

The gap in communication between what the child means and what the child is able to orally express creates a personal gap between the child's communication and the teacher's understanding. The teacher must employ active listening to prevent too many gaps in communication. In order for this teacher to actively listen, she needs additional training to hear the child's exact words. Learning to listen to exact words offers the speaker and listener a better opportunity to communicate intended meaning. *Listening to one's own utterances or hearing a child's utterances requires that the speaker has learned to separate out what is exactly said from what is intended.*

Listening skills provide the speaker with the opportunity to begin to hear the language. Further training in how to change the *language* to match one's communicative intent is provided in subsequent sections of this chapter as well as in other chapters. Communicating between a speaker and listener requires not only understanding of each other's personal (self) constituents, but also the use of interpersonal communication strategies that avoid faulty assumptions and communication fallacies. From creating positive interpersonal communication, the speaker and listener learn to share communication so as to be thoughtful or *respectful*.

Activity

1. **Describe active listening.**
2. **Describe one strategy that helps adults learn to hear exactly what they say or what a child says.**

Interpersonal Language Strategies

Complex concepts such as "respect" require multiple language experiences to be developed. So, classrooms and homes need to provide multiple communication opportunities to develop the language of respect. Learning to hear the child's exact words is helpful, but there are also a number of recognized interpersonal language strategies (e.g., see Adler and Towne, 1996) that also assist in active listening. These interpersonal language strategies help the listener take an active role in the communication process. Because the communication process is described as existing between two or more people, then interpersonal forms of communication that support the active listening process are beneficial in honoring the speaker and the listener. This section will describe three useful interpersonal language strategies: perception checks, the use of "I" language (see Adler and Towne, 1996), and the use of picture-based language (Arwood and Brown, 2000).

Perception checks give a way to evaluate the meaning of what is said. The child says, "I went to Boston." The teacher says, "You went to Boston?" The rising intonation is a nonverbal signal for the child or other speaker to take a communication turn. These perception checks can be used to understand content as well as intended meaning. If a student says, "Learning is brain based" the teacher might say, "What does brain based mean to you?" When a student says, "Are you going to the game, Mr. A.?" Mr. A. could say, "Am I going to the game?"

Even though *perception checks* offer ample opportunity to check on whether a person is an active listener, it also *gives the student validation.* (Other examples of this process will be described later in the text.) Using perception checks creates a win-win form of communication, if used by both the speaker and listener in a dynamic event of learning about each other's personal "who" constituents (passions, desires, thoughts, beliefs, past experiences, learning system, etc.), not just about a person's "what's." By using perception checks, the listener is saying, "I *respect* you for what you say whether I agree with it or not. It is your perception. And you have the right to perceive ideas in your way. I *honor* or *respect* your right." Perception checks are often used with "I" language.

"I language" is a counseling form of interpersonal communication that shows *respect* for one's own feelings as well as the right of the other person to feel differently. But, using "I language" is not always easy. *"I language" requires the speaker to be able to state personal feelings separate from the behaviors.* For example, how a person feels about a child's behavior is not the same as the behavior. "I feel sad about not being able to read your poem today" is different from "Your poem is late." *The feelings must be **sincere** and the "I" statements must show personal responsibility.* An example of taking responsibility might sound like this, "Claire, *I* really liked reading about the hot air balloons because *I* hope to ride in a hot air balloon someday." This statement about hot air balloons is specific to the speaker and not a judgment about Claire or the writer. This following statement is not an "I" statement. "Claire, your ideas are very clear in your essay." Perhaps, Claire did not like the essay she wrote. The teacher's judgment about Claire's clear ideas may result in a communication gap between the teacher and the student since the student had a different interpretation of her performance than the teacher's words indicate. However, the previous teacher's statement about how she enjoyed reading about the hot air balloons opens the communication between Claire and the teacher.

"I" language assists in helping the speaker accept responsibility for the speaker's own ideas, own behaviors, etc. The teacher *respects* her own right to like hot air balloons while honoring Claire's right to feel the way she does about her own poem. If "I" language is not used about Claire's poem, then the "I" becomes a "you." For example, "Claire, *your* ideas are very clear." In this latter example, personal responsibility for the teacher's feelings and ideas are transferred to the listener. It is the teacher's judgment that the ideas in the poem are clear. So, Claire is responsible for how the teacher thinks about the poem's clarity. If Claire were asked, Claire might say the ideas are not clear.

When "I" language is **not** being used, then blaming, critical types of judgmental communication is often used. The "I" becomes a "you." For example, a judgmental utterance about a student's interest in rap music might sound like this, "Your music is fun, but you can't dance to it." The speaker does not take responsibility for his or her own music likes and dislikes. However, this judgmental language disappears with an "I" statement, "I enjoy different types of music, especially dance music." Both utterances are referring to "rap music." The teacher thinks that rap music is not dance music, but the student thinks that "rap music" is a type of dance music. *The "I" statement opens up discussion about the music. With the communication open, the two can further discuss the merits and limitations of rap music. However, the "you" statement places judgment on the student's interests and therefore becomes a "closed" ended form of communication.*

An active listener who frequently uses perception checks and "I" types of language statements is on the way to communicating with the **language of RESPECT** *with students and not "at students."* Just putting the pronoun, "I," into the sentence does not necessarily make an "I" statement, if the subject is really "you" or the listener. For example, "I think you should work harder on your spelling" is really "You should work harder." *A real "I" statement takes personal responsibility.* The same "you statement" when spoken with real "I" language has a different focus. For example, "You should work harder" becomes "Juan, I see that the words are difficult to spell. What can we do to help you learn how to spell?" Juan says, "I don't know." The teacher says, "You don't know...um," with a gentle-rising inflection and open tone. After a pause, the teacher takes personal responsibility for the communication, "I look at the spelling word as a whole idea. I close my eyes and try to remember the way the word looks. If I can't remember, then I frame or outline the word and put my meaningful picture on top of the word. If I still can't remember the picture of the word in my mind, then I write the word on my picture dictionary. Do you still have a picture dictionary from the last story, Juan? Oh, yes, I see it. Well, I will help you make another dictionary for this spelling list."

By taking personal responsibility for the communication and the child's learning, the teacher establishes an adult-child relationship designed to *respect* the child's needs, but limited to options given by the teacher. In other words, it is not okay for Juan to fail spelling. Telling Juan to work harder at something he is not doing well at means that Juan's needs, as a learner, are *not respected*. In order to *respect* Juan's learning needs, the teacher listens and hears Juan's silent requests for help. Failing spelling tests is a quiet way of saying that the task is too difficult. The teacher then accepts responsibility for helping Juan be successful by providing him with alternative ways of doing the spelling task, alternative ways that match Juan's learning needs. (Subsequent chapters will offer suggestions of alternative learning methods.)

Understanding the learner's needs is based on knowing the learner as well as knowing how to communicate so as to "learn about the student." When the teacher matches his or her language to what the student needs, then the learner's needs are heard and are therefore respected. (Chapter Two defines the learner.) Perception checks and "I language" statements work to help the educator place responsibility for the communication with the adult in a win-win way that *respects* both the student and the teacher.

Many children and adults do not always understand the spoken message the same way that it is given. So, picture-based language is also needed as an interpersonal language strategy for fostering *respect* in the classroom. For example, the teacher says, "Be sure to take home your social studies work." When Dahlia arrives at home, her mother asks, "Do you have any homework?" Dahlia says, "No." When it is time for Dahlia, a 10-year-old, to go to bed, Dahlia power struggles with her mom because Dahlia hasn't completed her social studies work. Earlier, Dahlia's mother asked about "homework," not specifically about social studies. Dahlia's head *language* in response to her mother's spoken statement was a mental picture of doing work at home, but not necessarily "homework." In other words, Dahlia created a set of mental images different from the mother's verbal statement, "homework."

So, in addition to perception checks and "I" statements, teachers and parents also need to be *respect*ful of the child's way of *processing or understanding spoken language*. Students or even adults who think like Dahlia will need communication that *respects* their way of mentally understanding spoken ideas.

When teachers and parents become active listeners, then language strategies other than verbal or spoken language become useful communication tools. For example, facial postures, hand gestures, writing on the board, cartooning out behavior or academic tasks, flowcharting formal ideas, diagramming constructs, showing written instructions with tasks, drawing ideas before writing, etc., are all very important in communicating (Arwood, 1991). Using the visual, more picture-based ways to communicate in the classroom meets the needs of students like Dahlia. *Respecting* Dahlia's language needs, as a learner, is part of helping her develop her personal constituents. Listening to her learner needs and addressing these needs through positive interpersonal communication strategies (perception checks, "I" language, picture language) respects the learning process, the classroom environment, the teacher's need to be successful, and the right of Dahlia to be who she is.

Communicating with others is only respectful if the listener checks in with the perceptions of the speaker, uses "I" language, and tries a variety of language tools to communicate with the speaker. Sometimes educators participate in a peer supervision process (e.g., Acheson & Gall, 1980, 1987, and 1992) to create a support system for enhancing positive classroom communication. Having a peer educator who listens, videotapes, and supports a colleague helps educators learn to listen and to use interpersonal strategies to foster the **Language of RESPECT:** *the Right of Each Student to Participate in an Environment of Communicative Thoughtfulness.* Learning to use language to listen to student needs and to enhance learning is part of the educational process. Barriers to positive interpersonal communication often stem from underlying assumptions or fallacies. The next sections discuss how to eliminate these barriers so as to emphasize the **language of RESPECT.**

Activity

1. **Define perception checks, "I" language, and visual forms of communication as part of the Language of RESPECT.**
2. **Give examples of perception checks, "I" statements, and the use of visual forms of communication (other than spoken) to create the Language of RESPECT.**

Removing Communication Assumption Barriers

Positive interpersonal language strategies are sometimes negatively affected by assumptions learned through past communication experiences. These assumptions may act as *barriers* to creating the *language of respect* because speakers tend to assume that past ways to communicate are acceptable. *Speakers also assume that past experiences are okay even when disliked at the time of the initial experience.* For example, a child raised by a screaming parent may think it's okay to scream at teachers and other students in the classroom. This child grows up and, as an adult, is not able to discern screaming as being unacceptable behavior. This adult may become an educator or parent who thinks that screaming is part of the nurturing process. This adult may even recognize and dislike screaming by others without realizing that he or she also screams.

Even though adults may dislike past communication experiences, they may still use these past experiences as a basis for communicating with children. For example, an educator may believe that school is to be difficult for students because school was difficult for him. The educator may not like the way he was treated as a student who struggled, but the fact that the teacher "made it" means that it must be okay to make students struggle with learning. Such past experiences that are further communicated as "assumed" acceptable behavior lose sight of the individual needs of the student and the *respect* for those needs. If a learner's needs are not respected, then the learner's personal development is also negatively affected. Likewise, *the speaker who makes assumptions about another person's needs based on personal past needs suffers from a lack of personal development.*

A person's "self" consists of those previously mentioned "who" constituents—passions, interests, desires, thoughts, feelings, past cognitive experiences, a unique socialization experience, a specific learning system, etc. A communicator's success with each of these constituents fosters a high regard or high self-esteem for the speaker and assigns a positive regard for the listener. Successful communicators feel confident about their communication. Such success continues to result in better development of the speaker's and the listener's "self." Therefore, *past "positive" interpersonal experiences are more likely to produce positive communication in the present or future.* Past experiences that result in a speaker having been negatively affected result in the lack of readiness to produce positive interpersonal communication in the present or future.

Ideally, educators who have had positive past interpersonal communication, so as to develop themselves personally, make the best interpersonal users of the language of respect. However, many educators possess a low self-esteem. *Low self-esteem comes from not being able to achieve as well as one might expect in one or more of the constituent areas.* Language usage based on low self-esteem lacks *respect* for the achievement of others because the person with low self-esteem does not expect to do well and therefore does not expect others to do well. Past negative experiences result in assumptions that create *barriers* to communicating with the **language of RESPECT** and to perpetuating low self-esteem.

Past negative communication experiences may perpetuate expected negative communication experiences. For example, a child might grow up into an adult who screams because screaming was a form of communication used in childhood. But, that adult lost some self-esteem or *respect* as a person when he or she was screamed at as a child. As an adult, the adult tells the child who screams to "shut up." The assumption is that the past childhood communication experiences are okay and may be replicated as an adult speaker. Using these past ways to communicate ignores the *respect* for one's own "self" as well as the *respect* for the needs of others. The use of "shut up" says that the child's screaming behavior has no value, *but* all behavior communicates (more examples will follow in later chapters). These devaluing types of language utterances represent low self-esteem on the part of the adult, not the child. The speaker does not believe that a positive meaning can be assigned to the child's talking and therefore feels incompetent to communicate in any way other than the past way of screaming, "Shut up!" Unfortunately, the child or listener will also learn the lesson that he or she has little control over self-achievement or competence. Therefore, this child will also develop low self-esteem.

Since self-esteem has to do with personal achievement or success, why would a person with low self-esteem want to be a teacher, a person hired to assist students in achieving? Sometimes, individuals who struggle to succeed in a given area want to help others to *not* struggle. The irony in this thinking is that unless the adult develops more positive ways of using language, then the adult will communicate and teach with the same language that they experienced as a child, resulting in their students developing low self-esteem. *For positive interpersonal communication to occur, an adult makes a conscious effort to use thoughtful language not based on past assumptions of unhealthy or negative communication.* Students learn the **language of RESPECT** from adults who consciously model positive, language-based interactions representative of the adults' high self-esteem. So, to use the **language of RESPECT**, the adult's communication evolves from replicating past communication experiences to using positive interpersonal language strategies.

Changing the way an educator communicates with others may require more of a paradigm shift than just identifying the communication barriers based on past interpersonal experiences. *Educators may find that the barriers have roots in a culture that emphasized the products, not the person.* The communication was about the person's what, not who. Therefore, a shift from teaching students' skills and products to helping students "learn" may also be necessary.

Teacher education focused on how to teach the products to *all students* during the 1950's to early 1990's. This emphasis on products meant that the teacher learned to communicate about products...reading comprehension, multiplication tables, science facts, etc. This emphasis on the student's performance or the student's "what's" does not necessarily provide teachers with language training about how to communicate with the child or student. Outside school, the teacher's own family of origin (see Chapters Three and Five) may also have communicated about the "what's." Therefore, the teacher may have past experiences in school, home, and in training that emphasize the use of language for the efficient production of tasks, but not for the development of the speaker's or listener's "self." Setting up a classroom based on the **language of "RESPECT"** necessitates changing the emphasis of communication from being on a product or a "what" to being on the person or "who." The **language of RESPECT** focuses on the development of "the person." So, interpersonal communication focuses on the person. The **language of RESPECT** is about the person. The skills and content are byproducts of respecting the learner as a competent person.

Emphasis on production and not on the person's development results in negative interpersonal communication. These forms of communication create "fallacies" of thinking that often result in barriers to the language of respect. The next section describes the thinking fallacies that create barriers to the **language of RESPECT**.

Activity

1. **Describe communication barriers based on assumptions from past experiences.**
2. **Explain how past communication experience affects the development of self-esteem.**

Removing Communication Fallacies of Thinking

Past communication experiences affect not only the assumptions and resulting style of verbally interacting, but also the beliefs of a communicator. Therefore, *an adult who wants positive, **respectful** language needs to examine thinking fallacies developed from past communication experiences.* Adler and Towne (1996) describe many of the communication fallacies. The authors find that some of the *most common fallacies among educators include working from perfectionism, using "can't" statements, using irrational self-talk, and using debilitating emotional language.* This section will discuss these four types of fallacies. When educators identify these fallacies as part of their language, they can begin to change their styles of interacting with students in a way that *respects* more open, free-flowing communication. Chapter Six describes free-flowing communication.

Many educators do not realize that they are communicating from a perfectionist viewpoint. **Perfectionists are very serious at making sure that the tasks are "right" or "correct" in form, not just substance or accuracy.** Perfectionists want all the snowmen to look alike, the letters during writing to be of a single form, the paper to be on the desk a certain way, just a certain amount of glue on the art task, etc. Perfectionists may not separate their needs from the needs of their students; and, they use a lot of judgmental language since they are so needy to be right or correct. "Liz, you use too much glue. Your paper looks messy. Put your paper on the bottom of the bulletin board." Emphasis on the person and the process *and not* on the glue might have been said, "I like your family picture. Tell me about this person." The child says, "My mom." "Oh yes, let's wipe off a little glue. Now, I can see your mom's face better." As students begin to be unique in adolescence and independent as young adults, perfectionists can be quite punishing to students' constituent development. The emphasis on making "things" look perfect creates a negative message about being a unique, competent person.

As shown in the previous examples, statements about what a person "can" or "can't do" often accompanies perfectionist language. For example, when given information, many teachers respond with an "I can't" attitude. Mrs. Lee, might be overheard after a new methods inservice saying, "Oh, if I had only known that technique for those students. I am such a lousy teacher." A second teacher, Mrs. Fleish, might say, "Oh, I have some students for whom I could try that technique." A third teacher, Mr. Ubert, might say, "I can't keep changing my techniques every time someone comes to do an inservice." Only one of these three statements is a half-full, *respectful* statement. Mrs. Fleish recognizes that she "can't" do anything about the past, she realizes that she has plenty of tools to use, but she also realizes that maybe some students could use something else to be even more effective. Her view of the material is a half-full perspective. Mrs. Lee is caught in believing that she must be a "perfect" teacher and therefore is saying "I can't change because that means that I am not perfect so I am a bad teacher" and Mr. Ubert knows that he "can't" because he "won't." Such "can't" language by Mr. Ubert and Mrs. Lee places limits on their *respect* for what some students might need from their teachers. This type of language limits the teacher's personal growth as well as the development of the students. All belief fallacies limit *self-respect,* which, in turn, limits the *respect* for others. Such limitations may be expressed through "I can't" language.

The most common cause of failure in communication among parties attempting to meet special needs of school-age students is the result of personnel saying "I can't." These authors have found that accepting another person's ideas as a valid perspective develops strong interpersonal relationships. These relationships provide the basis for meeting the student's needs. For example, an 11 year-old was functioning at a sensory-motor level of cortical deafness and blindness. However, by the end of a three-week summer program, he was observed using speech and manual signs to explain to his mother what he did during the day. In other words, the student was beginning to function as a higher developing child and beginning to relate to others in a more independent way. However, the child went back to his school, in another state, and the parents telephoned, more than once, to explain that the district personnel "could not" help their son. The district had been sent numerous report pages about techniques, communication objectives, and learning recommendations. The district personnel saw the child a certain way and assumed that the child could do no more. Furthermore, they had not reached the child in the past so they could not do more in the present. Their "can't" language placed limits on this student's learning.

Unfortunately, no one "can make" a person try alternative techniques or new ways of working with children unless it's by physical coercion. So, unless a teacher has developed an open, *respectful* way of honoring and therefore accepting differences in students, all the methods, plans, and training may not help a student or the student's family gain the services they need, expect, or deserve. The child's district personnel believed that they "couldn't" help the child, so the child couldn't be helped. The fallacy in this type of "I can't" thinking is that the district personnel are not *respecting* themselves as competent educators who "can" meet the student's needs.

Sometimes, students or parents ask for "something" that seems "far reaching." For example, a family was asking for their adolescent to be schooled by the district personnel but at the student's home, because the student "didn't like the school building." The district personnel immediately said, "We *can't* do that." And, the parents sought legal assistance in forcing the school personnel to do what the parents wished. The legal counsel asked for a third party evaluation. The authors were involved at that level. So, in a room for mediation, the parents were asked what they expected for their son. Their answers were accepted in terms of what the parents' needed. Then the parents were asked, "How do we serve your son the best?" given the son's needs. At this point, the student's real learning needs were identified. Other options besides home began to be offered and finally the needs of the student, parents, and school district were met. If the school personnel had used positive communication strategies with the parents' initial contact, instead of an immediate "I can't response," then legal involvement would not have been necessary. Because the school personnel immediately rejected the parent's ideas by saying, "We can't," then an adversarial role was established. A third party had to be used to negotiate *respect* for all parties' needs. As part of removing the fallacies of perfectionism and "I can't" from one's communication, a rule-of-thumb for communicating might be...*respectful language accepts all ideas and all utterances as okay.*

Irrational self-talk is also limiting. This type of self-talk takes several different forms. In education, this language might sound like this: "The curriculum forces us to teach this way." But, how could an inanimate object, the curriculum, coerce? "The principal made me teach handwriting this way?" Did the principal physically force you? "The parents should know that Billy is just that way!" How can a person know what another person's background might be? And why would Billy be a particular way? Billy is a learner, as are his parents. "The district should give us time to collect adequate data." The district is an inanimate object so the person who says this statement must mean something else.

Irrational self-talk often includes a lot of "should" statements, generalizations, and stereotypical statements that cannot be understood or explained with logic. Examples might include: "You should know better." "It should never rain on the weekends." "All little boys have difficulty sitting." "Girls are just that way." "Teachers are greedy." *These types of utterances create meaning that leads the speaker to more irrational thought.* Replacing these types of *utterances is important in learning to respect others and to use language in the classroom that is responsive to respect.* For example, "Mary, you 'should' try harder. I know you can do better" lacks logic since no one really uses a crystal ball to know what someone else can or cannot do. If Mary already "feels" that she is trying hard then this statement also devalues Mary. This utterance could be replaced with a number of options. For example, the teacher notices that Mary hasn't written anything on her paper. He says, "Mary, I saw that you spent 20 minutes on your paper. Could you tell me about some of your ideas?" Mary tells about a couple of ideas. "Thanks, Mary. Let's see if we can get those ideas down on paper before we forget them. Let me start drawing out the ideas and you help me remember what you said, etc." Instead of judging Mary, the teacher switches focus to *honoring or respecting* Mary while helping her produce the products. The teacher replaces the fallacies of perfectionism, "I can't" language, and irrational thought with positive interpersonal language strategies of perception checks, "I" statements, and picture-based language to meet Mary's learning needs.

As the reader may discern, *language responds to the past experiences through an emotional channel.* Learning to recognize one's own emotions and then knowing the language that goes with the emotion is important. For example, feeling that one needs to be correct or right results in perfectionist language. Or, believing that oneself is limited in sharing power results in "can'ts for won'ts" and the use of "should statements" or other irrational self-talk. *Language* that responds to unrecognized emotions may result in behavior that colleagues, parents, and students have difficulty understanding. These episodes seem inconsistent to the listeners. For example, the teacher or parent seems jovial one minute, but is yelling at another moment. Such inconsistent behavior on the part of the adult causes three unhealthy patterns of communication: 1) the adult expects the student or child to please the adult so that the child must parent the adult; 2) the child cannot predict behavior so there is a lack of trust; and 3) adult relationships lack the respect integral to shared communicative power. Examples for each of these three communicative patterns follow.

The teacher or adult (could be parent) expects the students to behave and think just as the teacher wants. So, the teacher says, "I expect you to study really hard so that I am not disappointed." Now, the students must be parents to the feelings or emotions of the adult to maintain a relationship. Each student's performance on the task is mixed with the teacher's emotional needs. For example, a student, who really studies hard but performs poorly, must rationalize the teacher's disappointment. "It doesn't matter." "I don't like that subject." "The test was stupid." "The teacher is a control freak." On the other hand, students may rationalize their poor performance as needs to please others. The authors have seen young children actually try to take care of a teacher who has flipped the roles of child-adult (parent) around. For example, a child says, "We must be quiet because the teacher will get mad" or "I brought

Ms. Jones a sandwich so that she will like me." "Mr. Allen told me that I can't come to see you anymore. He says that if he sees us visiting with you before school, we will get detention. Why doesn't Mr. Allen want us to visit with you?" The students are judged by their ability to please the adult. This attempt to please the adult is called "gaining approval," not personal acceptance.

Because the child cannot control or predict the adult's verbal behavior, the child seeks approval, a form of control, not power. In the example of Mr. Allen, he punished his students for wanting to visit with former teachers. He needed all of his students' attention. Instead of encouraging students to respect all communicative acts with all people, Mr. Allen's attempt to control students' communication was thoughtless and selfish; therefore lacking *respect* for himself as a competent teacher, lacking *respect* for his colleagues, and lacking *respect* for his students' abilities to make wise communication decisions. *Not being able to predict or count on the teacher to respond in a logical, rational way also results in a lack of trust.* The students cannot trust the teacher to share personal needs and therefore to help meet their needs.

Students either decide to try to meet the adult's needs or assume that the student's own personal needs do not need to be met. For example, Mr. Allen tries to control his students' likes and dislikes of teachers. He says, "I do not want to see you visiting with Mr. Lancaster before school." So, the students then feel like their desire to meet with Mr. Lancaster must be underhanded, "Let's sneak in to Mr. Lancaster's room." But, the students may feel like they are disobeying and doing something wrong. So, they will try to seek Mr. Allen's approval by not seeing Mr. Lancaster or they will disregard their own needs. "It doesn't matter anyway." Mr. Allen does not trust the students to make personal decisions about their talking to Mr. Lancaster and the students do not trust Mr. Allen in caring for the students' desires or needs. Because they lack trust, the relationship among students and Mr. Allen is further strained. Mr. Allen does not trust himself to share power with the students.

*Respecting one's "self" and the "self" of others requires that communication be shared, not controlled. When parents or teachers use language that accepts all ideas and statements, then there is shared communication. But, when parents or teachers need to control communication by approving what is okay or not okay to talk about, then the **respect** for all ideas is lost.* For example, when the adult needs the students to perform well to show respectful behavior, then the students don't trust the teacher. "Sharon, you need to do better." This teacher's statement implies that Sharon is not working hard and that the teacher will only approve of Sharon's work when Sharon is able to meet the teacher's expectations. Since Sharon, an eight-year-old, thinks that she is doing what she is suppose to be doing, then she tries to please the teacher so that the teacher will accept her. In essence, Sharon is looking for approval. Because the teacher flipped roles, Sharon now believes that her role is to be "what" the teacher wants, not "who" Sharon is. Once approval for Sharon's production of work is mixed with her own feelings about her "self," then Sharon is learning poor communication skills, developing fallacies about communication and making assumptions that result in low self-esteem. She is confused about what to expect from the teacher. This same teacher also says to Sharon, "You will go to the party if you get 100% on your spelling test." Sharon, who has difficulty hearing the vowel sound differences, begins to think irrationally. "My teacher doesn't like me." What Sharon is really saying is, "If the teacher wanted me to do well she would show me another way to do the spelling and then I could get 100% like the students who will go to the party."

Sharon is learning more than spelling. She is learning that she is not in control of her thinking, actions, or academic success. She is beginning to see approval as acceptance, an unhealthy mixing of "what" a person does with "who" the person is. *Respect for oneself requires that a person is able to separate the approval of doing something from the acceptance as a person. A teacher or parent's language that is void of perfectionist, "I can't," emotionally debilitating, and irrational self-talk helps to develop positive communication that respects all parties' constituent needs.* Being aware of such fallacies and replacing the half-empty language with half-full positive interpersonal communication strategies leads to the **language of RESPECT**. With the **language of RESPECT**, *the adults and students or children share communication.*

Activity

1. **Define the fallacies of perfectionism, "I" can't, irrational thinking, and debilitating emotional language.**
2. **Give examples of each of the fallacies.**

Shared Communication

Once an adult begins to identify self-constituents and begins to recognize positive ways to communicate, thus leaving behind fallacies of thinking and past communication assumptions, the adult develops trust. **Trust requires shared power. Shared power results from the development of positive interpersonal relationships. Trust is actually a belief that each person is competent.** Communicating trust occurs across time. Anytime the communicative acts are unbalanced or not *shared* then the relationship between the two people is also unbalanced. Since healthy communicative acts are necessary to respect a relationship, then trust is also necessary. In the example of eight-year-old Sharon, Sharon is beginning to "distrust" the teacher-student relationship. If Sharon is the child, and Mrs. Jones the adult, then it is the responsibility of the adult to support, nurture, and protect the child. The child doesn't have to meet the adult's need of obtaining 100% on the spelling test. The teacher must meet the need of the child who is not getting 100%. The teacher must find a way to assist the child in being successful.

Lowering the expectation does not help with the trust of the relationship or *respect* for Sharon's differences in learning. For example, telling Sharon that she only needs to get 50% allows Sharon to not be embarrassed in front of those who do go to the party, but it doesn't help

Sharon's self-esteem. Sharon's self-esteem is dependent on achievement. However, using a way different from letters and sounds to teach Sharon how to write the words honors or respects her by allowing her to be successful on the test and to learn about who she is. Then, Sharon trusts the adult to be there. The adult is protective of how Sharon learns while supporting her to be successful, thus nurturing Sharon's "self." *Sharing the power between what Sharon needs and what the teacher expects will nurture, protect, and support the communication resulting in the* **language of RESPECT**.

Colleagues who work from their "unrecognized" emotions also may violate the basic trust of their adult relationships. For example, the teacher says to her colleagues in the lunchroom, "That family is a disaster. Phil is just like his brothers." Sure, genetics and past experiences provide many similarities among siblings and their parents, but all individuals *deserve the respect* of being treated as separate from such familial judgments. The colleagues ignore this generalized statement and so the teacher assumes that such a statement is okay to say. Later in the day, the lunchroom teacher runs into Phil's mom after school and says, "Phil is just like his brothers, don't you think?" Mom replies, "Well, no, I think Phil is a lot more sensitive than Jeff and Marc." The teacher continues, "Well, I mean, he can't read and write just like his brothers." The mom says, "Jeff and Marc have been receiving therapy from a private individual. They are now reading and writing at grade level. Are you saying that you can't teach Phil to read or write either?" The teacher's face turns red and the teacher is now in a defensive communication situation. "Well, it's up to Phil if he wants to learn to read." The parent walks down to the principal's office and says, "I want Phil out of Mrs. X's (lunch room teacher) classroom. She can't teach Phil to read. I don't trust her. She wants Phil to teach himself and that means I will pay for private therapy like I have for Jeff and Marc." So, now, Phil's mom is viewed as a "difficult parent." The discussion among faculty and the principal continues to lack responsibility for *accepting* Phil, his mother, Jeff, and Marc for who they are, separate individuals with human needs. **The teacher's language says that she does not respect the differences among siblings and therefore does not see Phil as a separate individual. This lack of sibling separation tells the mom that Phil won't learn to read, just like Jeff and Marc.** The principal's lack of accepting responsibility for the teacher's error in judgment blames the parent for the teacher's issues. And, finally, the colleagues in the lunchroom also had a responsibility to speak up and say that they do not see the siblings as the same people.

The teacher's generalized use of language ends up in a blaming situation, an adversarial scenario of "no trust" among the parties. The teacher in the workroom forgot to look beyond the siblings' abilities to produce products. Each sibling has a unique "self." A positive interpersonal relationship between teacher and child honors or respects that relationship so that shared communication is based on accepting each sibling for who he is. The teacher's own past experiences, fallacies of beliefs, and communication assumptions interfered with her ability to "see" the siblings as individuals. Likewise, the teacher's own personal development did not allow her to *trust* herself as a competent being, able to positively communicate with the parent about the siblings' learning needs. The teacher's own lack of a high self-esteem resulted in her inability to recognize the siblings' achievements, independent of their family membership. *Respect for the individual is separate from the identity of the group.* A person's language reflects a healthy separation. "I enjoy working with each of your sons. They each have such interesting hobbies."

Separating the individual from his or her membership group (e.g., class, home, family, and church) is an important part of the process of *respecting and honoring* diversity. *Communicating positively about the child, not the child's products or lack of products, allows all parties the right to learn and to create a thoughtful, trusting environment of shared communication between two or more people. Conscious language about the individual creates positive interpersonal relationships through the use of strategies that model the* **language of RESPECT.**

Activity

1. **Define the trust of shared communication.**
2. **Explain how shared communication depends on trust.**

Communicative Thoughtfulness

The **language of RESPECT** in the classroom is viewed as the *Right of Each Student to Participate in an Environment of Communicative Thoughtfulness*. Such language requires that the teacher or parent be aware of his or her own developmental readiness for promoting *respect*. Promoting *respect* means that the reader is able to communicate based on honoring one's self-constituents discussed in this chapter as well as the self-constituents of others. Use the following questions to determine whether or not you are developmentally ready to use the type of "language" necessary to create a classroom environment based on **RESPECT**. Each question is based on a principle of developing the **language of RESPECT** in order to honor and respect the development of adult and student learners.

Are you developmentally ready to respect others?

To answer the question "Are you developmentally ready to "respect" others with an affirmative response, you will need to use the *language of respect*. Read the following 12 questions. After each question give examples from your language that either support or reject the existence of such language in your speech. If you are not sure about your answer, go to the next question.

1. I consistently use "I" language to talk about my ideas, thoughts, feelings and desires; e.g., "I like your idea about butterflies." "I feel sad about not having the opportunity to read your paper."
2. I use language that *avoids* the use of "should statements"; e.g., "You should read more" is replaced by "I like to read about 'X.' Do you like to read about 'X'?"

3. I *avoid* stating generalizations; e.g. "All boys are active" or "All girls are verbal." These generalizations are replaced by specific language about individuals. "Mary is very active at PE. She says she enjoys running."

4. I use perception checks; e.g., a statement such as "I like snowmen" is checked with "You like snowmen?"

5. I share the power of the communication with my students through active listening. For example, I write down exactly what students say sometimes so I can see their exact utterances. I match their exact statements to my perception of what I thought they intended to say.

6. I use language that emphasizes the child's personal development (self-constituents). "Aziz, I enjoy listening to you play your violin. Thank you for sharing your musical interests with us."

7. I try to accept all utterances and ideas as valid. For example, I write down the students' words on the chalkboard or on their paper. John says, "That's my cow." I write down, "John says it is his cow."

8. I trust myself to honor student differences. I look at how to allow all students to be successful. For example, I allow all thirty students to accomplish the same task in 30 different ways, if necessary.

9. I accommodate all learners' ways of thinking by validating all ideas. For example, a student says he can't read. "Oh, you can't read. Let's see if there is another way to get the information from the page."

10. I avoid utterances that are judgments of what the child thinks, feels or believes. In other words, I replace judgments with natural language about people. "John thinks he can't read" is replaced with "John has difficulty saying the sounds with the letters. But, he is able to make mental pictures of complete ideas."

11. I focus my energy on ways to meet students' needs. In other words, I replace perfectionism, "I can't," and irrational self-talk with positive perception checks, "I" language, and visual forms of language.

12. I try to devise new ways to meet a student's needs by asking the student to draw, write, read, or talk about his or her needs. In this way, I am learning how a student thinks.

Based on the aforementioned questions, the reader's own assessment of his or her developmental readiness may be predicted. First, if the reader thinks his or her language is congruent with the questions, then the reader is an adult who thinks that he or she has language that is developmentally ready for a classroom based on the **language of RESPECT**. The real determinant of readiness is finding out what those with whom you communicate think? Give the checklist to someone else to give examples about your language for each of the questions. Or develop some peer supervision types of experiences. If the answers match between what the reader recorded and those of at least one other source, then the reader's communication patterns are ready for developing a classroom based on the **language of RESPECT**.

If there are any areas of language weakness, be aware that this language weakness may sabotage establishing a classroom based on the **language of RESPECT.** Later chapters will continue to demonstrate the language *of respect* while maximizing learning. The key to knowing how language is working is to ask the students to share power in communicating through all of the basic language arts modes...reading, writing, talking, drawing, presenting, and listening. The **Language of RESPECT:** *Right of Each Student to Participate in an Environment of Communicative Thoughtfulness* comes through shared power. Chapter Two provides the reader with information about how the learning system develops *"language"* so that the classroom and the teacher may *"respect"* the individual learner.

REFERENCES

Acheson, K. & Gall, M. (1980, 1987, 1992). *Techniques in the Clinical Supervision of Teachers.* New York: Longman Press.

Adler, R.B. & Towne, N. 1996. *Looking Out/Looking In: Interpersonal Communication* (8th Edition*).* New York: Harcourt & Brace.

American Heritage Dictionary (New Dell Edition). 1987. Boston, MA: Houghton Mifflin.

Arwood, E. Lucas. 1991. *Semantic and Pragmatic Language Disorders* (2nd Edition). Rockville, MD: Aspen Systems Corp.

Arwood, E. 1991-1993. *TEACUP (Teacher Education: A Clinical University Program to Promote Successful Integration of Children with Disabilities).* US Dept. of Education, Grant # H029B-00074.

Arwood, E. 1999. "Brain vs. Mind: The Culture & Function of Language." Presentation for APRICOT, Inc., February 26-27.

Arwood, E. and Brown, M. 2000. *A Guide to Cartooning and Flowcharting.* Portland, OR: APRICOT, Inc.

Grandin, T. 1995. *Thinking In Pictures.* New York: Vintage Books.

Lucas, E. 1980. *Semantic and Pragmatic Language Disorders* (1st Ed). Rockville, MD: Aspen Systems Corp.

Chapter Two

Learner Outcomes

Upon completion of this chapter, the reader should be able to do the following:

1. Describe how students learn based on social and cognitive underpinnings.
2. Describe how learning is a neurobiological process.
3. Describe how learning, language, and behavior fit together.
4. Describe how understanding a learner's system is one way to begin to respect others' differences.
5. Explain how honoring learning differences allows the teacher to show more respect for the student.
6. Describe how the learner represents ideas through language.
7. Explain how language is the tool of the learning system.
8. Explain how learning and language are related.

CHAPTER TWO

Respect for the Learner

How do we respect the learner?

The apple is held in front of a hall of mirrors,
Neither the apple nor the mirrors change.
But, the images of the physical world appear to be different.
A different apple or a different image?
Only the student of the apple can find the core.

A veteran first grade teacher sits next to the wall at a table in the lunchroom. Her head is hung down and she is quietly reflecting about the morning. Keith, one of her students, has dismantled the principal's office after being referred for misconduct in the classroom. Unfortunately, Keith then dismantled the school secretary's office for the last 10 minutes. Keith reads better than other first graders and he is constantly in trouble. Who is Keith? Why does he act this way? What can be accomplished by the adults to help Keith?

The teacher education literature and research is currently focused on the restructuring of schools, curriculum, and the reshaping of the classroom to meet the needs of students, their families, and society. Task forces designed to "study" the current school system come away with various topics such as how many students per teacher, how to restructure curriculum content, how to select philosophies about teaching, how to weigh the needs of teachers and students, how to evaluate teachers, how to diagnose students' problems, how to design methods to match learning styles, how to involve parents and business, how to create site-based management, how to raise academic standards, and so forth. Examination of such a list reveals that the emphasis is on the teacher, the administration, and on the structure of the classroom. Emphasis on the student and how the student learns best is lacking. Chapter One described how the teacher's language is affected by how the teacher knows him or herself and how the teacher affects the development of the student.

But, who *is* the student? What is our population today? How does the student learn? Why does the student appear to be different than in past generations? Why do different students exhibit the same or different behaviors? What are the student's learning strengths? This chapter will address each of these questions in attempt to better understand the student as a learner, the learner's differences, and how the learner uses language as a tool so as to begin the process of showing *respect* for the diversity of learners in today's classrooms. In this way a theoretical learning basis for establishing a classroom is offered. In order to honor the diversity of the learners in a classroom, understanding the differences must come first. To understand differences of learning, a theoretical set of learning principles are established in this chapter that demonstrate the link between learning and the learning tool, language. **RESPECT:** *the Right of Each Student to Participate in an Environment of Communicative Thoughtfulness* begins with the student. Therefore, **language for RESPECT** also centers on understanding the student as a learner.

Who is the Student?

Most of the students are biologically equipped with all of the necessary equipment to learn--eyes, ears, skin, nose, tongue. Such external equipment has been designed to connect the incoming information to the internal system that will process, organize, and utilize information. *These sensory systems or receptors make up the only way that information can enter the learner* (Arwood, 1991; Demasio, 1994; Greenfield, 1997). Information does *not* come in the form of words for reading, writing, numbers, charts, maps, workbooks, ditto sheets, tests, texts, memorized material, and so forth. Information comes in the form of sound, light, smell, taste and touch. Therefore, **the student is a receiving agent for what can be heard, seen and touched, and to a lesser extent for what can be smelled and tasted.**

As a receiving *agent*, the student can only function in the way the student is able to process sound, light, and touch. Therefore, *the student will only learn what the student is physically able to process.* The student, the learner, is the only person responsible for what *can* be learned. When the student's environment matches with the student's ability to process the input, then the student is a successful learner. When the student's environment does not match with the student's ability to process the input, the student may not learn from that environment. The environmental stimuli must match the student's way to learn so as to maximize learning and to respect the student for how the student learns. Skills, knowledge and subject matter do *not* determine how the student learns. A student is not personally successful unless the environment places the student central to the classroom. In other words, the student is the learning machine, not the curriculum, content, or skills.

The learner's processing of the sensory input produces interactive development between the environment and the student. The input is what *can* be seen, heard, or touched. *The interaction is the way that others assign meaning to what is seen, heard, or touched. The processing of the input is the way the learner organizes past information with new information.* The environment includes all people and things that change physically to produce input. Within this environment, the teacher is the facilitator of change to maximize the input for the student as a successful learner. **The student's learning system is the neurobiological way the student is able to process information.**

When the student learns, there is a physical change in the student. This change is evidenced by biochemical changes in cells (e.g., Greenfield, 1997) as well as by surface changes in which some cells may be etched through stimulation. This etching may produce cellular grooves that facilitate the speed of processing for information that is old or has already been recognized by the cells. These grooves establish a "trough principle" which **states that when old information is brought into the learning system so as to connect to new information, the student is more likely to demonstrate learning.**

Research about the learning system suggests that the learner connects past to present input. The **"building principle"** states that **in order for a student to learn new material, the new material must be connected to the old.** This building process overlaps the past to the present so that the student not only recognizes the patterns of input, but also begins to conceptualize patterns. Such processing of information develops the sensory pattern from the input but also develops the concept. **This "bridge principle" allows for the input to be processed through past interconnections. The student's ability to remember, retain and recall is based on how well such bridges are designed through their various phases of construction.** Just as there are wooded bridges, steel bridges, rope bridges and pontoon bridges, so there are a variety of learning bridges to "connect" prior knowledge with new concepts or experiences.

The **"networking principle"** states that **the ability to create a variety of experiences from similar input is the result of being able to use the input in a variety of ways.** For example, the student who learns to write ideas about a variety of subjects will possess a variety of ways to express his or her ideas. Furthermore, if the student writes for a variety of different reasons (journals, notes, thank you, research, business, pen pal writing), then the student will have more knowledge about how to write.

How the learning occurs is based on what the neurological system of the learner can perform. Therefore, being familiar about the composition of the learner's thoughts allows the educator to understand how the student can learn. Before a description of how learning occurs, a population profile will be provided in the next section.

Activity

1. **Name and describe each of the four learning principles.**
2. **Why are these principles important?**

Who is Today's Population?

Sometimes, teachers remark that today's students are not like the students 20 to 30 years ago. True, the culture is changing thus affecting family styles and life styles; but, there are also variations within the learning system of today's learners. Understanding these learners' changes may help educators to understand that the population of students today is different from the population one to two generations ago.

Research about sound deprivation in animals has revealed that when the animal is deprived of sound then the animal's behavior changes (Webster, 1977). In fact, the animal's way of learning changes. Similarly, the American Pediatric Association (1984) suggested several years ago that there was a connection between children with history of ear infections and their later academic problems. Recent research of the auditory system which connects what is heard with what is seen suggests that this system is developed by stimulation and that this occurs within the first two years of life (Greenough, 1987). Thus a child who has fluid in the middle ear as a result of allergies and/or viral infections is a child who is being deprived of some speech sound patterns. Today's medicine provides antibiotics for the infections so that children do not die from the bacterial infections, but there is definitely the possibility that such acoustic deprivation within the first two years of life does result in permanent changes in the child's neurological system and thus permanent changes in the learning system.

More recent research has indicated that the physical make-up of a human's learning system may correspond to different diagnostic labels. For example, PET scans show differences that correspond with differences in the brain activity and subsequent diagnosis (Volkow and Tancredi, 1991). Other research, for example, suggests that boys diagnosed with ADD (Attention Deficit Disorder) show brain stem activity differences with or without medication, retalin (Leavy, 1996). Therefore, there is little doubt that different behaviors that result in different diagnoses have underlying differences in neurological make-up or function. These differences in the learning system also show up in academic areas. For example, some recent brain research at Yale University in 1998 showed the cortical site of difficulty for dyslexic patients corresponded to problems with sound and letter connections. In other words, as more research data about the neurobiological aspects of learning is offered, educators recognize that learning has a biological basis (ASCD, 1999). Having the brain research is only one step in understanding the learner. Being able to interpret the data in terms of learning is crucial to understanding the learner. The next section uses this data to explain the student's learning system.

Activity

1. **Could physical changes in a learner result in learning differences?**
2. **How is learning related to the way a student is able to process incoming stimuli?**

How Does the Student Learn?

The literature about how the brain works is currently rich with data that can be applied to how the mind (e.g., Calvin, 1996; Carruthers, 1996; and Greenfield, 1997) is developed. Some of the data describes the working of the cell while other data describe the networking of the cells to construct complex thinking patterns. Whether it is the cell or the cellular network being described, there exists some fundamental constructs:

1) *Sensory input must be received by the receptor organs in order for the brain stem cells to begin to develop patterns of transmission of information;*
2) *Patterns of transmission are fully developed only when enough information has been recognized or processed by the upper brain stem and brain;*

3) *Recognized patterns are further integrated with future patterns for increasingly more complex thinking skills;*

4) *As the neural complexity of patterns increase, the cognitive or thinking complexity increases;*

5) *As the brain (cerebrum) increases the complexity of patterns, the inhibition between hemispheres increases; and*

6) *Maximum inhibition leads to maximum integration of patterns for maximum cognitive development (Arwood, 1991).*

<u>Sensory Patterns</u>

The *learner's system is equipped to provide input from the environment.* Research about the sensory system indicates the learner recognizes raw input when the input is processed by the neurological system. In other words, the student may complain of not hearing the teacher or the student may say "I can't hear words." However, when the student's ears are tested, the student can hear. The student is actually saying that his or her learning system is not processing spoken material. Often teachers and parents complain that the student or child is selectively attending or not listening. *Selective attention or not attending can only occur once the listener has recognized the input. If* the student can't process the input the student can't select out what is not to be recognized. The student's problem with attending or listening is a matter of whether or not the student has the ability to physically process the input, and not as many often believe, a matter of student choice.

Many teachers have compensated for students who could not process the spoken word. For example, the teacher finds a pen on the floor and asks, "Whose pen is this?" Most students are focused on the material in front of their eyes, or the material seen at their desk. Therefore, when the teacher says something about the pen on the floor, most of the students do not process the teacher's words. The teacher asks for the students' attention--which really means that the teacher is asking for the students to look at her. To get the students' attention, teachers learn to use different environmental strategies such as lights, whistles, raised or lowered voices, clapping hands, etc., to change the students' focus from their desk to the teacher's face. In a classroom of mutual regard and respect students are encouraged to ask for others' attention, "May I have your attention please." Language is used as a convention.

The change in focus by the student from the desk to the teacher provides a "bridge" between what the teacher's input looks like and what the student has experienced in the past. Students who cannot process the traditional input of spoken words appear to be inattentive, easily distracted, unmotivated, or physically "hyposensitive." In other words, these students do not process the spoken word because the neurological system does not internally connect patterns of sound. There also exists another type of student who does not recognize the incoming sound as meaningful because the student cannot filter out enough of the nonmeaningful sounds. This inability to filter or inhibit the sound is called "hypersensitivity" to sound. For example, this student may put his or her hands over the ears or complain that certain sounds hurt. Sometimes, the same student who doesn't recognize sound is the student who complains in the cafeteria or in the band room of the sound. It's as through the speakers for the sound system are working but the filtering system for what is to be amplified is not working. Therefore, all sound appears randomly presented. *Ideally, the first stage of learning consists of clearly received patterns of sight and/or sound (includes other sensory systems) with good inhibition and integration.* **Inhibition refers to the neurological ability to suppress nonmeaningful patterns of input. Integration refers to the neurological ability to connect more than one set of incoming patterns.**

Activity

1. **Explain how sensory patterns relate to learning.**
2. *Explain sensory integration and inhibition.*

Patterns of Recognition

Once the input from the sensory system is recognized, then the input begins to create patterns so that "words" and not just sounds are heard. These new patterns are connected to old patterns so that meaning is assigned from previously developed patterns. For example, in the neurological hierarchy of development, each input is overlapped and connected to other forms of input in a specific order. *The most complex pattern development requires recognition of patterns from not only the visual system of what is seen, but also from the acoustic system of what is heard.* This most complex set of patterns is developed by the auditory pathways that communicate not only within each hemisphere of the brain but also with a specific area of cell concentration and development in the left hemisphere (left temporal lobe of the cerebral cortex). In this way, a young four-year-old asks the same question over and over to acquire the pattern of relationships between past ideas and present ideas. Likewise, rhyming books, repetitive storytelling of familiar tales, choruses, and songs, role playing of family activities, dress-up activities, pretending roles, etc., are all ways for young children to show adults how concepts are developed. *These concepts are acquired from connecting past with present patterns (**trough principle**), building new ideas from old ideas (**building principle**), creating multiple connections (**bridge principle**), and finally having a variety of ways to represent the ideas (**networking principle**). Language consists of these learned concepts.*

If a student has a problem being able to connect the patterns of incoming input with past learned experiences then the student may exhibit behavior that the teacher might interpret as being inconsistent or inappropriate. For example, one day the student does well on an assignment. The next day, the student may fail a similar assignment in the same content area. Or, the student may answer all of the questions right on the homework and then fail the exams. This type of inconsistent behavior is perceived and interpreted so that the student is said to be "lazy," "ornery," "underachieving," "stubborn," "obnoxious," and so forth. But, the student's behavior represents the student's learning system. *The learning system only recognizes those patterns that have been developed through past experiences.* Likewise, the student's use of language also shows what concepts are learned.

In other words, changes in the spoken words by the teacher or changes in the way the material is presented determine the way the student is able to respond. The student's inconsistent pattern of behavior is predictable. *The student always responds the way the student is able to process the input.* Therefore, *it is the teacher's responsibility to find or recognize the way that each student processes the information* so as to provide suitable opportunities for learning. *Knowing how a student learns is part of knowing what constitutes that student's "self."* Understanding each learner in terms of how the learner acquires information also respects the learner's self. Respecting the learner for the way the learner is able to process information in turn assists the student in being successful.

The student can only process the information in the way the student is "wired" and therefore can only perform within his or her neurological limits. These limits mean that some students cannot process word patterns or the traditional spoken classroom lecture. These same students also cannot be over stimulated by the structure of the environment. In other words, the learner's neurology places the ceiling, as well as floor, on what will or will not be understood. If the student cannot process the patterns, then simplifying the input will only make the input more difficult. For example, teaching vocabulary can be very difficult because the student may have no previous connection to the pattern of the word. Breaking the words into more isolated pieces such as their definitions, letters, etc., only compounds the problem since the student may not have a way to recognize these isolated patterns. Without applying the basic **"building principle"** to the task, vocabulary means "nothing" to many students. Since teachers have already acquired or learned the concepts of the vocabulary, the task seems "simple;" but, without stopping to find out what patterns the student is able to process, the task can become even more difficult. In other words, there must be a "blueprint" to the acquisition of the vocabulary. This "blueprint" shows the structure of the student' learning system matched to the strategies of the teacher. **The blueprint is the way the student is able to process information. It is how the student learns concepts or language matched to the way the student must be taught to be able to learn vocabulary, for example. The way a student learns is therefore developed by matching language strategies to teach the student in the way the student learns.**

These language strategies are then based on what the student can do **(trough principle)***. These strategies are developed from what the student can build from past experiences* **(building principle)** *connected to other curriculum tasks* **(bridge principle)** *and to what can be used in a variety of settings.* Traditional vocabulary tasks that are not based on what students already know, can connect, can build from, and use in a variety of ways (**networking principle)** do not show long term learning because the patterns are not connected into concepts or language.

The student's ability to connect patterns will determine the type of academic work the student can process. For example, if the student is capable of connecting what is seen with what is heard, then the student is able to connect "letters" (seen) and "sounds" for phonetic reading or for phonic drills. Educationally, the teacher can try to make the student's learning system connect the sight and the sound by practice drills, memorization, pneumonic devices, associations, etc., but *whether or not the child learns these connections is dependent on the student's learning system.* Educational devices act as coping mechanisms but are successful for only some students. For example, some students with rigorous drill and practice can learn to say the sounds of letter combinations or "word call" the words on the page, but still not comprehend what is said or read. More importantly, such educational drills and practices will not create a different neurological system in the learner. *The way the student's learning system functions is the way the student learns. Drills and practices may create pattern recognition, but not necessarily comprehension or long term retention. Pattern recognition does not necessarily result in concept or language development. In other words, pattern recognition does not necessarily use complex interconnections or language for learning.*

The types of tasks that require the most complex use of connected patterns or the most complex form of learning include spelling, multiplication tables, worksheets, mathematical story problems, alphabet applications, grammar applications, and so forth. These tasks are separate from external stimulation of the learner. To do these tasks, the learner must bring interconnected patterns or concepts "called language" to the task. In other words, the learner must use past learned experiences as patterns connected with the present task patterns to successfully perform. These interconnected patterns are in the form of a mental language, spoken or seen. For example, "Oh, the teacher wants me to fill out the first three sentences on this worksheet just like the first three problems on the last worksheet." This type of internal language connects the present task with past learning experiences either by visually seeing the ideas or hearing the mental spoken ideas. Such tasks are considered to be beyond simple pattern recognition of sight, sound, etc. These tasks are referred to as "being out of context," out of the realm of simple external pattern recognition. *These complex tasks are the most difficult to neurologically acquire (**trough principle**) because the learner often lacks the opportunity to build ideas or concepts, "**bridging**" and "**networking**."* Ironically, these types of tasks are often provided early in the curriculum as easy or fundamental skills. From a learning perspective, these are the most difficult types of learning activities. In fact, *any task that requires some use of internal language or symbolization necessitates a more complex use of patterns or concepts.* Under these complex pattern conditions, the student is more likely to try to cope. For example, the teacher gives the student a multiplication table to learn as a set of mentally spoken words in phrase form (e.g., two times two is four). The student who cannot connect what is seen as a number pattern on the page with the mentally spoken pattern or words, must figure out a way to store the idea on the page as well as recall it.

Multiplication tables taught as memorized auditory patterns are out of the context of how this student learns. So, the student must use internal language to try to cope. Some students cope by attaching a mentally-pictured concept or idea to the number. For example, one student always could mentally picture a shoe when she saw the number "8." Such coping can become elaborate and neurologically taxing. Students who are taxed also need more time than the other students to translate their system into the expected set of patterns.

Activity

1. **Explain how the learning principles apply to recognizing sensory patterns.**
2. **Explain how recognizing patterns relates to learning with language.**
3. **Explain why patterns that require mental language are the most difficult. Give examples.**

Integrated Patterns

Once there is sufficient pattern recognition from a sensory system, then complex patterns begin to build through adding other sensory inputs. It is this type of integration that allows a child to spell using phonic systems and phonetic rules. The child starts with sound patterns for the names of letters added to sounds of letters in words that the child can see. The integration of the sound with the printed or seen pattern allows for phonics. Otherwise the learner may have to cope with whatever the student can figure out will work. For example, in the classroom, one child is able to say the letters (acoustic) to the spelling words but can't write the words during a spelling test. Even though this student has learned to say what is heard, such as "cee" for the letter "c," the student can't integrate what the letter looks like with what the student hears when the letter is spoken. Or, for example, a student may be able to write all of the spelling words at home during practice but when the teacher gives the test aloud, the student can't write the words. Again, this student can see and recognize the patterns but cannot integrate the visual pattern of letters to the spoken or heard pattern of the spelling word. If the student struggles, then the student may not feel like he or she fits into the group who is able to connect the letters and sounds. The lack of feeling like part of the group results in the student's own self-esteem being negatively affected. Self-respect and respect from the group may be jeopardized. To be able to use integrated patterns as concepts or language to be able to spell in the way the student learns allows the student to be successful and to feel self-respect as well as respect from the group.

In both of the aforementioned examples, the students struggle with certain academic tasks because the students are given tasks that require a different neurological learning system than what they, as learners, *can* do. In other words, most teachers expect students to automatically be able to integrate patterns for spelling, inferring, writing, reading and so forth. The reality is that more than three-quarters of today's school population is *not capable* of learning by integrating visual with acoustic patterns (Arwood, 1991). This means that there may be 20 out of 25 children in a classroom that all appear to be able to recognize the letters, say the words to the letter patterns, and write the letters; but only one out of five of those children can really hear the sounds of the word separate from the letters of the word. Therefore, there are only four or five students in each Kindergarten through 12th grade classroom of 25 students who can follow spoken instructions to perform read or written tasks without additional input to get the work initiated or finished. In other words, out of 25 students in a classroom, only four or five students will follow spoken instructions while the other 20-21 students will need some additional input to make the task match with the way the student learns best. Respecting the student means to honor the student's way of learning best. Therefore, teachers must find ways to not only to listen to what students say about their learning systems (Chapter One) but also find ways to help the students succeed through the way the student learns.

Some research (Eberhard, 1998) shows that the number of students who can hear and see the concepts simultaneously is even lower than 60 to 90%. In one urban middle school, as many as 98% of the population showed the ability to connect or integrate visual patterns to sound, but *not* the ability to connect sound patterns with visual patterns. In other words, as many as 90% or more of regular school children (K-12) need to see what is said to understand sound; spoken instructions, discipline rules, academic tasks such as spelling, phonetic reading, etc. "Respect" for the majority of the population necessitates the use of visual language structures that are meaningful and will validate individual students.

Activity

1. **How are integrated patterns different than simple sensory patterns?**
2. **What type of academic tasks require integrated use of patterns or language?**

Complexity of Patterns

As the student's past and present patterns increase, the complexity of ideas also increase. These increases in patterns require more integration of patterns and more connections of patterns for complex learning. Without the connections of patterns and the integration of patterns, complexity does not increase. **For example, concepts are acquired or learned, not taught.** Teachers may attempt to teach a word that represents the concept but only the word pattern, definition, etc., is learned; not the concept. Or, an educator may "teach" a student the multiplication tables, but the student may not be able to use those patterns to compute a percentage based on the inverse relationship of addition and division, derived through multiplication. Or, a student may be able to word call the taught sounds and letters on a page but not understand the meaning of what is read. **Complex sensory patterns are integrated from past patterns and are interconnected to form concepts or language.** *Language is the product of the learning process as well as the tool of the learning process when such complexity of patterns occurs.* *Concepts are meaningful integrated patterns that connect the human learning system to its function as a person in society.* For a person to feel like part of society, for a student to feel like a successful person in school, for a teacher to *respect* the needs of his or her learners; concept development must occur at a high enough level that the learner is able to understand ideas that can't be seen, heard, touched, tasted or smelled with single sets of patterns. Such ideas or concepts include words such as "respect," "responsibility," "trust," "integrity," "justice," and "love," to name a few.

The addition of meaning to past integrated patterns allows a learner to acquire more depth of understanding. In other words, **concepts develop through the same layering of the learning principles (trough, bridge building, and networking).** For example, during a health lesson, a class of fifth-grade students discussed priorities **(trough principle)**. As the lesson progressed, the teacher introduced Maslow's hierarchy **(bridge principle)** (for an explanation of Maslow's psychosocial hierarchy see Maslow, 1970). A couple of weeks later, the class was studying the arrival of the colonists in Jamestown. One of the questions posed by the teacher, was "How did the colonists spend their first ninety days?" This question could be answered in terms of a list of events, a measure of limited understanding. But, the students began to apply **(networking principle)** the stages of Maslow beginning with the "need for basics."

The students discussed the colonists' need for shelter, the need for provisions, safety, security, and finally the need for some form of government. Before the lesson was over, the students had generated multiple ways of examining the colonists' situation in Jamestown by utilizing concepts learned from a health lesson **(networking).** Such opportunity to create conceptual frameworks can only be generated by a truly "integrated curriculum." A curriculum that allows for worksheets that covers health and social studies *will not meet* the same higher conceptual standards of an integrated curriculum that generates the information from students across the content areas in multiple ways of delivery. *These multiple ways to discuss or share old information with new information in a variety of ways creates more conceptual depth for greater learning.* Greater conceptual learning contributes to a child's self-respect through increased achievement or better self-esteem and through increased self-worth, better *respect* for one's ability to be a successful learner and a resource to others. The students' multiple ways of using *language* generated multiple concepts that increased in complexity and resulted in *respect* for the learner as well as the content.

The ability of a student or learner to connect past concepts (Maslow, for example) with current ideas (Jamestown colonists) results in increased concept development. Likewise, by increasing what the student can perform increases the underlying use of the brain. There is some research that shows a healthy brain is one that is active. Furthermore, the learner's ability to produce ideas in a variety of ways also increases the amount of neurological inhibition. In other words, a child or student may appear to be "hyperactive," even diagnosed as attention deficit hyperactive disorder (ADHD), until the same child is able to cognitively organize information in enough different ways so as to seek multiple solutions to social problems such as sitting in one's desk during spoken class discussions. As this student is able to increase cognitive development of concepts about social behavior such as sitting and listening, then the student uses mental visual language to think about the discussion while doodling on paper so as to connect the motor system to the *mental visual language* (Arwood, 1991). This doodling allows the student to focus on the movement of the hand parallel to the movement of the child's mental pictures. The student's *mental visual language* typically races through the student's head. Some students say that the information is so quick and uncontrolled or unfocused that they aren't even aware of the *mental language.* Drawn pictures allow for content to be recognized while the doodling may allow the student to focus on the content of mental concepts. The student then learns what to do to be part of the group. In this way, the student becomes more of a self-advocate about what the student needs to learn. The student is learning to *respect* his or her own learning system because the adult or teacher is offering a way for the student to be successful as a learner. Respecting the child's learning needs contributes to the overall classroom **RESPECT.** *Using the student's own visual language as a valid learning system respects the student as a learner.*

Activity

1. **How are concepts developed from patterns?**
2. **How do concepts become more complex?**

Maximum Cognitive Development

When a student is able to think about more than a single set of integrated complex patterns or concepts (idea) at one time, then the student is also able to do more than one thing at a time. Real life experiences are filled with the opportunity to perform multiple tasks at a time. For example, holding a job for a long period of time while also maintaining family relationships requires a person to perform multiple tasks. Attending college while also taking care of family responsibilities also requires a person to engage in multiple tasks at a time. Being a loyal and responsible employee while also taking care of home chores and responsibilities requires a person to think in more than one set of complex patterns at a time. However, "going to school" does not always offer a student the opportunity to engage in maximum cognitive development. The classroom is often structured to enhance separate skills in a longitudinal way so as to make learning a linear hierarchy of skill building. For example, the student "does" reading, then the student does "social studies." The reading content is not integrated into the social studies content. A linear approach to content does not integrate complex patterns together for maximum cognitive development. Likewise, the linear approach to adding one skill to another skill also does not provide for maximum cognitive development. **Maximum cognitive development means that the learner is acquiring the language that represents multiple ways to view an idea as well as multiple ways to represent an idea**. For example, a learner is able to connect complex ideas such as Maslow's psychosocial stages from health to a social studies lesson. Furthermore, the student can not only read about how these concepts relate but also is able to talk about the relationships, draw out the relationships, and even write about the relationships. The student is able to represent his or her ideas in multiple ways (Chapter Four explains the cognitive stages that parallel this growth).

From a neurological perspective, maximum concept development requires integrated cellular or **trough building** through **bridges** and **networking**. To acquire the ability to do multiple tasks at one time or to think about multiple tasks at one time, requires multiple opportunities for the learner to use *language* to integrate ideas and multiple opportunities to represent those *language* ideas. To understand advanced concepts of *"respect,"* the learner would have to have advanced language ability, representative of maximum cognitive development. For example, a college student was recently arrested for thousands of dollars of graffiti destruction. When she was asked to face the business people to explain her actions, she said she drew on business properties as part of "her artistic expression." The business people were amazed that she did not apologize for the destruction. The college student was able to think about her own actions but not about the business people's needs. The student's lack of *respect* for her community, the other people's property, and the other people's perspective was a result of her not being able to use a maximum level of cognitive understanding. Her language at the town meeting was about *"her"* artistic expression, a complex concept created from multiple patterns of "personal" experience. (It is from these types of experiences that she was able to attain the test scores and grades to attend a well-respected independent college.) But, she did not have multiple experiences about artistic expression from other's viewpoints. Furthermore, she had not acquired a maximum understanding of the concept of *respect*. Even though her crime was a felony, she still believed that she had not done anything wrong. (Chapter Four describes the cognitive levels associated with this type of personal, self-centered development.) Maximum cognitive development results in better understanding of oneself as well as others' needs. Such growth offers the learner with more ability to engage in multiple tasks at the same time, understanding complex concepts such as "respect," and be able to take others' perspectives.

All conceptual development, especially complex pattern development, is not linear. There is a spiral staircase of concept learning from scaffolding old information about complex patterns to new uses of those patterns. Multiple cognitive experiences about the same concepts or ideas increase the concept development. Likewise, the neurological system is not linear but is an overlap of cellular patterns as well as an integration of cellular networks that create complex conceptualization. For example, a high school or college student might be ready to register for classes but there is no one to "walk the student" through the process. The student has all of the splinter skills needed to register. The student has the concept of registration and may even know what classes to take. But, the student has to engage in a new physical experience of registering without someone to assist. *To successfully engage in such an experience, the student must use mental language to connect past concepts and skills to the current "registration" situation.* By mentally integrating old information with new information the student is able to independently register. From this cognitive experience, the student has a more complex understanding of the concept of "registration." *The student has used language as the tool for acquiring additional meaning about the concept, "registration."* **To be successful at using language**

as a tool, the student has to have multiple uses of language as a resource tool for learning.

The majority of school children cannot use language as a tool for maximum cognitive development. Therefore, the majority of school children are not able to engage in multiple tasks at the same time, take others' perspectives, or understand complex concepts at an advanced level. The reason these students are not able to perform maximum cognitive developmental tasks is that they have not had familial, school, or other opportunities to increase their integration of complex patterns through multiple uses. The linear structure at school does not offer such opportunity. Many families are not structured internally out of "respect for family" but are structured externally. In other words, the family members do what comes next (linear) based on the clock...it's time for work, it's time to go home, it's time for piano, it's time for the Dr.'s appointment, etc. Later chapters describe this external structuring in terms of cognitive (Chapter Four) and social development (Chapters Three and Five). Because the family "sees" what has to be done, doing more than one task at a time or being internally structured is a type of cognitive development that few people experience. To experience such cognitive organization, the family member or learner would have to have multiple experiences of organizing through their language system. Since most K-12 students today are able to connect visual patterns with other visual patterns, then the integration and organization of complex ideas would have to be acquired through visual language activities. Because most teachers *respect* their own past acquisition of concepts, most teachers use the spoken or auditory language system for teaching. Classroom experiences that are primarily auditory in nature leave behind those students with visual motor "artistic expression" since they are not learning the "bigger concepts" through language that matches their learning system. On the other hand, the 25 to 30 percent who could follow those oral instructions in the early elementary grades are also the 25 to 30 percent who are functional in circumstances that require the use of developing new auditory concepts from past spoken ones. These students typically do well at multiple tasks. The student who can handle multiple tasks simultaneously with spoken words can also use those words to create multiple applications. Therefore, this student is able to register for classes from past experiences without additional information. Or, the student is able to use past spoken rules as guidelines for behavior. For example, "Wow, I would really like to paint a picture on this blank wall but the building belongs to someone else. They may not want the painting. After all, what I think is artistic expression, they might view as graffiti, etc." *Internal "head language" functions to create new cognitive experiences that maximize learning.* But, the language and the learning must match in order to respect the learner's needs. Maximum cognitive development of concepts occurs through the neurological integration of the way the learner thinks. *If the learner thinks in patterns that integrate sound and vision, then the learner is able to use auditory or spoken head language. If the learner thinks in patterns that are seen connected to other visual patterns, then the learner thinks in a pictured "head language."* Respecting a learner for the use of language to create maximum conceptualization also recognizes or honors the diversity among all learners.

Activity

1. **What is maximum cognitive development?**
2. **Give examples of how maximum cognitive development respects the learner's development.**

Respecting Today's Differences in Learners

As suggested earlier in this chapter, many veteran teachers ask themselves and their colleagues if the students of today are truly different from those of past years? The present day teachers are seeing differences in behavior that are often thought to be the result of societal changes. These changes have evolved from differences in economics, family styles, life styles and mobility. *But within the same society not all children demonstrate the same behaviors.* Therefore, the teachers are left wondering why an average student doesn't have adequate academic background, has to be retaught material, is lacking in basic skills and in social responsibility for self-managing behavior. Overall, many veteran teachers feel or believe that students have a general lack of **respect** for learning. In a classroom based on **respect,** the students, certified teachers, and parents work side-by-side sharing power (see Chapter One). Students are constantly reminded that the goal is for learning. They are given strategies to learn complex concepts in the way that they think or use underlying patterns. *Respecting all learners in this type of classroom means that students are challenged to integrate complex patterns of concepts in multiple ways.* Someone is always able to perform better than someone else including the teacher. This classroom represents the Shakespearean notion of "I meet superiors each day."

In classrooms that foster the overlap of concept development, students are more self-managed. The learning of advanced concepts in these classrooms helps the students stay focused on the class content. The learner is neurologically challenged to use their language to connect their past experiences with the present classroom activity and cognitive development is improved. Ironically speaking, many of the unwanted student behaviors seen in the schools are fostered by linear classroom models that are authoritarian in nature. In these authoritarian models the material is taught in separate chunks so that students do not cognitively develop the maximum depth of concepts about academic material and thus have to be retaught unrelated skills or simple concepts, year after year. The learning principles are not fully utilized in these classrooms. Because the material is not student directed and is not highly meaningful, the students use unwanted behaviors to keep the classroom relevant and to cope. And, finally, complex concepts such as "respect" and "social responsibility" cannot be taught in an authoritarian system that tells students what to do, how to do it, when to do it, and then devalues the student by telling the student the work does not fit the expected model thus perpetuating mediocrity (Chapters Three and Five discuss the authoritarian system and offers alternative ways to manage a classroom or family). *Perpetuating mediocrity does not respect the individual learner for who he is and what he is able to learn.*

In other words, the current system of education encourages the kind of student that does not develop ways or means to self-advocate for their way of learning. **However, it is important that respect for the learner's needs be kept as the focal point of the classroom and respect for the individuals be kept as the focal point of the family.** If the student is to be respected as "a learner," and the learner is the important piece of the community or family, then maybe the differences that teachers see in behavior are also "real differences in learning." *These real differences need to be honored in the individual as well as in the group in order for the classroom or family environment to respect both the individual as well as the group. In other words, differences in learners provide opportunities for more integration of complex ideas by allowing students to use their learning systems to communicate.*

Opportunities are planned and executed on a daily basis to "showcase" all learners with *language* that *respects* the individual learner as a contributing member to the group. For example, the typical classroom "show and tell" activity is often fraught with disrespectful behaviors, students talking to other students while a person in the front of the room is talking, teachers who are doing three or four other tasks rather than attending physically and personally to the speaker, etc. Rules for the "show and tell" situation requires *respectful language* that positively assigns meaning or explains why the person at the front is talking. For example, "Suzie is standing at the front of the room so we know that she is ready to share her ideas with us." A reason for listening might be as simple as "When Suzie is finished sharing her ideas with us, it will be our role to show her how well we understood. One way to show that we heard her ideas is to ask her questions about what she has shared." As students become more sophisticated in reasons for participating and as learners are valued for their contributions, they shift their behaviors to those that are more acceptable. The shift in behavior occurs as language is used to show respect for student's learning behavior. For example, Suzie is finished talking and Sean yells out a question. The teacher thanks him for his idea and writes the question on the board in Sean's words. The teacher also lets the class know that it is easier to hear ideas when people take turns by raising a hand. The teacher connects Sean's behavior to Suzie's behavior, "Suzie, I think you might have a better idea on who is ready to ask a question so I will leave the calling on students up to you. Who would you like to record the questions?" Suzie is helped to start the process. There is also respectful language for how Suzie will answer the questions or who will resource, etc. It's fun to watch Sean's behavior change as he sees students accept his ideas and he is complimented for being part of the class. Shy students are often discouraged to speak out because they are literally embarrassed by having to participate. In a classroom where all learners are respected, being shy is acceptable behavior. Students are given an "assigned expertise." For example, the teacher might say on behalf of a "shy" student, "Elizabeth might tell you that aluminum is a very light metal. Yet, that metal is very strong. Isn't that right, Elizabeth?" Elizabeth nods her head. The teacher gives more examples and thanks Elizabeth for her thoughts. Elizabeth is then asked if she would like to work with the teacher on a project on aluminum. She is allowed to hold up some pictures, point to vocabulary words on the board, or simply call on other students who have comments or questions about aluminum. The teacher answers the questions and still refers to Elizabeth as the teacher's associate. Soon, Elizabeth is participating because she has found that in a classroom of respect all ideas are valid and accepted. All learners' needs are respected. All learners are encouraged to raise their cognitive level of concepts by representing ideas in a variety of ways. Students learn that any sort of work may be refined...drawings become written papers, posters become reports, pointing to vocabulary becomes a way to cue a visual idea, etc.

In summary, the neurological learning system develops concepts that form language. These language concepts become a tool for more in-depth learning. It was pointed out that the changes in the learning system could occur within the first two years. It is apparent from correlational work with different disciplines' research that many of the students in today's schools are different in their ability to learn. As previously mentioned, only 25 percent of the students will learn from the typical spoken or oral language system which emphasizes the teacher talking, the students listening, and the teaching of reading and writing being based on a spoken or auditory language system of words. Therefore, if the methods, delivery instruction and activities do not capitalize on how students learn best as well as on the way that all students *are able to learn*, then the schools may be restructured and retooled but the system will continue to fail the students. For the students to be respected as learners, how the students learn must also be respected when setting up the classroom. When the students are respected for their ability to learn and to contribute to the classroom through respectful language, then their behavior reflects such positive assignment of meaning.

Activity

1. **Describe how patterns of visual complexity and complex auditory patterns result in differences in language.**
2. **Explain how respectful language honors differences in learners.**

Respecting Similarities in Student Learning

It's apparent that students are different in the way they respond and in the way they relate to previous experiences or information because each student's past is unique. The developmentalist will quickly point out that students are different in social backgrounds, genetics, environmental learning, etc. But often the students are more alike than different if the students' learning systems were considered in the development of the curriculum. For example, a teacher selects the activity of having the students complete a "coat of arms" in which the students list interests, ambitions, leisure activities, name, age, etc. But, when the teacher is asked if the activity is "developmentally appropriate," the teacher responds philosophically by saying: "The 'kids' like it." "We always do it." "Third graders are expected to do it." These types of responses do not address the cognitive level, the social level, or language level of the individual child or student within the classroom. *Doing the same task with all of the students presupposes that all students are at the same developmental level, functioning in the same way, and learning with the same neurological system.*

The *task is respected* by setting up elaborate rules for how to have all students doing their individual coat of arms, but the individual learner's understanding of "why" do the task or how the task relates to past or future learning is not respected. The same task could be set up differently. For example, on the first day of instruction, the students learn that they have a prolonged opportunity to do an ethnic report on their own background. Students are provided all sorts of sources in addition to the classroom and the parents. At back to school night parents are given more supports and guidance. Students and parents are shown samples of ethnic reports. Sensitivity to adoptive students is offered by being sure the report is about "today" and not just a chronology of events. Students are asked to collect songs, recipes, letters, documents, data from interviews with anyone who is considered "family," pictures, vocabulary lists, etc. Nothing is rejected...and students are expected to refine their work to a minimum of 20 pages, no maximum. Students are encouraged to find out about other families and other places as well as their own since many students in some schools lack the family support...or may have an embarrassing situation such as an incarcerated parent, alcohol abuse at home, etc. So, the emphasis is on "What do you know and what can you find out and what would you like to know?" Students are encouraged to chart, draw, write or graph any of their ideas as ways to organize their material. Format is discussed in class and students are given visual models to help form a mental picture or language about the tasks. The activity on "coats of arms" becomes a "by product" where each student is allowed to choose different aspects of the coat of arms. Some are historians. Some are artists. Some are collators. Some are publishers. Students self select working with others who have chosen the same aspect to research. Students become learners in a process that uses language to respect what we have in common as members of families but also what we have that is different as learners. Setting up this type of classroom results in students who continue beyond class assignments. With older students (fifth/sixth grade), Mr. Young has had students request extensions of time to continue the process even though the students requesting extensions might have 60 to 70 pages completed. *When students' learning systems are respected for their differences as well as similarities, the content becomes easy and the desire to do "personal best" increases.* The family "who factor" is also extended with these types of activity adjustments. Respecting family and student differences and similarities allows for a stronger development of oneself.

Students also respond differently to the same situation because their learning systems are neurobiologically similar, but the processing of incoming sensory patterns can be different. In other words, learners behave differently because they have learned different things. And, they learn different things in similar situations because learners process the sensory patterns differently. Children or students think differently about the same task because each person is at his or her own level of conceptualization. Even though each student is able to assign meaning to incoming patterns and concepts, each student symbolizes or attaches meaning to the patterns and concepts differently because each student has different information. Finally, learners or students are similar because they are "human." They are social agents within a community, not instruments to be manipulated like tools in a factory of "coat of arms" makers or "snowmen" duplicators. *Only if the classroom is structured to meet the developmental needs of all learners in such a way as to honor learning differences and differences in past learning will a classroom respect the similarities of all learners' needs to be successful. Being a successful learner within a classroom or a successful citizen within a community or family respects the individual.*

Activity

1. **How are students similar in their learning needs?**
2. **How does respecting students' learning needs respect the individual differences of learners?**

What Does the Student Bring to the Classroom?

The student brings an innate as well as developed learning system to the classroom. The innate system has been developed neurologically since his or her second birthday, to that neurological system is added past conceptual experiences. These past experiences include both academic as well as nonacademic situations that were originally nothing more than sensory input. The sensory input later evolves into complex patterns that form concepts. Language represents the development of these concepts for all learners. So, the student's learning system functions as well as the student's language is developed.

The student's past academic background assigns meaning to what the student expects of school as well as of teachers. If the background has been authoritarian then the student has learned the basic **authoritarian lesson: The student is as successful as allowed.** If the student's background is based on **authoritative** *respect* for individual similarities as well as learner differences, then the student has learned a different primary lesson: **The strength of the neurological system allows the student to be successful** as a learner, as a member of the classroom community.

The authoritarian system filters the student's needs into specific roles and expectations. These roles include being shy, quiet, reserved, or lazy. Such roles often extend into functions of the classroom, such as the nonreader, the "kid" who can't write, the obnoxious "kid," or even the class clown. Since all of the students in an authoritarian system must make up a whole, the only individuality is the way the students combine to represent all of the possibilities of the bell shaped curve. Therefore, there always has to be failures as well as a few successes. Because the students from these authoritarian classrooms have learned that they will perform only as well as the system allows, they also bring fears, anxieties, and uncertainties. For example, one student was reluctant to answer in class and actually cried when her name was called at roll on the first day. She was unskilled in how to belong or to join a group. *The authoritarian classroom perpetuates these past fears by expecting the student to be like all other students academically, socially, and behaviorally. However, in a classroom of thoughtful communicative events where each student is successful, the anxieties, fears, and uncertainties diminish within the first 60 days.* The safety from success, the support from the respect of fellow classmates, and the nurturance of what the student is able to do protects the student's individuality within a healthy group process called the community. *This pattern of safety, support, nurturance, and healthy protection repeats itself day after day, thus changing the student's concept of what the classroom is all about. The students actually learn the more complex concepts such as "respect" from the overlapping of language patterns that assign positive support, nurturance, and healthy protection.*

In a classroom, which is authoritarian, the student is restricted to specific roles and functions previously experienced. So, if the student believes that he can't read, then he can't. If the student is unskilled in belonging or joining the group then the student stays excluded all year. As long as the environment is similar to past environments, the student's self-concept will not change. The student will repeat past learned patterns that simplify the learner's development into feeling excluded as a learner.

Furthermore, the noncommunity-authoritarian system promotes specific survival skills so that the student functions at the median or a mediocre level. The student does not anticipate being in charge or being responsible. These are the advanced types of complex concepts that require a setting that uses language to respect the learner's maximum cognitive development. In the simplified authoritarian system, the teacher is the patriarch or matriarch in charge. The built-in restriction in roles creates a hesitancy to break out of these roles and to be different. Students are hesitant to do "more" cognitive development. Limitations from these past academic experiences necessitate validation from peers and from the teacher for verification. The student believes only what others verify. The truth lies in the past, not the present. *In the classroom of respect, the system exists to promote the individual learner so that with success, the student learns that he or she is in charge of the group process as well as individual learning.* The teacher offers ways for the student to learn that matches with the way the student *can* learn and there is a "win-win" experience for both the teacher and the students. Such win-win experience comes from the use of language to respect the learner's needs.

The communication lines are open among students and the teacher within the respectful classroom so that the students gain enough strength to take risks, to wonder about information, to problem solve, to critically think for the good of the entire classroom. These new experiences allow the students to feel empowered in making choices about the classroom activities. The students learn that the teacher is not omnipotent but a learner as well. The ability to be responsible for one's learning is seen as a "natural motivator." This natural motivation changes the student from someone seeking external approval or rewards to someone who is intrinsically motivated.

The feeling of being empowered as a learner also allows the student to select behavior that is conducive to making friends that are intrinsically valued. These friends are valued for their social support as well as expertise in specific areas. Community respect is built from the development of these natural friendship alliances as well as from the need to work with each other for what the other person has to offer. There does not exist a need to manufacture a sense of group identity or individual recognition because built into this community are so many opportunities to gain recognition naturally. For example, when the shy child speaks up with a louder voice, the child is not isolated from the group; but, the group is praised, "So many of us are learning to use louder voices." This message is like a natural consequence since the peers will usually say, "Oh, you mean Mary." There is no one right answer in the classroom where the learner is respected. The teacher may respond, "Why do you think it is Mary?" The process of becoming an individual within a group system is a win-win situation for both the student and the teacher. These natural ways to support one another creates the boundaries for maximum social development through respectful language that improves cognitive as well as social development.

In the classroom focused on the curriculum and its parts (not the learner), there are artificially imposed boundaries and limits through external rewards, praise, grades, and rules. Those students from noncommunity or authoritarian families and classrooms pair up with students in a whimsical way so that they are "buddies" only because of some common denominator. For example, peers or buddies who are working off of what is externally valued will seek solutions that are personally based and self-centered much like the college graffiti artist earlier reported. No matter how well the teacher tries to group the students, the teacher's grouping still belongs to the teacher and the rationale for working with someone else is artificially imposed therefore limiting social development. In other words, the externally motivated student connects only through the material world. There is little student involvement that builds the connections for maximum learning. Building socially and cognitively for superficial reasons does not create the depth of social responsiveness necessary in a respectful citizen (a complex concept that is acquired through the use of maximum learning principles applied to multiple cognitive experiences developed in multiple ways). Past cognitive experiences exist for all learners. It is the teacher's responsibility to tap into that cognitive wealth by open communication with the student, the parents, the bus drivers, the school secretary, etc. *The open communication develops a* **language of RESPECT** *for the learner, the learner's differences as well as the learner's similarities to others in the same group.*

Activity

1. **Since students differ in past experiences, and not just neurobiology, how does the classroom setting allow for these differences to exist?**
2. **What does a student bring to the classroom?**
3. **How does language work as a tool to honor individual learner's cognitive development of complex concepts such as respect?**

Summary

Most teachers are trained to teach skills and concepts. But the use of *language to respect* the individuals within a classroom requires the teacher to shift emphasis from teaching to learning. Therefore, central to an educational community is the individual learner. If the community is supportive of the learner, then "who" the learner is, must be defined beyond the constituents of the "self." The learner's system of concept acquisition demonstrates how the learner thinks and uses language to learn. *Respect* for the learner as different but similar to others comes from the use of *language* by others as well as by the learner through multiple cognitive experiences. Finally, the learner must be provided opportunities to successfully participate within the community so as to gain personal self-respect as an achiever as well as a community builder.

This chapter has discussed the student as a learner who comes to the classroom with a past. The past has already determined the way the child is neurologically able to learn. The past has also defined the way the student behaves. If the classroom is designed to define the student in terms of the past, then the student is what the system defines. If the student is allowed to develop as an individual learner within the classroom community, then the student brings a thoroughly developed learning system, intact constituents of "self," a knowledge base from past experiences, and the power to learn through concept development. By using learning principles of networking, building, bridging and troughing, the educator or parent can provide multiple opportunities for the learner to successfully use language to succeed. Learning is therefore a social as well as cognitive process. Chapter Three describes the social characteristics of the learner who has basic needs of being supported, nurtured and protected. In this way, the *respect for the learner* is magnified in the group process. Chapter Four describes the cognitive characteristics of the learner for maximum success and self-respect as an individual within a group.

Activity

1. **Describe the learning process. Be sure to talk about neurobiological, social, and cognitive aspects.**
2. **How does concept development through the use of language respect the learner's needs?**

REFERENCES

Association for Supervision and Curriculum Development. 1998. How the Brain Learns. *Educational Leadership,* 56, 3:8-92.

American Academy of Pediatrics. 1984. Statement of Middle Ear Disease and Language Development. *Journal of Pediatrics* News and Comments section.

Arwood, E. Lucas. 1991. *Semantic and Pragmatic Language Disorders* (2nd Edition). Gaithesburg, MD: Aspen Publishers, Inc.

Calvin, W.H. 1996. *How Brains Think: Evolving Intelligence Then and Now.* New York: Basic Books, A Division of Harper Collins Publishers.

Carruthers, P. 1996. *Language, Thought, and Consciousness: An Essay in Philosophical Psychology.* Cambridge: Cambridge University Press.

DeMasio, A. 1994. *Descartes' Error: Emotion, Reason, and the Human Brain.* Lecture in The Institute for Science, Engineering, and Public Policy. Portland, OR: November.

Eberhard, N. 1998. *Analysis of Oral, Read, and Written Language in a Middle School to Determine the Access Feasibility for Students with Visual Metacognitive Systems.* Thesis in partial fulfillment of a Master's Degree, University of Portland, OR.

Greenough, William T., J.E. Black, and Christopher S. Wallace. 1987. Experience and Brain Development. *Child Development* 58: 538-559.

Greenfield, S.A. 1997. *The Human Brain: A Guided Tour.* New York: Basic Books, A Division of Harper Collins Publishers.

Leavy, J. 1996. Mother's Little Helper with Ritalin, the Son Also Rises. *Newsweek*, March 18, 50-59.

Maslow, A.H. 1970. *Motivation and Personality* (2nd Edition). New York: Harper & Row.

Naugle, R., Cullum, C.M., and Bigler, E.D. 1998. *Introduction to Neuropsychology: A Case Book.* Austin, TX: PRO-ED, Inc.

Santock, John W. 1997. *Life-Span Development* (6th Edition). Madison, WI: Brown & Benchmark.

Volkow, N. & Tancredi, L. 1991. Biological Correlates of Mental Activity Studies with PET. *American Journal of Psychiatry* 148: 4, 439-443.

Webster, D.B. 1988. Human Central Auditory Pathways and Human Brain Dissection. Kresge Hearing Research Laboratory, New Orleans, LA, August 5-8.

Webster, D.B. and M. Webster. 1977. Neonatal Sound Deprivation Affects Brainstem Auditory Nuclei. *Archives of Otolaryngology* 103: 392-396.

Chapter Three

Learner Outcomes

Upon completion of this chapter, the reader will be able to do the following:

1. Describe what is meant by "language of social respect."
2. Explain how the individual learner gains from being a part of the social community.
3. Explain the various components of the "self" in terms of social learning.
4. Explain the differences between authoritative and authoritarian social development.
5. Explain how support, protection, and nurturance of the individual within a classroom are expressions of respect.
6. Describe the use of language to assign social meaning to the individual.
7. Describe the use of language to assign social meaning to the group.
8. Describe the process of socialization.

CHAPTER THREE

The Language of Social Respect

How do we respect socialization?

The wonder of the child--
A self, a person, an agent!
Oh, should we gaze not into the eye?
To see is to know the self of the child!

The master teacher stands and watches the classroom function. Each student is busy. Each student is engaged. Each student is working within the expected classroom framework. Such group activity results from providing each student the opportunity to grow and to learn. As learners, each student is independently becoming part of a group as well as struggling to be an "agent," separate from the others. Group members assign meaning to individual student's behavior. Each student's personal "self" takes on social characteristics. **This process of being an independent person who fits within the expected norms of a group is called socialization.** Every person is socialized through the parameters of others' language use. The purpose of this chapter is to provide the reader with a description of a learner's socialization process. Examples of how families or classrooms can use language to respect the socialization process of a learner are provided. Social characteristics of a classroom determine the type of socialization process of each child or student. These social characteristics support the respect of the individual while honoring the social needs of a group or community. In other words, *the community nurtures the individual's development. The community members actively participate in assigning meaning to the individuals within the group through the use of language. Language use becomes the tool for the social development of individuals.*

A student's learning is based on the cognitive connection between others' external assignments of meaning to the student's internal cognitive development. Therefore, **the respectful classroom is designed to recognize and honor the learning process. Opportunities for the assignment of meaning establish the learning process, which consists of each student's socio-cognitive development.** Chapter Four describes the cognitive characteristics of the individual learner.

Social Development

What is social development? The main social concepts acquired include *self-esteem, self-concept, self-worth, and self-discipline. A learner's social development is fostered by others in the learner's environment. Other people assign meaning to what the learner accomplishes. Such accomplishments are related to what society members value as important. The interactive process between the acquisition of the concepts and the development of these social areas is called socialization.*

All concepts are acquired through a cognitive learning process, which allows the individual to socially develop as he, or she interacts with others. For example, being able to jump rope might be a valued accomplishment of a first grader. The first grade child who can jump rope then is viewed as "fitting" into the group that "jumps rope." A high school student who can join a gang is valued by the other "gang members" who fit into this group. Gangs provide the feeling of belonging or fit that sometimes family and school can't provide.

The ability to achieve a "fitting" talent provides a first grade student or a gang member with better esteem about oneself (**bridge and trough principles of learning**). In addition to developing higher self-esteem for being able to fit into a group, the value of how the student or learner perceives him or herself within the group provides the development of the person's self-concept (**building principle**). For example, high school athletic students wear their jackets with letters because of the pride and feelings of "belonging." At many high schools today, providing the same type of jacket for academic endeavors has followed the athletic jackets.

Whatever meaning the members of a group has assigned to certain behavior or actions determines what the values of membership are for that group—gangs, sports, academics, etc.

When a student is aware of how the community or group values these achievements, then the student's perception of how he or she relates to those values begins to take shape. The student begins to value him or herself accordingly. Recognition of how one is valued by others is "self-awareness." Self-awareness contributes insight to one's self-concept (**networking principle**). The group's recognition of a person's achievements may not hold the same value as society's value for the group. For example, the first grader who can jump rope is aware of how the community values the achievement of jumping rope. Therefore, the child is aware of how jumping rope helps the child fit into the greater whole. The jumper fits into the first grade which also fits into society's' values. However, even though a gang member builds self-esteem because of individual achievements as a gang member, society or the greater whole does not approve of gang membership. Therefore, a gang member may have high self-esteem from his individual gang achievements, but poor self-concept. The poor self-concept is the result of the gang member being aware that the "whole society" does not value gang membership. *The ability to be accepted by a group for individual contributions as well as the group being accepted by society provides for social development of the individual's self-esteem, what a person can do, as well as self-concept, who the person is. Self-awareness is the individual's recognition of how he or she fits into the various groups.*

Language is the cognitive tool used to assign meaning to what a child or student does. Individuals, family, school members and "groups" assign meaning. From these externally assigned meanings, a student or child organizes the language patterns as social concepts about his or herself. A learner's development of each of these social areas may be fostered in the family or classroom that uses *language* to *respect* each learner as well as the group. Classrooms that show such social respect are often viewed as "different" or "unconventional." Families that use language to develop a child's social "self" are considered "healthy." A classroom, which is able to use the language of social respect, might be considered a "pseudo-family." The following sections describe each area of social development.

Self-Esteem

When a child begins to connect to the classroom, then the child is beginning to be an "esteemed" member of the community. **Self-esteem is, therefore, an attribute of how well the child is able to succeed within a group.** For most students there are four social groups: the family, the school, the peers, and other social agencies (soccer, boy scouts, and church, for example). And, most students have begun to identify with one or more of these groups by preadolescence (grades 2-6; social development age of 7-11).

When the student accomplishes tasks within a given group, then the student is paying dues to become a member of that group. For example, if the requirements of membership in a classroom are that the student is able to read, then the student who cannot read does not have anything of value to contribute to the membership of "the readers." Therefore, the student does not fit into the group value of being a reader. The nonreader will then need to socially find something else to make him or herself feel like a contributing member. Likewise, the student who is already a reader fits into the group of readers. Developing oneself begins with being able to fit into a group followed by learning how one becomes unique within the group. Such a change in social development is part of the socialization process. Being able to fit must come before being unique. The reader fits into the group and so the reader can continue to socially develop.

When a student is able to accomplish the tasks valued by the membership of a group, then the student's self-esteem is developed. For example, the reader's accomplishments increase self-esteem so that the student who reads is nurtured by the group that values reading achievements. The student who is able to read contributes to the membership of the classroom that values reading. Reading might be something that is valued by a group. Likewise, *respect* may be something also valued within a classroom. If "respect" is valued, then students will begin to participate in behavior that is deemed respectful so as to engage in behavior that "fits the assigned meaning of respect."

On the other hand, if teachers are not ready to respect themselves or do not know how to be respectful to students then respect is not valued and the class members will demonstrate behavior that society views as not respectful. For example, when a student asks a question of the teacher, the teacher sighs and puts his hands on his hips and says, "That is the dumbest question I have ever heard." The teacher's verbal and nonverbal behavior assign meaning to the student's "self." This student does not feel successful as a learner. The student will now begin to make his behavior fit so as to not be successful. The same teacher later asks a question in class. The student rolls his eyes, slouches down into the chair, puts his feet up on the back of the desk ahead and sighs. The student has *learned* to act out the meaning of "dumbest." The teacher assigned meaning to *not* be successful, and so the student fits the meaning. The student acts "dumb" and loses self-esteem, the ability to achieve as expected.

The student knows that the "rest of the world" expects the student to achieve, to be successful. But, in this classroom where the teacher says that the student's question is the "dumbest," the student is receiving the opposite message, how not to achieve. The student's self-esteem does not develop, but may actually lower. If the student received credit for needing to ask a question and the teacher had assigned a positive meaning, then the student could have been given the opportunity to fit into the group and to feel like an achiever. Self-esteem increases when the student "fits." *When a child or student does not fit into a group, then alternate ways of fitting are sought.* For example, the nonreader will need to seek socialization in a way other than reading, perhaps from being designated by his peers as the "class clown." The student who asked a "dumb question" might need to quit participating or completing class assignments.

It's the adult family member or classroom teacher who provides students with the opportunity to fit by assigning meaning to whatever level of achievement the child is able to perform. For example, one student transferred into a fourth grade classroom late in the year. The students were producing handwritten letters in their best penmanship as part of another project...sending out thank you's to community people for assisting in class activities. The new student said he could not produce the letter, as he did not have good penmanship. The teacher said that was okay and wrote an "A" on the top of the student's blank paper. The teacher told the student to turn in his "personal best" letter sometime before the end of the year. The student looked shocked. The teacher asked the fourth grade student what was the problem. Before the student answered, the teacher said, "Oh, it should have been given an A+." So, he made the "A" into an "A+."

The next day, the thank you letters were turned in. The parents of the new student called or stopped by to ask if handwriting was a major part of the curriculum. The parents were stunned when the teacher said, "No, we spend 10 minutes a day discussing our writing and allowing students to work on it." The son of these parents had spent three hours writing his "personal best" letter. The "A+" was well deserved. *This student needed to feel like he fit into the class and he needed to be able to do the work that the other students did.* The teacher assigned positive meaning and gave the student the opportunity to be successful, to not be judged for his product by others which is why he was given the A+. But, the other message given by the teacher was that the student's own achievement would be a valued contribution, whenever it was turned in and whatever way the product looked. Office staff, janitors, and bus drivers used to watch this teacher's students make transitions without adult supervision. Even middle school students were able to move from classroom to gym or to the bus in a quiet line. These students were part of a classroom based on the **"Language of RESPECT."**

When students are given the opportunity to fit within a group and to achieve by the standards or values of the group then students feel the pride of fitting but also being exceptional at the same time. Students in this type of classroom or family structure develop a high self-esteem. They learn that they are important contributors. The adult members' language places emphasis on the child or student, not the rules or products. Achievements are seen as products of the learning system. And, the learning system is developing what the child or student knows about being able to achieve.

When the student is not able to perform a task according to group expectations, then the student no longer feels like a part of the group. In other words, the student has no value within the group's standards, so the student's self-esteem begins to decline. For example, in school, the student is expected to perform certain academic tasks such as reading, writing, and arithmetic. If the student cannot achieve at one of these tasks, then the student begins to lose membership in the school community and the student's self-esteem begins to decline fostering a "I can't do it (the school work)" attitude along with other social stigma such as "I don't want to" and "I won't." At the end of the preadolescent years (7 to 11 years), students move into junior high or middle school. At this point, it is not uncommon to find the majority of students have either developed an "I can't" or "I won't" attitude from failures or feelings of not being successful in a given area. "I can't do math." "I hate school." "I like school, but I don't like homework."

Students "bond" with similar students. The authors have seen students at the end of these preadolescent years swing both directions--- become better students and citizens or become worse students and citizens. The fulcrum appears to relate to self-esteem. *Students who feel challenged to achieve and who do achieve at higher levels, and who fit into the group, find satisfaction and pride with becoming better students and citizens.* Students who are not fitting and who do not feel like they are achieving, often are not challenged and begin to show worse grades and behavior.

Self-esteem is a direct product of achieving within a valued set of members, whether it is in the classroom or in the family. A child's self-esteem is high when this child is producing what is expected. Therefore, the classroom's expectations often determine a student's self-esteem for academic success. Research results have often suggest that a child with higher self-esteem will academically do better than a child with lower self-esteem. *The obvious dilemma is that a student's performance within the classroom is also dependent upon how well the teacher is able to provide success for the student.* When students are provided the opportunity to be contributing members to the classroom, then the students develop higher self-esteem.

Teachers who offer an open concept of expected outcomes provide the flexibility for all students to achieve and for all students to show a higher self-esteem. For example, the previously mentioned teacher allowed the fourth-grade student with the opportunity to produce a letter at any time. The only criterion was that the letter writing be the student's personal best. The student already had a grade, so the product really didn't matter. It was the value the student placed on the letter that mattered. The student's opinion of his personal best was valued. *When the value is for the process (respecting oneself, others, the classroom, society, other's opinions, etc.) rather than the products or achievements, then the emphasis is more on the learner or student, and less on the products.* For example, when students in a classroom based on **RESPECT** are mixed with students from other classes (for example, music or PE), there sometimes appears to be little transfer of respectful behavior. The other classroom is not used to functioning with respect since the convention for society as a whole is not to use the language of respect. However, when teachers talk with students about this difference, the students say that the other students "laugh at them" when they show respectful behaviors such as holding open doors, offering others the opportunity to share, etc. The authors' observations confirmed the students' feeling that others laughed at them. The authors have noted that the "language of social respect" is often not a part of the other classrooms. However, there is a relationship between each student's social development and the variety of places allowing for respect. The more groups that allow a student to achieve, the higher the self-esteem. In other words, socialization is more likely to allow for higher self-esteem if more classrooms, families, and social groups expect the **language of RESPECT.**

To assist students in accepting a different way of behaving in other situations that may not foster the **language of RESPECT***, class discussions about goals and about how students view themselves becomes a recurrent theme.* By the end of the year, older students are able to separate themselves from peer pressure to be disrespectful. For example, Dr. Arwood's daughter, a second grade child, visited Mr. Young's fifth grade classroom on the second-to-last day of school. The fifth grade class got ready to go to PE in the gym. The students asked Miss Arwood to go with them to PE. She went to the gym with the fifth graders while the authors, Dr. Arwood and Mr. Young, remained in the classroom to discuss student-writing projects. When Mr. Young's students returned, one of the students quickly reported, "Mr. Young the other fifth graders were teasing and laughing at Miss Arwood." Mr. Young quietly said, "Did you handle it?" Several students said in chorus. "We sure did." He said, "Thank you. I knew that you would know what to do in a situation like this and I am sure that you took care of it." Miss Arwood looked happy and a part of Mr. Young's group. Later, she was asked what happened. She said that the fifth graders were running relays and that the 'kids' were laughing at her because she was younger, smaller, and not as capable. When asked what Mr. Young's class did. She said, "They told the students that I was a visiting guest and that they were not to laugh at me. Mr. Young's fifth graders are nice. They aren't like my school's fifth graders or the ones in the gym." She was asked, "What type of fifth grader will you choose to be?" She said, "I will be like the nice ones." She is in high school as this chapter is being written, and, so far, she has chosen to be different, to be respectful of younger students.

When a student is successfully earning his or her right to membership in the class or the school, then the student begins to connect personal worth to success. While self-esteem may be connected to achievement, the child's perception of personal worth based on others' expectations offers the social challenge of growth within the self-concept. *The self-concept is more about the child's personal "who" constituents. Respecting oneself and others in a classroom helps develop the self-concept as well as self-esteem.*

Activity

1. **Define self-esteem.**
2. **Explain how self-esteem is developed. Give examples.**

Self-Concept

Whereas self-esteem refers to the ability of a student or child to achieve within a group, **self-concept refers to person's ability to value personal fit within a group as an unique contributor to the group.** *The student's self-concept develops from an interaction between the meaning assigned by members of a group to how the student feels about his or her contributions to the membership.* For example, the group members offer verbal and nonverbal value to what the student is able to do. Even through the student may be achieving and therefore may possess a high self-esteem, if the student feels like he or she is not worthy of such achievements, then the student will develop a negative self-concept. Students often exhibit a gap between self-esteem and self-concept. For example, students who easily achieve, often feel that they do not deserve the rewards of the successes. On the other hand, many students work harder than their peers only to come up short in receiving recognition for their hard work because they lack the products to show achievement or accomplishments.

Personal compliments are often difficult to accept when a student experiences a gap between his or her ability to achieve and how they view themselves, their self-concepts. To assist students in learning to feel valued as individuals, compliments about interests, desires, learning systems, or any other personal constituents lace the curriculum. For example, photographs of students doing something to help other students are taken with a Polaroid or digital camera and then printed out with a written thank you or compliment. "Jane is helping Mary with the computer. Thanks for your extra computer work." Or, young children are given such praise, "Thanks for putting your coat on the hook when you walked into the classroom today. Now, other students will see what to do with their coats." At first, the compliments can appear to be awkward and superficial, "Nice jacket, Bill." But discussion about how we all need to feel good about our ideas, interests, choices, etc. helps students to begin to feel the familiarity of offering compliments and accepting compliments. Compliment giving as well as receiving is valued as part of the "**language of RESPECT,**" *the Right for Each Student to Participate in an Environment of Communicative Thoughtfulness.* **ALL** students are featured as being significant contributors to this type of environment every day. Compliments become more frequent, common and mature in giving and receiving. Even guests receive such "sweet surprises."

Rewards are similar in function to compliments for helping students to socialize themselves. Students are often extrinsically motivated; they feel they must receive outsider's consideration because that is what they have experienced in the past. However, the successful child or student is capable of gaining recognition by peers and others, thus multiplying the sources of recognition tremendously in a classroom where there are many people.

Making the social shift from externally assigned value to an intrinsic value of oneself is difficult. Parents and educators have the power to help children and students make such a shift. For example, after a discussion about self-esteem, a college graduate student in a human development class said, "Dr. Arwood, I know I would feel more comfortable in this class if I knew I had an A." Dr. Arwood asked, "Is an 'A' grade more important to you than your learning?" The student

replied, "I can't learn because I am too scared that I won't get an 'A'."
Dr. Arwood responded, "Well, I believe that all of you have 'A' grades
right now. If you get less than an 'A' grade it is because you chose not to
keep your 'A.' Do you want me to put an 'A' in my grade book? I will
do that so that you know you have an 'A'." The student sighed and said,
"Yes." Dr. Arwood pulled out the grade sheet and recorded an "A" next
to the student's name. Dr. Arwood then showed the student that the
grade was under the "final grade" column and that it was in ink next to
her name. The student said "thank you" and began earning the grade.
Her work was far superior than expected for all assignments.

At the time of the student's request, the other students said, "Wow is
that all it takes...just ask for it?" Dr. Arwood said, "I will write an 'A'
next to anyone's name. It will be up to you to decide to work up to that
grade or choose not to. It is okay to chose not to do 'A' work. We all
have different needs, desires, schedules, priorities, etc." One of the
students came up that same evening during the break and said, "My wife
is dying of cancer, my son is hospitalized after leg surgery, and I had to
miss teaching school today to be with my wife and her doctors. I have
chosen to work for a 'B.' Is that okay?" Dr. Arwood queried, "What are
you doing to work for a 'B'?" The student, still worried about how he
might be perceived said, "Well, I just can't do my personal best right
now, but I will turn all the work in and I am learning a lot."

Concerned about the student's need to justify his behavior, Dr.
Arwood asked, "Is a 'B' okay with you?" He quickly responded, "Oh
yes, I will be thrilled to have earned a 'B'." Since his choices are
personal, Dr. Arwood replied, "Then it is okay with me. Now, what are
you doing for yourself?" Somewhat surprised that Dr. Arwood didn't
care if he worked for a "B" but was more concerned about him, he said,
"What do you mean?" She explained, "Well, what are you doing to
handle your feelings about your wife, son and work?" Relieved to be
accepted for his choices, he sighed, "I am coming to class. Class is for
me. I learn so much about 'who' I am and I am learning to be okay with
'who' I am." Thrilled that the student was learning about himself, Dr.

Arwood asked, "How does that affect your teaching?" Whimsically, he said, "My students are having more fun. We laugh a lot and they are learning more. Right now, they are my inspiration." By studying his own development, this teacher was also developing as a person, and so were his students. His changes in his self-concept were affecting his interactions with his students. His self-esteem had always been high, but now his self-concept was beginning to match.

In order for students to feel successful and worthy, then the classroom must provide an atmosphere that is safe for all students to risk and to be rewarded as individuals who fit within a group. A child who is able to develop a way to achieve and who feels worthy of the success is a valuable member of a society. When the classroom consists of such valued members, then the community emulates a healthy extended or pseudo-family. If each student is aware of what he or she is able to contribute, then the classroom offers protection from self-devaluation. Such self-awareness bridges the gap between knowing what is expected and how to achieve. In this way, **self-concept is about who the student is...the student's personal values, likes, dislikes, feelings of worthiness, desires, etc.**

Activity

1. **Define self-concept and explain how it is different from self-esteem.**
2. **Describe how self-concept is developed. Give examples of self-concept development.**

Self-Worth

When the members of a society are aware of how each person contributes to the whole, then each member is aware of his or her social self-worth. For example, one student member may illustrate beautifully, while another student is able to orally articulate a story. If the illustrator understands how he or she contributes to those who do not illustrate while the orator understands how he or she is able to contribute to those who do not orally participate, then these two members have acquired some self-awareness of how they might be valued within the group's membership. Such awareness of one's "self" provides the individual with sufficient self-worth. To be worthy of membership within a group offers the possibility of being socially acceptable. *Acceptance as a group member feeds the constituents of the "self" whereas working for approval of products leaves the student needy for further social development.*

Social development is at its best when the student is achieving membership within the community (using the student's own standards). Each student then is a valuable member who is successfully determining the structure of the group in terms of what is to be valued. For example, the gang sets the standards for who achieves or is a valuable member just like specific classroom methods often determine who will read or be successful. The gang or school, as an organization, may determine who may be successful and whether students feel worthy of membership. The individual member has no self-worth unless the member can socially consider him or herself as a valuable member. For the individual member to feel worthy of the group standards, then whatever the individual can contribute must be given an assigned value so as to create the group standard. For example, a child cannot read aloud well. But, perhaps the same child is able to tell about what he or she mentally pictures from seeing words, not saying the words. If the child is allowed to look at print and draw pictures about the ideas seen on the page prior to reading aloud, then the student may be a successful oral reader.

By being able to do what the other students do in the way the student learns best, the student has begun to demonstrate how he or she is worthy of being a member of this community. But, if the child fails at reading aloud, then the membership of the classroom becomes exclusive rather than inclusive. The student who cannot read aloud is not part of the group. It should be noted that in some schools or classrooms, there are more students who can't real well aloud than there are students who can read aloud well; so, two or three students and the teacher become "readers" for all of the students. This type of action really destroys self-worth. The teacher values reading aloud "so much" that the students' need for alternative ways to take information from the printed page is not recognized. Students who don't read well feel a loss of being able to achieve, day after day. Those who read quickly and silently, but not aloud, are not recognized. Only the teacher's needs of being sure the students orally "read" the material are being honored or respected. *Individual learning differences are not heard and therefore not respected.* **Respecting individual differences means allowing students to feel worthy as contributors.**

Students are given opportunities to contribute by taking lunch count, opening the door, unlocking the door, taking guests jackets, changing the temperature of the room, calling for class meetings or reviews, asking others to assist, etc. But, it is the class who decides how the group will honor and respect everyone who shares the "power" or work in the room. When the teacher assigns these tasks, then the teacher is still controlling and the student feels little self-worth as a contributor. Just as children at home need the opportunity to manage tasks they know how to do, so do the students in a classroom. For example, a teacher may want to set the tone of the classroom "physically" belonging to the students the first day of school by explaining that there will be times when the room is too warm or too cold or the hallway too noisy and then asking the students what the rules should be to take care of these types of needs. Even Kindergarten students are able to brainstorm about ways to set up the room so that the person closest to the door, closes the door if the hall is too noisy, etc.

By offering the responsibility of caring for the physical space of the classroom to the students, the students learn to manage themselves in relationship to others and to give support to the group as a contributing member. This shared power also gives the teacher tremendous opportunities to compliment class members for helping. For example, it's a warm spring day in an inner city neighborhood. The classroom windows were opened by the fourth grade students as they came in that morning. By 9:00 A.M. there is a maintenance person outside mowing the lawn. Jack has to use his inhalant for asthma because of the pollen. Jenny is sneezing and wiping her eyes. Arnie can't hear the "guest speaker" and is beginning to talk with Sarah who sits next to him. Bahrom notices the noise and Jack's asthma medication. He quietly slips over to the windows and pulls each one shut with very little disturbance to the guest speaker. He is not the window monitor. This classroom has "no monitors." He is the person who happens to be sitting in the front seat closest to the windows. He is occupying the seat that the class has chosen as the "most convenient" seat to the windows, and therefore, the person who would be most likely to create the least disturbance in opening and closing the windows. As the speaker is finishing, so is the mowing. Bahrom moves over to the windows and opens them again. The students have developed some thoughtful questions for the speaker but the other classes are now moving to recess. Char moves over to the door and closes the door. She is the one closest to the door. At any given time of the day, a student may call for a class discussion, ask for a class meeting, or express specific needs to the peers. In this type of room, *the students' language is used to assign meaning to each other as contributors to the whole.*

When *all students gain membership to a group then the social atmosphere is conducive to shifting external motivation to individual or internal motivation.* The shift is from external rewards such as grades, value judgments, praise, and tokens to an internal desire to successfully compete against oneself (Chapter Five describes more of the cultural component of social rewards). This shift in locus of control from the external world to the student's internal power is imperative to preparing students in problem solving, learning how to learn, critical thinking, and being a productive citizen. *Self-worth becomes a product of self-esteem and self-concept. When students with high self-esteem and positive self-concept feel accepted as students as well as citizens then they also feel worthy of such acceptance and membership. The* **language of RESPECT** *for students assists them in becoming giving and sharing group members who value their membership. The students are learning to socialize themselves as contributing members of society.*

Activity

1. **Define self-worth. Give examples.**
2. **Describe how self-worth and self-concept are related in the process of socialization.**

Self-Discipline

A student's power to be his or her own learning advocate is the goal of self-discipline within the school system. The student with self-discipline learns how to achieve within a group's expectations while maintaining his or her own dignity in developing uniqueness. For example, the student with an internal locus of self-control has learned how to ask the teachers for what he or she needs to best learn. Perhaps self-advocacy might take the form of a music student who cannot read notes until she hears the music played. Once the music is played, then the visual configurations called "notes" come to life on the page. The student is able to mentally "see" the music and, therefore, the student is able to play or sing the notes. The student may need to ask the teacher to play the music prior to playing or singing the note symbols. This student may be able to protect her dignity as a musician within the group provided that the teacher honors the uniqueness of how she learns.

Self-discipline is often mistaken for "responsibility." Self-discipline is knowing what one needs and knowing *why* one needs something. For example, a student may ask the teacher for all of the teacher's lecture notes because the student thinks he needs those notes to pass the test. The student says, "I can't take lecture notes." The teacher's responsibility is to help the student be successful in the way that the student learns best. "Just not being able to take notes" does not represent the way the student learns best. So, the teacher helps the student learn to take notes. Now, the student can take notes "his" way and pass the exam. This student will show self-discipline for being able to take lecture notes his way in future classes. Self-discipline has to do with learning to take care of one's needs in a healthy way. However, it is also the student's "responsibility" to be the advocate for one's needs.

Using the notetaking example again, teachers in the intermediate grades (grades 4, 5, and 6) usually try to help students understand that when teachers talk, the students must take notes. The teacher's assumption is that the student is able to hear what the teacher says, and is able to write while the teacher talks. As described in Chapter Two, most of today's learners are not able to connect what is being heard with mental visual language simultaneously. So, most students are *not* successful at taking notes the way that the teacher assumes is a natural developmental progression from hearing the words to writing what is heard. Some students learn to write verbatim the spoken patterns. As long as the student can scribe fast enough, the student is able to write what is heard. This latter student does not know why the notes are being taken. In fact, some students have to take the notes home to look at the print to see what was said. In other words, the student who writes the words verbatim is writing patterns which are not recognized as having meaning until there is time to see the ideas on the page.

With notetaking, the student who scribes in a verbatim way does not know that he or she needs to put what is being said into his or her *own language* in order to learn the meaning of the word patterns. These intermediate teachers who show *respect* for differences in learning have often set up some sort of opportunity for students to learn how to take notes in the way the student learns. One teacher starts the year by having the students write down their interests, etc., on cards. These cards are used then for adding information, changing information, or removing information during the first six weeks. The cards are then organized around themes...e.g., outdoor sports, indoor sports, home activities, etc.

Students arrange cards by groups. Then the teacher asks the students to go to the school library and research a couple of topics within each cluster. The students are asked to record new information on new cards.

As the year progresses, the students learn many principles about notetaking including how to draw ideas before writing ideas, how to organize ideas into a cartooned-like story before writing, how to resource from others, and eventually how to take notes (using drawing, writing, etc.) when someone is speaking. They learn to divide their paper into quadrants (topic analysis), how to scan for meaning before a lecture, and how to fill in space during a presentation. Another teacher uses a five to six week testing, notetaking process. The students work in groups with texts, then later with other sources, with each other's notes, and finally with spoken language. Testing from these notes begins as a group and is gradually changed over the five weeks into a final individual test with individual notes with no talking or sharing.

In these examples, it is apparent that students are guided into becoming their own advocates for how to learn best. The teachers give the students the necessary *language* tools and the students are responsible for trying the tools. *However, the students won't be responsible until they have the tools to be self-disciplined, that is, they can advocate for what they need based on what is best for learning.*

When students become self-disciplined, they also take responsibility for being where they need to be, when they need to be there. For example, one of the criteria of knowing whether a class has developed a respectful environment that fosters self-discipline is attendance. Teachers say that when the students are learning many parents report that their son or daughter want to go to school despite the matter of being ill, having a cold, etc. In TEACUP, many parents reported during the third year that their child was disappointed to have summer school come to an end. Several years later, some parents still report that their son or daughter talk about attending that summer school. It was not designed to be a "play" school. It was designed for students to learn in the way the students learn best.

Students or learners who appear to be self-disciplined may not be responsible. For example, a student knows that she is not able to arrive on time without some visual structure to help with her mental visual language. So, she writes an appointment time down on a piece of paper. The piece of paper is by the phone. She never looks by the phone to gain information about her appointment. So, as a learner, she knows she needs some sort of visual aid, but she doesn't know why she needs it. She doesn't use what she has written. The result is that she is not on time for her appointment, even though she wrote the appointment time (Arwood, 1991; Arwood, 2000). To be responsible and self-disciplined means that the student needs to know how she learns best, be able to advocate for what she needs, and be able to feel comfortable using what she needs. In other words, the student is more likely to be successful showing up for the appointment (self-esteem) when her own self-concept values herself as a member of society.

Activity

1. **Describe self-esteem, self-concept, self-worth, and self-discipline.**
2. **Explain how social development relates to the acquisition of the concept of respect.**

Support

One of the purposes of a group is to provide other members of the group with basic psychosocial support. **Support of a child or an adult may be defined as providing credit for what a person can do while validating the "who" of the person's "self" for what he or she can do.** Support is crucial for healthy socialization of oneself. Support begins in the first moments. For example, during the first hour of the day of school, each student is provided the opportunity to say something about him or herself. Most students begin talking about one or two things that the student likes to do or does well. These likes and dislikes are typically about objects or things or "what's." If the teacher recognizes each student's contribution by saying something about the student's willingness to risk, to talk, to contribute rather than just about the student's interest, then students begin to value the other students for their "gifts," their "talents," their "contributions," their "participation," etc.

Crediting and validating are forms of support. Such crediting and validating might sound like this. John says, "I watch a lot of TV...that's all I do." The teacher says, "I am unable to watch a lot of TV. It must take a lot of concentration to watch?!" The student says, "Nah, it's just there." The teacher adds an idea such as, "Perhaps, next time you'll share with us some of the things you see on TV. I would like to learn about what you watch." On the other hand, if the teacher deals with the child's "what's," then the teacher might have said, "Oh, surely you do something besides watching TV." The former option opens communication about the child. The communication about the TV or the object closes the communication by placing a value judgment on the child's "self," on the decision to watch TV as being a "bad choice."

Support of a child or an adult means crediting and validating or valuing the individual for what the person can do. For example, when a student is moving a desk, the teacher might say, "Jim, you may want to move the desk closer to the window, where you will be able to join your research project partners. So, you don't injure your back, ask some of your buddies to help you." The emphasis in this example is on what the student can do to meet his needs...move the desk. But the teacher doesn't want the floor scratched so the teacher offers the student consideration for the student's worth; not on the object such as scratching the floor. Such support is also a recognition of what is known about learning. **Optimum learning occurs when the learner is able to connect something meaningful from the past with something meaningful in the present** (Arwood, 1991; also see Chapter Two regarding learning principles).

This process of learning therefore connects the social aspects of the learner to the thinking or cognitive components of the learner. For example, a social studies topic might include upcoming Olympic games. For a specific ten-year-old, the Olympics might be a vague concept (**trough principle**). So, to allow the student to discuss games that he or she already knows will identify a base level of past knowledge to connect to the Olympic games (**building principle**). The learner builds mental bridges from his bank of past experiences of games to the concept of the Olympics (**bridge principle**). From here, the teacher and other students guide the relationship of one concept such as javelin throwing to another concept such as throwing a ball (**networking principle**). These relationships about throwing may then be connected to cavemen who might have thrown spears at animals. It is a natural step from the student's own throwing of a ball to the modern event of javelin throwing in Olympic games. The student's learning *supports* the child's improved cognitive and social development.

Shuttling from the present to the past and back to the present also strengthens the development of the curricular concepts being learned. Whether the educator subscribes to the philosophy that "practice makes perfect" or the theoretical knowledge about the "pathways of the brain" connecting overlapping related ideas, **learning occurs best from connecting what a person knows to something new.** Therefore, beginning with something a child or student can do provides a personal historical reference (Chapter Four will describe the cognitive development that relates to this learning). With this ownership comes the possibility of higher internalization levels for the learner. The student's learning experiences *supports* the student's way of thinking as well as the student's development of "self." *Respect for one's accomplishments is important, but when the child or student begins to develop respect for the individual learning system, then the child or student is becoming a life long learner.*

Since learning is based on how a student actually thinks, then connecting meaning gained from classmates or teacher (social component) to what the student is able to think about (cognitive component) maximizes the student's learning parameters. To illustrate this point, consider the student who would like to have a foreign pen pal; yet, this student is not certain about how to gain such as friendship. During a class discussion about the similarities of children from around the world, the teacher encourages the class to picture a friend in a foreign land. Then the teacher places mailing envelopes on the desk for those who would be "willing" to write a short note to a potential pen-pal. The teacher concludes with the statement, "Someone in another country is anxious to be your friend, but does not know how to start the relationship. This is your opportunity to show him or her how to begin this special friendship writing or drawing ideas for him or her."

Some students seize the opportunity. Others politely are "willing" to write a note. One student has always wanted a foreign pen pal. Now, the option is brought into the world of possibilities. The teacher creates the opportunity via the electric excitement of integrating language arts with the social studies purpose. In other words, the content of social studies provides a reason for writing (language arts). The anxious clamor of excited classmates as well as the matter-of-fact assurance of the teacher has joined "wish and fact" in a delicious stew of possibilities, imagination, and action for this one student.

Within minutes, the reluctant student is writing a rough draft letter to a potential pen pal. Imaginative comments seem to gush from his pen, as the student discusses the members of his own family, the world's best "wiener dog," three guinea pigs who live in a aquarium in his bedroom, the league winning baseball team he belonged to, his beginning band class, his up-coming birthday, a boy scout jamboree at Valley Forge, Pennsylvania, and, oh, so much more!! He is getting to showcase who he is for someone else. A sealed letter tossed into a mail bin, an anxious waiting period; and, finally, the most wonderful letter received from Taiwan opens up new vistas of possibilities for this student who then seeks to gain friends in Greece and other countries. The student has found a purpose in relating himself, and who he is, to others across the world.

A simple *supported* opportunity opened a whole series of successes for one young man. Suddenly, fifth grade became a new world of exciting discoveries, real challenges, and sweet successes. Even the student could not explain to his teacher why his grades were escalating in the ensuing days. This student's parents were at a loss for words, but were ecstatic at the "new" student in their home. The teacher continued to use this opportunity to extend past learning into new avenues of art, acting, and writing humorous stories. His teacher sent samples of his artwork to a well-known university in South Bend, Indiana where the teacher's friend shared this young student's work with others. He needed to know that there was *support* for him as a person in other avenues.

This aforementioned student is headed for a very bright academic future. *A mixture of social competence and cognitive competence stirred in with a good dose of friendship brought the support needed for success.* The best news is that this student is not an isolated case. There are more students who are classmates of this young man who have their own true-to-life successes to share with the world. A few of these successful student stories could be considered to be minor miracles by many teachers but these successes are the expected norm in a classroom that uses the **language of RESPECT.** Recently, one of the authors attended an Eagle Scout court of honor that focused on a young man. This young man had found school to be very difficult in the elementary years. But, when he began to share who he was with the teacher on the first day by listing his interests, the teacher and student developed a shared reference. They discovered that there was a mutual area of interest, martial arts. Both could converse about martial arts, which spilled into the class time. The teacher used this shared set of ideas to allow the student to successfully participate in front of the group. The student's ability to be in front of the class and to share, even though he had originally isolated himself, soon turned into his desire to perform plays and to act.

Socially, the student was developing from one area of interest. But, this one area of interest, when supported by the teacher helped the student grow in other areas. The student began to share his computer expertise. Finally, he became the class computer expert. This student's martial arts, drama, and computers created a positive context from which the teacher and student could share meaning. By the end of the fourth grade, this student had come into his own "self." His difficulty in school no longer existed and he headed into the next grades as a competent person with lots of positively recognized self-constituents; worthiness, esteem, positive concept and self-discipline. The support afforded him in the one class made a difference to this student's social development.

All learners need to feel the support by a teacher, parent, or other adult for who the person is. Without the support, the learner will not develop socially into the higher levels. Some of the social areas of development may remain weak into adulthood without adequate support. Different styles of "parenting" provide different types of support and result in different social development.

Activity

1. **How is support important to social development?**
2. **Define support and give examples.**

Authoritative Parenting Style

Supporting a learner within the framework of a school or social agency necessitates an authoritative style (Santrock, 1997) *of parenting, much like a pseudo-family.* This is to say that each student shares himself or herself with the "family" in a give-and-take communication network. The authoritative pseudo-family provides opportunities for support so that any behavior might be turned into a success. For example, a student who reads about snakes while others get ready for social studies class might be valued for his reading ability. The teacher might say, "John is so careful to read all the details. Everyone may read for ten minutes on any subject. Now when you break up into your smaller groups, be sure to ask John for any help that you might need, in gaining details for the social studies projects." The teacher may validate this support by asking John if that arrangement is suitable for him. A potential behavior problem has been averted while the student gains support and learns respect for his ability to control choices.

This ebb and flow of personal exchanges of ideas, negotiations, jokes, comments, concerns, news, frustrations, successes and the endless tide of interactions that any family may face; seems to fuel this perpetual motion machine constructed with real, live, breathing personalities, a kaleidoscope of events, a warehouse full of needs, schedules that are on collision course and all coordinated in an elbow-to-elbow arena, the classroom. Using well-thought out language to assign positive meaning to John's behavior results in all four of the learning principles coming together to connect (**build**) old information (**trough**) [reading about snakes] to new information (reading social studies). Once John is involved with the other students, **bridges** and **networks** are built. The ability to collectively bring students into an authoritative classroom based on the language of respect is much like being a philatelist.

Just as each stamp is a valued collection item, each stamp is an integral part of the whole collection. The other stamps in this collection gain in value with the addition of each successive stamp. For the stamp collector, each stamp (large or small, foreign or domestic) is reviewed, examined closely, and appreciated over and over and over again. With time, each stamp will become a unique and familiar entity. Most of all, each individual stamp becomes a very important part of the overall collection. The individual stamp, of and by itself, seems to boost the value as well as becomes the philatelist's appreciation for the total stamp collection. The class is a community of valued individuals and the environment is a "pseudo-family."

It would be very encouraging if most classrooms took on the family values of most teachers. Dr. Arwood often asks her graduate students, who are veteran teachers, what they socially value for their students. The teachers often list content goals, state standards, and behavioral expectations. Then she asks the same teachers what they want or value for their own children. The teachers typically list different goals: protection, social success, to be a good citizen, to be successful academically, to feel good about themselves, etc. The two lists are different, but don't have to be different. In a classroom based on the **language of RESPECT,** students and teachers are given the opportunity to bring their personal constituents into the classroom so that all members are *supported* in an authoritative structure.

Shared relationships in an authoritative setting go beyond the matter of proximity. **Authoritative support is a style of relationship in which options or choices are frequently offered with an attitude of mutual benefit and unselfishness.** Too often, in some teaching situations, the student is offered "choices" designed, calculated, and limited by the teacher who has stacked the deck of "so-called" options in his or her favor. In reality these skewed choices are not real options for the student. These so-called choices are in actuality, preplanned alternatives, in most cases, acceptable only to the teacher who is consciously or unconsciously controlling the situation.

An honest, real choice should be an option that suggests an alternative that is beneficial to the person(s) offering the choice. Such a consideration should be mutually beneficial to both parties for a truly authoritative climate. In an authoritative system, the parties are supported from within the group by the individuals who provide such options. For example, choosing to work with someone familiar, may seem reasonable to a student. But, the teacher gives the instruction, "Work with the person next to you." The person does the work with the student next to him or her even though the student may never learn about that person. The student sees options limited to the teacher's choices. Respect comes in the form of compliance, a valid form. But, self-respect for one's own choices may not be validated. The classroom may look like the students are developing because products are generated, but the student's own socialization may lack development.

In many of today's classroom, choices belong to the person creating the structure. Options are not provided by the adults. The classrooms reflect choices designed, created, and executed by teachers with the best of intentions. The students in these noncommunity, authoritarian classrooms must pick their way through a minefield of "do-it-my-way-or-else" choices that are not real options thus forcing the student to give-in to the teacher's approval rather than to be supported by the teacher's gifts of knowledge and acceptance. This "do-it-my-way" classroom does not offer real choices. Too, the obvious looks of disappointment and the façade of "I guess I'm stuck with you," dampens what could have been a Mardi Gras spirit and attitude.

With the authoritarian classroom, respect is expected from top down. Everyone loses because respect is often not earned from a shared process. A shared process respects the individual's needs as well as the group's needs. For example, "windows of socialization" must be created as opportunities for the teacher and students to "just chit chat," to have "human being time." These windows of time are for being genuine, open, free, sensitive, safe, and warm. Instead of grading papers or attending endless before school meetings that run up to the moment the bell rings, create a 20 minute window where the students may *always* find the teacher available and accessible. If necessary, stand by the door so as to step out into the hall to have a private conversation. For some students, this is the *only* time that they are able to share personal messages. Total confidentiality is exercised here. In two to three minutes of just allowing students to be part of creating the day's context, the teacher can find out about student's concerns, family issues, curricular obstacles, and even analyze the spoken language (with training for this latter one) for how the student is developing or learning. These windows must be scheduled in as part of the school day and they must be available for *all* class members. Students who have found it difficult to self-advocate or to be a part of the class will use this time with the teacher to create adult to child student bonds that are healthy and offer support.

A healthy, supportive, respectful classroom accepts the fact that its members are involved in a variety of sports, leisure time activities and hobbies. *Authoritative structure necessitates knowing its members as part of the whole group process. Knowing the members provides internal structure of healthy limits and boundaries.* Thus, in the authoritative classroom a student with an interest in playing the piano is respected and accepted as much as the student who prefers to play a major team sport such as football or baseball. Both are seen as being strong personalities in his or her own chosen field of endeavor. Both are fine human beings who enjoy doing what they have chosen to do.

The primary concern of the healthy, supportive, community classroom would be to champion the unique value of its multi-faceted students. But, knowing the class members requires knowing the individuals. The feelings, preferences, growth, learning, safety, comfort and dignity of its valued student-members are prime. Genuine support of individual needs, wants, and values within the classroom acknowledges the individual persons as well as his or her interests.

In this supportive environment athletes as well as nonathletes are valued, recognized and prized. Shy as well as assertive students are appreciated. For example, the authoritative classroom welcomes the news of an up-coming first year musician's violin recital featuring one of its quieter students. This student's contribution to society is just as important as the all-American basketball team center who is clearly well-known and popular on the court and in student government roles.

Besides being supportive, the respectful classroom is responsive to student needs. It is a safe, supportive haven for equality. **Equality is translated into frequent encouragement, spontaneous celebrations, and genuine demonstrations of moral support during all phases of class members' involvement.** There is no priority for praise, support, and cheers among its members. For example, each person earns praise for any genuine reason such as the person who brings his books to class.

For bringing books, one student may be complimented while another student is complimented for solving a math problem. All members observe a full quota of attention. All members are worthy of group recognition, acknowledgment, support, and validation. *Supportive praise* is a natural part of the *language process* of *respect* and comes from the members, not just the teacher. The teacher sets up opportunities for sharing praise as well as models how to praise. Praise comes to all students, but not at the same time. In this way, all students are also unique.

For being a unique or "one-of-a-kind" individual, the authoritative classroom offers *respect* for differences of opinion and tolerance for diversity. *The only way to have a classroom of individuals within a group that functions successfully is for all of the individuals to guarantee that such individual diversity is supported within the system.* For example, the first day of school might be designed so as to set the tone for acknowledging each person's unique "who" which also allows each student to honor the diversity of his or her peers.

One popular technique of promoting the "who" is the verbal introduction strategy. In this technique, the student introduces himself or herself by name, then connects some personal preferences such as specific sports, favorite pastimes, and foods. One student might introduce himself as "Fearless Frederick" who enjoys soccer, skydiving, and chasing butterflies. He then informs the class that he enjoys eating anchovy and sardine pizzas, and toasted-almond chocolate ice cream.

The students are taught at the onset that they may disagree about preferences, but that they may not express their disagreements in the form of negative comments or booing. Language is important! Acceptable comments from those who might not enjoy Fearless Frederick's favorites might suggest that their personal favorites include baseball, football, pepperoni pizzas, and vanilla ice cream. Again, each individual is guaranteed his or her right to be unique; while the colorful diversity of the total membership is maintained, in a positive light. To bring "acceptance" home, the teacher may ask for advice when traveling to a foreign country and being introduced to unusual foods or entertaining guests from a foreign country. How should they react? How may a person from China react to catsup on fried rice? How should true feelings be expressed or should the true feelings be expressed?

As the teacher encourages the student for risking and for participating, the students learn that all ideas are valued and that all opinions are accepted. These ideas and opinions are accepted because they represent the uniqueness of the individuals in the class. At this point, it really doesn't matter whether the child speaks about a recent TV program or relates a story about visiting the Smithsonian Museum in Washington, DC. The absolute value for the entire class lies in the very fact that a member of its group is sharing his or her life's experiences, ideas, thoughts, heart-felt opinions that represent him or her! Because each child is a valuable asset to the community of the classroom, each contribution has equal value. The value of the child is greater than the content of the contribution, thus modeling for the students a form of citizenship that empowers all individuals.

Being supportive of all individuals allows for the celebration of individual uniqueness that provides the first steps of social development. Meaning is assigned from the support of the individual to the group that the individual supports. The class members improve their socialization as citizens with more positive self-concepts, higher self-esteems, better self-discipline, and improved feelings of self-worth. Part of this socialization process requires that the learners also be protected.

Activity

1. **Define authoritative support. Give Examples.**
2. **Explain how an authoritative environment respects individual differences as well as the group process.**

Protection

Support within a classroom is also a form of healthy protection for all members of the group or community. **This protection is provided by the teacher who understands the student as a person or agent who has basic needs and wants**. These basic needs are "human rights" which are granted through the interaction of the members of the student's community, itself. For example, as the students begin to share something about themselves the first day, some students may make sniping shots of ridicule which are value judgments learned from authoritarian classrooms and unhealthy family structures.

These ridiculing remarks are necessary for the child who is using them to fit in the system. When the teacher explains about how we all have contributions because we are all people and all people are important in this community, then the teacher is attempting to *protect* the student who is being sniped. Sometimes, the other class members can provide the support by the teacher asking the classmates to help the sniper. For example, "Class, John really needs your help. John, please say that again." John is then allowed to rethink his comment. The class empowers John with a specific teammate of John's choice to help him with the thinking process. The message to the class is clear. Sniping is not accepted, "Who would like to help John?"

This feedback is repeated often to reinforce the notion that each child has the right to be *protected*. Sometimes teachers have difficulty recognizing a sniper. Sniping comments cut into another person's self-esteem—either through devaluation, name calling, judging, or other closed communication. Sometimes, teachers are the snipers. Examples of teacher sniping might be, "John, don't you think before you talk?" This type of statement means that John is a thoughtless person and perhaps not intelligent. Another example, "Mary, that was a really stupid question." A qualifier of a product, such as "stupid," used to describe work, is internalized personally as being called stupid, etc. Sometimes, closed communication also signals a lack of interpersonal integrity. For example, the teacher says to the class, "We have a lot of work to do today." A student raises her hand and asks, "Are we going to get to finish our writing projects?" The teacher closes the communication with the statement, "We aren't going to talk about that now."

The teacher thinks that her communication is justifiable since she already told the students that there was a lot to do. What the teacher was saying was this: "I have a plan for each of you today. I will tell you what to do, and you will do it; so, that, at the end of the day, I will feel good about all that you have accomplished." The feelings of the student who asked the question are not considered in the teacher's use of language.

The use of terminal communication or language that stops the learning process lacks consideration for the students' needs and feelings. As students' needs and feelings are "shut down," their body posture and language begins to show the effects of being "shut down" and being devalued. *Even though such communication may result in work production, the means do not justify the end since students lose their interest in being successful learners and competent citizens.* The student is developing as a person, not just a robot. When socialization is not positive, students will often try to manipulate the context to do the bare minimum to fit. Their attitude becomes, "Just tell me what to do and how to do it." This attitude goes with them into the workplace; and, if they become teachers, the same attitude is perpetuated in the classroom.

Often, students have learned these negative ways of fitting into a group from family or past authoritarian classroom structures. *Negative patterns of interaction are a result of a difficulty defining roles and responsibilities.* The lack of socially positive language and interaction increases members' insecurities and incompetence. For example, "John is too stupid to do anything right," says that it is okay to name call, devalue someone's contribution, and to expect little from John. Allowing such a comment does not provide a safe environment for *all* learners. John is not protected, and healthy individuals will realize that they, too, are not protected.

If the interaction is not supportive so that individual's ideas and values are protected, a third party tends to be brought into the situation.

The language then becomes a triad of communication. For example, the teacher sends the student to the vice-principal for a discussion about being late. These triangles or triads within the school perpetuate the insecurities so that individual members cannot grow without the approval of the other triad members. For example, a mother may quit her job to accompany her five-year-old to Kindergarten each day because she knows that her son will be like his mentally-ill father. Even though the mother has no basis for her belief, her own insecurity about her ability to get nurtured and protected by her spouse has been placed upon the child. The mother expects the child to be like the father. In other words, the child must meet Mom's expectations or the mother will not be able to nurture and protect the child. The teacher or another supportive adult will need to bring both the mom and her son into the room as competent individuals before Mom will be able to let the son succeed in Kindergarten without her presence.

The triad in the aforementioned example is the overlap between mom and the spouse with the child in the middle. Dad cannot become well because Mom's relationship with the son is based on Dad's mental illness. Mom cannot change her relationship with either her spouse or her son because her value as a person is based on the relationship between the dad and the son. And, the son cannot be healthy because his relationship to Mom as well as his relationship to Dad is based on being like Dad. So, the classroom offers the opportunity to Mom to demonstrate the healthy boundaries and limits of how all are successful.

The most common triads in the school are based on teachers assigning value to a student's behavior in relationship to the teacher's own needs. For example, the teacher hears a student making comments that the teacher views as being annoying. So now, the student is "annoying" to the teacher. The teacher cannot relate to the student without expecting to be annoyed. The student finally does the expected work, but the teacher is annoyed. So, the teacher talks to the parent who is the third party. Because the teacher's problem is between the teacher and the child, the teacher has now set up the triangle. The parent must take on the identity of her child or be the scapegoat for the teacher who has tried to shift the problem to the third party, the parent.

A third type of triad often exists among colleagues within the school setting. These triads express themselves in the faculty lounges, in the hallways, in the parking lots, behind closed doors, and in faculty meetings. For example, many teachers may not want a certain curriculum idea implemented in their building, because of their own lack of knowledge or personal insecurities. So, these insecure teachers must name-call, devalue, and build a case against the supporters of the impending curriculum; rather than acknowledging that they do not have the needed skills and information. Teachers who oppose a curriculum change but are not insecure or lack knowledge do not name call or devalue others in trying to share their information about why they don't want the changes. *Respect includes the value of open and honest communication that uses supportive and protective language.*

The triad exists between those teachers who are willing to try a new curriculum idea, those teachers who are not willing to try, and a third party being an administrator or a parent group. And there may exist one or two teachers who don't fit into any of these groups. Any time there is a triad, there also exists the possibility of using value judgments against others who are not present. This is the adult form of "tattle-telling." "Suzie's ideas are way out there...I don't know why she has to impose them on us...maybe she needs to go on vacation." This type of devaluing allows the speaker to not have to think about the new curriculum idea.

A fourth kind of triad may exist among students who are enabled by an adult such as the teacher, paraprofessional, parent, coach, specialist, neighbor, bus driver, principal, counselor, etc. For example, two boys are sent to the counselor's office because a teacher saw the boys fighting on the playground. The problem is between the teacher and the two boys. Since the teacher has a need to involve the counselor, the teacher has now created a triad. In this triad, the counselor is expected to take care of or fix another person's problem. The boys are learning how to shift responsibility for their behavior to other people to be fixed.

In this type of triad, by sending the boys to the counselor, the teacher has already told them by action, that the boys do not need to take responsibility for their behavior, because the teacher has not taken responsibility for the teacher's behavior. The real issue is that the teacher probably lacks skill or expertise or confidence in dealing with the boys; someone else, the third party, must take care of the teacher's problem.

The counselor now has the choice to accept his position in the triad between the boys and the teacher, or to decline. If the counselor accepts the position, then the boys are guilty of fighting. If the counselor declines, then the boys can now talk to someone about each boy's perception of the situation or circumstances. Often the students in these triads do not have adequate language to explain their perspective of "fighting" or whatever rule they have broken.

The authors have often found that students do not believe themselves to be guilty of fighting or of breaking a rule. When students are asked to *draw* about their understanding of a situation, often they draw behavior that an adult would call fighting. The students don't have the language to match their mental understanding of a rule to what fighting looks like. The perception of each student is based on past experiences. For example, the boys know that fighting is bad, but they do not believe themselves to be bad, therefore they could not be fighting.

Allowing students to express their ideas in a way that represents their mental language allows for cognitive expression of what they really understand. If students don't have the oral language to express the accepted meaning, then drawing often works. Otherwise, students will give back "empty language" such as saying, "I don't fight." Within the drawn picture, the boys show their real understanding, "I hit the boy with my hand." Then the adult can assign the meaning. "You hit a person, this boy, with your hand. Hitting with your hand is called fighting." Socialization comes through the language that supports, protects, and allows the individual to grow into society's expectations.

Furthermore, *this type of respectful protection sets limits on what is considered support versus what is personal devaluation for students.*

Many students do not have histories of success as individuals and therefore they do not see themselves as agents. The classroom that provides the protection through support also values the child as a competent being who is nurtured because the child exists--not because the child does what the teacher wants, the way the teacher wants it. **To adequately protect an environment as "safe" for all members, the teacher must use assertive assignment of positive meaning to all students, avoid unhealthy communication triads, take responsibility as an adult for all actions within the teacher's boundaries, set positive limits, and offer real choices.** Each of these skills will be expanded upon throughout the text. Supporting individuals within a protected environment provides students the opportunity to be nurtured.

Activity

1. **Define healthy social protection.**
2. **Describe how healthy protection respects the individual as well as the group. Give examples.**

Nurturance

The child who is supported as an individual, and is uniquely protected by the community, is provided nurturance. For example, when a child offers an opinion on what might be a good dessert for the evening meal, the agreements and disagreements, by the other members of the family, encourage the child to become involved. The very fact that the child's contribution was heard, accepted, and included in the discussion affords the child a definite screen of protection. The child learns quickly, that his or her contribution is a valuable one in this family. Also, the family members are aware of the positive support that they are handing to this member. The true value of the family's acceptance lies in the fact that a human being's opinion is valued more than the dessert choice, itself. The child is protected; but, even more, the child is nurtured. In all likelihood, this child will participate in future contributions.

A higher form of nurturance, internal nurturance, develops from within the individual. This form of nurturance is a form of maturity and a sense of security within oneself. One might imagine a family discussion revolving around the need for a particular individual to buy an expensive baseball glove, or even a new car. The family budget does not provide funds for the purchase of either of these items. The family discusses the options and the individuals willingly give up something to allow for the eventual purchase of the glove or car.

The real maturity in this situation is found in the agreement by the family members to provide the funds. The family takes into account, the impact of their wishes, on the shoulders of the individual. The internal nurturance of the individual from past experiences allows each member to feel important in the decision-making process. There are limited ill wishes, harbored resentments, or competitive value judgments. **This form of nurturance requires the development of one's own values within the framework of the total community. This insight of the individual within the total community is the integrity of the community itself.** *Decision-making then becomes each individual's contribution, valued as a part of the whole.*

Nurturance comes from respect within the responsive classroom. Each member is sensitive to the others' needs and "gifting" becomes part of the class's values. For example, some children come to school without their hair washed and in "hand-me-down" clothes. When teachers see these students, they often feel pity or sympathy. The teachers' faces do not light up. But, the third grade girl who walks in with a new dress, new shoes, and well groomed hair receives an open greeting, smiles of approval, and personal acceptance. Students read teacher and parent nonverbals. The students quickly learn that the child from the poor family does not deserve support, because of lack of approval of the child's hair and clothes. The child is left alone, at best, ostracized and teased, at worst.

To be nurtured, the adult (teacher) must take the lead. First, privately talk with the student about feelings and options for seeking solutions. For example, these authors have been part of a before school clothes change, wash, shower activity for many students. This activity becomes nurturing when the whole class learns to participate in service learning activities. To understand differences in the economics of families does not mean that persons from those families deserve less. Sometimes the students will begin to openly share what it is like to be homeless or from a poor family eventually resulting in gifts of understanding in return for gifts of respect and nurturance. Without *nurturance,* a student sometimes drops out and may not grow to meet society's expectation.

A lack of *nurturance* within the classroom can often be seen in the jousting for position, status, popularity, etc. This type of jousting tends to be different for boys and girls. Boys tend to be more physical…pushing, shoving. This type of physical jousting may last for a short duration, as the confrontations are easy to **see** and **feel.** Because of the physical aspect of jousting, boys tend not to use the "heady" strategies of girls. Girls tend to use verbiage, physical appearances, social standing, and what is "stylish" or popular as ways to joust for nurturance. This type of jousting seems to take a lot longer. Both types of jousting cross over as girls can also be quite physical and boys certainly figure out that name calling results in a lot of attention, even if it is negative attention. Classrooms with cliques, loners, inseparable groupings, etc. are the result of a *need for nurturance. Increase the nurturance of all classroom members and the individual need for such jousting is left at the door when the students enter the room. Control the individuals' needs, and the jousting, physical or verbal, increases. When all members of a classroom receive the opportunity to be supported and protected, then all members receive the type of social nurturance to feed the individual's self-esteem, self-concept, self-worth and self-discipline.*

The classroom may be the only place a student receives nurturance. The home and other settings for the student may not offer such caring. From an educational standpoint, we are educating students to become citizens. *Citizens need to feel protected, supported, and nurtured to feel like they belong.* Littleton, Colorado is an example of nurturance needed at a simple level. Students who are wearing trench coats or WWII outfits need the emotional support of the whole group based on a discussion of what those clothes mean to others. They were "outcasts" who needed the emotional support from the teachers and the classrooms to fit. They needed to be nurtured!

Activity

1. **Define nurturance.**
2. **Describe how nurturance respects all classroom members.**

Summary

For social development to be fostered within the classroom, each individual member must be valued for achievements (**self-esteem**), for fitting into a group as a unique individual (**self-concept**), according to the individual's own **self-worth,** and personal standards (**self-worth and self-discipline**). Each individual is **supported, protected** and **nurtured**. Such socialization is half of the learning process. The way the individual thinks in order to achieve social success is the other half of learning. This processing or thinking is the student's cognitive development. Chapter Four provides information about the cognitive portion of learning. The **language of RESPECT** offers learning that is both social and cognitive in nature.

REFERENCES

There are many readings about self-esteem and social development. Each of these references also refer to other readings.

Arwood, E. 1991. *Semantic and Pragmatic Language Disorders*. Gaithersburg, MD: Aspen Systems Corp.

Arwood, E. 2000. Strategies for Adults, in press.

Brooks, R.D. and Dalby, R.K. 1990. *The Self-Esteem Repair and Maintenance Manual*. Newport Beach, CA: Kincaid House Publishing.

Hodges, L. and Wolf, C.J. 1997. *Promoting Self-Esteem in a Caring Positive Classroom*. Master's Action Research Project, Saint Xavier University & IRI/Skylight.

Kimmell, E.B. and Killbride, M.P. 1991. *Attribution Training for Teachers*. An inservice workshop publication, p. 8.

Kaufman, G. and Raphael, L. 1990. *Stick Up for Yourself! Every Kid's Guide to Personal Power and Positive Self-Esteem*. Minneapolis: MN.

Mayer, N. 1999. People Who Can, Teach. *Oregonian*. Living Section, C1-3.

Santrock, J. W. 1997. *Life-Span Development* (6th Edition. Madison, WI: Brown & Benchmark.

Schall, J. 1985. Teacher, Are You Too Tough on Yourself? *Instructor* 94: 42-46.

Stevenson, H.W. 1992. Con: Don't Deceive Children through a Feel-Good Approach. What's behind Self-Esteem Programs: Truth or Trickery? *School Administrator* 49(4), 23-30.

Chapter Four
Learner Outcomes

Upon completion of this chapter, the reader will be able to do the following:

1. Define cognition as it relates to learning.
2. Explain how cognition relates to respect.
3. Explain how language strategies facilitate concept development in the classroom.
4. Explain the relationship between learning and cognition for concept development.
5. Explain what is meant by an event-based classroom.
6. Explain the relationship between classroom use of language and cognitive development.
7. Explain why refining a student's ideas allows for better learning through improved language use.
8. Explain how concept development relates to cognition.
9. Explain what is meant by the phrase "the language of cognitive respect."
10. Explain the difference between visual cognitive symbols and auditory cognitive symbols.

CHAPTER FOUR

Cognitive Respect

How do we respect cognitive development?

Thinking is seeing or hearing--
A self, a person, an agent!
Knowing is understanding
What a person does, feel, believe!

Most educators think that *respect* consists of social skills. But from a *language* standpoint, **respect is a formal, cognitive concept.** As a formal concept, *respect* is acquired from an external assignment of meaning or socialization as described in Chapter Three and also through many overlapping layers of internal meaning or cognition as described in this chapter. *"Cognitive respect" describes the notion of being conscious of one's "self" in relation to others and their perspectives, viewpoints, and needs.* In a way, *social respect for one's environment and community comes from attaining a high level of cognitive development. Cognitive development refers to the way a person uses mental tools for processing information, for learning, for knowledge, etc.* This chapter will describe the development of "cognitive respect," the way social and cognitive development connects in learning, through the use of language.

Cognitive Development

Since **learning is a socio-cognitive process** of developing how one fits into a society based on how one thinks, then the classroom must consider not only the social parameters but also *how individuals think.* In order to understand the way students think, it is important to recognize that **knowledge about cognitive processing is based on how the brain functions. Cognition is the way a person processes information or the way a person thinks based on the way the brain functions.** From this research, it is apparent that there are those individuals who are able to hear and simultaneously see what is being received. These auditory language learners are able to hear another person's words as well as their own spoken words without first having to create a visual or pictorial image within the mind. Other learners find the acoustic or heard signal to be jumbled, lost, or sometimes not even consciously heard, even though the sound is available. These latter visual language learners have difficulty hearing without being able to first see a visual or pictorial image of an idea in their mind.

Table 4.1 How do different people learn language for thinking?

Visual Language	Auditory Language
• I *see* what you say (high context)	• I understand the *sound* of words (low context)
• I think in *graphics* (e.g., I see movies, shapes, etc., in my head)	• I think in *sounds* (e.g., I use sound internally)
• I use spatial concepts (e.g., ground to physical parameters) or *space*	• I use temporal concepts (e.g., ground to the timing of sound words) or *time*
• I use my *body* as a physical reference point in relationship to papers, etc.	• I use my *sound words* as a physical reference point
• I have a *photographic memory* and sometimes a *phonographic memory*	• I have an *auditory memory* (e.g., alphabet, spelling, multiplication tables, etc.)
• I *organize by sets* and *cross reference* by what I *see* (e.g., I see what I write)	• I *organize by category* and *cross reference* by using *sound* words (e.g., see and hear)
• I can *infer from seeing the whole* picture, e.g., I can use flow charts to see the "whole"	• I can *infer from the use of words* in the spoken or written language, e.g., I can use outlines
• *I can see myself* do what I can visually depict	• *I can hear me* say what I do or what you say I do

Adapted from <u>Semantic and Pragmatic Language Disorders</u> by Dr. Ellyn Arwood, 1991.

These two types of language cognition create a challenge for the classroom teacher who insists that all students must be able to perform a task, in a specific way. For example, a student who cannot hear the sounds of the letters seen on a page will remain a nonreader until the classroom offers protection from such failure. When protected, the student is allowed to create mental pictorial images of the whole set of letter configurations, so that ideas are visually graphed as a mental construct instead of being heard as words. This student may then participate in the community as a fully practicing member. The student is *respected* for who he is--a student with a different way of thinking. The added benefit is that the student acquires the expected skills as well, so he learns to read!

A classroom that provides adequate protection for both of these kinds of thinkers accepts the notion that not all individuals must fit a norm. In other words, **conventional products may come about through several different ways of processing the information.** *All processing methods are respected and honored as possible choices.* Furthermore, trying to force a student to perform a task in a way the student's brain does not work, actually punishes, frustrates and even confuses the student; thus reducing self-esteem, challenging the student's self-concept, and making the student fit into the group of "have not's," "can not's," or "will not's." Since most of education is designed to work with an economic system based on the auditory way of language thinking in time, not space, then it is not surprising to find that the educational system is also based on auditory thinking parameters. *To honor both types of cognition, the educator needs to know the characteristics of each type.* The following section describes the characteristics of Table 4.1 in more detail.

Visual Language and Auditory Language

About 60 to 90% of the school population (K-12) learns best when an idea is represented in some picture or graphic form (Arwood, 1991). These students grow up in the auditory culture of the US with the ability to function *only* as well as education or family have provided opportunities for accommodating their way of learning language.

Unfortunately, this visual type of thinker is not just dependent on the material being presented in a visual form, but is dependent on the way information is symbolized (Arwood, 1991). So, *if the classroom allows the student to think as well as use language in a visual way, then the student will be conceptually successful.* For example, many students who think with visual language prefer to read comic books to chapter books with limited pictures. To respect their way of thinking, they are encouraged to read classics that are in comic book form to allow them the opportunity to see what they read. Likewise, they are given additional exposure to foreign language films with subtitles to allow for a cross match between the spoken idea and the written notion. *Allowing students to think in visual language or symbols allows these students to be respected for how they learn.* **Language is the tool for academic, behavioral, and social functioning. The language of the mind is conceptually in the form of the way the student processes concepts into symbols.**

Visual symbols (language) do not depend on sound words but on mental visual patterns or configurations, or mental pictures of what can be perceived by the eyes. For example, a student who needs to *see what is heard* will create a picture of the idea that is spoken before hearing the pattern of the word. So, this student really doesn't hear words but sees a visual representation of what is associated with the acoustic pattern. If the classroom teacher presents material on an overhead projector, then it is assumed that the teacher's visual representations (words) are the same as the students' visual concepts (pictorial images) of the mind. Unfortunately, *mental visual symbols are unique and complex integrated patterns, mental visual configurations, acquired by each student.* Just putting ideas on the overhead may not mean that the student's mental pictured language has the same meaning as the overhead visual patterns.

In other words, making something so that it is seen does not make the visual concepts understood. **Only the language of the patterns will make what is seen understandable. Such meanings or semantics of cognition takes on the characteristics of the way the person**

cognitively processes learned ideas. Visual language uses visual cognition. *Such cognition necessitates that the learner is able to process the incoming visual material into symbols or language that is constructed mentally.* These "head pictures" may be in still form, moving videos, or even multiple videos on separate mental screens like TV's. The actual visual idea is seen BEFORE sound is added, if it is added at all. However, **the person with auditory cognition is able to use the sound of a spoken voice as a meaningful set of patterns called auditory language.** This thinker is able to hear sounds and connect the sounds to visual images, or to other sound based patterns. For example, the auditory language thinker is able to use phonics, sound interconnected to letters, spell from hearing the word and seeing it written, learn vocabulary easily out of context, play with mentally spoken words for grammar exercises, and manipulate numbers within formulae for algebra, etc.

Since English is characteristically an auditory language, most school norms for the language arts are based on auditory language characteristics. However, most students (60 to 90%) do not use auditory cognition for processing information in the classroom. What are the effects of this mismatch between methods and language? A person with visual cognition can hear but does not necessarily remember spoken instructions, spelling words, vocabulary lists, when to turn something into the teacher, simultaneous time based-tasks, time inferred instructions, etc. So, the student figures out how to cope or is referred for special diagnostic evaluations, assessments, and support services. On the other hand, a student with auditory cognition enjoys and appreciates verbal words or instructions in learning a task, academically as well as socially. But, if only math examples are provided without a worded explanation, this auditory student must cope in the math class by getting others to give spoken explanations. But, once the ideas are understood, the auditory person enjoys silence as the spoken words are recorded mentally. The auditory thinker uses his or her own mental spoken language to connect mental auditory language to tasks. The visual language thinker uses the recorded mental pictures as graphics, videos, etc., for their use of determining meaning of tasks.

Examples follow for how these two cognitions differ on social as well as academic tasks. The social example is the learning of specific ice skating moves. *A child who uses visual cognition likes to see the skate instructor show the skating moves with few verbal comments.* Concentration is on how to mentally match the way the learner's body looks compared to the instructor's body. The skate instructor says this is a backspin and then executes the backspin for the learner to observe. The visual thinker creates a mental visualization of the instructor's backspin and then tries to physically match his or her body to the pictured backspin. However, the child with auditory cognition can't really see how to match his other body to the instructor's move without the instructor breaking the task into verbal parts, "Put your left toe pick into the ice," etc. If the visual language child is being taught by an auditory ice skating instructor, then the child will imitate over and over what the instructor is doing instead of listening and then executing. This behavior is often viewed as inattentive and disrespectful. The student is not listening but trying to match a mental picture to movements of his or her body. On the other hand, if an auditory language user is being taught by a visual language ice skate instructor, all of the demonstrations in the world will not help as much as a few *spoken, but specific, words.*

In the classroom, *the auditory cognitive language user learns to read with letters (visual) combined with sounds (acoustic) through a phonics or "see-say" approach.* The first presentation of phonics to an auditory thinker is easy and this auditory thinker is successful at reading and spelling whether or not such tasks are enjoyable. *The visual language user learns to read English through being able to see the whole pattern of an idea or concept as a mentally pictured idea matched to the printed word form.* If this type of cognitive thinker does not learn how to see the patterns of the concepts so as to look at the page and create mental "head pictures" then this child may fail multiple reading attempts over many years. Even if this latter child learns to finally connect sounds (isolated skills in a visual language system) to letters (isolated skills) through repetition of patterns, the comprehension may be lower and/or the ability to word call aloud may be difficult since comprehension is based on cognitive development. Reading through letters and sounds for a visual language thinker is very difficult, and, in some cases impossible even when the skills are rehearsed and regurgitated back to the educators. *However, learning to see what the visual patterns on the page mean in context (Arwood, 1991; Arwood & McInroy, 1994; Arwood and Unruh, 1997) is a possible, viable way to be conventional as a reader and writer.* Allowing students an alternative way to read and write, than is typically expected for English, **respects** the student's way to learn. The student who is afforded an alternative way of learning which matches to his or her thinking may become fully included into the classroom since there is no discrepancy between what the child thinks he or she should be able to do and actual performance. *The child's success allows the child to fit into the classroom. The child's cognitive achievement supports the child's social development as a person. Thus learning is truly a socio-cognitive process.*

Activity

1. **What is cognition?**
2. **Describe a visual thinker. Give examples.**
3. **Describe an auditory thinker. Give examples.**

Auditory and Visual Language Development

Educators often realize that students are able to do more than what they are producing, but the students don't seem to be "reachable." It is not a matter of reaching a learner, but honoring a learner. Reaching a student implies that the educator must take responsibility for the student's actions. In reality, the learner needs to be responsible for his or her own actions to be empowered. Furthermore, cognition becomes enhanced only when the learner is actively in charge of his or her learning acts. So, if the educator does the work, the educator improves the skills, knowledge, etc. If the student does the work, the student improves skills, knowledge, etc. **To honor a learner is to respect the way the student learns or thinks.** The following section describes how auditory and visual language is cognitively developed through differences in thinking.

Students have educated both of the authors about students' needs for support of their cognitive development. *Since cognition has to do with how a person "thinks" and since language is used as an academic process for thinking, the use of language in the classroom is critical for cognitive development.* The previous two chapters described why the assignment of meaning is important from a social standpoint, **but** the assignment of meaning is also cognitively important. The student or learner acquires new meaning, adjusted meaning, and corrected meaning for academic, social, and behavioral purposes from those who assign meaning. For example, the infant cries and the mother says, "Oh, you want the bottle." Even though the infant may not know what the pattern "bottle" means, the parents assigned meaning by giving the baby the bottle, saying the pattern, showing the visual pattern to help the child develop cognition about "bottle," about social issues such as who is the bottle giver, and about how to behave. In other words, the baby does some act that gets a change in the other person's behavior.

This type of interaction provides a continuous development of cognition as the basis for future language (Lucas, 1981; Arwood, 1991). The stages of such cognition are described in many studies, but are typically thought of as developing from the **sensory input** with infant **motor output** (0 to 2 years) through the need to be separate from space or to **preoperate** from the environment (3 to 7). Then the rules on how to operate become **concrete** (7 to 11) finally creating a **formal** understanding of a concept (e.g., Piaget's Stages of Cognitive Development, Santrock, 1997; Arwood and Unruh, 2000).

Cognitive development results in actual concept differences between those who process in auditory language (visual with acoustic features or patterns) and those who process with visual language (visual with visual features or patterns). For example, a young child is looking at the toys while sitting on the floor. The child's mother says, "Cindy, pick up your toys." The child who can process the spoken words with the visual objects or toys begins to act on the toys. The child who is visual in conceptualization may not even process the mother's spoken ideas. If the child recognizes that there is sound input, then the visual thinking child will turn to look at the source of the sound to wait for visual clarification. The visual thinker turns to source of sound, Mother now points, and adds visual cues to her words.

These thinking differences continue into school and even into adulthood. For example, the teacher says, "Students, please put your books into your desk so that we can get ready to go." Those who processed the spoken directive will typically try to comply. Some students may not even process that there was a spoken directive. Some students recognize that the teacher is talking so the students look around to see what everyone is doing in order to comply. If the teacher "reads" the students well, the teacher will begin to create visual class cues so that directives are not lost. For example, the teacher may announce that the time for an event is quickly running out and that there is 30 seconds left, then 20 seconds, then counting backwards, the students develop an acoustic (not auditory) cadence or pacing that allows for the students to begin to "feel" the closing spaces of times...10, 9, 8, 7, 6, 5, 4, etc. Or, for example, hand cues may be used to show that it is time for recess. Students who use the visual thinking see the hand and immediately start to move. Without such a cue, they must wait and look around to see what others are doing.

The visual thinker does very well with sound (acoustics) as long as it is not tied to the meaning of the spoken language (visual with acoustic processing). For example, if the visual thinker is tested for hearing loss, the test results will indicate that there is no hearing loss of acuity; but, in the classroom, the visual thinking child may appear to not respond to verbal directions. As adults, the visual thinker is quite talented at mapping the building architecture, but may not be able to use spoken English (auditory language) to explain the details of the architectural plan. *Mental cognition is composed of concepts, whether the mental patterns are of visual or auditory characteristics.*

*To develop cognitive concepts, the classroom activities must provide students with opportunities for manipulating the concepts through a hierarchy of tasks beginning with basic use of the idea (**preoperational**), through the rules of reading, writing, talking about the concept (**concrete**), to finally acquiring the adult meaning (over 11 years or **formal**).* In other words students aren't taught concepts but *acquire concepts* through the opportunity to use concepts in a variety of language based activities. For example, if students study earth science through reading a chapter and then answering the questions at the end of the chapter, there exists all sorts of learning possibilities. Some students may answer the questions found at the end of the chapter by matching patterns with little or no conceptualization, therefore with very little learning. When these students are asked "what" they are studying in class, they will say, "I don't know." Sometimes they will say "earth science?" as if to make a guess. When asked about what earth science means, they typically can't answer because they haven't acquired the language of the earth science concepts, even if their grades are good. Using the same example, some students may have copied from the book or from others' papers by matching and using some internal mental language (either auditory or visual) so that there is some awareness of the topic but little development of conceptualization. Auditory thinkers may have used their own internal spoken language to slowly read and reread the language concepts, gradually acquiring knowledge of earth science based on their internal matching of meaning about the concepts being read. These auditory thinkers may use their mental spoken patterns to match with reading. They, too, may not have learned the concepts.

The students with little learning or conceptualization will say they are studying "earth science or science." They can say whether or not it is easy or hard and even talk about the types of activities. "First, we read the book. We do questions and answers." But these students have difficulty with being able to tell about the concepts except as rules. For example, "Earth science is about the earth." "It is about the ground, water, dirt, weather." If they are asked how weather is related to earth science, they will not be able to answer in complete, relational answers that show complete language use. However, *if a child reads, writes, and talks about the content in earth science, then they will be able to answer the questions using language about the learned concepts. A variety of language ways to use concepts creates the development of concepts.* Even a Kindergarten child is able to say, "Well, I study the ground, how to plant things, how to pick things, and how the plants need water, air, and sun." If asked about the words used, "What is air?" This young child will try to give a definition. "Air is breathed. I breathe oxygen. Oxygen is what I breathe. My body needs oxygen. Plants make oxygen. All living things need oxygen." ***Language consists of concepts so that the child's cognition improves with increased use of language about the topic.*** *Since language is the tool for better learning, then increased use of language also increases learning. Therefore, to increase learning in a classroom, cognitive developmental stages for concepts must be considered. Allowing students to use concepts at all levels of conceptualization maximizes language use for maximum learning.*

Students who use visual thinking are able to see the concepts in their heads...pictures of the earth, rain, past experiences, present day weather, etc. Students who use auditory thinking are able to hear their own mental spoken language, "It's fun to study about how the earth revolves and moves...how the climate is related to the earth and its properties." *The classroom that respects the cognition of learners provides both of these types of thinkers with multiple opportunities to use language to increase conceptual development or thinking in the way they learn.*

Activity

1. **How is concept development related to cognition?**
2. **How does the way a person thinks affect the understanding of concepts?**
3. **How is language related to concept development?**

Classroom Language for Improved Conceptual Development

Chapter One provided an overview of the type of language used by the educator to create an atmosphere of *"respect."* However, language goes beyond the basic way to be socially acceptable with interpersonal language techniques previously described (Chapters Two and Three). *Language also needs to assist students in learning concepts.* **Concepts are organized from the meaning of what is provided by the learner's environment.** *So, how an educator or parent provides meaning also determines how well a child's learning may be respected.* In other words, the teacher may be very respectful of the student in terms of language related to social development, but if the child fails academically because the child's conceptualization as a thinker does not match the way the educator is presenting the material, then the child begins to be excluded for cognitive reasons. Allowing a child to read in an alternative way was offered earlier in this chapter as an example of how to respect the child's thinking. *There are many ways to assist the language development of students so that the ways a child conceptualizes language are also emphasized.* The following examples provide ways to use language in the classroom to improve conceptualization or the **language of cognitive respect.** Better use of language helps all types of thinkers!

1. **Use "because"** as a way to explain rules, behavior, situations, etc. For example, "Yes, we can't chew gum during PE **because** we might choke on the gum while running or yelling." "Even though the sun is closer in winter, the temperature of the days is cooler **because** the

rotation of the Earth, etc." "I think Jessa is asking for someone to help **because** she has too many things to carry." Reasons for how concepts fit together are connected by "because" in a way that helps give limits to the parameters of the concept. Adding time and space concepts such as "because," "during," "between," "while," "after," "so," "when," etc., also helps *create additional relationships between cognitive and physical experiences through language.*

2. **Use specific referents** when talking, explaining, showing, demonstrating, etc. For example, "Sam and Rory have built a volcano. Sam and Rory, do you have something to share with your classmates?" This utterance uses specific referents for the agents (Sam, Rory, classmates), the object (volcano), and the action (share). The same idea could have been said without these referents, "Listen up...you're on." Such *colloquial use of language is suitable but it does not offer the students with language that shares the **respect** of the agents, actions, objects within the classroom environment.* Perhaps the student does not use referents very well. Chatauqua says, "Here's my experiment. Any questions?" Chatauqua's lack of referents is a cue for the teacher to have a class chat about the expectations. If the task is to demonstrate and tell the class about the demonstration, then Chatauqua needs more information about what that type of task sounds like and looks like. The other students need to become the "keepers" of the classroom, not the teacher. The teacher facilitates by saying, "Chatauqua, I am not sure what you did in your experiment. Chatauqua, please tell us about your demonstration. Begin by describing the first thing you did. Then give your classmates the opportunity to ask you questions." (The class will have already had a discussion and practice on asking appropriate questions). Now Chatauqua may still need a prompt, "So, the first thing you did was...." After Chatauqua's demonstration is over, it is probably a good time to review with the whole class how "we talk about what we do." Always give the students the "because," "You know, next year, when you are in the fourth grade, the teacher will expect you to stand tall so everyone can hear, to speak loudly so the teacher in the back of the

room can hear, and to talk about everything you see in the experiment. We are practicing what it is like to be older. You are all so capable of doing such fine work. Thank you for giving each of us the opportunity to practice. Who is on the list to practice his or her skills next?" *Teacher and student use of specific referents in oral language results in clearer student writing and in better respect of the whole learning process because language is focused. Referents add clarity, rationale, and improved understanding for better concept development through the better use of language.*

3. **Use possibility language.** Learners need to know that each student or self is "competent" as a human being. Since all human beings learn, then there is always the **possibility** that the learner hasn't met all challenges and that there is yet more learning. This sets up the student to be a "life long learner." "Doug, I see your project has a thatched roof house. I wonder what plants were used for the thatch roof?!" Doug responds, "These were bought at the store." Teacher replies, "I didn't know the Klamath Indians in the 1700's had stores!?" The possibility exists that the stores could be real but unlikely. Doug shrugs his shoulders. Teacher adds, "Well, why don't you look in those books for 10 minutes to see if you can find (*possibility*) some information about those thatched roofs." The purpose of the assignment is not to prove the teacher right and the student wrong but to offer the student the opportunity to learn more information about the roofs. It's usually not long before the student discovers that the thatch is made out of plants, not bought at the store. Then this creates the opportunity to raise the question about why the Klamath Indians did not have stores, as we know them. Students *love* the opportunity to research a question. Both authors have had the experience of students turning in multiple "unassigned" research projects in all sorts of forms. Students are given the opportunity to expand on these reports, share with classmates and others, and post them where all can see. In return, the students are given written notes of gratitude, lavish praise, and a title of expert. All students become experts...researchers, writers, typists, model popsicle house builders,

musicians, recess organizers, due-date-keepers, best users of materials, illustrators, computer experts, etc. *The combination of the socially assigned meaning as an expert with content rich projects developed from possibility language increases the student's conceptualization through the use of language.*

Possibility language also refers to the use of language for future learning. For Kindergarten students, "Let's think about what we might look like next year in first grade?" Third grade students, "When we go to the cafeteria we want to look like we know how to be third graders. What does a third grader look like?" After brainstorming, and "How will we look like in fourth grade?" To some fifth graders, "We will tell our stories to the first graders. They are younger than we are. They will help us learn how to tell our stories. Each first grader story partner will ask us one question about our stories. When we answer the question we will want to tell them the 'whole idea' so that they will be good writers and story tellers when they are in fifth grade."

These possibility language examples for future learning requires some "run through" practice. Students are using spoken language as well as mentally pictured visualization to think about what behavior and academic expectations "look like." Possibility language about the future also offers the opportunity to set goals. For example, "Sam, you are such a fantastic artist that you might consider a career in an art design field. If you are interested, I will bring you some information." Learners need the opportunity to *think* about how they will fit into the future. *Possibility language is rich in providing future opportunities.*

The reader should be reminded that a student who uses auditory thinking as a mode for language uses "time" as a way to plan for the future through spoken mental language. However, a visual thinker uses the way he or she mentally looks doing a past or present task to plan for future tasks. *Possibility language offers spoken words as well as a method of visualization based on the present to see the future.* The majority of school age students do not plan for the future because they use visual thinking without anyone providing a way to visualize the future. Possibility language helps visual thinkers see themselves in the future.

Possibility language has the built-in factor of being safe, as there are no absolute or rigid answers. The student is out on an equal status of power with the teacher so they both explore the possibilities. Many students relax during these moments compared to math drills or spelling tests. Humor, imagination, and creativity are easily employed in possibility situations. So often, peers attribute strengths to these possibility explorations, to shy and more private students. Possibility language is a powerful strategy!

4. **Walk in the student's shoes.** To walk in another person's shoes means to treat that student the way one would like to be treated. Some people say this is the essence of the Golden Rule. For example, "The student blurts out when the teacher is talking." There are all sorts of ways to respond to this student but the teacher needs to think, "In what way would I like to be responded? Would I like to be shut down by someone saying 'Alex, sit down. You are not to talk out when I am talking.' Or, would I like to be punished in front of others with 'Alex you are always talking out, go to time out?'" As a learner who has social needs, I would probably like to be treated as if I didn't know better and I could probably use some adult direction, so as to feel like I fit into the group. The teacher could respond to the blurted out ideas with the following, "Alex, what did you want to say about the recess?" Alex responds and the educator thanks him, "Alex thank you for your idea. You always have a lot of ideas to share. When you first shared your idea, I didn't hear you because I was talking. Next time when you have a really good idea and want to share it while someone is talking, draw or write the idea on paper. That will help you remember your idea to tell when there is no one talking. We don't want to miss any of your ideas. Christy, I see you writing some ideas down, maybe you could show Alex how to take down ideas on paper after we have recess." Christy says, "Alex, I used to always talk at the same time as other people, but, now, I talk just when I want to. I will show you how to write 'visual notes'."

The respectful language exchange between Alex, Christy, and the teacher only occurs when the classroom environment respects all learners' needs, cognitively as well as socially. If Christy's language sounds formal and caring, it is meant to be such language. Christy is learning to use this type of language from the teacher who **"walks in the students' shoes."** *The teacher uses rich and explanatory language to build conceptualization about behavior as well as academics.*

5. **Facilitate friendship language.** "Jarold, I was really impressed by the way you let Monica go first in the cafeteria line. This shows me that you know how to be a friend. Friends give their friends ways to be first." These types of *friendship statements* in response to something the teacher observes or "sees" connects both the spoken message with the cognition of what the concept of "friends" means. Such a message is spoken privately and warmly to Jarold as the teacher and Jarold walk along. Or, for example, "Becka, I like to see you giving Anita the ball before recess. You are growing up. (Becka is a first grader) I don't even see second graders be so kind to their friends. You are very kind. Thank you for sharing with Anita." The concept of friendship is like all other concepts. It must be acquired over time so multiple opportunities throughout a child's school year helps the child develop a more sophisticated level of cognition about the concept of friendship. *Again, language is the tool for concept development.* These types of friendship behaviors may also be drawn out as a cartoon (Arwood & Brown, 1999) to show the student what the friendship behavior looks like. The authors have often used Polaroid pictures to snapshot moments that are later explained to parents and students as important learning moments. A single warm, friendly, thoughtful note on the back of the snapshot provides language that encourages conceptualization of the formal concepts of **respect,** responsibility, consideration, cooperation, etc. These concepts are important in the "language of respect" because they represent what the behavior of *respect* looks like, sounds like, and acts like. For example, Alisha is standing quietly in line. A picture is taken. Later, Alisha is handed the picture. On the back her teacher has written,

"Thank you for being a leader in this class." Attached to the photo is a 3 X 5 index card with the written statement, "I see how thoughtful you are to wait for everyone to get ready to go to lunch. Thank you!" The student is given a choice of what she wants to do with the picture, maybe she will take it home, maybe she will post it, and maybe she will hang it in her locker. It is a gift to her. The authors have heard many stories about students keeping crumbled up papers and pictures in their billfolds through adulthood as a reminder of a teacher "who cared." Scribbled on these papers are thank you notes, goals, inspirational language that all people want as a *friendly* reminder of being competent and worthy of such praise. These pieces are kept because the language to students typically is lacking in such friendship statements. *All learners deserve such language and the frequent use of friendship language offers a social model of being competent cognitively.*

6.   **Use measurement language. Measurement language defines the place, time, quantity and quality properties of ideas or concepts.** Because visual and auditory cognition results in differences in concept development, **visual language creates concepts based on space (acquired through the use of eyes) and auditory language creates concepts based on time (acquired through the sound properties connected to vision)** (Arwood, 1991). Because the visual thinker uses the cognitive development of points in space or measuring, then students with visual cognition need to see what the organization of space looks like. For example, the mental concept of a "due date" might be mentally picturing the person "doing" the task on that date. The result of such metacognition is the student starts the project when the project is "due." By helping the students see what the "whole project" pieces look like and then putting those pieces on a calendar working from the finished project backwards to today, the starting point helps measure the "due date" as separate parts, each requiring certain tasks, time and behaviors to meet the "due date." Therefore, to the visual thinker, "time" is measured by the space on a clock. So, there is no physical "hurry up," but there is a way to measure each activity as taking so much space on

the clock. (Chapter Seven will discuss more about using time in the class.)

Understanding that there is a difference between space and time according to differences in thinking, measurement language for the visual thinker might sound like this. "Janelle, I need to see your bottom in this chair by the time I walk to your desk." Or, "Mark, I see you have written the due date on your calendar but I don't see what you are going to 'do' to get to that date." After Mark tells the first piece, "Mark how much time on the clock does writing a note card take?" By using measurement language, students learn how to organize and plan. They learn about the past and the future. They learn to be responsible and to respect the auditory culture of a time based economic system. The use of picturing the steps in each space (e.g., cartooning) goes hand-in-hand with visualizing successful people who reach their goals such as athletes, business people, etc. "Being on time" or "punctuality" cannot be visualized. But people, actions, and objects, such as the students walking into the class when the clock's hands are at a certain point, can be visualized, drawn, and pictured. *The English language is full of time measurement words which is why auditory language thinkers have an internal sense of time; but, visual thinkers in the English auditory culture, struggle with time concepts unless language showing what measurement looks like is offered.*

The following activities are additional examples of how visual measurement of time occurs in an auditory culture. For middle school to high school students, setting career goals is a two-week activity: 1) visual timeline; 2) education or training required; 3) what can I do NOW; 4) salary; 5) job specifics; 6) role models; 7) disadvantages (e.g., travel, strenuous, long hours, dirty working conditions); and 8) advantages. Students love finding out the details in looking into the future through spatial, visual components. For activities to occur in the future, all preschool, elementary and most middle school students need visual timelines that show what happens at each step, not necessarily the date. These are used for preparing for reports, fieldtrips, and parties.

Parents often pick up on drawing out the steps for their students. Cartoons for any behavior even for "before-going-to-bed" for students helps them pack their backpacks, recheck backpack for assignments, select school clothes for the next day, and put clothes in the appropriate place. Parents really appreciate these types of visual structures. Even exercises on "preparation" help. These might include baking cookies, going camping, having friends over for a slumber party, or cleaning a bedroom. In these exercises, priority ranking is given to those preparation activities that are "absolutely necessary," "good to have," "helpful at times," and "just in case." *Any activity that involves more than one step and/or requires planning is helped by visually showing the learners the steps through measurement language.*

7.   **Use rich language. Rich language describes, evaluates, assesses, and creates ideas for learners.** For example, "Mack, a frog is a living creature" is an utterance that is a statement of information that the student may already know. But, "Mack, when I see your hands gripped around the middle of the frog so the frog can't move, then I know that the frog also can't breathe. If the frog can't breathe then the frog will die. Put your hands loosely, 'like this,' around the frog so that the frog can't hop away and hurt himself, but also so the frog can breathe." This latter example provides more information and creates mental pictures to explain why a student should hold a frog differently. Rich language also helps with behavior and discipline in a classroom. For example, nine-year-old Priscilla walks into the classroom and slams the door behind her. "Priscilla, when you slam the door so that I see the door shake, the pictures move on the walls, and all of the students turn to see what caused the noise, then I know that slamming the door is disturbing other people. The teacher next door is probably sitting with her students reading a story. When you slammed the door, then the students next door forgot the story that the teacher was reading. The teacher across the hall was probably doing math with her students and when you slammed the door, then the students couldn't do their math, etc." *This type of rich language establishes boundaries, limits, and provides tremendous*

meaning about how to act and behave by classroom or societal standards.

The spoken ideas sound a little redundant for auditory language users but the richness provides the mental pictures for visual thinkers. These ideas can also be drawn and cartooned for students who continue to have trouble with behavior (Arwood and Brown, 1999). The drawings hold the information still or constant for better assigning of meaning. At times, the redundancy is brought up by the students who do not need the repetition or overlap. This provides the teacher with the opportunity to ask the class why parents, teaches, coaches tend to repeat ideas. The students are usually right on target. They realize that hearing an idea isn't the same as remembering an idea. It is the responsibility of the teacher to guide the students toward possible answers or considerations. Here is another chance to offer respect and develop bonding as a result of respecting the diversity of others.

Spoken rich language also models the boundaries and limits for students. For example, two third grade boys came running into a room talking frantically about "something." The teacher said, "Wait, Sean and Eric. I see you both run past me and I see your words also run past me." The teacher gestures the course of the path the boys are running. She continues, "I can't hear you. Your words are also running past me and I don't know if you are talking to me. If you want to talk to me I need to see your face to know you are talking to me." Both boys walk back to where the teacher is standing next to the open door. Instead of the boys slouching for being punished, both boys stood up straighter and taller. The teacher smiled to each of the boys. "Now, I can see your faces and I know you have something important to tell me." Sean says, "My mother is coming in a minute. She is looking for a place to park." The teacher replied, "Your mom is coming in today?" Sean says, "Yes, she wants to watch." The teacher says, "I am so glad you boys told me about your mom coming to visit. I am looking forward to seeing your mom. I also feel good about the way you stopped to talk with me. I can really understand your ideas a lot better when you stop and look at me while you talk." *Rich language is not punishing. The richness of language gives additional meaning to the activities, the behavior, the rules, etc.*

8. **Supplement oral language with visual structures**. *Spoken language needs to be supplemented by some sort of visual assists in order to respect the different ways that learners think.* These assists could include drawing the idea or behavior (Arwood, 1991; Arwood & Brown, 1999), using graphics for content, using gestures (also known as "g-signs"), enhancing visual facial postures, using sign language, and creating flow charts. All of these visual structures assist the students to "see what is said." Creating meaning so that the learner can "see as well as hear" helps to *respect* the mental *language* of the two types of thinkers. Classrooms that have more layers of different visual structures tend to reach more of the students' learning needs at higher cognitive levels of development. These external structures are created by students and teachers as ways to enhance the richness of the spoken language.

9. **Use language of visualization.** *Create opportunities for students to mentally reflect on a situation through visualization. Visualization helps students see the relationship among spoken language, written language, and physical experiences.* Mr. Young used to take writing samples at the beginning of the year. He discovered that many of his fifth graders had minimum success. He would begin to use visualization into the curriculum. For example, "You are in for a treat. Every sense will be triggered. You will hear beautiful sounds, sense temperature changes, become aware of the special smells of a forest, its flowers and more. All you need to do is close your eyes, relax your body, and just let your minds flow with the words as I turn off the lights, shut the door, and begin with a raft trip down a lazy river during the month of July. (Telling the students about the task with spoken words helps the auditory students see the mental images as the visualization task proceeds.)

You launch your yellow, two person, rubber raft onto the South River. As you climb gently into your raft, your bare feet nudge your only luggage, a Styrofoam cooler filled with soft drinks and fresh fruit. You lean back and look up at the clear blue sky; not a single puffy cloud in sight. The fingers of your left-hand trail casually in the cool, clear water causing a pleasing, gurgling sound as you float down the tree-lined river. The sun feels great. It must be 85 degrees. Dressed in your favorite, green and white striped soccer tee shirt and dark green shorts, and Notre Dame cap, the day seems to be perfect in every way. Overhead, a circling, redtail hawk with steady, outstretched wings and twitching tail seems to be watching you as you relax and float your way south. Cheep, cheep, cheep! You raise up on your right elbow and notice a mother duck swimming along the low bank with her five, fuzzy yellow ducklings with brown patches on their heads and wings. Mother duck leads the straight line of inexperienced swimmers. She seems to glide along effortlessly while her ducklings paddle with all of their energies. You glide toward the bank with a few strokes of the aluminum oars and watch the family of ducks swim by. Mother duck quacks a friendly greeting to you. Each cuddly duckling seems to smile at you as they parade by at a close range. The nearby forest floats a special aroma of pinecones, and flowers on a wandering, cool breeze blowing down from the distant, tree-covered hills. The area is a picture perfect scene. Pushing off, you aim for the middle of the river. Leaning back you notice a curling column of gray smoke from a lonely log cabin in the distance. As you approach the cabin made of hand-hewn logs, you hear someone calling out "Stop for awhile." You wave back and soon meet the Linn Family. Mr. Linn is wearing a pair of worn, blue overalls and a tattered straw hat. Mrs. Linn wears a free-flowing dress with bright yellow sunflowers on it. You're invited to stay for lunch. Seated at a wooden table under a spreading apple tree, you enjoy a garden-fresh salad, some freshly caught and fried-in-cornmeal trout, as well as some, tall, frosty glasses of iced tea with refreshing mint leaves. For dessert, Mrs. Linn brings out a steamy, freshly baked pie while Mr. Linn heaps generous scoops of homemade vanilla ice cream on each delicious slice. The mouth-watering, flaky crusted pie filled with sunshine-ripened berries and tasty ice cream hit the spot. You share some of your fresh fruit from your Styrofoam cooler with them as you wave a good-bye to your new friends. The cool water feels good around your legs as you step back into the river, slip skillfully into your raft and head toward Burrisville where friends will meet you for an overnight camp at Frog Lake in a few hours. Sipping a cool beverage, slipping your cap over your eyes, you lean back and simply enjoy your quiet, restful ride down the South River.

Using such visualization helps students see as well as hear the mental pictures. Auditory thinkers use the sound of spoken words to create visual images. Visual thinkers readily process the spoken words as mental pictures. All of the students are asked to draw and/or write what they visualized. Class discussions about differences in how students perceived the various ideas result in empowering discussions about how different students think and learn. From the overlap of mental cognitive experiences comes the attachment of the written ideas. Students learn to use their way of thinking for such writing tasks. Soon students are given a writing task for which they create their own mental language for success.

10. **Use consistent language.** *Consistent language connects one set of ideas to another set of ideas in a variety of ways.* "Tell the students what you are going to do, then tell them about doing it, then tell them about how to evaluate it, then tell them about what was completed, and then connect the work to the next task. Review the last talk with language, review what was learned and how it was learned, then connect the learning to the next task." These connections create an atmosphere that is predictable or consistent. The students "know" the structure of the classroom in terms of socialization as well as cognition. The students

know what to expect, how to behave within the set up structure, and how to use language to improve behavior or academics. This type of connected language also creates a class environment based on the **language of RESPECT**—*the Right of Each Student to Participate in an Environment of Communicative Thoughtfulness.*

Consistency or predictability of another person's behavior is the primary basis for "trust." When a teacher's behavior is predictable, not to be confused with routine, then students feel more open to trust the teacher and the classmates. This type of trust generates a risk-taking atmosphere that creates fun and learning. Furthermore, activities are in context of what the students are doing since the teacher and students use language to connect ideas. This consistent use of language allows for the class to move from one activity to the next with minimum transition time since all activities are connected. *Connected language also allows all students stay in contact with what is expected.* If these connections are drawn as parts of the whole event, it will also help students who are struggling with staying on task. The language connections provide the child an external description that can later be visually used as mental language.

Consistent language includes social as well as cognitive acts. For example, instead of class discussions always being about content, class discussions can center on social or academic behavior. It might be common to hear, "Why do you think that Cindi enjoyed PE class today?" or "Jim, why are you finding it easier to write sentences these days?" or "Class do you have some ideas about why we are taking less time to get ready to go home at the end of the day?" or, "Does anyone have an idea of why the substitute teacher wants to return to this class?" Students learn to expect to grow both socially and academically. They are learning to expect language that respects them as learners and as citizens.

Consistent language also connects social and cognitive acts. The use of videos and photos to catch both cognitive and social moments of pride are very popular. The students are provided the opportunity to use the cameras on the playground, on field trips, getting off the school bus, everywhere. These videotapes and photos offer visual structures to assist in talking about social as well as academic behavior. *Learning to respect all students is part of the consistency in the language of respect.* Students learn that they are responsible for their behavior as well as for assigning positive meaning to their classmates' behaviors, academic and social.

11. **Use grateful language.** *Grateful language shows appreciation in all acts, big or little.* Thank the students for being in class, for coming to school, for being helpful, for sharing ideas, for smiling, for wiggling with excitement, for wanting a sharper pencil, for bringing something from home, for talking with you before school, for asking a question, for participating, for anything and everything. *Each human being deserves to be in a safe, appreciative context. Create opportunities for being appreciative.* For example, Max brings his model plane from home. "Max, I like your model plane. Would you like to tell your class mates about the plane?" "Yes, I want to show them the plane." "Okay, when I call your name for roll call, will you please tell everyone that you would like to show your plane and we will then discuss when it would be a good time. Thank you for helping me remember to show the class your plane." It's really important that the teacher **not** forget to follow through so that the students see how to share their personal interests with others.

Opportunities may be set up for students to receive all sorts of *appreciation* for sharing family and friends with the class. The teacher as well as students quickly dash off thank you notes for such sharing. This becomes part of the writing curriculum. When visitors come to class, opportunity is given to individual students to write a thank you note on behalf of the class. The content of such notes is shared with the whole class...copies are sometimes posted on the board. Students quickly learn that *gratitude* is the other half of giving. The teacher also models this by writing notes to the students, their families, and by even making 30 second phone calls. Parents and families become accustomed to hearing about their son or daughter's successes, not just their problems.

Successes might include talking about smiles, skills, presentations, work, and anything that can be captured in words or a picture. For example, the teacher calls home and leaves the message, "I enjoyed having John at school today. He asks wonderful questions."

Gratitude can also be "awarded" as long as all students participate. For example, all students even the older middle school students appear to *appreciate* being a caregiver for a stuffed animal. So, when a student is "caught" doing a kindness for someone else, the teacher might say, "Sandy, you are so kind to help Janice with her math. Sandy, pick out a stuffed animal to sit with you today to share your kindness." It is not long before all students have had a stuffed animal. Eventually, volunteers from the class become the people who award the stuffed animals. This task can be turned into quality time having the recipients justify why they were awarded the animals. Justification is created by having three **other** witnesses (students) attest to positive reasons. The practice of giving positive reasons helps in creating ways to use thoughtful, appreciative language as well as helping students learn to accept positive language. These are opportunities to use the **language of RESPECT**.

12. **Use humor.** *Humor should be age appropriate and generous.* Sometimes, teachers reserve all humor to what the teacher brings to the classroom. This is literally "hogging" center stage. **Shared respect for communicative thoughtfulness means giving all individuals the opportunity to laugh and be humorous.** Some students are more comfortable sharing than others are, but all students like to laugh. Humor brings about a level of informality that seems to relax students. It shows them, in a very acceptable manner, that their teachers make mistakes and are human too. From laughing together, students tend to bond as a class.

One drawback to humor is that some nearby classes may be disturbed. Colleagues may even ask that the class be "toned down." Some colleagues even complain that such fun makes their students also want to participate in the humor. So, a watchful eye for closing the door, for keeping the loudness to a certain level is necessary. The closing of a door or a watchful eye must be part of a class discussion about other's rights. In other words, it is okay that the other classroom teachers do not want to hear the laughter. There is no devaluation of their needs, only a discussion about how to honor their needs. *Respect is a reciprocal role between being honored and honoring others.*

Using humor requires a finely honed personal technique of being comfortable with students, enjoying the classroom atmosphere, and feeling positive about teaching. Humor has to come naturally and be part of the classroom management. Contrived humor is deceitful and students see the teacher as "cloudy" and a lack of trust ensues resulting in power struggles and management problems. *Humor comes from the personal strength of character, not from a mask on stage.*

Humor comes in all forms. Since humor is so personal, then teachers may want to develop the type of humor that works for them. Simple examples of humor follow. Sometimes, the teacher can use a deliberate misunderstanding tact to illustrate that "things" in life are askew. The student asks for a book and the teacher says, "Why do you need a hook?" When the flustered student begins to explain that it is "book" then the teacher says "Oh I must be getting old...I didn't hear, is it possible I am getting old?" The students begin to laugh and the teacher quickly says, "It is time to get back to work." With this type of humor, the students learn to laugh and immediately return to task. Another type of humor tells the student that peculiar things happen to us all. It's a humor of "I do that too." A student says that she has gone to the library in the past and then forgot what to do. The teacher says, "Oh, yeah I have found myself running up the stairs at my house to come to a screeching halt wondering why I am not downstairs tidying the living room." Laughter usually follows with other testimonies of such predicaments.

A third type of humor evolves from using language to try to understand an idea. For example, a student says that the Columbia Gorge was formed by giant dinosaurs. The teacher says, "I don't understand. Is the Gorge the foot prints of dinosaurs?" Everyone chuckles and the student giggles, "No, I mean the Columbia Gorge was formed after the dinosaurs were 'gone.'" The only comment necessary is a simple, "Oh, I understand now."

Sometimes, the students see the teacher as someone who also gets confused and such human behavior is acceptable. One of the authors once had a third grade boy walk out of the classroom and tell his dad, "That lady doesn't know anything about baseball." This young man typically spoke in one to two word phrases and had not been successful with academics. The author had been invited into the classroom to help assess the young man's academic and social needs. The author had used the "I don't understand" form of language to help the young man realize that his spoken language did not match with his mental pictures. In reality, the author knew a lot about baseball, but by not assuming what the student meant, the student had a need to clarify his language. The author, student, and the student's teacher really laughed and enjoyed the session. *Even the father respectfully laughed to hear his son use a complete sentence* with such exasperation. The young man remembered that day for many years. In high school, he wrote a letter to the author to ask for more help. The respect between him and the author stemmed from the author using language to show the young man that he could cognitively express more than he typically did. Their shared humor was a way to make the task feel comfortable and the people accepted.

Students are encouraged to bring humor to the class with readings from *Reader's Digest* magazines, selections from other books or articles, creating humorous thoughts of the day, etc. The major rule about humor is that it should never be aimed at anyone as a put-down. Funny put-downs are still put-downs. Put-downs are degrading, negative, and unwanted. The immaturity of put-downs should be discussed as well as the maturity of humor of good taste. Ethnic and class jokes are absolutely forbidden. Laughter can be about the ridiculous, the peculiar, and even jokes, but **never** at the expense of another person. Name-calling is not funny and not tolerated. Differences in humor are also accepted. Visual thinkers and auditory thinkers will show differences in what they find humorous. For example, visual thinkers like to show peculiar visual displays such as a picture of talking frogs advertising lemonade. Auditory thinkers enjoy these pictures especially for the spoken words by the frogs.

The more variety of language used in the classroom, the better the conceptual development. Language is the tool for helping to create concepts that are used for learning in the way that the students think. Therefore, teachers and parents who improve their language also see an improvement in the conceptual development of learners.

Activity

1. **List the various types of language strategies used in a classroom to help concept development.**
2. **Give examples of each type of language strategy.**

Event-Based Cognitive Development

Most recent teacher education pedagogy focuses on the shift from "out of context tasks," such as worksheets and fill-in-the-blanks, to more student-centered activities such as working with peers on projects. **Changing the methods without regard for cognitive development may be more socially appealing to teachers and students but may be limiting with regards to learning.** For example, the third grade teacher divides the classroom into groups of three students each. Each group of three students is to work together to create a project. The project has three parts--the writing about the pioneers, the drawing about the pioneers, and the telling about the pioneer project to the rest of the classes. All groups are responsible for selecting their topic about pioneers. Even if the teacher uses "good" language to visually show (drawing/writing) the tasks and to tell the students when the project is due, there are still pieces missing. What are the rules for working together? Is this an event where all students are equally empowered?

What are the steps to complete each of the parts of the tasks? Do all of the students have equal skills? If any of these questions resulted in a "no" answer, then imposing an arbitrary "three person group" structure onto the students' interpersonal development within the classroom may result in limited effectiveness of individual students, cognitively and sometimes socially. Note, the students and teacher may still prefer the imposed grouping over traditional tasks.

To respect the individuals as well as the learning process, within each small group of three students, all pieces of the assignment must be completed. It is assumed that there exists equal skills among all groups and within groups. The task is to do the same activity divided by three, which does not account for differences in learning systems or individual needs. For example, Marietta is quickly able to do all three parts while Joshua doesn't know how to start. Even if the task is part of a classroom theme such as "wild animals" some students have more knowledge than others do. *Instead of imposing an artificial structure on the students, set limits for the event.* **The event is defined as people who are doing something with objects or within a place.** *The classroom of students are the agents. Their actions include a variety of options to include drawing, acting, talking, writing, journaling, playing instruments, etc.* The objects are the individual tasks that are developed within a content area. The English convention is assumed to be oral language or written English. So, the final level of dissemination is expected to be in that written *and* spoken form from each student, even if a student starts with drawing or making a decorama. Individual interests dictate the direction of interest about the pioneers or the theme of wild animals instead of the small group projects. In this way, talented and gifted students are challenged just as much as the ones who have never learned about the topic.

Within a classroom where the **language of respect is used to foster cognitive development as well as socialization,** the fiber of the weave is set from the first day. All students are competent and deserve individual *respect*. Therefore, all students are agents for other students, their ideas, their gifts, and their ability to resource for others.

The teacher's responsibility is to serve as a facilitator to provide students the opportunity to use language to learn from sources and to learn to resource. The teacher might say, "Adam, Anna has a picture of the wagon train. You could ask her to help you put that picture into your report about pioneers." This provides opportunity to learn how to work with others without a structure that may actually interfere with learning. *In small groups designed with the single purpose of completing an activity, but often multitasked, students elbow to be heard, to show what they know or sometimes what they don't know, and sometimes the effort of working with others overrides the learning.* For example, Ashrad, Jake, and Sheena are in a third-grade-group. The project task is about insects. Jake has been studying insects since he was in preschool. His mom and dad both have doctorates in field biology. Jake is also diagnosed as attention deficit disorder (ADD) without hyperactivity. Ashrad's family comes from a Middle Eastern culture but all family members are professionals and speak English fluently. Ashrad is interested in computers and Legos. Sheena really doesn't care about insects except she doesn't like them killed. She has just been to see an animated movie about ants. The teacher has instructed the groups to decide on an insect that they want to research. Jake grabs a piece of paper and begins to draw a detailed dragonfly while telling the group everything he knows about dragonflies. Ashrad is sort of listening to Jake but really doesn't care. He is thinking about how he will make his moving Lego robot when he gets home. Sheena keeps telling Jake that she wants to do ants. Neither Jake nor Sheena are listening to each other. When the time is up, the group will be doing the dragonfly since Jake jumps up and shows his beautifully drawn dragonfly. The teacher is not aware that the group is not working together but independently to produce the project. Sheena goes home angry. She throws her coat in the door and asks for a snack. When her mom questions her, she says she has to work with boys. The real lack of communication is not discussed.

After all, Sheena is too young to protect her ideas. It is the responsibility of the adult to protect Sheena. Ashrad goes home and works on his Legos. He has no homework.

The next day, the teacher gives the students time to go to the library to look up material about their chosen insect. Jake finds a really interesting book and begins to draw a black widow spider. Ashrad is looking through the books that show how insects "come apart." Sheena is trying to find information about a dragonfly. Disillusioned and frustrated she is trying to stay with the topic chosen by Jake.

On the third day, Sheena is further frustrated by the fact that Jake is not helping with the research. In reality, why should he? He already knows about the insects. Sheena is copying from the book onto her paper. Ashrad is telling her that her writing doesn't look nice. He will write. Jake is talking about the preying mantis. Ashrad grabs the book and starts to write. Sheena sits. She looks around. The teacher sees the group writing and all busy with insects except for Sheena. The teacher walks over, "Sheena, you need to be helping Ashrad with the writing." Sheena has learned a valuable lesson. School is arbitrary and frustrating. None of the students are cognitively improving their concepts, knowledge of insects, or people skills. Jake, who is never really on task, may be learning the most since he already knows the most about insects. He is able to take past information and assign meaning to what he draws or talks about (learning principles are self-imposed). The others are struggling to "get the task complete." Sheena goes home again angry. She throws open the door, tosses her backpack, grabs a snack, and plops down in front of the TV. When she is asked about her day, she says, "I don't like science." Her mom asks, "What don't you like?" She says, "Insects." This lesson of working with Jake and Ashrad has nothing to do with liking science but everything to do with *"language use in the classroom." To be an event-based classroom with supportive, nurturing language, Sheena needs to find her learning skills first.* Then the teacher needs to facilitate the use of Sheena's skills within the whole classroom.

From the previous description of the activity, it would be difficult to realize that Sheena has several learning skills that are strengths. She is compliant, is able to follow spoken instructions, a hard worker, and has excellent oral language. But given peers who don't have good listening or language skills with whom to solely work, Sheena's learning is shut down and the purpose of the small group activity is lost for her. In an event-based classroom, Sheena becomes an agent who writes, reads, works, acts, demonstrates, etc., about a topic, insects, for example. Then each student becomes a supporter of the other students' strengths, as needed. In other words, the class works as a big group and all students work with the other members as needed, in small groups. Jake is able to do multiple illustrations about insects and the teacher is then able to direct him into more challenging content. Ashrad could easily be assisted to develop a Lego insect display that he would then write and talk about. All three students would learn more, work together better, and their strengths would be better facilitated through language directed at their personal skills and cognitive level of development, if there were not an imposed small group.

To set up an event-based classroom, the initial social atmosphere of all students being contributors to the whole and having expertise must be established (see Chapters Two and Three). **From a cognitive standpoint, the lowest common denominator for classroom language use is to develop concepts that are "I based."** Since language development of concepts begins at the preoperational level, then an activity that uses the preoperational level of instruction is the best for beginning any lesson, at any content level, even college. Since preoperational cognition is about the speaker, then "I" language works well. **Storytelling** is an excellent way of pulling all the students into the teacher's context. The teacher tells an "I" story with rich language and visual properties so that students can self identify with the teacher. For example, "Last night, I sat on my front porch (drawing a stick figure sitting on a chair on the porch on the chalkboard or storychart paper). I looked across the street to my neighbor's porch and I saw a really big person. This person (while continuing to draw stick figures) was bigger than the porch (use of hand gestures and facial postures). I wondered who could this person be?" A pause signals the students to raise their hands and take a turn in guessing...their ideas are validated by the teacher saying back the words and writing their ideas on the board. Student names are used to personalize the ideas. "Jane said she thought it was a bear." **All students** are given the opportunity to draw and/or write about their idea of who this person could be or about one of the ideas on the board. This gives **all students** the option of being part of the group since there is plenty of visual and auditory language options to structure all learners. For upper grade students, the same sort of story could start a discussion on perspective, shadows, perception, reality, etc.

From this first set up, the lesson goes to a language arts lesson that incorporates reading, writing, fiction exploration, possibly some integration of science (shadows), math (measurement), etc. Working from a preoperational story given by the teacher to individual work (self "I" stories about what the students know or draw or research) establishes the students' own stories. The teacher then works back to big group discussion, followed by student sharing to allow opportunities for students to use each other as sources of information, knowledge and expertise. Usually, intermediate grade students (4-6 grades) and higher are able to lead the class by November of the school calendar. To check for the students' ability to know the learning process, the teacher brings up a topic and sits back to watch the students take the topic through the steps. Teachers also can facilitate the student leadership process by giving the topic to a student who is asked to find out how much the class members know about "topic X." The student gets the members' attention with a positive directive such as "May I have your attention." Then the student asks the question, "Does anyone know anything about 'topic X.?'" The students quickly raise their hands or walk to the reference books. The student leader arbitrarily sets a time limit by asking, "Do you need more than 10 minutes?" Any member may request an extension of time at any point. The students learn not only about the topic but they learn about themselves as competent learners as well as about how to be a leader. The students are active agents within an event-based learning environment.

Sometimes teachers will use a theme to help with the learning process. But, sometimes themes are too high a level of cognition to include all students. For example, "Today we are going to talk about shadows" is more formal than preoperational or concrete in language concepts. The result is that some students (about 30%) will not be on task with this start up.

To create an event, agents must be part of the language. **The agents must also be doing something active.** Therefore, language that uses non-specific verbs such as "going to talk about," when it is the teacher who is probably going to talk, results in a higher language level. If the students are assumed to know about the topic so as to be able to talk about "shadows," then there is probably little left to learn. The best use of class time is to begin at the lowest common denominator for language use, preoperational. This preoperational use of language is "self based" and incorporates the class members one by one into the whole. Additional resources and opportunities for the individual students to use their meaning and understanding helps the learners improve concept development. **Trough, building, bridge, and network principles of learning are being met through setting up events within the classroom.**

As the students generate their own writing about what they see and hear (story base), then each student becomes an agent doing an action (writing, reading, etc.) about the topic. The concepts of the topic are refined as students are facilitated to work between whole group (sharing what they know) to individual work (sharing on a one to one with others in the group). In this way, they also learn to trust themselves. Daily, the students are building concepts through each of the stages—preoperational, concrete, formal.

Visual structures as well as appropriate levels of language must be used to create an atmosphere for all to succeed. Responsibility for success rests with the teacher. The teacher, an agent, determines the tone of the classroom as well as the content for what the students are able to learn. *In the event-based classroom, there is the opportunity for more natural use of respectful language to create better learning.* Learning to use concepts at a more advanced level requires the overlap and layering of ideas. The next section defines each of these cognitive tools.

Activity

1. **Define event-based cognitive development.**
2. **Give examples of how to establish event-based learning in the classroom.**

Cognitive Overlap and Cognitive Layering

The previously described learning principles (**trough, building, bridge,** and **network**) accounted for a basic understanding of how to create concepts. But **concepts also have depth, the type of depth described as increasing meaning from a preoperational to concrete to finally a formal level of understanding.** *The depth of a concept comes from allowing a student to use language. The language originates with the learner who uses concepts in a variety of dimensions or ways (preoperational), moves to a shared way to use the concepts (concrete), and finishes in a formal way to disseminate learning.*

Original language occurs when students have the opportunity to read, write, and talk about **their** ideas related to the topic as well as offer ownership. So, within an event, there are many opportunities for students to offer their ideas. Assignment of roles can occur at many junctures. One such juncture might be when writing, drawing, and researching is discussed with the entire group. Another juncture might occur naturally as students need to share information or make connections between and among other students who are working on similar topics.

Working with other students and learning about their projects and work is important to providing additional layers of information about a topic. Through this type of additional information, the student is cognitively layering one idea about a particular concept with other related ideas that follow the basic learning principles. For example, a student is working on a project about the planets while another student is working on asteroids. These students will want to share information before dissemination since Pluto may or may not be reclassified as an asteroid rather than a planet. Beginning with the student's own ideas is defined as the preoperational level of understanding. "I live on Earth." Adding information from multiple sources (students) creates a concrete or rule governed understanding. For example, "Planets are not the same as stars. Earth is a planet, it is not a star." Once a student acquires multiple layers of concrete information, then a formal definition of a planet versus a star begins to emerge. This type of natural layering for better conceptualization can be quickly stopped with activities that do not use original student language. These activities are devoid of feelings, creativity, and energy. They are sterile and "boring" for learners. For example, fill-in-the blank sheets, most teacher-generated worksheets, copying from the book or board, are examples of tasks that lack the student's original language.

The authors have seen too many students who think that writing what someone else says and changing a word or two is original work. These students arrive at college eager to please but without the ability to use their own language for writing and talking from what they know. Some of these students are even punished for plagiarism at college without understanding "why" such punishment occurred. To provide the "why" for plagiarism is not only a kind thing to do, but also a humanizing event. Taking the time to explain the "why" announces to the students the teacher's philosophy about education as a professional (effective role modeling), and, too, a chance for the student to perceive the teacher as a flesh-and-bone human being with a heart that "understands," and a soul that "cares." To create the overlap of meaning is an investment in the student's cognitive as well as social development. *To acquire depth of a concept, a student must have the opportunity to use his or her own language through the layered cognitive stages of development.*

The **overlap** of one use of a concept with another use of the same concept allows for **layers** of deeper conceptualization. *Such overlapping occurs as different modes are used to express ideas--reading, writing, making a poster, writing a song, etc.* If different students engage in different activities, but are not facilitated to share the information or to create layers, then each student learns only what he or she creates (preoperational.) For example, in a third-grade-classroom, students are involved in solar system projects. One student works on the topic of the moon while another studies asteroids, etc. Each student is an agent engaged in an activity (preoperational). A concrete understanding develops if a student understands the relationship between Mars as a planet and the concept of planets having moons (two or more reports). Since the concept "solar system" is a formal concept, most of the classroom learners will know pieces. Few students, if any, can define the solar system.

One might argue that third graders do not need a formal understanding of solar system. True. But, if the students repeat this same process year after year, then science becomes "boring" because there is too little learning and too much "teaching" taking place. **Learning is a neurobiological high** (Arwood, 1991)! *Students are biologically predisposed to learn. An atmosphere that allows for learning through the challenge of acquiring layers about concepts is personally rich for each learner.* Even preschoolers with good language can tell about the basic constituents of a solar system and explain basic relationships about the constituents when given the opportunity to learn.

To create maximum cognitive learning in an event-based classroom, then the students each work on projects that are continuously refined, shared and disseminated. Dissemination refers to the use of reading, writing, and talking to explain what a learner develops or understands about his or her project. The juncture of dissemination also allows for more overlap. *Even discussing why overlap is needed for raising conceptualization with students older than the third grade is another way to create layers of information.* Whenever the class is determining how to share information, students are given the opportunity to layer and overlap concepts. The students proudly engage in these types of activities and grow in "leaps and bounds." Parents often comment on their children's growth and their "true love of learning." *A solid **respect** for concept development allows students the opportunity to take responsibility for better learning. Better concept learning comes from acquiring more depth about concepts by using **language** to layer meaning as well as overlap the use of the concepts in a variety of ways. Retrieval of such concepts is easier and allows for better **bridging** and **networking** in future situations with this type of learning.*

Activity

1. **Define cognitive layering and overlapping. Give examples.**
2. **How does language develop layering and overlapping of concepts for better learning?**

Refinement of Concepts

Students learn as concepts increase in depth and use. To change the development of concepts in this growth process requires refinement. **Refinement is the semantic correction of ideas.** All ideas are valid but the content may always be refined. **Semantic corrections are positive ways of refining ideas, understanding or meaning.** For example, the young child says that the cat is a tiger. The adult says, "Yes, it looks like a tiger because it has four legs, long hair and stripes; but, it is a cat, because it is smaller than a tiger and lives inside the lady's house." As the child's concept of "cat" grows, so does the refinement process. A parallel with this type of academic refinement may be found with championship quality athletic teams or outstanding corporations. In these situations, discussions bring out an overlap and natural layering of individual strengths within the group process as they relate to the classroom, the athletic team, and the business workplace. Each person's ideas are valued and the group process is used to refine the work of the group.

The refinement process validates the person while changing the content whether it is used with very young children or adults. Allowing students to give inaccurate information results in a lower level of expectation of them (a form of devaluation over time) and a lack of respect of human learning. Inaccurate information represents a "breakdown" of the development process. The lack of refinement is a dangerous "poison." Everyone loses self-respect for the lack of semantic accuracy. While inaccurate or unrefined material represents downward growth, refinement represents an upward momentum! Figures 4.2-4.6, at the end of this chapter, show the relationship between refinement of mental ideas that are drawn, redrawn, written and finally rewritten ideas for an eight-year-old followed by Figures 4.7-4.10 (end of the chapter) for a thirteen-year-old. The time to work each of these students from being "non readers/non-writers" to the final level of production was about 40 minutes for each.

A teacher who uses moments of thoughtful language throughout the day to refine students' ideas is gifting the students in a variety of ways. The students are learning that they are empowered through the use of their own individual learning systems. They are learning that the process is never complete. Ideas are always changing. Learning is continual and life giving. These students' ideas are being validated but their ability to continuously improve is also being validated (social development). This use of refinement allows students to learn to set goals and to continuously work toward the better use of ideas, language, conventions, etc., (cognitive development).

For all students, *the use of refinement is a respectful way of negotiating with others and of learning to set up win-win situations.*

Group refinement also is encouraged within the classroom. For example, students are told to propose alternative assignments, projects, and even activities. Anything that affects the group is discussed by the group. Individually, the teacher encourages refinement with simple probes such as "I wonder why this works?!" or "How can you be creative in this project?" or "Which parts are missing?" Students are encouraged to leave unsigned notes on the teacher's desk or in a box to make recommendations. It is okay for the teacher to act "stumped" to encourage students to lead in the assignment of meaning. Between the use of probes and the teacher-student exchanges, the teacher can also determine the level at which a student is learning. In this way, the teacher is aware of who is learning at what level and which students need more challenge. Students are encouraged to be honest, "Mr. Tran, I am lost. I have no idea where you are leading me." Hearing the student, Mr. Tran finds himself on "equal footing" with the students. The teacher assumes the role of the student and probes, "What do you know about the pioneers?" This is a healthy role reversal where the teacher is now the learner. Bonding is possible and trust is obvious. Mr. Tran will use the student's confusion as a way to help the student and others refine Mr. Tran's sharing. Learning becomes a universal currency for both the teacher and the students. Sharing these positive exchanges at times of refinement empowers both the teacher and the students.

These points of refinement or clarity act as compass points directing the teacher to the water that is smooth and fluid for learning to progress. *Refining what a student says, writes, or talks about is the responsibility of each person in the classroom. The language for such refinement is respectful and explanatory.* For example, "What types of questions do we ask when Shari is finished presenting her ideas?" The class brainstorms and comes up with the types of questions, who will listen for what types of information, and then how Shari will call on the classmates to ask the questions. Finally, the class decides what Shari's options are for dealing with the questions, how she will answer, that it is okay to not have an answer, that she may want to find the answer but someone else could find the answer, or the answer may not exist. *Refinement through* **language** *is the essence of* **respect** *for cognitive development. An activity that does not include refinement cannot assume that the students are learning.*

Activity

1.   **What is refinement?**
2.   **How does refinement work to increase cognitive depth?**

Summary

The **language** *of* **RESPECT** *for cognitive development allows for maximum learning in the classroom.* To adjust the classroom to meet all learners' types of thinking, presentation of materials must include consideration for mentally seeing spoken ideas. Opportunities for allowing students to present ideas in a variety of ways also allows for students to use their own way to cognitively organize their work. In addition to accommodating differences in thinking, the classroom must be ready to layer, overlap, and refine concepts. Chapter Five describes the cultural context in which students are developing a cognitive respect to learn, followed by Chapter Six which discusses more language strategies followed by how to assess students' or learners' cognitive development in Chapter Seven.

REFERENCES

Arwood, E. Lucas 1991. *Semantic and Pragmatic Language Disorders* (2nd Edition). Gaithersburg, MD: Aspen Publishers, Inc.

Arwood, E. and Brown, M. 1999. *A Guide to Cartooning and Flowcharting.* Portland, OR: APRICOT Inc.

Arwood, E. and McInroy, J. 1994. *RISES I. Reading: It's So Easy to See.* Portland, OR: APRICOT, Inc.

Arwood, E. and Unruh, I. 1997. *RISES II. Reading It's So Easy to See.* Portland, OR: APRICOT, Inc.

Arwood, E. and Unruh, I. 2000. *Event-Based Learning Handbook.* Portland, OR: APRICOT, Inc.

Lucas, E. 1981. *Semantic and Pragmatic Language Disorders* (1st Edition). Gaithersburg, MD: Aspen Publishers, Inc.

Santrock, J. 1997. *Life-Span Development* (6th Edition). Madison, WI: Brown & Benchmark.

Figure 4.2 – Male 8.7

The student read aloud a grade level passage and then used oral language to tell about the passage saying, *"Fire."* The student was then asked to draw about the passage. He drew three trees on fire, one person, a wall of fire and a stream.

The student told about his drawing saying, *"This is a stream... he is throwing water on the fire."*

Figure 4.3 – Male 8.7

Since the student omitted many of the passage ideas, he was asked to silently scan the passage for additional ideas to add to his drawing. The student drew a second person and a tent.

When asked to tell about his drawing he said, *"Fire, trees, two people, tent and stream."*

Figure 4.4 – Male 8.7

The student was asked to write about his drawn ideas.

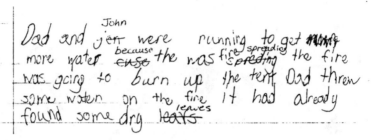

Figure 4.5 – Male 8.7

The student's written words did not semantically match his drawings, so the drawn ideas were semantically refined by the adult through the addition of lines and arrows to connect the actions to the agents and objects. The student added written names to the agents.

Figure 4.6 – Male 8.7

The student was asked to redraw his picture in a cartoon strip sequence. Afterwards he told the story to the adult who wrote his words. The adult added the circled temporal markers.

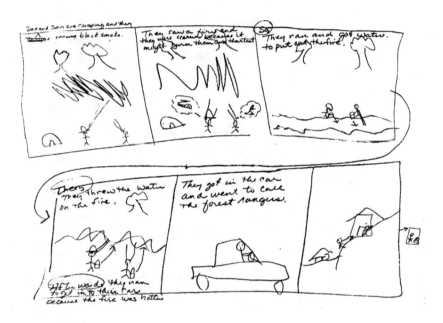

> **Frame One**: Dad and John are camping and they see black smoke.
>
> **Frame Two**: They saw a fire and they were scared because it might burn them and their tent.
>
> **Frame Three**: So, they ran and got water to put out the fire.
>
> **Frame Four**: Then they threw the water on the fire. Afterwards, they ran to get into their car because the fire was hotter.
>
> **Frame Five**: They got in the car and went to call the forest rangers.

Figure 4.7 – Male 13.2

The student was given the choice to draw or write about something he read. He chose to struggle to try to write some ideas. After 15 minutes he produced a number of ideas that are not connected.

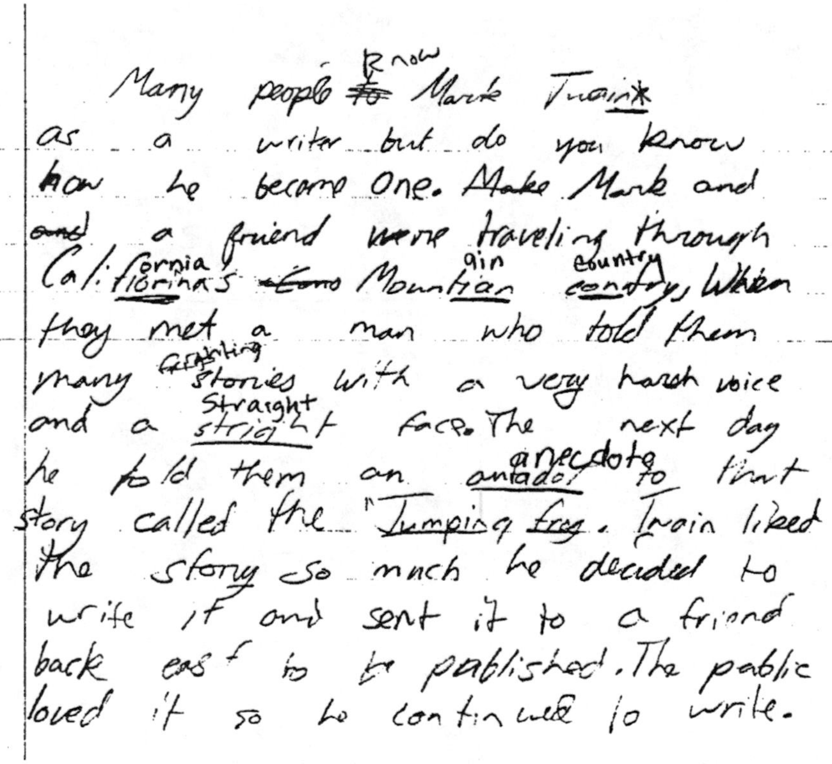

Many people know Mark Twain
as a writer but do you know
how he became One. Make Mark and
a friend were traveling through
California's Mountian gin country, When
they met a man who told them
many stories with a very harsh voice
and a straight face. The next day
he told them an anecdote to that
story called the "Jumping frog. Twain liked
the story so much he decided to
write it and sent it to a friend
back east to be published. The public
loved it so he continued to write.

Figure 4.8 – Male 13.2

Next, he was asked to cartoon the story.

Then he told the story. His ideas are both literal to what he sees ("he's writing a book") and general to the story ("one day he was hiking through the mountains).

"Many people know Mark Twain as a writer, and he's writing a book. And this is before when he was in the mountains with his friends and then there he had many jobs, he was a publisher, an editor, um, a "something" pilot, and a printer. And, uh, one day he was hiking through the mountains with his friends, one's name Jim, and they went into a tavern and Ben Cook, an old associate or something and he told them long tedious, not tedious, what's the word, end-less tales, and he had a very serious face, and then the next day, after he tells him the stories, Ben tells him an anecdote to that story called the "Jumping Frog" and Mark Twain likes it a lot and decides to write about it and then he sends it off to get it published by a friend back East, and the public loves it so he becomes a writer."

Figure 4.9 – Male 13.2

This student's spoken words do not match his cartooned pictures. This indicates that he has more information than he is able to express in an organized way. So he was asked to flowchart the story.

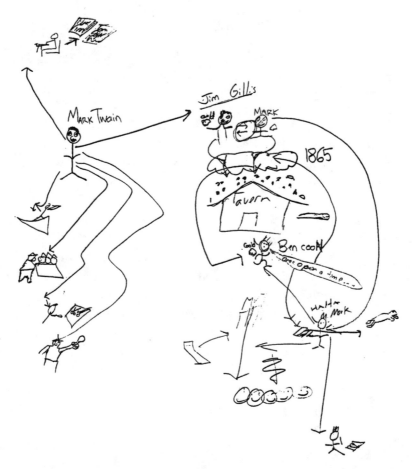

Notice the detailed drawings. The left side lists Mark Twain's various jobs sequentially. The right side is a flowchart showing the relationship of Mark Twain's experience to his job as a professional writer.

Figure 4.10 – Male 13.2

After flowcharting, this student sat down and fluently wrote a story that was clearly organized, connected with appropriate grammar and punctuation. His spelling was clear and the task was easy. The entire reading, writing, and drawing process took the student 40 minutes (including the first 15 minutes in which he struggled). Prior to this work,

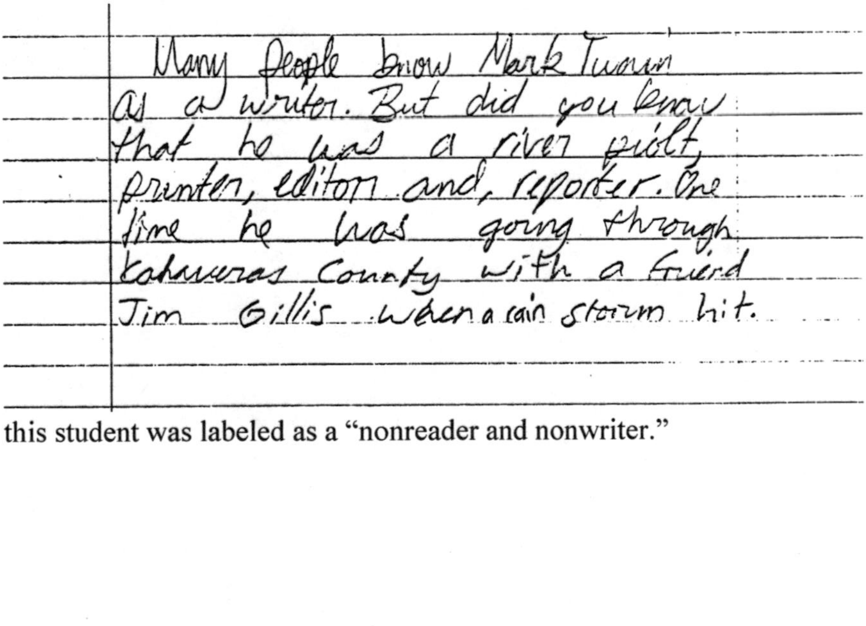

> Many people know Mark Twain as a writer. But did you know that he was a river pilot, printer, editor and, reporter. One time he was going through Calaveras County with a friend Jim Gillis when a rain storm hit.

this student was labeled as a "nonreader and nonwriter."

Chapter Five

Learner Outcomes

Upon completion of this chapter, the reader will be able to do the following:

1. Explain the concept of cultural respect.
2. Explain the dominant use of an authoritarian culture.
3. Explain the difference between an authoritarian and an authoritative culture.
4. Explain why different classroom cultural styles result in differences in the concept of respect.
5. Explain how authoritarian language affects the respect for individuals.
6. Explain how the individual learner succeeds within an authoritative classroom.
7. Explain the concepts of shared power, intrinsic learning, and healthy parenting.
8. Explain how parenting styles affect language use.
9. Give examples of using language to respect and honor cultural differences.

CHAPTER FIVE

The Language of Cultural Respect

How do we use language to create a culture that respects individual differences?

The students look into the teacher's face
Changing eyes from oneness to many
Why can't we see but together?
Why can't we hear but one?

An observer walks into the classroom. There's a quiet air of *respect* as each student participates in being a member of the classroom, while each student feels validated for his or her contribution. Students are focused on individual tasks within group projects that nourish the classroom's content. Even though there is a new person in the room, there is no change in students' participation, activity levels, or behavior. Another observer means another adult from whom to glean new ideas, resource research projects, and to aid in the process of learning. This group of students is a classroom of focus and participation. The focus is on how to do one's job; the participation is on how to be a member of this society. *The purpose of this chapter is to provide the reader with information about how to use language to create a culture of respect while honoring the diversity of individuals within the classroom.*

Authoritarian Culture

The majority of US population is raised in a society that suggests the individual is part of a whole. The whole group might be a family, an organization such as church or school, or a group of organizations such as the military. Being a member of the whole group necessitates that individuals give up their identity for the identity of the whole. For example, the teacher wants first graders to color fire engines. The teacher shows her fire engine's color and then expects the students to make a fire engine that looks like her fire engine. The resulting product is 28 similar, to exact, looking fire engines and three fire engines that don't have a close enough fit to count. These three might have been the wrong color, the wrong size, or even the wrong shape. More importantly, the right way to "do" a fire engine suggests that there are wrong ways. The right ways are within the group norm of approval while the three wrong ones are not within the group norm. Chapter Three described how not being able to be successful with an activity affects social development in terms of the learner's self-concept, self-esteem, self-worth, and self- discipline.

If there are students who do not fit into the modeled behavior, such as making a certain type of fire engine, then there are some students who do not fit into this micro society called "the classroom." If these students don't fit, then where do they belong? In Chapter Three, it was stated that by the time a child is about seven to eight years of age, then the child has already begun to socially try to fit within the comfort zones of society. However, if a society suggests that the child cannot fit, then the child has nowhere to go within the school as an agent. Perhaps the child will fit within the norm outside school. Maybe it will be the family norm, or with peers, or with some other group. These other groups will find a place for the child.

When a classroom begins to be subdivided into those who can and those who can't, there cannot be a sense of warmth and acceptance within the group. There cannot be a community atmosphere. What are we teaching these students? We are replicating the authoritarian parenting style (Santrock and Santrock, 1997) that most of the U.S. families use to raise their children.

Characteristics of the authoritarian style of interaction include: a) directive teaching (do the fire engine my way); b) adult centered tasks (the fire engine has to look like an engine the adult would make); c) external rewarding to *control* behavior (you did the engine my way so you did a good job); d) guilt and punishment instead of encouragement (your engine should not have so much blue); and e)

fault or blame instead of accepting responsibility (you didn't listen to my instructions…). The next sections of this chapter describe these five characteristics of an authoritarian style of classroom culture.

Activity

1. Describe which parenting style is used most often in the U.S.
2. Give examples of how authoritarian style would sound like in a family.

Directive Teaching

The authoritarian model of parenting revolves around one person. In the family, this one person might be a male or patriarch, or it might be a female or matriarch. If this person's control is strong enough, then this person might even be outside an immediate family cluster or outside the generational boundaries. In other words, any person who has the strongest or largest number of options, or even the most immediate number of options, may become central to the family activities.

In the school, the teacher is usually the parent, whether this is at the elementary or high school level. The teacher holds the largest number of options: the curriculum, the schedule, the assignments, the rules, "In my classroom, we…." "My students are doing well at…." "Our play was a success." "We are having fun in science because…." "This is a great class because they always do what I ask…." *Central to these options is the teacher's feelings, beliefs, tasks, etc.* Whether in the family or in the classroom, there is room for only one "General-in-Command."

These leaders in the authoritarian system provide direct ways for the members of the group to be right. If the member cannot be "right," then the member has no option but to be wrong. So, the leader, who also must be right, has ownership of the group. It is his or her classroom or his or her family. And, unfortunately, if the student cannot be right, then the student's problem belongs to someone who can fix "it." So, the teacher works diligently to make sure that all students are right and can be fixed. After all, the teacher must "direct" all behavior into a certain form that is the way the teacher would do the task.

The message over and over again is that "My way is the best way and I am trained to be the model to follow." This teacher has been "directed" to follow others and to therefore set up paths for students to follow in the same way. This teacher has a community mandate--that is, the teacher assumes that when one student answers a question, then there is a consensus by the class members. One correct answer means that all students can do the task and that all students should be producing right answers. One correct answer validates the teacher into directing the students into the teacher's own perception of reality. However, one's reality may be smoked mirrors. But, knowing that there is a false cover and knowing that there is truth are valuable lessons. As one teacher said, "Performing to yourself in front of a mirror is teaching, but not necessarily learning."

The teacher who directs the students into producing his or her responses, products and or answers is providing an authoritarian cultural model. Those students and or teachers, who fit into the authoritarian model, perpetuate the "follow the leader" syndrome; and, those who don't fit, fall into other groups of society to include gangs, nonreaders, dropouts, nonconformists and so forth.

Some people "endure" these types of authoritarian educational environments but the joy in learning may be forgotten. The authoritarian model is often referred to as "cookie-cutter mentality." There is probably a place for this type of authoritarian classroom, but *respect for individual differences can only be honored if there is a classroom where directive teaching is not the focus.* A later section discusses the alternative type of teaching experience that allows for the **Language of RESPECT:** *the Right of Each Student to Participate in an Environment of Communicative Thoughtfulness.*

Activity

1. **Describe the characteristics of "authoritarian teaching."**
2. **Describe how directive teaching fits into an authoritarian culture.**

Adult Centered Tasks

Classrooms around the country play the same scenario, day in and day out. It begins with the teacher announcing the next activity of the day. Then, in one smooth command, the teacher goes into the "rules" of the activity. As you might expect, *the teacher is the judge, jury and Supreme Court in an authoritarian classroom.* Once in a while, a youngster might ask why the game couldn't include another rule, one not mentioned by the teacher.

The youngster does not have to wait very long, to learn that the "youth's rule" is not acceptable. The teacher has set the basic rules, and the class will follow those rules. This youngster soon becomes a "quiet" youngster. The quiet youngster learns very early in an academic career, that the teacher sets the rules, calls the shots, and controls the entire school scene. The youth learns that the student's role is that of "faithful producer." The youngster's role is to do as he is told, and those new and innovative ideas are not welcomed because student-ideas can result in labels such as "trouble-maker." Being wrong, being obstinate and being a troublemaker brings about negative consequences in this "teacher-rules-only, world."

So, many of the young students learn, all too soon, that in order to achieve, the student must be a mirror image of the teacher. The teacher directs the class in not only the spoken rules of the "right way" to do a task but also in the unspoken rules of an authoritarian system. As the student becomes older, he or she may rebel against the lack of identity. In the meantime, the student who doesn't rebel is learning how to "play the game," to figure out some of the "unspoken rules."

Some of the unspoken rules or hidden agenda of this type of group include the following: a) the teacher knows all of the right answers; b) the students do not hcve a say in what is right; c) the student is the emotional nurturer for the teacher (the students work at gaining the teacher's approval so that the teacher is happy with the student); d) the adult is only a parent when a child or student can make the adult happy. It is in this adult directed system that the student is really not allowed to be a child. The developmental creativity of exploring one's potential so as to excel within a group, is not allowed. Furthermore, the adult may yell, reprimand, scold, shame, belittle, devalue or use any other behavior that represents a tantrum when the adult does not get his or her way. If the adult in the authoritarian system feels out of control, then the child is sent to someone else to be fixed. *The adult depends on the child's ability to take care of the adults' need to be right.*

The child as a caregiver of an adult has no value except for what the adult might receive and thus transfer on to the child. For example, "Mrs. Jones, your daughter completes all of the worksheets just the way I like them." In this example, there exist only the needs of the adult. The daughter assumes the identity of the teacher. The teacher may not even know the child as a person separate from the task of the classroom. The teacher likes to control what the child does. It should be noted that "teacher control" can be strict or permissive and still be authoritarian. For example, the third-grade students are told to choose a topic about "space" and to research the topic. The teacher gives written instructions. The students are to write three pages about the topic. These ideas are to come from two sources. The child's name and the teacher's name and date are to appear on the upper right hand corner of the first page. Joanna, a third grade student, is very artistic. She learns best by creating mental pictures. So, Joanna draws some pictures about her topic and then she writes her three pages. She inserts the pictures and, makes an elaborate cover for the topic. The third grade teacher uses strict authoritarian control, she gives the report back to Joanna and tells her that she will not accept the project. Joanna had completed what the teacher wanted and had actually accomplished more. But, the teacher could only see that Joanna had not followed the teacher's way of doing the report. Conversely speaking, a third-grade teacher across the hall uses permissive authoritarian control. For example, she announces to the students that all third graders in the district do a project on space. The students are yelling out ideas, talking to one another on the teacher's words, and attending to "whatever they see or hear." The teacher attempts to control the class, "If you don't raise your hand to request permission to talk, I will make you stay in at recess." Two boys immediately shouted out ideas. The teacher wrote their names on the board and said, "You two will stay in at recess." They become quiet as others shout out ideas. Some ideas are heard and some aren't. Some ideas are recognized as the teacher calls on students who have their hands up, but sometimes the teacher accepts ideas shouted out. Her rules are "permissive." She sometimes follows through and sometimes doesn't. Either way, she is still trying to control what the students do through what she wants. When the projects come into her, some students have written three pages, some haven't. Some students have not turned in a project, others have worked all weekend to complete the project. Depending on the teacher's mood and whether she is personally irritated by the behavior of the students, she either punishes or rewards. For this assignment, the whole class is given two more weeks to work on the project. The students who have their projects completed are now "spending time" keeping busy in class while the other students spend class time to complete their projects.

Probably the best example of permissive authoritarian control is seen in public. The child is running around the store. The parents say nothing until the child knocks over a display. The child is reprimanded or spanked and there is no responsibility taken by the parents for the damaged goods. The child and parent leave that store for the child to go to another store for the cycle to begin all over. *The adult is attempting to control another person's behavior or actions in either a strict or permissive way is called an authoritarian style.*

Adult directed teaching or parenting is a reflection of the person in control and not of the learner. Authoritarian parenting promotes mediocrity since new ideas, problem solving, and creative thinking are not welcomed. Even consensus is substituted for individual work that is separated from the teacher directed tasks. In the authoritarian culture, the center of the classroom or of the family revolves around one member so that the society is a monarchy with the unspoken rule that consensus reigns. With the adult centered model, the student's needs are "invisible." Some youth try to be compliant at the expense of giving up their own needs until they have to shout, kill, fight, or get the adults' attention in some violent way. Other youth lose their identity to drugs, teen-age parenting, dropping out of the school system, or accepting some other group identity. Those that endure such a system either replicate the quiet, teacher or adult centered "violence," or become motivated to change the system. A later section in this chapter describes how to move the direction from the teacher to the students while *respecting* both the curriculum and the individual differences. If the learner does not move from the teacher directed system, then the learner must depend on external *rewards*.

Activity

1. **Define who directs the flow of the classroom or family for an authoritarian setting.**
2. **Explain what is meant by teacher directed control.**

External Rewards

The authoritarian system advocates for rewards for specified tasks, behaviors, and situations (for explanation of these systems as parenting styles, see Baumrind, 1971; 1991). *Such advocacy suggests that there is going to be some sort of "carrot" at the end of performing some task.* The student does the work, for example, to get the grade. There is no internal motivation for doing the work, perhaps to just learn (for explanation of external stimuli and reward mechanisms, see Skinner, 1961; Martin & Pear, 1996). When this externally controlled student gets a job at a restaurant, he cleans tables until 4:00 P.M. and then walks out even though there are still many more tables to be cleaned, because there is no external reward for continuing past four o'clock. Or, for example, the teacher leaves the building as soon as the principal allows, even though there is a parent who feels a need to talk. Such rule-based mentality fosters the need to always have a reward for an act. There is no need to internalize a set of principles or guidelines, since rewards are dispensed for "norm approved" tasks, behaviors and situations.

The authoritarian system suggests that a reward be given; such rules for the rewards are not always well thought out. For example, there is a rule that all students who are late to school must stay in at recess. When a student is late because the parent's car does not start, and, the student misses recess, it does not appear that the rule for the behavior is logical. Why isn't the parent asked to sit in the room during recess? Furthermore, the rule defines an expected behavior. If a student can't behave in a certain way, the absence of the reward becomes a punisher. For example, "If you don't earn your Friday surprise this week, you can try again next week." This type of logic doesn't follow since next week brings a different Friday surprise. The enforcing of the rules becomes punishing. If a student is kept from receiving Friday surprises but other students receive Friday surprises, then the enforcement has also created barriers separating those who can from those who can't.

One of the most observable factors is that the enforcers of rules often have little or perhaps "no" idea of why the rule is being enforced. For example, a group of fifth-grade-students are being kept in from recess. One of the students raises his hand and asks why the students are losing their recess. The enforcer, the teacher, says she does not have time to deal with his question. He is to put his head down like the others and be quiet. As an enforcer, the teacher must follow through with the expected punishment. The flip side of the coin is that this very situation may take away a very positive opportunity for the enforcer to learn from the student, what he or she actually feels about the incident. *Putting the punishment into action robs the enforcer of the opportunity to gain personal insights, to empower the students, and to gain valuable information about the incident from those being punished.*

Group punishment results in total loyalty among group participants. Adolescents will not tell on other members of a group because they must support each other. This lesson of "loyalty at all costs" is the result of too many rewards turning into group punishers. These same authoritarian adults are amazed when middle and high school students engage in crime which could be prevented if some other adolescent would have reported the crime, either before or after it happens. Today, many students will not break their "unspoken code of loyalty." For example, some high school students committed dozens of robberies in a local area. Even after the police knew the names of the robbers, the thieves' school acquaintances would not "tell" the where abouts of the criminals or give information about the crimes. Once, some of the students began to be arrested, it was obvious that parents and educators who knew information also were loyal. Community members were "shocked" at the loyalty of the professional parents of these "thieves," as well as the loyalty of the high school students and educators, who knew about the crimes, but said nothing. After many months of investigation, it was apparent that many students knew about the robberies even before the crimes were committed, but said nothing because of "group loyalty." *When rewards become confused with punishers, as a result of group versus individual recognition, then the individual's identity is lost to a group mentality of what is appropriate or acceptable social behavior.*

Dependence on external rewards such as grades, stickers, happy faces, praise, candy, points for parties, foster a psychological dependence on others providing the gifts of life. Such psychological dependency is the same as addictions to food, exercise, and drugs (including alcohol, caffeine and nicotine). In other words, the classroom that provides external rewards without an attempt to shift the responsibility for learning, from the reward to the student, is perpetuating the American authoritarian culture of society. This type of society is dependent on material, external pay off systems that promote group collateral instead of individual contributions. So, the group owns social problems such as pollution, garbage, homelessness, disease, and famine; but, individuals have no responsibility, and, therefore, no reason to work to alleviate these problems. A later section in this chapter will describe ways to shift the need for external rewards to internal desire, motivation, pride and respect for others, one's "self," and the learning environment.

Activity

1. **Define external reward.**
2. **Explain what external rewards do for the individuals in an authoritarian classroom or society.**

Guilt and Punishment

In an authoritarian family, one cultural consideration is that the individual should fit into the whole. When the individual cannot fit, there is no choice. The members of the group or family then try to control the individual's behavior so as to make the individual fit. If the individual still cannot fit, then there is a punisher. The punishment is to stop the person from doing the undesired behavior. The assumption is that the punished person can produce the desired behavior and that by producing a desired behavior, the individual will "fit." Unfortunately, if the desired behavior cannot be produced, then there is also guilt for not being able to be correct, right, etc. In the classroom, a child who tries to spell with auditory strategies, but who cannot mentally hear the sound differences, is being punished over and over again for trying to decode sound. A child, who wants to learn a foreign language, but continues to be taught with auditory, out of context vocabulary and grammar drills, which the student cannot cognitively use, is being punished over and over for not hearing the sounds of the foreign language. A child, who likes math, but is being taught with visual patterns and can't learn from the multiple visual patterns, is being punished for liking math, because the child can't do the patterns, and so forth. *Guilt for not being able to perform as expected is a result of punishment.*

In society, for example, the military has a need to be sure that a person does not think independently when there is a crisis. Such control and conformity covers clothes, hair, schedules, manner of movement, etc. There is a need to indoctrinate all individuals so that the military functions as a whole. If the individual cannot march correctly, then there might be an immediate punisher--physical, emotional, etc. The individual feels guilty because the individual has tried hard to fit, but has let down the officer, other soldiers, etc. The lack of emphasis on the positive is desirable so that individuals do not differ from others.

In the school, individuals who don't match with what is expected are punished. For example, the student who doesn't write, draw, or do math as well as the others, may be punished much like the military. Laws are developed to protect students from severe physical punishment, but emotional punishment still exists. For example, a child's colored picture is put at the bottom of the bulletin board because the child's fire truck is the "wrong color." Or, one child is told that she can't write as well as another child; the child is told that she should try harder to be like someone else, an older sibling. A child might be told that if he would "just try harder," etc. These are all punishing types of statements since the child already feels guilty for not being able to perform as expected. And, if the child could perform as expected, the child would comply.

The emotional punishers are effective at producing feelings of guilt. Feelings of guilt limit the individual's development of the "self." By the time a child is in the third grade, the student's feelings of guilt determine what the child will and won't try. For example, one of the authors attempted to sample oral language for all children in an elementary school by asking each child on an individual basis (away from peers and the classroom) to tell a story about a pictured event. By the time the students were in the third grade, the students were becoming reluctant to try. By the fourth grade, the students showed physical signs of oppression--shoulders bent, furrowed brows, slid into the back of the chairs, quiet voices, partial statements, etc. The fifth graders wouldn't even try unless they were told to make the story a pretend story and to start with "Once-upon-a-time." *These students had learned to be just like the adult so as not to risk any individuality. Being oppressed in thinking is worse than being punished for an inappropriate behavior, because the oppression keeps a student feeling guilty. The guilt limits the person's creativity and even the willingness to try.*

Encouragement to be like another person often adds salt to the wound. Not only does the student feel guilty for not being able to produce as expected, but the teacher's kind words "to try harder" are heard by the student as the teacher not accepting the student's attempts. So, the student feels more guilt for not being able to meet the expectations of what is being encouraged. The child, as a person, is being oppressed even more by the "good intentions of encouragement." *The guilt and punishment are so interwoven that the child doesn't know who he or she is in relationship to what the adult can do and what the adult expects the child to do.* A child who is "trying as hard" as the child is able begins to believe that something is personally wrong. **Guilt and punishment strips the individual of "who" constituents. Therefore, guilt and punishment has no place in a classroom where all students and their contributions are to be respected.**

Activity

1. **Define guilt.**
2. **Explain the effect guilt has on the learner.**

Fault and Blame

When the classroom does not protect individual diversity, there is an increase in guilt and subsequent shame. Feelings of shame typically result in more of a need to place the responsibility for acts on others. For example, the student who does not read well, who works hard, but still cannot achieve the rewards, may begin to pass the responsibility. "I hate reading...it's stupid and boring." In other words, it is not the student's fault that the student doesn't read, but the student *believes* that it is his or her fault. The only way that the student feels competent as a person, and still not able to read, is to blame someone else.

The student in the aforementioned example feels ashamed of his inability to succeed. The teacher may also model this authoritarian belief. In other words, the teacher may also pass the blame to the student by making comments that assign blame. For example, "Oh, if you would only try harder" means that it is the child's fault that the child can't read. This teacher may also feel shamed by the child's lack of reading ability and so the teacher willingly passes blame. In the faculty room, the teacher says, "Why don't these parents read to their children? Ian is never going to learn to read without his parents' help." It's easy to pass judgment onto someone else without complete data. Have the parents been asked if they read to the child? How many outstanding student readers have never had anyone read to them? Why are there so many illiterate high school students who have had people read to them their whole lives? The blind judgment is made without the data because a cultural authoritarian lens covers the teacher's good intentions.

Such a lens assists teachers and researchers to gather data to prove such judgments. For example, most literature says that children who read well had parents who read to them. But, the data is incomplete. How many children who don't read well also had parents who read to them? And, how many who read well did not have parents read to them? *The authoritarian culture tends to encourage individuals to blame outside sources when goals or expectations are not met.*

Authoritarian education supports the notion that the teacher must have the right answers, fix all others' problems, and be the "bearer" of news on whom to blame. By passing on the pecking order of "Who is at fault?" and "Who is to blame?," the middle school teachers wonder why the elementary teachers did not properly prepare their students for middle school while the high school teachers don't understand what is wrong with the middle school teachers, etc. And, the college professors find something wrong with the whole education system when some college students cannot read or write at a third grade level or above.

The authoritarian system perpetuates the need for passing fault so as to blame someone else or something else. Even labeling a child provides a point of blame that removes individuals from responsibility. For example, a child labeled as dyslexic doesn't need to learn to read. Instead, others are expected to do the reading for the dyslexic student even when there are ways to teach reading that would be successful. *In the authoritarian culture, there is the constant juggle for finding the right thing to do, in the right way. Any mismatch between the right thing to do or the right way to do something is passed on to someone else in the form of fault or blame.* More professional development, inservice training, new programs, curricular revisions, revisiting the mission statement, etc., are requested as "hopes" for fixing the students, the curriculum, the teachers, the parents, and of course, the administrators. When fixing is not the solution, then blaming is easy to do.

The authoritarian culture perpetuates the cycle of caring for others by passing judgment or blame. **Fault is always expected as an outcome of blame.** Someone else can always be found to be responsible. The individual is responsible only for those acts that the individual *chooses*. In the authoritarian culture, social responsibility to the group does not exist. *However, knowing the limits of an authoritarian past and present offer hope for finding a future that is culturally different, a society that fosters respect of the individual while honoring the group.*

The preceding sections discussed the authoritarian culture as consisting of directive teaching, adult centered tasks, external rewards, guilt, punishment, fault, and blame. As difficult as it is for the authors to write about the authoritarian system, it is important for all of us to realize what our current culture believes. The preceding section is about where we have been. *The next section describes a paradigm shift, a move toward a different cultural set of values that honor the individual as well as the group through respecting individual diversity.*

Activity

1. **Define fault and blame.**
2. **Explain how fault and blame are perpetuated in an authoritarian classroom.**

Authoritative Culture

The characteristics of authori*tative* culture are very different from the authori*tarian* system in several ways: 1) The individual is assisted in becoming part of the whole so that the classroom is student centered, not teacher directed; 2) The group functions as a system of individuals, not a group of similar individuals; 3) Learning is a process among individuals, not teaching; 4) Strengths rather than deficits, are emphasized; 5) Correction is based on what is meaningful, not on what is judged to be wrong or right; 6) Adults are expected to show the characteristics of healthy parenting, not the focus of blame and guilt; 7) Learning is intrinsically developed, rather than extrinsically rewarded; and 8) Students share a respected hierarchy of power with all others, including classroom visitors. The following chapter sections discuss the characteristics of the authoritative cultural style of parenting and teaching.

The Individual

The authoritative system values the contribution of each individual within the group. In this way the individual is a part of the whole. Instead of 28 students with similar fire engines being credited for value, as in the authoritarian system, the authoritative or respectful classroom sees students producing a variety of products related to fire trucks. Some of the students might be producing some type of artwork, but others might be reading books, doing reports, making field trip lists to go to the fire station, practicing songs related to the fire station field trip, etc. Because all students' contributions are credited and valued, there is no "single" right or wrong way to represent what is learned. In the authoritative classroom, students are encouraged to make creative models of a new fire truck or to look up what past fire trucks looked like. Reading and writing are always incorporated as conventional ways to layer and overlap the child's knowledge about fire trucks with what the teacher and others know. (This emphasis on the conventions of language helps facilitate cognition [see Chapter Four] and learning). Even oral dictation for the teacher to write at the computer is an acceptable way to represent what a learner knows about fire engines. *Each individual is valued for his or her contributions.*

Whereas the authoritarian system expects a norm from which to measure progress of the individual compared to a norm, the *language of respect* assigns value to the process of individuals picking out ideas, choosing to work on products to share with others, and refining work on their own projects within the authoritative system. *The authoritative expectation is that these individuals will share their projects with others so that there is interconnectedness among the individuals of the group, of their products, and of their learning.* At the end of the year, the learning pieces fit together much like a jigsaw puzzle. Instead of one piece being added each year to make a puzzle that fits the expected norm of 12th grade, there is a real puzzle or picture being created at each step of the way. The puzzle adds dimension, richness, others' qualities, others' experiences, etc., to create a whole. The pieces represent the diversity and richness of each individual's past. The whole group is a collage of individual's cognitive experiences. *As individuals, their products come from a process of using language to respect their individual contributions.*

*The students within the respectful classroom give and take from each other as well as from the whole so that there is a **shared flow of communication, teaching, validation, and credit giving**.* There is a strong interconnected fit among the individuals. This interplay becomes a catalyst for the group because the individual's contribution is often seen as not only valuable but unique. The child's uniqueness is often a "first" experience where the child rediscovers the information. For example, the authoritative classroom teacher might say, "Oh, perhaps you can get together with me and we can talk about some piano music for our class." The student who has a past experience with playing the piano is not only valued for sharing this information but for the student's ability to provide something to the classroom as a whole. Now, the individual feels a "fit" within the group, so the individual also discovers his or her own source of uniqueness. Such uniqueness will occur over and over as the contributions of others are valued.

The individual's value and contributions function for the good of the group. The group works to incorporate the individual. In this way, the interactive process between the individual and the group creates a microcosm of a healthy society or a healthy pseudo-family. The individual is seen as fallible, unique, caring, and special. *This combination of characteristics is modeled by the teacher who doesn't know everything, who makes mistakes, and who welcomes learning opportunities from the students.* For example, the students in an authoritative classroom may be told the first day of class that the classroom is a "practice place." It is a place for all individuals including the teacher to practice learning. "We may make mistakes in our classroom just like a musician makes mistakes when practicing music. We will want to learn from our mistakes, just like a musician or an athlete learns from their mistakes." By the end of roll-call, the authoritative teacher has mispronounced at least two names and has established the philosophy of making corrections part of the learning task. "Whose names did I mispronounce? Thank you for providing the correct pronunciations. Please be patient with me while I learn these names. I appreciate any corrections whenever I mess up. I am learning too." It's the role of the authoritative teacher to model options for learning through individual success. Chapter Four discussed ways to develop layers and overlaps of cognition to helping the individual succeed. When an individual is allowed to cognitively be challenged and to contribute to the whole group, then learning is becoming part of the success of the group. *In the authoritative classroom, it is the teacher's responsibility to find out about each student's needs and then to honor those needs, individually, as well as through the group.*

Activity

1. **Explain how the individual is important to an authoritative classroom. (Reminder: authoritative is *not* the same as authoritarian).**
2. **Describe why authoritative classrooms respect the individual.**

Society

The authoritative system values the function of society in relationship to the individual. Within the authoritative classroom, language of respect is used to assign meaning to the individual in a way for each individual to form the community. The classroom communities form the social component of the school. This school is then a contributor to society in a way that represents the total culture of all the rooms. For example, different authoritative classrooms work together to form the whole picture. The whole picture might be how all classrooms work together to make a field day successful, or how writing projects fit together for a school newspaper, or how the classrooms work together to contribute to preserving the rain forests. *In the authoritative unit, the function of the whole is more successful, because ownership is at the individual level of contribution. In other words, each person contributes his or her piece to the whole. Each individual contributes to each group. Each group contributes to the whole of the society.* More pieces are welcomed opportunities to grow and develop.

In the typical graded schools, micro cultures rather than a society of communities diversely rich in heritage are developed. These micro cultures might be "fifth graders," "the girls," "soccer club," "chess club," "the Title I students," etc. Therefore, to be a contributor in these groups, the individual must do what fifth graders do, must identify with soccer, chess, non-readers, etc., or the individual may not fit in with what these groups value. In authoritative classrooms, the grade level, or classroom does not dictate the cultural schema. The culture is determined by the children's likes, dislikes, passions, interests, heritage, experiential past, etc. For example, Sarah's statement, "I play soccer," is different from Mark's utterance, "I like to play soccer." The first student may be on a soccer team, but never plays the game or hates the game, but the parents like it. The second student, Mark, may not be on a team but loves playing the game with friends in his neighborhood. In order for the group to contribute its values to the school, then utterances like those by Mark and Sarah are equally important. Finding out what each student, Sarah and Mark, meant by each of their statements is invaluable. *In an authoritative classroom, there is a system of individuals whose likes, dislikes, needs, desires, and other **personal constituents** contribute to the function of the whole classroom.*

In the classroom which fosters cultural respect, the instructor learns about the students so that the group's collective attempts are developed out of the strengths and abilities of its members just as a productive society might recognize the business, academic, social fellows for their contributions. So, one student is interested in directing a play about the people of the 1600's in America. But, for that student to be successful, he or she will need researchers, writers, actors, actresses, prop gatherers, prop makers, stage helpers and a lot of adult resourcing. In a respectful classroom, through adult facilitation, the students are provided the opportunity to develop, act out, invite others in the school or out of the school, etc., to work with the producer. Others in the classroom may "see a need" to set up a museum of what the 1600 colonists might have built, eaten, seen, etc. The classroom members become interdependent on each other because of individuals' strengths, not because of artificial or externally offered rewards. Strengths emerge as part of the value system. *The individuals value one another for their contributions. And, all members are assigned individual value as a contributor to the whole.*

Out of the contributions of these individuals comes the "societal whole." The good of society is a result of the contributions of the individuals to the good or to the whole. If the students are contributing members of society at school, then they are also expected to contribute to the workplace in a similar role. The school becomes a microcosm of work fields in which adults are leaders and students are the work force. The business world, as a profitable site, is an extension of the nonprofit development of skills and knowledge by the students in the schools.

A classroom based on respect is the child's work place--a safe microcosm of what society expects, skilled workers with many strengths and with the flexibility of working at many roles. From this microcosm comes skilled members capable of contributing to the good of the whole community. From these respectful classrooms with authoritative values come the school whose members are valued by the society at large, as contributing citizens and societal members. Such classrooms allow students to see the value of the learning environment as it connects to the culture at large. For example, students' papers may be collected to send to a town in China where penmanship is valued, so that student's may learn the value of their own handwritten papers. Students may work with classrooms with older or younger students so as to learn about being a "different age." Members of the community are welcome to attend class, any time, so students learn to respect the contributions of the community at large. Students receive praise and credit for bringing parents and others, even if for a couple of seconds, so that students learn that they are respected for their family contributions, as well as their own contributions. As students' family backgrounds are learned by the teacher, the teacher may ask the student to bring a parent who is a fire person, a cardiologist, a ditch digger, a secretary, or a professor to come to class to talk about what it is like to be a part of society. Student projects receive classroom or public attention for bringing society into the classroom. For example, "Class, we need some time out. [This is a cue for all students to direct their attention to the whole group...a well oiled classroom whose values are based on respect will take 30 seconds, at most, to become focused on the speaker]. Miss Copp has written an idea that I've asked her to share. Miss Copp, please go ahead." Miss Copp reads her idea. The teacher says, "Class, what do you think that Miss Copp is really saying about the Civil War?" When the discussion is over, Miss Copp is thanked by the teacher for the thoughtful idea. During the discussion, the individuals' ideas are validated and Miss Copp is used as the "expert" about her statement. Most of the time, the students are not aware that they are producing a great idea, a profound statement, an unusual and creative piece of art, and so forth. *Halting the proceedings of the class to assign positive meaning to the individual's contributions models what the individuals within the group will contribute to society.*

Bringing societal members (bus drivers, secretaries, staff, parents, friends, relatives, and volunteers) into the classroom helps offer accolades to individuals. All class members are offered the opportunity to receive recognition. *The use of language to assign positive meaning to individuals, their contributions, and their values, is central to an authoritative classroom. Society is the benefactor!*

Activity

1. **Explain how individuals within an authoritative classroom contribute to society.**
2. **Describe how society's values are influenced by students being educated in authoritative classrooms.**

Learning

In the respectful classroom, teaching becomes a product of the learning process rather than an initial goal. And, language is the tool of learning. The members of the group use language to assign meaning to the learning process. For example, instead of trying to teach students (Arwood, 1991), the teacher acts as a facilitator to help students learn. The students then become responsible for their own learning. With ownership, the students are empowered as individual learners. *Each individual learns to respect the process, not only for her or himself; but, also, for other students' contributions to learning, as well as the teacher's contribution to learning.*

The common learning goal for the authoritative classroom based on the language of cultural respect might be stated as follows: The students shall demonstrate changes in learning through reading, writing, demonstrating, drawing, singing, signing, etc., in content areas of science, math, history, social studies, health, etc. In long term learning, the changes in behavior (reading, writing, drawing, calculating, etc.) are observable and permanent (Arwood, 1991; Santrock, 1997).

Student work samples are authentic assessments which demonstrate where the students were in knowledge and skill at the beginning of a time frame and where the students are at the end of the sampling period (see Chapters Seven and Eight for additional information on individual assessment and classroom organization). *With learning being respected as a socio-cognitive process (see Chapters One through Four), the classroom based on the* **language of RESPECT** *offers multiple opportunities to be a successful learner and therefore to fit into a group. Such group development is based on individual differences so that there are also group commonalties. The group commonalties form a culture that honors the individual differences within the group.* ***Whereas the process of socialization (Chapter Three) refers to similarities among all people, culture refers to identified differences shared by groups of individuals.***

The rationale for promoting an authoritative type of emphasis on learning, and not on teaching, is based on the neurobiological research. This research shows learning as a permanent cellular change developed from external or environmental input as well as from internal cognitive stimulation (see Chapter Two). The external input is the way the people and environment assign meaning **socially** (see Chapter Two and Three) and the internal input is from the way the learner thinks **cognitively** (see Chapter Four). *Language is the tool for learning which is why the goal for the overall classroom of cultural respect is stated: The students shall demonstrate changes in learning **through reading, writing, drawing, singing, signing, etc.** All of these acts are language-based processes.* This socio-cognitive way of developing change is the way all students learn. Chapter Four discusses the differences in the way these internal ideas are formed for students and Chapter Seven discusses how the classroom is organized so as to provide respect for the opportunity for learning for all students. How the students interact with one another teaches more than the content. *The students learn that interactions within the classroom can be safe and that the learners can be protected.* As learners, the students discover that learning is fun and that they are good learners. *They learn how to learn in an authoritative classroom.* The students also learn that the classroom values the individual as well as the individual's unique contributions. Being a learner who is successful also teaches the student about his or her own strengths. The individual's "self" becomes part of the strength of the whole group. *Individual strengths are therefore honored and respected as part of the learning process.*

Activity

1. **Describe learning as a valued entity in an authoritative classroom.**
2. **Describe the learning contributions of the individual to the whole group.**

Strengths

The cultural respect of an authoritative classroom is set up so that individuals' strengths are emphasized. Academic tasks are based on a learning framework rather than on teaching. So, the typical deficit model of teaching a child to do what the child can't is eliminated and students are encouraged to do what they <u>can</u>. For example, instead of trying to teach decoding skills to a child who is struggling to read, the child is allowed to sketch about what the child mentally sees when looking at the code on the page. The sketch is then assigned value by what the child can tell the listener about the sketch. The information about the sketch is then refined through the initial writing by the listener, to refining the pictures by talking and additional drawings. Eventually, the student learns to take material off the page by looking at the printed patterns on the page and associating mental visual language pictures rather than by trying to say the sound patterns of the written words. Because the child's strength is in the mental visual images, and not in the mental spoken or auditory symbols of saying what a letter sounds like, then allowing the child to first sketch ideas also offers validation for the child. Someone writes the symbols to the child's description of the sketch, which in turn teaches the child strategies for using these visual structures (written/drawn symbols) as whole thoughts, representative of the child's mental ideas. In a short time, the child is reading and writing through the child's learning strengths.

Emphasizing students' strengths also models authoritative parenting. Instead of telling students how right and wrong they are doing a task (authoritarian parenting), the teacher is demonstrating how to nurture and support peers for what they can do. For example, "I notice how you have added a lot more information to your story" takes the place of "Your story still isn't complete." Positive protection creates by-products of students feeling valued for who they are as well as the classroom atmosphere becoming open, kind, giving, and supportive to nurturing differences. By emphasizing students' strengths or differences, accepting cultural diversity then becomes a part of honoring each individual's strengths. For example, a student who is reading a comic book during social studies may be assigned the positive contribution of being able to draw or sketch the social studies into cartoon strips. The cartoon strips, in turn, allow many of the students to see the social studies as relational, one idea connected to another idea. The cartoon becomes an external visual structure commensurate with the student's mental visual language. *The student's individual strength is assigned positive meaning so that the group benefits from the student's difference.*

Being different means that the products aren't always the same, correct, or right. *Not having all of the "right" answers sometimes feels uncomfortable for students or teachers who are used to being in an authoritarian culture. But in the community (authoritative culture) classroom the student and teacher are expected to not have all of the answers; otherwise, there would not be the need for all of these students and teachers to engage in individual learning.* As students are asked to call on other members for help, for work, for contributions; the individual members learn that not all students learn the same way, and the students learn that cooperation is a necessity of life to "getting" things finished. Furthermore, "being lost" becomes a positive feeling. It's okay to not know where the next step might lead because the group will support the individuals. This "cooperative spirit" really creates the essence of a responsive classroom--where all students are learning to work from the diversity of each person's strengths. This cooperative spirit is facilitated through the **language of RESPECT.**

*In a classroom of **respect**, the teacher uses language to set up opportunities for students to routinely ask others for help* rather than to pass or to have to say, "I don't know." The teacher encourages students to take on more responsibility by the teacher giving away jobs as the year progresses. Students begin to ask to assume roles (e.g., calling for papers to be collected after tests; taking attendance; lining the class up for recess; going to music class; going to the library; going to PE class; fire drills; cafeteria/lunch duties; door, lights, and window adjustments; computer, VCR, equipment; etc.). Students take over the greeting of guests; seating them; conducting tours around class; providing tests, paper, pens and beverages for the guests; and even being the guests' lunch partners. The pride in assuming these roles is obvious from the students' personal demeanor of standing tall and speaking clearly to their own explanation that this classroom is special. The "sharing" of roles also allows students to gain more depth in concepts about "cooperation" and "working with others." Sharing in the answers, projects, and products encourages students to create a disciplined habit of work.

Students are in process of sharing and learning, so they are encouraged to do "just a little bit more." They learn to invest in the goals now, so that they are successful later. They are encouraged to see the parallels in the corporate formula for success. For example, a primary student used to swim each day. The classroom teacher encouraged him to do one extra lap each day. The teacher and student calculated what this extra lap meant. They discovered that one extra lap a day produces two extra miles a year. Another student produced a beautiful cover for her group's project. The teacher encouraged her to enter an art contest. The student won third place.

In an authoritative culture, there is no single patriarch or matriarch monopolizing the group, but a shared referent, the individual strengths interconnected through the social and cultural foundations of being in a group. These types of shared environments provide multiple opportunities for students to show strengths and to grow socially and cognitively. By assigning expertise, giving credit, and sharing roles; students' strengths build the respectful authoritative classroom.

Activity

1. **Explain students' strengths as part of a respectful authoritative classroom.**
2. **Give examples of offering opportunities for students to show strengths.**

Correction

Chapter Four discussed the use of language to assist with making semantic corrections. **In the responsive and respectful classroom, correction of behavior or products is expected. Semantic correction is the assignment of language to refining ideas.** *Since refining ideas is a known and accepted part of human development, there is ample reason for expecting refinement as part of the student learning process within the classroom.* This refinement in the classroom is based on what is meaningful, not on what is valued or judged to be right and wrong. For example, during a lesson a child says, "The Earth moves in and out around the moon." The child's contribution is credited by correcting the information given. "Yes, it sometimes seems like the Earth is moving in and out around the moon, but let's look in one of our library books to find out more about the movements of the moon and Earth." Or, a child looks at a picture and says, "There are two match sticks." The teacher says, "Yes, the green stems with the read flowers look like match sticks but they are probably flowers, maybe tulips."

In this way, there is no correct answer. And, if there is no correct answer then there is also no wrong answer. All ideas are considered a valuable contribution to the work of the classroom as a whole. *The teacher spends time on the content instead of on the contribution.* The content is the meaningful part of the classroom so that knowledge increases the students' levels of cognition rather than the teacher making comments on the accuracy of the contribution. *Because the students' ideas are all valued, there is also a social value to being a part of the classroom.* The students can't be right or wrong because the focus is on the meaning, not on the student, and the products may always be improved, but the student is always an okay person.

In the authoritative classroom where differences in learning as well as differences in the individual students are respected, all products are "in process of completion." There is no end point, only periodic evaluations (see Chapter Seven about assessment). In other words, a simple writing task may become a publishable work for some students with the teacher and peers continuously refining the student's work. *Learners appreciate semantic correction or refinement by examining content.* For example, "I read your report about the Earth's moon but I don't understand if other planets, like the Earth, have moons! Could you look in the books (activity and responsiveness is expected based on the tone of the way the classroom is set up) and find out if the other planets have moons?" This type of correction results in meaning being added to support conceptualization. *As concepts increase in depth, the child's ability to represent ideas (read, write, draw, etc.) also increases.* In other words, this type of interaction increases learning of content as well as development of basic skills. *The absence of judgmental right and wrong also helps the child be open to self-evaluation, another form of semantic correction.*

Correction is a *positive* assignment of meaning to the ideas and products and not to what the child is personally trying. For example, a child has missed most of the math problems. What is the child's thinking? Why did the child miss most of the problems? Giving the child a "right" answer or even an acceptable pattern will not change the child's conceptualization. Additional meaning or language is needed for the child to understand why the child did not answer the problems correctly. By having the student write or draw out the meaning of what the problems represent, the teacher can find why the student is missing the problems. Now, the student, armed with graph paper, is able to perform with better accuracy. *The child has discovered by correction of past work that the numbers he sees in his head aren't the numbers on the paper, if the numbers on the paper are not adequately lined up.*

Similar to the math example, many students do not realize that the words they have written do not match with their mental pictures. *Correction of the written ideas by adding meaning to drawings of what the child wanted to write, matched against the written words, improves the forms and structure of writing as well as the story line.* This type of correction offers improved writing, reading, and oral language skills, not to mention an improved understanding of content meaning. *Since learning is a neurobiological high, students who are actively learning through correction and other forms of refinement are also actively enthused about learning. Active learning improves the student's interest and desire to be in school and to be a part of the school community.*

Activity

1. **Define correction.**
2. **Give examples of semantic correction as a positive form of refinement.**

Healthy Parenting

Each adult in a society has a role to play with all children. This role is that of a parent. **In authoritative parenting, the adult nurtures, protects, and supports the child so that the child's psychosocial development is dependent on the adult's well being.** For example, when the adult shows appreciation for the child's contribution, the child is emotionally being nurtured as being a valuable contributor to the group. "John, thank you for sharing your idea about the Earth. It gave us the opportunity to read in our library books, so that we could better understand the relationship of the Earth and its moon." This type of language shows respect for John, a learner, and contributor to the authoritative classroom.

When the adult offers such nurturance, then the child is also being protected from devaluation. For example, the child offers the previously stated contribution about the earth and its moon. In a classroom where the adult does not protect, then some other child might have called out a "put down," e.g., "That's dumb. The Earth doesn't move around its moon." A healthy adult or parent knows the difference between a contribution and an attempt to detract from the classroom. The authoritative adult does not accept put-downs. "Andrew, I think that John has an idea and now we will look in the books about the moon and

Earth." Andrew receives no value in his put-down. Soon the children learn that only attempts to contribute will be credited. *Once children are protected, the room becomes safe for learning and for taking risks in contributing to the whole group.*

When all the students are feeling safe, then the support from the adult is at its best. The students make comments such as, "I love being in this room." "Mr. Smith really cares about his students." "I like school this year. Mrs. Jones likes the students." "This is my best year because Mr. Adams lets me learn." "We all feel good in this class." There are no shy children in a safe classroom and there are no "bullies." There are only children who are nurtured, protected, and supported in the quest to learn.

Because many families are not able to provide such parenting at home, the school becomes the one place where all students' ideas are honored. However, because of past experiences, students do not come into the classroom ready to respect all the others. There is always the need to discuss some of these tough past cognitive and physical experiences. There is time at the beginning of the year set aside to talk and brainstorm about bullies, shy students, defiant students, problem situations that don't feel safe, etc. The teacher leads the student discussion through behavior modification rules, modeling, learning and teaching techniques, respect for the "wee" folks, etc. The rationale for these discussions comes from the students' own experiences and feelings. For example, "We were all tiny at one time" opens a discussion about how all people mature as they get older. At the other end of maturity, a discussion about respect for the students' parents and the elderly provides wonderful opportunities for the students to open relations with grandparents, neighbors, etc. The students begin a path towards respecting all ages and all levels of people within the community. *The students are learning to be responsive to others' needs, to move from a position of self-centered, egocentric socialization to a more rule-governed shared community where language represents the respect for all individuals.*

Healthy classroom parenting places limits on what a child is allowed to do while fostering a child's "who." Therefore, the boundaries between "who is the child" and "who is the adult" are clear. The adult nurtures, supports, and protects the child. The children do not function to parent the adult, that is, to make the adult feel good, in control, smart, etc. The respect for the adult's role as separate from the student's role is critical in offering lessons that will be intrinsically learned. Ultimately, students learn that a safe environment can occur and that they have choices in how to respond to one's environment. *In the safe authoritative environment the students are learning lifelong lessons about themselves and how they will treat others and allow others to treat them. External rewards are shifted into a need to learn, an intrinsic motivator.*

Activity

1. **Describe healthy parenting.**
2. **Explain how healthy parenting assists in creating an authoritative classroom.**

Intrinsic Learning

*In a classroom based on what the children **can do**, there is an emphasis on the children's internal development.* Because the students can contribute from what they already know, then there is a strong commitment to intrinsic development. In other words, learning is the basis to the classroom and the learning is based on what the children know, rather than on what the children don't know how to do or can't do.

Because learning is based on a child's own neurobiological make-up, then a child's own development motivates the child to more learning. This learning is a neurological "high" because there is truly a biochemical change in the child's learning system (see Chapter Two for an explanation). For example, while discussing a word "momentum," the teacher asked students what they thought it meant. Immediately several reached for dictionaries, some went to the encyclopedia, some turned to the glossary of the science text, and a group of students huddled together to discuss the word "momentum." *This immediate response was developed from a discovery process that the teacher encouraged in the development of this classroom into a community where each student has contributions and each student has resources.* Built into the responsive process is the understood *language of respect* for one another. The teacher expects 3-4 minutes of quiet time so that all students have time to find the information before some begin to share. Those with extra time begin to write, draw, or represent their ideas in some way other than shouting an answer. In this way, there is no reward for being "right," "first," etc., only the intrinsic reward of being a valuable contributor. These contributors are participants in a safe classroom.

In a classroom for younger learners, students problem solve as a group on how to draw a map of their school so as to learn when activities occur, what the students in this Kindergarten look like walking to the cafeteria, etc. These Kindergarten students are learning to share power as they bring their own knowledge to the task of drawing the map. Shared power is the individual's needs to resource a topic and then to share it. *To protect, nurture, and support in an authoritative classroom is to trust the child or student in his or her own strengths to be the best at contributing to the whole.* Respectful teachers reduce the number of external rewards and offer healthy parenting through semantic corrections. The power is ultimately shared among all classroom members. *In the authoritative classroom, discipline shifts from control techniques to more powerful assignment of positive meaning through shared power that focuses language on the individual member.*

New students are brought up "to speed" in this type of classroom by their classmates using language to help new students feel comfortable. Rules even become intrinsic so that the room seems like a well-oiled machine. But, every little machine part has been assigned positive meaning in so many ways that the details of such a room seem monumental. For example, in this type of room, students may borrow others' (including the teacher) supplies or materials, *but* only with the owner's consent. Students may sit where they need to sit, *but* only if this place works for the student and the other class members. Limits to the classroom are by intrinsic value rather than by arbitrary rules that have been externally established. The intrinsic value comes from making all students learners while also establishing all working relationships based on the formal value of **RESPECT:** *the Right of Each Student to Participate in an Environment of Communicative Thoughtfulness.*

What values should have been learned at home are practiced and learned as part of the natural way to interact within the classroom. *There exists a shared, human right to be safe, nurtured, and protected that is part of the intrinsic learning for all.* Students learn that they are valued for their contributions, and therefore they want to learn. In this type of classroom, it is difficult to sometimes send students home. They come before school, they want to work on projects after school. They ask to increase the time and boundaries of assignments. They are seen meeting together on Friday evenings at the library to work on a project. *The students constantly look for more information as their contributions are valued and their individual rights respected.*

Activity

1. **Define intrinsic learning.**
2. **Give examples of how the use of language fosters intrinsic learning.**

Shared Power

Respect for shared power is part of the authoritative classroom. **Shared power is the right of each student to equal safety, protection, and nurturance through the teacher providing opportunities for success for each student, cognitively and socially.** These opportunities occur not only socially by sharing roles and responsibilities, but are learning opportunities for cognitively sharing academic tasks. For example, when the students gather their information for an assignment or task, they then have the opportunity to share their ideas with one another. The teacher in a respectful classroom wants to know from the students how this information will be recorded, transmitted, shared, etc. Artists may want to draw. The computer whiz wants to use the computer. Some want to read from the books, dictionaries, and encyclopedia. Now the classroom becomes dynamic. Even though the information may be identical, the power in the room is for the students to figure out what is redundant, and what is critical, so that all individuals are credited with their findings. The information is integrated across groups so that there is no right answer or single source, and, so all students are contributing to the final report to be evaluated and credited to all members.

The students begin to realize that there is even a hierarchy in the process of relating information. The process includes thinking, sharing, disseminating, and reorganizing information. This process is much like the process of scientific inquiry. The facilitator poses a situation, the students question the possibilities of answers, and the research is performed to determine what the options to answering the questions might be. The process becomes more important than finding the "right answer." Because the individual student is central to the process, the answers and products are as unique as the number of individual students. *This authoritative process overlaps with the concept of using an inquiry process in the classroom to facilitate natural learning.* Students begin to venture out from the original question "Are we going on a field trip?" to using the same process for answering a multitude of questions to include "Who do we invite to the field trip?" to "Why do you want to go to the planetarium?" There is always the opportunity to ask more questions.

Time is reserved for the whole group to discuss and ask questions. When the group decides to move on, the teacher may continue with an individual student's need to answer specific questions in more conceptual depth. It is interesting to note that most students recognize that they are valuable members of the group and will continue on a task for a short time before realizing that they can connect their work back to the group. For example, one fourth-grade student who really felt the need to find a particular reference point along the Oregon Trail asked for a class discussion to have more time. The teacher allowed the student to call the meeting and to facilitate the meeting. The student stated his problem and asked for more time. The students in the classroom immediately asked him what amount of time he needed. He said that he had been looking for a book on this place for two weeks. One student raised his hand and when the facilitator called on him, he said, "What is the chance that you won't find the place even after more time?" The facilitating student said, "Good point. I hadn't thought about how much time I was going to need. I guess I've tried hard enough for right now." He then thanked the class for helping him get focused. The students then began to share their materials, maps, songs, dances, reports, etc. As part of the listening process, the students had learned how to be active in asking appropriate questions, assisting in correcting, and refining others' works. As one of the class members showed a map, the student who hadn't found the specific place asked, "Is Mt. Whitmore on your map?" "The student responded with, "I don't know. Would you like to borrow my map?" Guess what? The student found the location on this other student's map. The group had shared power with him. They had helped him move on. By moving on, he had acquired more resourcing from the class members who helped him find the place. *Shared power is a by-product of a process, a natural way to respect and honor student differences in a classroom.* The language used to share this power directs comments toward the individual's needs and in response to others' needs.

Activity

1. **Define shared power.**
2. **Explain how shared power respects individual differences.**

Summary

Cultural respect for a responsive classroom is strikingly different from what might be found in the marketplace of America. It is respectful of the individual in such as way as to protect, nurture, and support the student as he or she is finding a niche in which to contribute. The responsive classroom supports the authoritative culture: 1) The classroom is student-centered; 2) The classroom functions as a whole; 3) Learning is a process; 4) Strengths of the individuals are emphasized; 5) Correction is based on what is meaningful; 6) All adults are expected to exhibit healthy parenting skills; 7) Learning is intrinsically developed; and 8) Students share the classroom power through knowledge, skills, and personal strengths. Competition is determined by how well one might do in seeking information rather than how correct or right one's answers might be. All answers can be improved, corrected, refined, negotiated, developed, solicited, marketed, changed, and most of all appreciated. *Language of* **RESPECT** reflects authoritative parenting values and thus develops the individual, refining the individual's contributions to higher levels of thinking about how to learn, and how to process what others are learning. Within the responsive classroom, learning is the ultimate intrinsic reward for being a respected member of this culture. The next chapter discusses how the culture of this type of classroom offers long-term societal benefits by using a form of language that communicates authoritative values.

REFERENCES

Arwood, E. 1991. *Semantic and Pragmatic Language Disorders.* Gaitersburg, MD: Aspen Systems Corp.

Baumrind, D. 1971. Current patterns of parental authority. *Developmental Psychology Monographs,* 4 (1, pt 2).

Baumrind, D. 1991. Parenting styles and adolescent development. In J. Brooks-Gunn, R. Lerner & A.C. Petersen (Eds.), *The Encyclopedia of Adolescence.* New York: Garland.

Martin, G. & Pear, R. 1996. *Behavior Modification: What it is and How to Do It* (5ᵗʰ Edition). Englewood Cliffs: NJ: Prentice-Hall.
Santrock, J. 1997. *Psychology.* Madison, WI: Brown & Benchmark.
Skinner, B.F. 1961. Teaching machines. *Scientific American,* 205, 90-102.

Chapter Six

Learner Outcomes

Upon completion of this chapter, the reader will be able to do the following:

1. Describe a variety of ways to use language to foster communicative thoughtfulness.
2. Describe the difference between acceptance and approval of students and their acts.
3. Describe how cultural styles of communication affect respect.
4. Describe how language represents how cultural respect is communicated.
5. Describe the importance of communicating respect.
6. Explain what is meant by communicative thoughtfulness.
7. Explain how concepts of recognition and consideration fit into a classroom.
8. Describe how to offer students the opportunity to have ownership and to make contributions in a classroom.
9. Give multiple examples of how to foster communicative thoughtfulness.
10. Explain how respect, culture, and language are tied together.

CHAPTER SIX

Respect Through Communicative Thoughtfulness

How do we foster acts of communicative thoughtfulness?

The child talks a riddle, sings a song,
plays through a dance.
Sad but true, the adult sees not
the child, just the dance or the song.

About 4000 BC, a desert tribe in North Africa discovered that to survive in a harsh environment, they would have to live in a community. Even more importantly, these people were being restricted by the larger society. So this tribe set up specific rooms for specific functions within the community providing each member with a way to fit within the society. The lesson to be learned is that the small community survives by the strengths of the individuals—the potters, the scholars, the cooks, the weavers, and so forth. Even as the ruins were uncovered, there was a predictability to the findings. Such community success has been found in other civilizations. The success of the individual was the foundation to the community as a whole.

In American education, the 1950's and 1960's emphasized that all individuals were equal and thus necessitated the same curriculum, the same books, the same teaching methods, etc. Contrary to what has been known for thousands of years, the individual was isolated from the needs of the community. Thirty years later, some people report the US is now 49th in the world in illiteracy, the social problems of the society are huge, and the individual is difficult to identify. The purpose of this chapter is to demonstrate how the classroom which *respects* the learner can promote a community culture that fosters the individual to grow within a group that protects, nurtures and supports. It is within this community culture that the individual becomes responsive to learning. **The language of RESPECT:** *the Right of Each Student to Participate in an Environment of Communicative Thoughtfulness* occurs within this "responsive" community.

Community Culture

The community is a mosaic of individuals with texture and color. The texture is the fabric of the past woven into the present network of communication, negotiation, and success. The color is the brightness of the individual's strengths, unique as a rainbow of hues. From the texture and color comes the design of the mosaic, with specific events spelled out boldly among the overlapping relationships of the individuals. **The difference among these individuals is the cultural value placed on the individual within a broader community.** Within community culture all members are valued for their contributions...the weavers, the fabric makers, the sellers, the buyers, the animal workers, etc. The community cannot pretend to exist independent of its members. Each member is expected to be valuable to the weave of the mosaic.

The final mosaic is a pattern of all workers' strengths. As mistakes are woven, their corrections are a valuable part of the process. Each refinement is another learning moment, so that future mosaics benefit from the past acts. The individual's experience is not only physical in making the mosaic but cognitive in developing the value of how to create a community, interdependent and healthy. Safe, protected, and nurtured, the individuals are part of the learning process of how to communicate to one another. The community is defined as all of its interdependent members. The community culture is responsive to all of the individual differences, honored as separate from the group culture, but also part of the group's identity. The individuals develop not only as competent members, who are successful, but also as part of the group's identity. All of the individual differences when honored create a group identity that is a community culture. Outside the community culture of the classroom, the student's differences are similarities with other groups and their culture. Truly woven between small and large groups are the individuals' identities and their cultural groups. Through the use of language, the class members define the value of individual differences as well as group identity.

Activity

1. **What is meant by community culture?**
2. **How does a community culture develop from the individual differences?**

Communication

The **language of RESPECT** *is used to communicate the valuable cultural differences of individuals; just like the group's similarities are communicated.* Through these communicative acts, the members of a group (school, family, church, sport team, etc.) begin to find a personal responsibility to help others meet their needs. Eventually, the group takes on a level of "responsiveness." **Responsiveness refers to the ability of group members to individually respond to the needs of the individuals as well as the group needs.** *The individuals of the responsive classroom are able to communicate with one another in proportion to their awareness and sensitivity for each other's contributions as human beings.* What is accepted by the teacher as a contribution is modeled for the students for greater awareness. *Language is used to recognize the contributions and to assign meaning to the value of all members' acts.*

In order for the teacher or adult to assign positive meaning to a student's contributions, the teacher or adult must understand how communication develops in the classroom. *The child's communication is dependent on the child's past understanding of how to communicate, as well as on what the child can contribute.* In other words, the child's own culture comes into play at the beginning of each school year.

Most US families are authoritarian in cultural style of communication, telling the listener the right and wrong way to respond.

And, most US families are too busy today to sit and talk during a joint task such as eating dinner, washing clothes together at the old-fashion neighborhood washing trough, preparing a family meal, planting of a crop, and so forth. Therefore, the student is used to being a responder to questions, commenting on quick bits of information, or being giving small phrases of information. For example, "Take out your books." "Don't be late." "Sit down and be quiet!" "Do your homework." "Start to work." All of these phrases reflect the authoritarian values about how to communicate. These phrases tell the listener what to do and, yet, do not give the listener a rationale.

Classroom communication can be authoritarian or it can be more authoritative, giving students a rationale for their behavior. As the classroom community develops its own culture, each child learns to communicate the way the classroom breathes. With each breath, the child shares a breath of past experiences with the air of others' past experiences. Providing a rationale for the child's acts, offers the child opportunities to benefit from others' past experiences, in essence, to breathe through others' lives. How much opportunity each child has to take on the character of the community is determined by the way that the teacher fosters the "free flow" of communication.

The teacher will offer only those opportunities that the teacher has learned to provide. For example, a student, Russ sees that there is a paper that needs to be picked up. He does not understand what the class is talking about. Russ thinks about what he sees, not what others' say. He gets out of his seat and the teacher says, "Sit down, Russ." The teacher's communication is phrased in a way to "tell Russ" what he should be doing. There is no doubt that Russ should also be thinking like the teacher. Another teacher sees Russ's behavior as a contribution, thus providing the teacher with information about how Russ learns best in this classroom. This other teacher realizes that Russ has a different way to communicate his ideas. And, even more fundamental is the notion that Russ may not even have the same ideas in his head as the teacher may.

The respectful teacher takes the opportunity later to walk over to the student and say, "I see that you were helpful by picking up a paper and throwing it away. Keeping our aisles and floors clean is very useful to all of us and I want to thank you. I think you and I could get together at noon and talk about ways to set up a recycling program in the classroom. Once we get the program in place, then you will be able to focus on the speakers as well as be helpful to keeping our classroom clean." Later a discussion ensues in the classroom, separate from Russ's behavior, about what "we" all expect from others when we are speaking, what our behaviors look like, what we ask after a presentation, how we use strategies for staying focused on a task, etc. Through several overlapping ways to assign meaning, Russ learns strategies for attending to a speaker and for dealing with paper that is on the floor in a more appropriate and mature fashion. The multiple ways to assign meaning with language to the various components of Russ's behavior is important to communicate to Russ "why" he is expected to be sitting in his seat during a student or teacher presentation. Russ is given the opportunity to benefit from many opportunities to connect his behavior with the "free flow" of communication in this type of classroom. The culture of the classroom is one of respect. It reflects the diversity of differences in thinking, learning, and beliefs through honoring Russ's needs as an individual while protecting the rights of the group.

In the US, teacher education programs train teachers in curriculum, methods, materials, evaluation, and the foundations of educational history and philosophy. Little training is completed in interpersonal communication strategies or in communication styles. The assumption is that all students will relate to the culture of the teacher's system. And, therefore, the teacher's communication style will match what the student understands. In other words, if the teacher tells a child to sit down the teacher who thinks in spoken words expects the child to comply with the spoken words. The assumption is that Russ as well as the other students will follow directions presented in spoken words, will learn to read words aloud as connected sounds and letters, will learn to write words spelled with letters and sounds, and will learn to do math with spoken mental words. The culture of the teacher is based on English auditory word thoughts (see Chapter Two) although the majority of American students come from a different cultural way of communicating to themselves and to others. The majority of students think and breathe in what is seen, not coded in spoken words of language or symbols (see Chapter Two for an explanation of auditory and visual language). There is little flow of communication between a teacher who has one set of values for learning and the students who think differently.

The breathing, responsive classroom is dependent on a free-flow of communication so that all students' past experiences as well as all students' present ways of communication and thinking are honored. Basic to this style of free flow communication is knowledge about group dynamics and leadership as well as about how the community is developed. Free-flow communication is dependent on five factors: 1) The use of "ownership language;" 2) The use of "nonverbal language" to invite students to take a role in the classroom; 3) The use of "verbal invitations" to the individuals to contribute; 4) The use of "resourcing" to improve contributions by the individual students; and 5) The use of "reflection" as a way for students and teachers to accept contributions as a natural part of the classroom. Each of these factors will be independently discussed in the following sections.

Activity

1. **What is responsiveness?**
2. **How does communication develop in the classroom?**

Ownership Language
The use of language to denote the responsibility of the activity of the classroom determines the source of power. For example, the teacher says, "Give me your attention" then the teacher is the source of power

and the activity belongs to the teacher only. If the teacher uses a group personal pronoun such as "we" then the students become part of the classroom. This use of who has power can be further extended by how the teacher allows the students to communicate their contributions. For example, the teacher sees a student reading a comic book, the teacher might say, "Jimmy is reading Gulliver's Travels and I want to compliment him on his choice of a famous piece of literature. A lot of people have read this book in foreign countries. So Jimmy and millions of other people around the world know all about Gulliver's Travels." There may be a student who says, "It's a comic book." But then it's the teacher's responsibility to accept both students' contributions. The teacher says, "Yes it is a comic book, but does it have some ideas?"

The value of ownership is also extended by bringing in other students to Jimmy's significant moment of being valued by asking the students to name other "classic books" that might be found in comic book form. The opportunity for discussion is further encouraged by the teacher who talks about when they might read a classic and in what form they might read a hard back book or comic book. Value of the comic book is culturally respected by the teacher also noting how the teacher enjoys the use of pictures, maps, and other diagrams to learn. In this way, the teacher is culturally sensitive to the way this comic book reader is learning information.

Ownership language is encouraged in the class through plural form (we, us, class, peers, colleagues, etc.) unless there is a reason for the teacher or student to show respect for an individual student. For example, in the aforementioned situation, the teacher wants to use the "I" statement as a way to relate how different students learn. In this way, the comic book reader is not isolated and the teacher places a personal value on what the child is doing. This comic book reader is not only encouraged to continue but to move into another form of reading or perhaps another classic story in the same form. Other students see that the teacher does not ridicule, does not judge, and does not isolate a student based on the student's personal reason for choosing a comic book. Ownership language fits nicely with the use of "I" statements (Chapter One) and storytelling (Chapter Four), this language encourages an individual's social and cognitive development, as well as the growth of the entire group.

The ownership of language as a group (we) or as an individual within the group (I) provides a level of storytelling that is at a preoperational to concrete level of cognition. *The preoperational level requires an "I" story about an event so that other people may relate to the storyteller's actions and experiences* (see Chapter Four). Even though students may be much older, even in high school education, it is easier to relate at the preoperational level for new material. The students generate their own ideas and the level changes from an "I" event to multiple speakers or agents, the concrete level of cognition. Finally, the teacher assigns additional meaning such as retagging the <u>Gulliver's Travels</u> book as a "classic." The concept of a classic can't be seen, touched or felt...but the students already have a real event to reassign the meaning of a "classic." In this case, the information of millions of foreign readers is also added information to the fact that a classmate reads the comic book. These other readers are agents just like the students sitting in the class. By the teacher using language to assign a positive meaning to Jimmy's use of comic books to read something that others, outside the classroom, find important, means that Jimmy has been given ownership for his reading. The other classmates are given ownership for being part of Jimmy's room and for also having ideas about these "classic" books. And, they are all given ownership for what they know about classics.

The use of "ownership" language molds the fabric and texture of the classroom into its own fabric, unique to the character of the students and the way each person becomes part of the "we" as an "I." **Language that assigns a group ownership to all the students is the essence of a culture of group respect.** "We are working together to form a classroom that respects the individuals through communication of the person's constituents—desires, interests, feelings, needs, etc."

Shared communication results in shared power (see Chapter Five) and the assigned value of all individuals being contributors to the whole learning process of the group. Communication acts create a climate of flowing from one student's needs to another, and so forth. The feeling of a classroom with a "free flow" atmosphere is one where the communication considers the individual as well as the group process.

Activity

1. **Why is ownership language important to establishing the classroom atmosphere?**
2. **How does language represent the values of the group?**

Nonverbal Language

Some students are content in allowing the classroom to revolve around their use of "I," and other students are content to listen to the teacher's use of "I." But, a classroom is not a community until all people are contributors to the well being of the group. To be a contributor to the well being of the group means an invitation is offered from the teacher to become a member of the group. The invitation to participate may happen through direct verbal statements addressed to the whole group, such as "What do you think about the recess after lunch?" or verbal invitations addressed to individuals such as, "Lenora, maybe you could bring your classical music to class for us all to learn about?" The first verbal invitation given by the teacher occurs when the teacher asks the students to sculpture a personal profile of them. The teacher calls on the students by name to supply the classmates and teacher with the students' favorite sports, leisure time activities, or other pertinent information the first day of class. This invitation allows each student in the class to be recognized by others for who they are so that they may be "seen" in different perspectives, roles, and situations than what academia traditionally offers. For example, Jaimie says she likes to golf, eat sushi, and play the trumpet. The teacher says, "Oh, we'll need a lesson in golf before the year is over and maybe you and I can talk about your favorite kind of sushi and music." A first grader, Jason, says, "I'm a big boy. I play with Suzie and I eat pepperoni pizza." The teacher says, " I can see you are a big boy. Who is Suzie?" Jason says, "My sister." The teacher says, "Maybe you can bring Suzie to class someday and we can have pepperoni pizza for lunch that day." Whether or not the two ideas go together doesn't matter as much as the offer of opportunity. The invitation is complete when the teacher has assigned meaning to Jason's *exact words,* thus validating him as a contributor of ideas, and has appropriately followed up on the intent of the conversation.

The students are always verbally invited to participate in the class discussions when communication is a "free flow process." The value of a discussion occurs when students' ideas are followed up. For example, the students' comments during the first day invitation to give a personal profile takes on value as an activity when the students' ideas are typed and copied and shared with other class members. Younger students may also draw and illustrate their ideas whereas older students are able to literally see their spoken ideas on the paper. The ideas would be lost if the teacher didn't go back to the "sushi," or the classmates could not see Jaimie's words on paper, or if the teacher didn't follow up by bringing Suzie to class, and so forth. The value of communicated ideas is always increased when additional meaning is given to ideas by following through with additional ideas, written comments, and thank you notes from the teacher, etc. The invitation extended to each child is not a one time "special day" for each child, but a constant, year long, reminder of "who" each child is. *Even though the written, drawn, and spoken ideas are important, so are the unwritten, gestural, and nonverbal signs of communication that add meaning to the verbal invitations.*

The use of nonverbal communication is also important in inviting a student to participate. For example, open facial postures encourage more activity from the students. An open posture may include big eyes, round smiles, open and relaxed body postures, open eye pupils as a result of feeling comfortable and safe in the classroom, and an open mind or attitude of approach. Voice is also a nonverbal. Changes in tone tell the students that there's a change in the setting. The vocal tone conveys different meanings, changes in feelings, teacher's personal problems, teacher's likes and dislikes, teacher's personal judgments of what is "proper" or "right," teacher's hidden agendas, and teacher's past ideas or experiences about how to "teach." *If the meaning is to be positive, comfortable, safe, and inviting; then the tone must be warm, interested, well-paced, and encouraging.* The students also tune into the teacher's understanding of hair, clothes, make-up, music, art, colloquialisms, humor, and general understanding of the culture of the students. *All of these nonverbal pieces influence the ownership of the classroom.*

The students are also given feedback as to what the teacher is "tuned" into in terms of dress, neatness, hygiene, manners, use of language, etc. For example, "I like your haircut." Sometimes, the teacher has to handle students in private to provide what is needed for students to feel like they fit—that is to get the guidance and direction in a safe way to handle the situation. The teacher cannot presume the students have hot water, soap, deodorant, hair supplies, etc. It is the teacher's responsibility to use one-on-one time to help the individual feel comfortable. For example, the teacher explains to the student that she knows how busy the student is and how difficult it must be to get cleaned up. The teacher gives the student 10 minutes of private bathroom time to become clean (see Chapter Two). Although there is a standard, value judgments are not made nor does the teacher tolerate such judgments by the students. Both authors have worked in inner city schools as well as isolated district schools where poverty is a value. *Baby steps toward the change in values are crucial to the success in altering perceptions. Community education begins with the students and their families. Through the individual teachers and their ability to assign positive meaning, changes in values become acceptable, even though different from the family.*

If a teacher is consistent in using nonverbal ways to communicate, most students are responsive to the teacher's nonverbals by the third month of the academic year. These nonverbals may include hand postures, facial postures, body postures, tone changes, etc. It's the teacher's responsibility to create a variety of different, distinctive nonverbals that are consistent. For example, in one classroom, the teacher would look in the direction of students talking on top of the words of a classmate who was presenting. This was a signal to the students that something else is important. They had learned about this nonverbal gesture from the teacher who had talked to them as a group about what kind of behavior "we" want to receive when we are sharing our ideas. The group had identified that talking while someone is presenting interrupts the flow of communication, etc. Therefore, the nonverbal eye gaze works as a reminder to the students' rule.

If there is not an agreed upon rule, nonverbal communication holds a multiplicity of meanings **In other words, nonverbal communication is specific to the situation or the culture; it is not a conventional language form.** One teacher's look is a reminder while another teacher's look is a disapproval. Therefore, all nonverbals come through assigned meaning. For example, "How will we know to move our desks back?" One student says that we can look at the clock and at 10:15 we know it's time to move our desks. The teacher accepts that answer and says, "What if someone isn't looking at the clock or we decide to quit early?" The discussion continues until it's agreed upon that a low voice that says, "Time to move" is a signal to all students to move the desks. The students and teacher also discuss the type of behavior wanted when desks are moved, how much time it will take, etc. The class agrees to try the move in 30 seconds. So, the class practices moving desks with the nonverbal and verbal cues of the teacher. "Time to move...30 seconds... 20...10, 9, 8...." Then the teacher checks in with the practice.... "How did we do?" The students discuss the fact that several people hadn't made the move in 30 seconds. So, the teacher asks the class what they could do to help these people. The teacher also asks those who didn't make the move in 30 seconds what they need. No one really enjoys being late. So, the students talk about "intentions." The class expects to receive a notification, "It's almost time to move!" In this way, the class members are trying to take responsibility for how to solve the problem of some people being late. Those who are late discuss what they need in order "to see what time it is" and begin to change behavior.

The tone of all of this time spent on "moving desks" is about **respect...** respect for others in the class, for the time needed to do the curriculum content, etc. By the third week of classes, the students **all** move within 30 seconds. The move is quiet, orderly, kind, and respectful for others as well as their desks, books, etc. When visitors come to the class, they are astounded by the fact that the group can be working on individual projects while working with others as resources when there comes the quiet, "It's time to move." In seconds, the students are grouped into a circle ready to share as a whole group. If there are guests, student members ask the guests where the guests would like to sit and if the guests would like to participate by moving into the circle.

There are some students who do not hear the voices in class; they see the voices. So, when the teacher says, "It's time to move," the student mentally sees or pictures the practice moves that took place. Without the time to assign meaning and to practice the activity in response to the teacher's words, some students would go the entire year not hearing the teacher and therefore having to match his or her behavior to what others do, perhaps always lagging behind. Always matching to others has a significant negative affect on the student's "self." Being able to respond independently increases a student's ability to feel empowered. *Connecting nonverbals to the verbal meaning is powerful for teachers to help students learn behavior that respects all classroom members.*

Activity

1. **How does nonverbal communication contribute to the learning atmosphere?**
2. **Describe how nonverbal communication augments**

Verbal Invitations to Contribute

The students learn that all contributions from students, parents, visitors, and teachers are accepted and valued. In order to facilitate contributions; open communication through questions, comments, and encouraged opinions are accepted on a regular basis. For example, during math, some students figure out how many flowers are in a design by multiplying one side of the design by the number of flowers in the other side. But, there are also those students who want to add the rows. And, there are some that count each flower to arrive at a valued answer. Some might even guess the number. There is no wrong or right way to answer the problem. Those who multiply are provided the opportunity to share how their multiplication works thereby validating the adders. Those who guess are called the estimators and those who count are the verifiers. Accepting all possible methods as valid accepts all personalities as contributing to the whole. For students' participation to be valued, students' activities (verbal and nonverbal) must be accepted and valued as a contribution. By openly sharing these different ways to find the flower design answer, all students are given more information. This additional information improves the math concepts, therefore improving students' cognitive development (see layering and overlapping concepts in Chapter Four).

Parents also need invitations to contribute in meaningful ways. Many parents want to be involved but the parents want to also be valued for their contributions as well. They want to know that they are welcome to offer any services or goods. Many parents fear school settings and an invitation to contribute comes as a threat unless their fear is culturally respected and invitations are real options generated from home visits, providing child care, transportation, etc. Other parents do not fear but value school. As professionals, they recognize that they are professionals because of their education. Their time is limited and their willingness to participate great. But most professionals don't have time to come and "tutor" students. They want to be a *"valued," respected* member of the class. Therefore, the invitations to the parents need to include the opportunity for parents to talk with the students about what they do professionally or in their job or career, about their educational experiences, and about their workplace. Parents need to know that pictures from the workplace, age appropriate books about what they do as professionals, or any other material contribution will be appreciated. Invitations to participate in evening activities are also appropriate, especially when extended by the student.

Sometimes, invitations to shy students or to students who have had little success truly comes through the everyday assigned meanings. For example, one fifth-grade girl burst into tears when her name was called the first day. The teacher was sensitive to the girl's personal needs and so the teacher did not ignore the tears but thanked the student for being at school. The teacher said she would return to her later when the girl felt better. The teacher chatted with the girl at the first classroom break. The girl was very shy and very afraid of speaking up in the classroom. The teacher said that being shy was okay and that there would be lots of opportunities to contribute which would not require speaking in front of the class. By the winter break, the shy girl was one of the most active verbal participants in class. Her parents were amazed, as they had never heard her share many of her ideas at home or in school. Discussion between the parents and teacher resulted in finding out that there were many cultural differences between how to communicate at home and at school. For example, females typically wait for males to invite them to contribute in their culture. At school, this shy student had been told in the first couple of years of school that she was not talkative like the other girls, a value not respected by the family. These mixed messages had resulted in confusion. Does she speak up when she has something to say or does she wait for the males to talk first? In a classroom where the teacher allowed the shy student to gain knowledge about how to participate, she flourished. She did not have a shy personality but a lack of understanding of how to be successful as a participant. The student needed a clear invitation from the teacher in order to participate.

Some students need invitations from the teacher that are more personal or are given in private. Being available the first 20 minutes before class, between class, on the playground, and at lunch helps students access the teacher in the way the students feel comfortable. As the group becomes more respectful of each other's needs, then these students feel a part of the group and are no longer in need of an invitation. Attending class is an invitation to learn! The students then use their language to invite visitors to participate in the same respectful opportunities in which the teacher invited them to participate.

Activity

1. **What is an invitation to contribute?**
2. **Why are invitations to contribute important to respecting students' and parents' needs?**

Resourcing to Improve Communication Contributions

There is another dimension to the invitation task… resourcing. *Part of the respected communication paradigm provides for ways to resource; that is, ways to obtain help from peers, books, the library, the home, etc.* For example, the teacher might ask for the students to share their work. One student begins to share but then hesitates. The teacher lets the student know that he is not alone. "Mr. Jones, who do you want to call on to help you?" This group effort allows the student to be strong within a group. *This type of support within the group is often called "contributive knowledge."* The teacher and the students talk about this concept of how we sometimes have to have many people involved before the task is finished, always remembering that each person shares in the glory or knowledge. No individual's ideas are complete, but each student's perception is valid. In this way, each individual provides a cornerstone to the class.

Each student and each student's contributions are part of the resourcing. To learn how to find information and how to value others' ideas is as important, if not more important, than the product. **Who can find the information is as important as what can be found. Where the information or contribution is found is as important as the content. And, finally, the process by which the resourcing occurs is more significant than the final outcomes.** For example, resourcing goes beyond the texts, library books, encyclopedias, almanacs, etc., into the home so that interview and survey techniques are developed even in the youngest preschool child. Using language to verbally invite others to contribute and to find information is important for all members of the classroom.

Family, neighbors, and friends are encouraged to come into the classroom as well as help with supplying information. The taboo of working off of others' systems is laid to rest as the students are encouraged to use others' ideas. Cheating doesn't exist in the *responsive* classroom where the **language of RESPECT** is used to develop community. Students are told that they are expected to do their best so as to see what they can do on their own. Likewise, they are also given ways to reference other authors' works and how to cite sources so that plagiarism isn't part of the process. Students are encouraged to use themselves in these situations in order to develop the methodology of introspection. **Introspection refers to reflecting on oneself in a context designed for maximum learning.** Questions about feelings, beliefs, passions, interests are asked to provide the student with insight for the activity. For example, in an ethnographic study of sixth graders, a student might be asked about how he or she feels to be Norwegian or what she or he believes to be a Norwegian passion. For second graders, a student might be asked about what he or she likes about walking to school.

Students are encouraged to use letters, the phone, computerized surveys, the World Wide Web as other ways to obtain information. All methods of gathering information are seen as verbal invitations to contribute to the knowledge of the class. Once the student feels important as a collector of information, as a resource agent, as paramount to the learning process; then the student's quality of work improves. It becomes almost "urgency" on the part of the student to "do the student's best job possible," because the student sees his or her effort in a craft, artwork, project, etc. When the student is an active contributor to the community, the student feels a certain amount of pride in being able to resource and produce work based on mature invitations to other sources to contribute.

Although it may seem natural to develop ways to resource, the need to resource is also a value that must be transmitted as part of one's culture. For example, one of the authors was consulting in an inner city school sixth grade. The teacher expressed interest in improving the students' reading skills for better science and math outcomes. But the classroom was a very closed system. All ideas came from the adults and the text materials. Even hands on experiments were designed for all students to recite the same answers or to copy the same words on their worksheets. The students were not given the opportunity to use their own language to create opportunities to learn through accessing other resources or to function as a source for others. As a consultant, the author suggested several ways for the teacher to set up more shared power opportunities where students would use their language to resource, therefore developing better concepts and better basic skills. To these suggestions, the teacher said, "I don't have time to resource or to let the students get library references." The author followed up on this teacher's statement, offering 15 to 20 ways to resource within the metro area, some of which were only a call away and free. Some even offered delivery to the school. It was quite evident that this teacher's values from her own cultural background would not allow her to share power with the students. She did not trust herself as a learner nor did she trust the students' ability to be learners. Therefore, she had a personal need to control the environment and to act **on** the content rather than **with** the content. She did not trust the students' abilities to be empowered.

Resourcing means that there is an umbilical cord between the classroom and the community at large. There is a tie to the society as students are members of that larger culture. Resourcing means students will bring in new information. Resourcing is a process of inviting other people to contribute to the whole. With open invitations to the community, teachers are not the vessels of all knowledge. Furthermore, some students may surpass the teacher's level of content knowledge or even "skill." Parents may even hold more advanced degrees in a content knowledge area than the teacher. However, this inner city teacher was part of a culture, a school that needed to control students' learning. She was part of a school that could not understand why its standardized test scores were so low and why the district might "reconstitute" its faculty and administrators. The school was ready to resource experts as long as they could offer a quick fix of the students. *But they were not ready to share power with the learners, to create a community of respect.*

This same teacher's values were being transmitted within the classroom. For example, the very next visit after offering ways to resource, sixth graders were "whining and complaining" about doing unchallenging art work. The artwork was a project assignment. Each student was to select something about a South American country and create a poster. The author casually walked over to the first group of five students at a table and asked the first student about her picture. The student said it was a "peso." The author said, "What country or countries use the peso for currency?" Marci responded, "Mexico." "Oh yeah, that's right I wonder if there are any other countries!?" Marci shrugged her shoulders. So the author said, "Maybe the next time I come you will be able to tell me if there are any other South American countries that use a peso. Ummmm, I wonder what a real peso looks like?" Marci's eyes sparkled, she straightened her shoulders and said, "I know. I have one at home." "How did you get a peso?" "My aunt brought me one from Mexico." The flow of communication begs two issues: These children may not be from upper middle class families economically but they are not experientially poor. They have been gathering knowledge for 11 to 13 years. Secondly, by the time the author left the table, these students were focused on new ideas and were excited about learning as they all had resourcing tasks to challenge them. From a learning standpoint, Marci was doing artwork about something she already knew. To color previously known ideas is not much of a challenge. *Doing something that a learner can already do robs the learner of personal worth and a positive self-concept about school achievement.* Without a teacher who values the resourcing strength of all members of the classroom, students plateau and are thus limited to what they already know. *The gap between ability and learning increases when students plateau. Their past is their future. Resourcing opens up opportunities and a wealth of experiences outside the past. Resourcing is a verbal invitation to assign meaning from many other sources. Learning to know what other sources have to offer or to contribute enhances the social development of how the learner is a part of the community as well as the learner's cognitive ability to respond in a variety of ways.*

Activity

1. **Describe resourcing as an extension of inviting class contributions from students, their families, and the community at large.**
2. **Define resourcing and give examples of how resourcing encourages RESPECT for the individual learner as well as the group.**

Reflection

The students who resource and who become contributors begin to recognize that they are part of the classroom's pseudo-family. Students begin to recognize the importance of all members. *They are able to reflect on how they fit into the group and how other members work in tandem to produce a group culture.* There is more "real cooperative learning" as students need one another to produce the products. *There is a team concept of how to work together to produce the best individual products. These individual products create a whole that is better than the parts formed from the negative competition of working against each other.*

Students are encouraged to reflect upon their comments so as to provide suggestions to one another as well as to generate creative options so as to improve the process. **The status of how the student is functioning is the state of the student's ability to reflect; that is, to self-evaluate as to how well the student feels about the process.** Self-evaluators are more confident and their work is produced at a higher level of quality. They begin to generate their concerns and their discussions about the content. These concerns and suggestions are not put downs or value judgments but actual critiques of how to do a job or activity in an effective, as well as efficient, way. For example, in a developmental preschool classroom, a child along with three of his peers were making a cardboard kitchen for his "house." These students returned to the whole group to discuss what all the small groups were doing. The teacher said, "I saw a sink but I didn't see any pipes for the water to the sink! How is the water going to get into the sink?" Several small hands shot up. The teacher skillfully assigned meaning to each child's utterance while helping the children reflect on how to remember to finish a job. One young boy, Eddie, said, "I'll get my plumbers and we'll build some pipes." The teacher said, "But you were working on the car. Shafer and Shonda were the plumbers." Shafer, a very low user of language and diagnosed with autism, said, "I make the pipes."

The discussion continued as the teacher quickly wrote, drew, manually signed their ideas and drew out the connections among the verbal contributions and what their spoken ideas would look like as pictures. The preschoolers were able to brainstorm through seeing and hearing what was expected and what was needed in a way to decide as a group how the kitchen sink would get pipes the next time they were working on building their kitchen. Even the youngest children need guidance in beginning a life long process of being able to problem solve by taking different perspectives and by seeing how other people fit into the decision making process. *Most value systems are developed by the time a child is five to seven years old. Therefore, it is very important that language is used to help students learn how to reflect on a decision or problem.*

Part of this reflective process goes home to the parents in the form of letters and/or drawings of appreciation from the students as well as from the teacher. The students connect this adult way of interacting between the family and school as being part of the community way to work in society. Cooperative styles and interpersonal assists provide the safety for all students to nurture and protect one another. The **respect** is for the process of how all students contribute. Students are also encouraged to make *reflection* as part of the overall learning process. "I wonder what the next step might be?" "What would we need to do to be able to take a field trip to the factory?" "I wonder who would help us understand the human body better?" "I like your idea to go to Hawaii but we live in Portland, Oregon. What would we have to do as a class to go to Hawaii?" "Chester, who would you like to help you critique your presentation?" "Is there anything about Chester's presentation that we would like to use or do when we present?" "What did you enjoy?" "What questions do you have?" "What would you like to learn from Chester's report?" After the presentation the students might ask, "What three things did you learn?" *Students learn that reflections about their work and other people's works are valuable contributions to their own development as well as to other individuals and consequently to the group's needs.*

The **language of RESPECT** communicates to students that they have ownership of their activities, that they can contribute to other's works, that they can resource from others, and that they can reflect on their own work as well as other class members' works. All contributions by learners are individually valued and group pooled as ways to offer opportunities for students to learn.

Activity

1. **Define reflection. Give examples.**
2. **Explain why reflection assists a student in functioning as a classroom contributor.**

Learning Opportunities

In order to maximize learning that emphasizes both social and cognitive development, *opportunities* for whole group work as well as individual work must be provided. *Many opportunities are provided for the students to assist one another in a big project that cannot be completed unless all individuals are valued.* For example, the students are given opportunities to go on field trips only if the students decide how to set up the committees to plan, execute, and evaluate the activity. When the teacher asks for help in planning these activities, the students are empowered and feel a sense of worth as active contributors. One teacher allows students to plan a banquet for outside school hours. The students are expected to figure out the menu, the invitation list, the place, the transportation, etc.

The act of the planning is offered to the students through open-ended forms of communication. The flow of communication is designed to offer *empowerment opportunities*, not advice. Another teacher creates an event from all of the individual projects. For example, when the students have their marine biology projects completed (could be plays, mobiles, artwork, etc.), she asks the students how they will represent what they have completed for others. Even second and third graders, realize that they will need to write about their work to make their creativity understandable for people outside the room. This use of the written form makes their posters, for example, a conventional form of language. Then the teacher asks who will see their work and suggests other groups who would want to see such "outstanding writing samples." Sometimes the students create an evening or daytime for parents, sometimes for other grades, sometimes for a whole school, to show case their work in the cafeteria, etc. Learning opportunities for social and academic development are offered to individuals and to groups through language.

Whenever a student is given opportunities to be a respected member of a classroom, a higher cognitive level is expected. If a higher cognitive level is not expected then the student will not be learning anything new and the project will seem tedious. While participating in these activities of opportunity, the student is expected to conform to the rules (concrete level) as well as to offer something to the class (see Chapter Four for explanation of cognitive levels).

Creating opportunities is probably one of the most powerful learning tools. Perhaps the reader is thinking that all classrooms are opportunities to learn, to be a member, to be empowered, **if** the student wants to be or is motivated. Yes, there is the assumption that the student's learning system is always in a constant need of being stimulated. Yes, the students therefore can use learning in a positive way to be stimulated, **if** the student is learning, or **if** the student has language of a formal, adult thinker. But, if the student is average or below average in language and/or conceptualization, then the student needs the environment to offer opportunities to learn to use language to self-create opportunities to learn. Without a lot of very sophisticated language, a student is not able to create opportunities alone. The head or mental language needed to be able to self-motivate would sound something like this. "Well, I guess I could answer the questions on this worksheet by finding the answers in the text. But then I won't remember the material for future use so I think I will try to study each of these questions. First, I will put my own meaning (language) to the answers, then I will write about the answers in my own words, finally I will connect these ideas to something I already know. In this way, I will remember this for future use and I will be learning." Many college students don't even know what they need to learn. Asking young students to convert tasks into meaningful learning opportunities is unrealistic. *It's the adult's responsibility to create the opportunities for students to learn.*

Teachers can offer opportunities by listening to the needs of the students and then by assigning meaning through the way students learn to think or use language (visual or auditory thinking). For example, one young fourth-grade male liked to play football. He had been identified as an "at-risk" student because he did not seem to follow through with his assignments. However, he never had trouble following through with football plays. So, the teacher helped him with the assignments to make sure the young man could do his work. Then they wrote a contract together which said that as long as he maintained a "C" or better in all his work, then the teacher would encourage the football coach at Notre Dame to write to the young man. Months later, a white envelope with a gold football helmet embossed on it arrived for the student. The student as well as his classmates were stunned. Coach Lou Holtz had written to him. The parent of the young man came in to see the teacher and to tell the teacher how inspired her son was to have Coach Lou Holtz write a personal, handwritten note to him. This teacher used the boy's interest to make a connection between the child's personal values for football and the child's ability to do the work. Given some strategies, the student maintained a "B" or better average. The note from Lou Holtz was an opportunity for the teacher to say, "I value you and your interests and I thank you for valuing the classroom work." The Coach's note was an opportunity for the student to become more connected with what school had to offer as well.

Opportunities to be respected by others, a coach, a parent, an administrator, for example, *provide students with social increases in their own socialization.* Such social opportunities to see oneself in relationship to the group also come individually. For example, individual opportunities are also offered students through displaying baby pictures and current pictures showing "sweet, old days" as well as "current successes and achievements." Every photo is a frozen moment of success. These photos like the note from Lou Holtz are visual "trophies." All show how the student is part of the learning environment.

*Even when a student has behavior that does not meet the standard,
there is an opportunity in that behavior "to respect"* how the child
learns. For example, a student in a middle school used profanity in Mr.
Dale's class. Mr. Dale told him that profanity was unacceptable in
school. There were school rules regarding profanity but even more
importantly, there were members of their classroom, including Mr. Dale,
who felt that it was distasteful and rude. The student continued to use
profanity. Mr. Dale told him that for each unacceptable and profane
word, he would owe 30 minutes of detention. The student appeared to
understand the rules and consequences as he repeated them along with
his "choice words." After school, he bolted. Mr. Dale raced after him.
The student climbed into his parent's car. Mr. Dale quickly introduced
himself to the parent and explained the situation. The teacher told the
student and his mother that he didn't care if the mother or son sat in
detention but that one of them owed the time. At which point, the mother
said she was too old to sit in detention. She dragged the boy back to
class and on the way told him that "after all, it was his dirty mouth that
got him into trouble, not hers."

The purpose of detention was not for breaking rules but to spend time
with Mr. Dale in a positive, safe, environment that would become the
norm, not the place you go when you break rules. The mother said she
would be back in an hour to pick him up. Mr. Dale thanked her. The
young man, Ryan, visited Mr. Dale years later and hugged him. Mr. Dale
didn't even recognize him at first. Ryan had become the manager of a
local firm. He was married and had his own school age child. He then
showed Mr. Dale his sports car. Mr. Dale and Ryan had set that car as a
goal during detention in 7th grade. Mr. Dale had used that one-on-one
time to help Ryan make some choices and to discover goals that would
require different behavior. Ryan spoke to Mr. Dale's class. "Listen to
everything he says. He is the best teacher."

Following rules are not only a part of "respecting" the group but they
are also about consequences that are opportunities for respecting one's
own choices in life. Ryan's unacceptable behavior was given detention

that became an opportunity to help Ryan find ways to fit into the classroom and later into life. However, *it should be noted that it was not the detention that changed Ryan's behavior but the language of respect that the teacher used during detention that helped Ryan understand consequences and make different choices.*

Several examples of students who quit the educational system come to mind. These students did not find ways to fit into academia or to be successful contributors to a classroom. *Their inability to fit or to be successful resulted in the loss of opportunities and eventually exclusion, often as angry outcasts.* These students who quit need opportunities to be agents and to be part of the group. Some are home schooled, some are schooled by the district in alternative placements, and some receive one-to-one schooling because their behavior is "out-of-control." All of these students lack the opportunity to fit, to learn in the way their system allows, to be part of the successful group.

Once students are given opportunities to fit and to be successful learners, they benefit usually as they are given opportunities in the way they learn. For example, Eric was a six-year-old who had been "thrown out" of three preschools and public first grade. He was given the opportunity to see himself and to learn through drawings. Within a year of help, Eric was placed in a regular second grade with a teacher who continued offering Eric visual learning opportunities. Today, Eric is a regular student in sixth grade. He makes opportunities for himself today.

Bentley was an 11 year-old-male who had never been schooled in a classroom because his behavior was too aggressive. He was given a summer three-week opportunity to **not fail.** Whatever Bentley did, he was given verbal, drawn, and manually signed consequences to all academic and social behavior. Most positive assignment of meaning resulted in verbal outbursts. Some lack of assigned meaning resulted in hitting. The adults used nonverbal body postures and facial postures to show their dislike of specific behaviors. The adults continued to reassign verbally and in drawing what they wanted Bentley to do. Academically, Bentley even tried to sabotage his work by doing something that didn't fit, such as putting Martians in his map of Pakistan. He was told that if he wanted to share and look like the other kids then he would have to move the Martians out of his clay relief map of Pakistan. He said he would by "Thursday" and he did. It was also obvious that he had the learning potential but could not read and write because he had not been given the opportunity to learn in the way he needed to learn. He recently graduated from high school with above a 3.5 average. He holds a job and has received awards for his job, his skills in chess, and his schoolwork. He still struggles with friendships because his learning system is different. But during that three-week summer opportunity, he learned that he could fit because he was given an opportunity to fit. More importantly, the teachers and specialists of his community also learned how to give Bentley opportunities to be successful at learning so that he could fit into the educational community. They, too, would not let him fail. And, his parents have never let him fail. For Bentley and Eric, opportunities to learn and to be successful as group members are tied together with being successful as individual learners and as successful citizens.

Informal reviews and class discussions can be fantastic "opportunities" for the students to demonstrate their skills, tutor their peers, and brainstorm about options. Students soon learn to lead these sessions individually as well as in small groups. Students also learn that when they are in doubt of how to do an activity, to follow a set of directions, or how to implement additional options; any student in the class may call for a review or class discussion. At times, the teacher may want to ask the class if they need a review. Students usually learn to speak up and explain enough for the teacher to realize whether or not the students understand the material. If there is a silence when the class is asked, or only a couple students respond, then a review may be needed to assess the teacher's effectiveness (see Chapter Seven on Assessment). *The teacher is responsible for providing the learning opportunities, not the students. However, the students are responsible for their learning, given strategies and appropriate opportunities.*

Always assisting students to meet the academic, social and behavioral needs of a group allows students to succeed. Setting goals outside the classroom and even into the future allows the students to cognitively succeed at a higher level. Each of the aforementioned examples, used the situation to help the students "see" into the future…what the student would look like, what the Coach of Notre Dame might do, what behavior does to allow for success.

Even product-based goals such as sports cars allow students to earn self-respect for future use. *It's the teacher's responsibility to offer students opportunities to learn and to be successful. Teachers and parents are also responsible for providing learners with healthy prevention from failure.*

Prevention

When the students are able to learn to be their own sources of learning by accessing resources, then the opportunities created for learning also protect the students from being devalued. Healthy protection from failure is a necessary part of socialization. Open-ended forms of communication within a safe environment help protect students from failure. For example, questions have no right or wrong answers. The teacher says, "What could we do to celebrate?" Now the group begins to discuss the possibilities. *The teacher restates students' ideas to validate all possibilities.* For example, one student says, "Let's go to Hawaii." The teacher might say, "What do the rest of you think?" One student says, "That's too far for one evening." The teacher says, "Nadine thinks that Hawaii is too far." Another student jumps in and says, "I think we have to stay in town." The teacher says, "Okay, then what can we do in town. Perhaps if we want to plan a fieldtrip to Hawaii we would need to take several days. Such planning would take a lot of time. I have helped students plan a fieldtrip to Hawaii." The student who offered the Hawaiian suggestion is addressed, "Aquino, what do you think?" The student replies, "Yes, I was really just joking, but could we plan a trip to Hawaii?" The teacher says, "Well, let's talk about it some more. Why don't you see my at recess. We could discuss some options."

In this way no idea is laughed at or rejected. All ideas are possible so that all students are valued. *It is the teacher's responsibility to include all students by guiding students' input.* Because students come to the classroom with past family and classroom experiences where parents, siblings, teachers, and peers allowed put downs, name-callings, and ridicule; students may attempt to use these disrespectful behaviors. In a *respectful* classroom, such behavior is not accepted as appropriate. When a behavior is not appropriate, a general student-discussion assists students to decide what is appropriate. For example, a student puts down another student, "Hawaii? Are you stupid or somethin'?" The teacher might say, "Okay, class, let's take out five minutes to discuss what has just happened. I have some feelings about being called a name, but I need to know what you think?" The students discuss under the teacher's leadership how they might feel. Then, the teacher says, "Let's decide what to do." Other questions might be, "What should we do with this?" "How does a third grade student handle this?" "How would this affect you in senior high?" "How would this affect you on the job?" "How will you want to look at recess?" This type of communication allows students to protect themselves as well as offer opportunities for others to learn to protect themselves.

Sometimes, individual discussions are warranted. For example, when faced with a put down, a teacher might ask the person responsible for the put down, "If you could do things all over again, would you purposefully hurt your classmate?" Most students would choose not to do it again. For the angry student who insists that the other student (the victim) deserved the put down, the teacher could say, "John, I'm confused. You have never put me down. I have never put you down. Which person are you really? (pause) Am I your next victim?" If the teacher has an open flow of communication and is helping students develop respect about themselves and the teacher, then most students have a change of heart at this point and a subsequent change in behavior.

The students will respond at the cognitive level the student can utilize. For example, the student often begins at what is meaningful to the student. The teacher helps the students relate the behavior to what others do and why. Finally, the students deal with the behavior at a more formal or abstract way by connecting it to the future. This developmental hierarchy of how formal concepts are acquired helps provide the structure for the discussion. The teacher recognizes that there is no "cookbook" to leading the discussion but a process of dealing with the situation based on what is appropriate for developing higher cognitive skills. Each student's self-image is protected by the process that encourages all students to learn to protect one another. Whatever the classroom decides, as a whole, also determines the consequence or impact on each individual student.

Inappropriate and unwanted behaviors are redirected into something that "works" for the community or group. One way to redirect an inappropriate or unwanted verbal or nonverbal behavior is to call on the contributor to reflect about feelings. "Marvin, how do you suppose Maria felt when you called her stupid?" The switch from the class activity to the reflection changes the demeanor—the person is valued, not the activity. The students' decisions of what is appropriate provide the individual student with self-acquired pride. The students' demeanors model the expectations of what is acceptable by the teacher as well as what is now acceptable by the student peers. This process provides the students with the framework for other situations.

Even though skills may be generalized; the knowledge of how to handle new situations is only acquired conceptually through language that mediates the learning process. Students are eager to solve problems so that they may try out the new skills. As the social skills increase in complexity, the students are challenged to deal with more than individual behaviors. The students are allowed the opportunity to be part of a safe group that protects all students through multiple practices.

Role playing also helps to direct students' negative comments or behaviors. These types of role-plays are often used to follow up on the class discussions. "How could you replay the last five minutes if we could do them over?" If no one shows the human hurt, the teacher could be the reflector, "If I were Mary, I would feel disappointed in myself, that maybe I wasn't worthy of others' friendship." Then the students are given the opportunity to see or act out how the situation could be different. *This type of class investment provides a preventative format that protects individuals and creates a safe community.* Cartooned pictures showing how the different individuals "look" helps some students take responsibility for how they look when they behave a certain way and how others look.

The concept of prevention is critical to the process of a group fostering open communication for self-reflection as well as for opportunities of learning. Instead of waiting for incidences to occur in the classroom that then need a fix (this is a typical authoritarian, not authoritative scenario), the teacher tries to model how to validate students beginning with the first minute the first day. Each student is encouraged to communicate about the student's interests, background, and ambitions. The teacher protects that piece of what makes each student special. "Sally, I also like to collect insects, maybe you could prepare an insect display for us someday. Get together with me at recess and we will plan it." Or maybe, "Mike, I'm glad you like to read so much." The latter child is actually reading below grade level material while students are working on academic tasks. "Since you like to read, why don't you look at the pictures of the experiment that Amy is working on right now and see if you can find some information to help her. You can draw the experiment like a story, similar to the kind of stories you like to read. Your drawings can be used to show other students in future years how to do this experiment" Or, there could be the redirection to higher level materials in other forms such as previewing science videos for the teacher or gathering information about the experiment topic off the world wide web.

When students feel like they are significant contributors, the classroom begins to take on a group identity. The identity of the classroom as a group of contributors protects the rights of the individual. Individual identity is the basis to a strongly developed democratic society. Without the individual protected, no student is safe. Instead, the teacher becomes the patriarch or matriarch with the students learning to comply with the status quo. *In a community classroom where respect is the basis of education, the students' abilities to co-create an environment of community protection and individual recognition is essential.*

Family hierarchies also have the need to find protection for their sons and daughters so that their youth feel like they fit into a community, a socially acceptable group such as school or athletics. When students are disenfranchised, they lose hope and express themselves in inappropriate ways to gain the credit and recognition of the community members who have allowed them to lose their self-esteem, their self-concept as a positive person, and their self-worth. The families, teachers, and students in Arkansas; Springfield, Oregon's Thurston High School; and Littleton, Colorado's Columbine High School certainly understand the negative power that comes from students who are not protected by society. Students who are not protected feel disenfranchised and lose hope to fit. They feel like they don't fit in families, groups like sports and scouts, and school. People who feel the loss of their right to be protected find ways to attack the ones who did not protect them...the parents, other classmates, and athletes. Anger against themselves may become channeled into anger against other groups. On the other hand, *positive protection is a learning process for both adults and children...it is an everyday assignment of meaning so that opportunities are created for all students to "feel" successful and to "feel" protected as competent human beings who contribute to the "welfare" of the community.* In this way, students gain their recognition in a positive way.

Activity

1. **Describe the purpose of protecting a learner.**
2. **Explain how healthy protection provides a life long process of contributing to the community.**

Recognition

The encouragement of students' ideas through individual recognition and self-direction encourages new perspectives on what are societally accepted values. Since students are expected to learn, students are encouraged to bring outside work into class to share with the classmates. For example, a student might draw a horse at home and bring it to the teacher. The teacher uses the opportunity for the student to study about horses and then to use the information to share her interests with other students. Now, this child becomes a very active contributor to the other students' knowledge and may find that other students are also interested in horses, creating a positive avenue for friendship. Because the students are encouraged to bring in outside contributions, the classroom decor becomes a hodgepodge of contributions from the students rather than an externally decorated, adult designed centerpiece. *These contributions are samples of recognition of students as individual contributors.*

It should be noted that contributions must positively contribute to the welfare of society. Students are not given credit and recognized for their drawings of armored tanks, bombs, the killing of athletes, etc. Instead, students are redirected by the adult who assigns a positive meaning to their skill, not their interest. Then, from the skill given to another set of students, their interests are reassigned meaning. For example, a student wants to show the class how to build a bomb. The teacher assigns positive worth to his need to contribute. "Robbie, I am pleased to see that you want to share some ideas with the class. And, I am really impressed that you are so inventive. However, the military do not need any help from us in building bombs, and the military is not here at school. So, I have an experiment that allows you to use your ingenuity. Let me show you." This conversation would occur on a one-to-one and the student would be followed closely. Through conversation about the experiment and about Robbie's ingenuity the teacher will probably find out where Robbie learned to build bombs, if he has other bombs built, and what he plans to do with the bombs. Outside authorities are contacted as necessary.

Both authors have been redirecting, protecting, and assigning positive meaning to students who want to destroy for years. Many, many special needs students who are labeled as emotionally disturbed or behavior disordered draw "destruction" constantly. Neither author feels comfortable when students "get into" the negative aspects of life so both authors have always redirected. It is a natural way to assign positive meaning. And, for both authors, there is no room for such destruction... which begins with put downs, name calling and devaluation. This is why students are also redirected into wearing clothes that do not reflect the negative aspect of society, e.g., T-shirts with the faces, logos, etc., of negative groups or even sit-coms promoting a counter culture to a healthy school or parent environment are replaced with more positive social items. Emphasis is on the recognition of the positive aspects of life.

Students are also recognized as individuals through numerous photographs of the students in a number of different situations inside the classroom as well as in outside activities such as on the playground, during field trips, music productions, etc. These photographs are used for auctions, for parent appreciation activities, for sharing with other students, for gifts to visitors such as parents, for information, for progress reports which are written on the back, for subjects of class material such as writing about someone the student thinks is very kind, etc. Each photograph says to the child, "I like who you are and the activities you do are worth remembering." Recognition of the student as a person along with the student's pictured behavior creates a positive community through the **language of RESPECT**: *the Right of Each Student to Participate in an Environment of Communicative Thoughtfulness.*

Role-playing may be used to recognize individual's values such as how we do not use "filthy" language or other unacceptable behavior. Instead of the teacher's values only being accepted, the students role play the meaning of behaviors such as picking on others, putting down others, etc. The teacher uses the time to help the students counsel one another and the final vote is given to the students. *Once enough information is given to the students, the students are able to give their stamp of disapproval or approval based on a reason, not a rule.* The teacher then extends the students' decision beyond the role-playing of the classroom into other situations in the community or into extracurricular activities, the home, etc. *Even very low skilled students can use role play with pictures, cartoons, and photographs to add depth to conceptualization of content within an event. The idea is to help the students "recognize" themselves as having choices and of being able to make choices.*

Recognizing students during class time is easy during monitoring. While the teacher is monitoring or working around the classroom, the teacher uses the time to do "30 seconds of individualized counseling." For example, the teacher might say, "I noticed that you have been on time all week. I've also noticed that you use to get "B's" on spelling but now I see "A's." Perhaps you would share with the class your secret formula for these grades." The teacher then makes sure that the student has the opportunity to share "the formula" in front of the class.

Written stories about noticeable and positive situations are also used to recognize the individuals. The students are helped with writing about the strengths of others. For example, Florence was a fifth grade student. She had a physiological problem that necessitated that she leave several times during the day. In the fifth grade she used these times to "cruise the halls." This was after the previous (fourth grade) teacher routinely "ejected" her from her classroom. Florence lacked reading, writing, and all grade level math skills. At the beginning of fifth grade, she would cry easily and usually forgot to turn in her work. Peers would say hurtful things to her on the way to school which would make school even more difficult. Florence and the teacher began to discuss schoolwork with drawings. Pictures and carefully chosen picturesque words seemed to help. Florence showed her amazing ability to use hand drawn pictures even more. Along with the pictures, Florence would spend an hour after school each day with the teacher. Soon another student learned that after school sessions helped to finish all the work in an hour. This student asked to come and work too. The students drew stick figures, colored major ideas, and made simple drawings on the chalkboard. By November, Florence was down to earning two bathroom passes a day. There was no "cruising" and by January she was on an honor system. By February, any external rewards such as points were eliminated. Figure 6.1 shows the type of language the teacher used to help Florence.

Figure 6.1. Letter to students by teacher about Florence's strengths.
Florence is one of our major social committee members. She decided to organize a social committee that would make two visitors in our class feel wanted and comfortable. She took it upon herself to assure us that one of the guests, an eight-year-oldster would find time to color pictures, have a gift of an ice skating pillow (the eight year old guest was an ice skating competitor), and be assured of a fun-filled recess in the morning and again in the afternoon. Florence's efforts were successful! All went like clockwork! In response to this written note, others in the class commented on how well dressed Florence was and how she had a "gentle-heart." Others commented on how Florence shared her snacks and how she had developed so many academic skills.

The teacher can also write letters and notes without naming the child. Figure 6.2 is an example of writing a story without naming a student.

Figure 6.2. Story about a classmate.
This student is very quiet. She likes to work often by herself, in the comfort of her own privacy. She likes to smile and nod her head in response to the teacher and classmates. Yesterday, the class applauded this student's effort on her homework. Who is this student? The class immediately said it was Harriett. At the end of the year, this was a note written to Harriett from the teacher. Here's wishing you the best of the best, Harriett. I just wanted you to know that we all know now, that you deserve the heartiest congratulations for a job well done. You have a ways to climb yet, as the top of the mountain is in

sight. We all want you to know that we are here for you, when you need a word of encouragement.

You can evaluate your own improvements. You are the expert on Harriett. Remember when you burst into tears when your name was called during roll call in September? Now, your confident voice shouts out "here."

How about the cheers that you heard when you solved a math problem at the chalkboard without any assistance from anyone? Didn't you feel great about accomplishing that math problem without a single bit of help? Good luck to you, Harriett! Keep up the great artwork too!!!

It should be noted that Harriett, like Florence, also used a number of drawings and pictures to learn how to be successful at school.

Students write notes as well as add to the ideas of the teacher. Sometimes, parents also write notes or add the names of other students to notes sent home. Again, the recognition is for how the student functions within the classroom. *Sometimes, the stories are turning points of empowerment because the students can see themselves on paper.* Even examples of what needs to be improved provide opportunities for change. Figure 6.3 shows how a need to improve a particular behavior resulted in a contract between school, home and the student.

Figure 6.3. A contract between student and teacher.

Each time I bring my work to the teacher's desk and put my work in the teacher's basket, I will receive an A for my homework. [Signed] Sean

I agree to give Sean an A grade for each homework paper that he puts in the teacher's basket.

[Signed]
The Teacher

Interestingly, some administrators have expressed discomfort with these success stories. Why? Perhaps, it is their own low self-esteem or education history that dwells on the deficits or negatives. In any case, *all* students and their parents deserve positive recognition for being part of the community. Students really enjoy learning how to assign "feel good" attributes to others as well as receiving such accolades from peers and the teacher.

Through these recognition forms come the benefits of the community, values that are shared and communicated among one another. Such benefits create an open environment that is safe and nurturing for the students while providing maximum support for the family to belong. Students learn that being part of the community is respecting oneself as well as others in the group. *To be part of the community requires not only the opportunity and the recognition but also the acceptance.* Some students and parents write letters of appreciation. See Figure 6.4.

Figure 6.4. Letter typed at home and given to fifth grade teacher.

Dear Mr. Aaron,

Thank you for all the nice letters you have written me, my dad really likes the notes too. I really like being in your class. You have tought me a lot so far and it hasn't even been two months.
Your class is the best class I have ever been in. I really do like you even though sometimes it doesn't seem like it.
I also thank you for the snacks you have given me awhle ago.

Sincerely,
Carnegie Smith

Students also learn to write compliments, letters of recognition, and appreciation notes.

Figure 6.5 Student to a Student (second grade).

This student wrote a note to another student. The teacher helped edit the note and put it onto the computer. This is the final edited note.

Thank you for helping me with my project. I liked the picture you drew. You draw very well and I hope you are proud about your drawing. I want to draw like you. Can you teach me to draw?

Even teachers write thank you notes to their colleagues. Such appreciation is unusual and therefore the thank you note is often kept and posted for years.

Activity

1. **Define recognition. Give examples.**
2. **Describe how recognition is a part of the language of respect. Give examples.**

Acceptance

When values are developed, then all activities, behaviors, and ideas must be accepted. The students are even encouraged to use a variety of ways to answer a task so as to value all possibilities. For example, a teacher may have students diagramming sentences in whatever their home language might be. One fifth grade student asked to diagram in Hebrew. This student then customized the roll into Hebrew, which was posted later in the room. Even the students' answers to the roll call may be individualized as well. When a variety of answers are possible, the students work hard to come up with a variety of appropriate ways to be recognized as part of the classroom. By the middle of the year, some students might say, "Good Morning" while another student says a phrase in French, etc. One second grade classroom had 15 different languages that students were using. For two girls from Russia, it was the one time of the day that they could participate, as they spoke no English when they were first assigned to this classroom.

The teacher who encourages cultural diversity also stops to ask the students what the phrases mean so as to show case their language expertise. The students who are encouraged to be individually accepting of the differences among students are creating the culture of the classroom. To inquire about such differences is a way to better understand cultures.

Acceptance of all students as members, of all opportunities to learn, of all learning systems, of all ideas, of all possibilities, etc., is a big undertaking for a teacher or parent who does not believe these essential truths of acceptance. An adult who does not believe that all students are entitled to be given opportunities to learn in the way that the students need to learn or who believe that there is a limited way to think will have difficulty respecting all students. Or, athletic coaches who believe that not all learners can benefit by participating on the team will have difficulty being accepting. Chapter One explored the need to understand oneself. Part of this exploration requires the adult to examine biases. All beliefs are biases, therefore all adults have biases.

If there is differential treatment based on these biases, then the person's actions are bigoted. *Acceptance is blind to bigotry. Acceptance knows only the child. Acceptance separates the child from the child's behavior or actions. Acceptance is unconditional respect. Acceptance is not approval (see Chapter One). While approval deals with activities, products, and what a person does, acceptance protects the person's "self."* In order to have an environment that is based on respect, acceptance must be part of the value system by the teachers and adults first, and then the students' and childrens' values easily reflect those adult beliefs. The students and adults use language that reflects the respect of accepting all learners as co-contributors to the community. Assigning meaning through language, creates values of respect. Creating values is dependent on the use of language to reflect or show acceptable community meanings. The **language of RESPECT** protects all community members.

Activity

1. **Define acceptance as part of the "language of RESPECT."**
2. **Explain how acceptance supports the learner. Give examples.**

Creating Values

As long as the teacher and students co-create an open environment that is honest, the students stay empowered and the classroom can function as a community. **This community is defined as an environment that allows each student to participate in communicative thoughtfulness. The community members, through their verbal and nonverbal actions, are responsive to others' needs and share their values through positive language.** When the environment is providing all learners with opportunities to succeed, with healthy prevention, recognition, and acceptance, then the community is safe. There is order within the community, not anarchy. There's anarchy when the students are not empowered to commit to the whole or when the classroom consists of 30 individuals doing only what the teacher demands. Then those students who can't fit into the teacher's model have to find other behavior to demonstrate how unique they might be. When each person is trying to contribute to the whole instead of trying to tear down or break the other individuals, the individual sees himself as important. The value comes from being a "contributor to the whole." **Co-creating the values of the environment is based on communicative thoughtfulness that is honest.**

Part of the honesty in a respectful classroom comes from dealing with what is and is not acceptable. **By the teacher setting the limits and boundaries of behavior as well as of the way to communicate, the students learn what is respected.** For example, to compliment a student on being mature for asking a question suggests that the student is growing up. The student then sees himself with greater expectations than previously thought. The students are asked once or twice a month to share verbally and in writing about what they have noticed to be improvements in other students as well as themselves. Again, only supportive and protective language that nurtures the development of others and fosters a high self-esteem for all is allowed. The students are encouraged to write and/or draw friendship stories about what they have learned from observing others as well as themselves. For some students,

262 THE LANGUAGE OF RESPECT

the task of writing about one's own improvements is too difficult, but the simultaneous task of writing about others improvements is often more comfortable. The teacher models such behavior by writing about different students and their contribution to the community from day one. For younger classrooms, the students draw and then write stories about friendship and the teacher models such stories with small groups as well as the large group.

Learning to be a valued contributor is learning to value one's environment to include all of the other contributors and their efforts. Being able to assess one's own beliefs and acts as well as others' acts and beliefs, and to offer all members of the group positive critique, refinement, opportunity, recognition and acceptance, allows a learner to value one's schooling, goals, and future. Assessing such growth is not always easy but essential for respect to be valued. Creating values which are community shared come from sharing the community, from modeling what is expected, from giving learners sufficient knowledge about the rationale for actions, and by learning to self-evaluate.

Activity

1. **Define how values that promote the language of respect are created.**
2. **Define expected values. Give examples of how to create values.**

Assessment/Evaluation

As students develop their own work from the nurturing environment that protects the uniqueness of being creative, the work is put into a student generated organization. Such organization is a viewfinder of how the student sees him or herself. The organization also is another way to say, "What you do and who you are is important to all of us." A popular form of such organization is the "portfolio." The student is expected to collect such work so as to demonstrate what the student has learned. Unless the work represents the student's own ideas, then the folder says how well the student fits into the teacher's system. In fact, the authors have seen portfolios of teacher-based work, a file of worksheets, fill-in the blank tests, multiplication skill tests, etc. When these students are asked about their portfolio, they usually say there is nothing that they want to keep…that is, nothing they value or respect.

If the student has developed a number of ways to communicate the student's own past, present, and future, then the student is a historian in a culture. **The history is the way the student represents the student's beliefs, interests, passions, etc., and the student's culture is the way the student represents his or her ideas.** These representations, when collectively assembled, are artifacts of the culture of the classroom. For example, if the students only draw about ninja turtles then that is what the students represent that they know about their society. If the students, on the other hand, write, talk, map, openly talk about others' ideas, philosophies, places of origins, then the students represent a broader way of viewing the world. If an anthropologist were to examine the ninja turtle room 1000 years from now, the classroom work would represent a narrowly focused, unnatural way of looking at the world—and certainly not a pragmatic way of viewing the world. *On the other hand, the classroom of honored individual work, represented at different levels, about different concepts would show a culture of diversity, breadth and concern for humankind, true artifacts of the classroom's set of values.* Learning to assess one's growth both cognitively and socially is part of growing up in an environment where the language of communicative thoughtfulness promotes **RESPECT.**

Summary

Culture is what makes human beings different. These differences are center points for bringing groups together. Brought together through similarities of difference, each student is honored for fitting into the school and different for being an individual. Each student is provided the opportunity to learn through a flow of communication that respects one's ownership of ideas. Invited to contribute, students are expected to succeed as their ideas are refined through reflection and resourcing. Over time, students' values are created and passed on to future generations. Such values include a respect for the process of learning, for others who learn differently, and for differences of ideas and products. Adults and children are only safe when there is adequate prevention from put downs, name calling and devaluation; when there is recognition for each individual as a contributor to the welfare of society or the community; when all ideas are accepted and valued for what they contribute; and when adults are willing to create acceptable values. Acceptable values model what society deems socially appropriate while cultural diversity of individuals is honored and respected.

REFERENCES

For a more in depth description of how to access higher levels of conceptual learning through the use of student events, the reader is directed to the following.

Arwood, E. & Unruh, I. 2000. *Event Based Learning Handbook.* Portland, OR: APRICOT, Inc.

Chapter Seven

Learner Outcomes

Upon completion of this chapter, the reader will be able to do the following:

1. Assess whether or not a classroom is functioning with **the language of RESPECT** principles.
2. Assess levels of interpersonal communication among the students so as to determine cognitive levels of interpersonal need.
3. Assess the tone of the classroom in terms of language and activities.
4. Assess the use of materials and activities for including all students.
5. Assess the outcomes of all students in terms of self-evaluation.
6. Explain the difference between testing based on a deficit model and assessment based on the individual's strengths.
7. Explain how assessment of learning is based on the use of language.
8. Explain how language facilitates respect.

CHAPTER SEVEN

The Assessment System of Language

How do we assess the language of RESPECT?

The child looks into wondering eyes,
Gazing, peering, searching...
The adult knows not the mystery or the magic.
The adult finds not the amusement or the fun
Of assessing what is in the complexity of the mind.

Jessa stands at the classroom doorway examining the new photographs that have been placed on the door. Each photograph is a lesson in time, an historic moment of Alex describing his favorite school activity, Joana leaping over a hurdle at P.E., Leonard doing the commentary for his group's production, Sue describing a scientific moment of discovery at home, and so on. Jessa is looking for the history of herself as well as the history of the others. After glimpsing at herself in a photograph with others at P.E., Alex moves toward her desk. As she walks, each foot completely settles on the floor before the next step is taken. Each hand touches something on her right or left side with each stride so as to make the room come to her center of gravity. As Jessa settles at her desk, the teacher has gained an assessment of this student's behavior from observation. The assessment is about the student, for the student, and centered on what the student *can do*. In this example, Jessa is able to move through space as part of the ground. She is literally grounding herself as she walks. The purpose of this chapter is to describe how behavior may be used to assess the individuals in a classroom. The assessment process allows us to determine if the **language of RESPECT** principles are being learned and if these principles are being used by the teacher.

Introduction to Assessment

Historically, the schools have tested students mainly to determine what each student knows or does not know. Areas of testing include everything from speech skills, writing proficiency skills, learning styles, to awareness of subject matter such as specific social studies content, and even handwriting. These tests are used for grade level placements, classroom assignments, support services, curriculum designs, special interests, and so forth. This type of testing works to identify what a child might be missing that a teacher wants to teach. For example, if a teacher wants to teach handwriting, then testing a child on handwriting skills logically follows. If a school district wants students to be chronologically placed into grades, then testing a child each year determines whether or not the child is at grade level for what has been or will be taught at each grade level. In other words, **testing is a predetermination of one's expectations of students.** *So, testing is most effective when an educator determines what is to be tested based on what the teacher wants to teach, and, also, based on the teacher's philosophy of how to teach.*

However, learning is not determined by the curriculum guide but by opportunity. There are no limits to learning, therefore, there is no way to test everything a child learned or will learn. But, similar to the student who stands at the doorway evaluating what she knows about the context of photographs, the educator may use his own theoretical base of knowledge to understand the student's behavior. *The educator uses this knowledge from which to observe each student in a context so as to evaluate how the student is learning, what progress has been made in the student's learning, and what techniques might work best for improving the student's learning.* Without this knowledge the teacher is left with using testing of skills and content as a way to determine the focus and development of individuals within the group.

How well individuals are learning to use *language to respect* society or its members or its products may not be measured with testing. Being able to assess the student's use of language to respect him or herself and others assists in knowing students and knowing what they will or will not be able to perform. For example, a student may be able to "make grades" in a high school but then attack his fellow students and teachers with guns, bombs, etc. The same student shows adequate ability to take tests and receive good test results. However, this same tested student may have developed a film that showed the killing of all athletes prior to an actual school attack. Killing peers, even in literary jest, is *not* acceptable because the film represents language that disrespects peers for their values. The film also disrespects the process of using language to honor others. Most importantly, the film disrespects the producers' own understanding of others' needs. In other words, such a film says that the student producers do not feel like they fit into a membership and therefore, where do they fit? Remember (Chapters Three and Five) that *all learners have a need to fit and must feel like they fit as they progress through preadolescence. In adolescence, learners must then feel unique but cannot do so if they do not fit. Without finding a societally acceptable way to fit, students will find an unique way to fit.* By using the student's own work as a guide for assessment, the teacher has a lot of information about what the student may or may not do, how the student feels, and possibly even what to do to help the student.

Using theoretical knowledge of how students learn as the basis to analyzing the student's film assists the teacher in recognizing that such a negative film does not fit into society's values. This assessment occurs in the classroom with the teacher referring the student for more professional counseling help so that the student producers find out why they feel so disenfranchised. Such assessment allows the teacher and support staff to use *language to respect* these students, and perhaps to avoid future Littleton, Colorado situations from happening.

Professional assessment by the teacher of how the individual functions within the group based on the principles described in earlier chapters about **RESPECT** provides the teacher with a developmental knowledge base for better language use. *The knowledge base provides for the development of language that respects the learner, the learning* *processes, as well as societal standards and products.* In order to determine the difference between assessment and testing, an historical description of testing is followed by the way assessment differs. *Respect for both types of evaluation, testing and assessment, is important. Each type of evaluation provides the educator with information.*

Activity

1. **Is learning best evaluated through assessment or testing? Give examples.**
2. **Are skills and content best evaluated through assessment or testing? Give examples.**

Testing Uses a Deficit Model

US American teacher education curricula are based on a deficit model. *In other words, when a student is tested for reading, the purpose of the reading test is to determine what the child can't do in reading. Based on such testing, the student is provided with the necessary remediation for such a reading problem.* Logically speaking, a reading deficit can't be remediated. But the testing for deficits logic is created by a western psychological principle of what is "normal."

In education, *the normal distribution of students is a bell-shaped curve that represents the lowest skills at one end and the highest skills at the other end.* So, the lowest readers, for example, are at one end of the curve and the highest readers are at the other end. Hence, groupings of students by skill, ability, grade level, and so forth can be literally spread out on the bell shaped curve for normal distribution. Unfortunately, a completed task may or may not indicate the way the task was performed, only whether or not the student received a correct or incorrect answer or whether the student completed the task. For example, a student may take a formalized test such as an achievement reading test that would place the student on the bottom third of the curve even through the same student's learning strength is in reading. Now the student is placed on a remedial reading program that actually punishes the student for having a strength that tests out as a weakness. In other words, the student reads to herself all the time but the test measures how well she analyzes the sounds and letters. Because the student reads by creating mental visual pictures in response to the printed words, she does not analyze sounds. She is then referred for resource work in sounds, based on testing of her ability to use sounds, which is not needed for her to read as she already reads above grade level material in the classroom.

Once punished for not doing well in the way that the student can really think or learn, then the student will begin to try to adapt or to accommodate to the environmental pressures of not reading. *The gap between performance on the test and the student's ability to do the task in a different context creates a punisher.* The reading student's self-esteem drops because she is unable to achieve in the way she thinks others want her to achieve. Testing her against others who think differently results in her believing that she is not achieving like others, and, therefore she feels excluded or "not normal." Most students who have been through such repeated deficit testing tell the authors that they feel stupid, even as adults. *Testing to find deficits to be remediated is an authoritarian way of looking for behaviors that may be approved. Such testing may punish rather than respect the student for who she or he is.* In other words, *respect of the learner is based on acceptance (see Chapter Six), not approval. Acceptance is based on how a student feels, not approval by someone else for what the student accomplishes.* Anytime that there is an emphasis on approval, the student's personal worth is negatively affected. Even college students who read silently to themselves but have difficulty reading aloud because of the letter/sound code interfering with the content often express they do not feel "normal." Punishment levied because of not being able to read in the same way as everyone else results in feelings of inadequacy as a normal person.

This type of deficit testing and corresponding remediation may or may not provide information on how a student learns best, nor how a student is able to compensate using different strategies to achieve, nor how a student may function in the "real world." In order for a student's learning to be determined, then *the student's learning system as represented by behavior, both verbal and nonverbal, must be assessed.* Assessment is a sample of where the student is at the time of the data gathering, rather than a comparison of the student against other students. *This type of sampling is a form of assessment used to evaluate the learning process of the person, not the deficit products. Such assessment respects the individual's learning within the group.*

Deficit testing does provide information about what the student can or cannot do compared to large groups. For example, testing on specific skills or specific standards attempts to determine if a student or a group of students are within a "norm." However, the assumption is that the students taking the test are "like" all other students in thinking and learning. The corresponding scores may be used to determine if there is a minimum standard that a student must offer to be included in a group. Such grouping may be for a grade, a program, a school, a college, etc. However, this testing does not look at the individual student's values, interests, desires, beliefs, or needs. *To assess the development of these latter types of self-constituents so as to use language to respect these areas of a learner's development, assessment practices are necessary. Assessment requires sampling verbal and nonverbal behavior.*

Activity

1. **Explain deficit testing. Give examples.**
2. **Explain how teaching and remediation practices are often based on testing. Give examples.**

Assessment Through Sampling Verbal and Nonverbal Behavior

When the student produces work that is developed from the student's own learning system, then the student is producing something that represents the way the student thinks, acts, and learns. **Such work is an assessment of how each student is able to use language to think. The use of language to perform an assessment task improves the cognitive understanding of concepts used.** However, when the student produces something that is designed by another author such as a worksheet, questions from the end of a chapter, a modeled art project, etc., then the student is not using his or her own language. The student is literally using someone else's language to produce the task or activity. Replications and/or reproductions require very little learning that is more than at a level of how well the student is able to match someone else's work. This type of matching does not foster advanced or higher levels of learning or conceptualization. So, worksheets or answers to chapter questions, modeled art projects, etc., do not assess the student's learning process, but how well a student is able to match patterns or copy patterns. *The student may or may not have meaning or language for such patterns.*

Learning may be best assessed or sampled through the works of the student...how a student creates a project, how a student illustrates ideas while another student writes a poem or acts out a segment of their social studies lesson, or how a student engages in activities with other students. However, *sampling such works is a matter of context.* What is the context? **A context is based on the teacher's assumptions of what the student interactions will be as well as how the activities will progress.** Therefore, in setting up the classroom, *the authoritarian educator assumes that the classroom exists for the students to do the teacher's activities, in the teacher's way and at an expected level, and that students will be graded according to any deficits in the production. An authoritative educator assumes that the classroom belongs to the students, that the students are all learners, that each student is able to participate only at his or her level of development, and that all participation may be assigned meaning that allows for acceptable verbal and nonverbal behavior for all learners.* Therefore, the context for an authoritarian classroom assumes that the individuals will automatically fit into a group that follows the teacher's activities. The authoritative classroom context assumes that the individual learner will contribute to the group process based on the teacher facilitating individual as well as group growth. *Creating a context that is suitable for sampling the* **language of RESPECT** *means creating a context that respects the learner.* Setting the tone of the classroom allows for a context in which students' work is valued. By the students doing their own work, then the teacher and students have multiple samples of each student's nonverbal and verbal behavior for assessment.

Nonverbal behavior includes the way the students walk, sit, play, run, search for answers, comply or don't comply with spoken directions, etc. Verbal behavior samples may be collected from what a student says talking to others spontaneously, talking during a focused group activity, talking about his or her own learning system, talking to peers, etc. Other forms of verbal behavior include the learner's use of drawing, writing, or reading to gain information, to share information, or to solve problems. *Only a classroom that respects the individual learner will have sufficient samples of nonverbal as well as verbal behavior on each student to be able to adequately assess the learner.*

Activity

1. **Explain why sampling is used to assess learning. Give examples.**
2. **Define authoritarian and authoritative contexts. Give examples.**

Setting Up an Authoritative Assessment Context

Setting up a classroom that respects the learner means setting up an authoritative room that honors the individual within the group. In this type of room, the teacher is able to gather lots of samples about individual students as well as group data. *Both authors encourage teachers to begin with a clean room with only the equipment essentials such as desks, tables, rugs, etc.* Mr. Young began his class with one thing on his bulletin board, the word "RESPECT," faded, discolored by the years, and to many first day students, meaningless. But as the year went on, that word was powerful. The students created the classroom's tone, its context through their things that they displayed. At the end of the year, the students removed all of their things...projects, art, photographs. As one student said, "Mr. Young shall I leave 'respect' on the board? I think the students next year will need it just like we did." **The context is the setting, all of the people, the way people interact with one another, the values, desires and all of the "self-constituents" of all of the people in that environment.** One might say that Mr. Young helped the students create their context that could best be represented by the single word "respect." This text is continuing to use respect as an acronym that refers to *the **Right** of Each **Student** to Participate in an Environment of Communicative Thoughtfulness.* Mr. Young's student expressed through his language that "respect" is a value..."maybe others will need this concept just as we did." Such a statement reveals that the student also needed knowledge about this concept and that the student learned about the concept throughout the year. This student also was "thoughtful" about other students and felt safe in "communicating" his interests to the teacher.

This context begins the first day as the teacher greets family and students and invites them to stay. The teacher then provides an initial structure of asking the students to take a seat and having them write their names on a card or on a paper, or, for little ones, the chance to draw themselves and their family. Then the teacher introduces "who" he or she is. The students are then invited to introduce themselves (a previous explanation was described in Chapter Two). After invitations to introduce themselves, older students are led in a discussion of their classroom while younger and lower skilled students are led through the drawing of the classroom. Then the classroom is literally built using those learning principles of the first two chapters. Older students are encouraged to put desks where and with whom they want to sit (limit of 5 to 6 desks together in pods). Younger students are helped with creating nameplates for their space so as to know where they are to be when they work. From these discussions and the rights of individuals to share their past, the classroom for the older students comes to life with potted plants, ribbons, medals, photo albums, and other personal artifacts brought by an invitation to contribute (Chapter Six). As academic projects are designed and completed, students select their "personal best" work to be put on certain bulletin boards. For the younger students, the class comes to life as events emerge. The third graders are building a library, researching the library, and creating their own classroom library which will be dedicated just like a community library after they research that process, create that process, and do the process. The first graders are turning their room into a community with a place for animals, their idea of how to care for a pet expanded to how others care for animals at a zoo, etc. Students are encouraged and assisted in providing invitations to bring parents or friends or siblings into the classroom. As outside agents are involved with the process, all sort of artifacts are brought to class to be shared and respected by all. This classroom set up creates a context through shared language that respects the individual person within the group. Creating an authoritative context also assists the individual in learning to fit within the group so as the respect the group process (see Chapter Eight).

The value of a student created context cannot be understated. The students are agents within this type of environment. They go on to middle school, high school, or college to return to tell how valuable it was for them to be "in control" of their context. Prior to that experience, most students report that their classrooms are covered with teachers' ideas and things and what the teacher values in terms of student works. Even Kindergarten children report feeling sad and left out when their work continuously is put on the bottom of the bulletin board because the work isn't approved of in the same way as others. "The teacher doesn't like me. She always puts my work at the bottom." "Why do you think she puts your work at the bottom?" "Because I use too much glue and can't color right." This type of competition to be "right" and "approved of" allows for devaluation of those people whose objects of art don't fit. The result is an authoritarian room with a controlled, teacher centered, context. Teacher designed and created classrooms are often manicured and lack the warmth of a classroom created by 30 empowered third graders. *Students need to be learning agents.* Even high school students need to be individually unique and respected for their "adult like" cognition, even if it does lack wisdom. *For all students, creating their classroom as part of the learning process is setting a context for the best assessment of learning.* The students learn how to know if they are learning, how to be successful as a learner, and how to value learning products as part of society or community needs. Such a context is often referred to as a "responsive context." *To create a responsive context, the teacher samples the students at the beginning of creating the context and then multiple times throughout the process.*

Activity

1. **Explain how setting up the context the first day helps to create an authoritative classroom.**
2. **Describe how an authoritative context respects the individual learner's needs.**

Pre and Post Sampling

The work of a student is assessed at the beginning of a unit, reassessed during the activity, and assessed again at the end of a unit. Students' works are assessed by what each student is able to show, demonstrate, construct, or think about. In order to determine where a student might be in the understanding of specific concepts, a developmental approach to assessment may be used. Looking at the student's ideas in terms of how the student represents the concepts through language allows for a natural quick assessment. The following section describes the levels of such language use. The purpose of this section is to provide the teacher with developmental knowledge so as to assess verbal and nonverbal behavior adequately. There are three levels of language development…preoperational, concrete, and formal.

<u>Preoperational Language</u>

1. *Preoperational language may be defined as "the big I"…the person speaking, drawing or writing is central to all activity.* For example, "I'll do it my way." "I have an insect at home." "I caught a butterfly Saturday." "I want to find some lady bugs." "I have a book on spiders." "I think that you need to clarify the material."

2. *Since preoperational language is used to describe events dependent on the student being an agent in a context, then, if something doesn't go as planned, external things or people are at fault.* For example, "You gave me that grade." "The judge sent me to prison…it's his fault." "I didn't lie. I don't lie. John lied." "My dog ate my paper." "My baby brother lost my computer disc." "You didn't tell me what to study." "You are the worst teacher." "You didn't give me anything new at that workshop," "Athletes are snobs," and so on.

3. *Preoperational language shows that the student is concerned only with how he or she relates to others.* For example, "I gave the community my artistic expression. I expected the community to appreciate my work" (verbal response to thousands of dollars of graffiti on business buildings). Unfortunately, functioning in society is based on how well external factors are responded to by an individual so that the individual can accept responsibility. The preoperational language user does not accept responsibility. For example a preoperational thinker might say, "They didn't give me the job." "They didn't tell me I had to apply." "The teacher isn't fair." "Everyone doesn't like me." "The teacher didn't tell us what was on the test." "The curriculum told us to teach that way."

4. *Preoperational language puts the person at the center of an event, which also means that the person is dependent on outside or external*

rewards. **Dependency on external rewards results in an external locus of control or in a victimized, controlled position.** For example, a preoperational learner says he doesn't want to join any group. The student lags behind others so then the student is the last to be put into a group. Because the student is the last to be put into a group he says, "Nobody wants me." The student scripts out failure so that the world is responsible for the student's failure or success. The adult or older student may use such preoperational language to fulfill the same victimized position. "I'm always a 'B' student." "I can't do math." "The principal doesn't like me." "I am an outcast. I like to be an outcast." In these positions of being controlled by others' actions, the victim is also dependent on receiving rewards from others. The cycle between being rewarded and being controlled continues since rewards in the authoritarian culture are dependent on production or achievement. Higher conceptualization allows a person to use language that moves him or her out of the cycle.

5. *Preoperational verbal or nonverbal behavior by the child or adult also shows that this learner is able to match behavior to what is seen, but may not be able to change behavior.* For example, a fourth grade class was dismissed to go to the media center. One very capable boy looked around the room and then performed the activities as he saw them. He would see someone put away books so he put away books, etc. He was the last person to leave the room even though the school perceived him as "impulsive" and "hyperactive." Therefore, for this boy, he worked as well in the classroom as he was able to match what others do. Even though he tested with an above average IQ, his ability to function in that classroom was minimal. His learning system was not recognized and therefore his behavior was dependent on what others did. He functioned with preoperational language skills without the assistance of language structures that would help him function higher. Preoperational thinking can result in nonverbal behavior or verbal behavior that reflects the need to depend on others' activities. For example, a thirteen-year-old tells the listener that he watches others.

"The others don't report to the office when they are late to school." Unfortunately, he also indicates that unless he can watch others, he isn't able to function on his own. The same student is late to class unless he sees his friends go into the classroom.

6. *Preoperational, but spontaneous language, may demonstrate lots of repetitious types of colloquialisms, faddish types of behavior, or socially inappropriate behaviors.* For example, "Well, uh, well, like it's a, like, well, every time, you know…they, um, well, I don't think it is fair." Or a coach being interviewed on TV says, "Well, the boys, uh, well, they done good. They showed their stuff. They did it right. Um, um, they are the best. They are the tops. Um, well, they are the bomb, you know, like they are phat." Or, a student is trying to explain an assignment, "Well, first, like first, well, the first time, the first thing, the first thing we did, well, like sometimes, we well, we think, well, I think, well the first time we did discussions." *The use of such repetitions, colloquial language, and faddish language takes the place of content.*

7. *Preoperational language represents thoughts that are underdeveloped.* However, these individuals know that they "should" be able to say what they are thinking, so they "talk." These individuals are socially trying to fit into a group typical of their age even though their thinking about a particular idea, concept, or event may result in preoperational language. The typical age for preoperational thinking and preoperational language is three to seven years of age. But a thirteen-year-old or a thirty-year-old may also function at the preoperational level of language use in certain or even most circumstances. As a result, the thirteen-year-old student who is functioning socially with preoperational language will appear to be immature and socially inappropriate as compared to societal standards. For example, a student blurts out, "I have three pencils to use at school today." This utterance as well as the manner of speaking may be perceived as socially immature. It actually just represents what the speaker is able to say at that moment. On the other hand, a whole classroom of students may set up a "controlled" environment that is undermined by the students' own use of

preoperational thinking. For example, a number of graduate students who are veteran teachers decide that they have nothing to learn in a given class. Such decision making is very preoperational and sounds like this, "That teacher is a waste of time." "I am going to do something else during class." "I don't need this, I already know how to run a classroom." Ideally, such individuals would give a more concrete or advanced thinking response to their colleagues, such as, "Yes, I've heard a lot of this material, but the class time gives me the opportunity to be affirmed for what I do know. I think I will ask Professor Smith what he thinks about using small groups to foster respect in the classroom." This latter use of language is *not* preoperational but more concrete...there may be an opportunity to share ideas between what the professor and the veteran teacher have in common. *Preoperational language represents underlying thinking and the use of preoperational language limits higher thinking.*

8. *Students, older than seven years of age, who socially and regularly function with preoperational behavior and language, are apt to also be in trouble with societal expectations. Society expects language and behavior to be shared or conventional, at least a concrete level of functioning.* For example, a thirteen-year-old was expelled for the remainder of his freshman year of high school after only three days of school. On the third day he had brought a bag of marijuana to school in his pocket and had showed his drugs to others. Even though the student had a history of learning/language difficulties, he was expelled on the first count of drug possession per district/state policy. The student's family argued that the student did not have the language for understanding his actions and therefore should not be expelled. The district stuck to their policy even though the mandated drug screening and several week participation program found the student clean and basically unaware of his violation. However, every time a person asked him what he did *wrong*, he said he brought a bag of marijuana to school. He could even show where such a rule was written in the student handbook. The parents were still not convinced that the student

understood his actions. So, a third party evaluation of the student's language was requested. The student told the assessment party that he had learned to buy marijuana in his middle school DARE program. He described how he knew others used marijuana but that he never did. He drew out the day he went to buy the marijuana. He described how he knew that these people possessed marijuana because a friend told him. He then remembered what to do to buy a drug as shown by the DARE sessions at school. He then visually matched his mental pictures of how to buy the drug to doing the activity. He rode his bicycle to the house and asked for the marijuana. He gave them the money he had and they gave him the corresponding amount of marijuana in a bag. He put it in his pocket and wore those pants to school the next day to show his friends his "achievement." Not one time, either verbally or in drawing, did he connect the rule of not bringing drugs to school to his activity. He *did not understand the conceptual connections beyond the preoperational level* of what he did. To connect the rule to his activity he would have to have been able to use a higher level of cognition such as a concrete or formal level. Once the evaluator drew out the connections in a cartooned form to show how the specific school rule pertained to him and his activity, he didn't want his parents to fight the expulsion. He knew what he had done because he could see himself in his pictures. *Respecting how a person thinks in relationship to their language use helps to establish respectful relationships.*

9. *Preoperational language may also be sampled in forms other than spoken language.* In addition to sampling oral language as a way to assess the preoperational student's level of understanding both academic and social skills, other types of samples such as writing and reading may be used to demonstrate the level of functioning. Exhibits 7.1 and 7.2 are written and drawn samples of two children the same age, eight-years-old. Exhibit 7.1 shows a preoperational level of drawing while Exhibit 7.2 for the same age child shows a concrete set of writing skills.

Exhibit 7.1 – Eight-year-old at preoperational cognitive level.

Exhibit 7.2 – Eight-year-old at the concrete cognitive level.

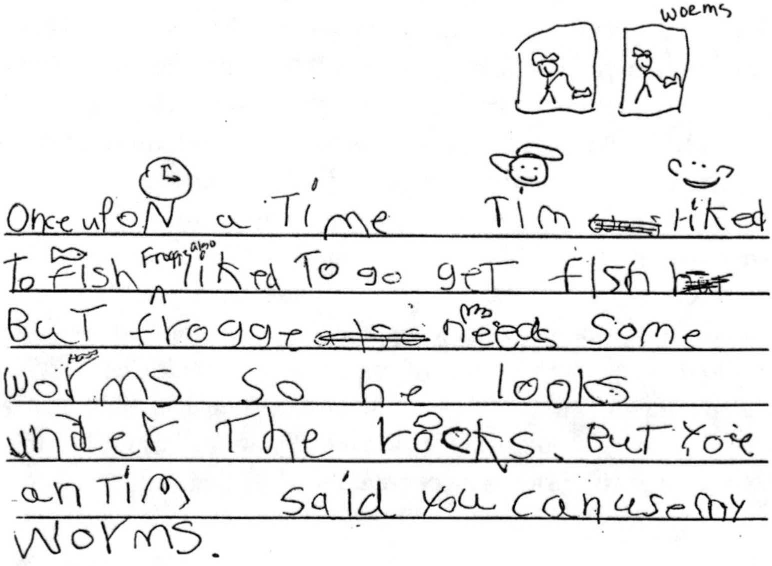

Exhibit 7.3 is for a twelve-year-old who is functioning at the preoperational level socially but capable of functioning at the concrete level cognitively. Exhibit 7.4 is a twelve-year-old who is functioning at the concrete level socially but at the formal level cognitively. This assessment for these students would suggest that these students need refinement from the teacher to move into a higher level of functioning. Note that the language lacks clarity, completeness, and connectedness. Because preoperational language is from the learner's perspective, the writing and reading are also limited to unconventional ("I") forms and structures. Even though these students are in regular education, these samples represent what the student is able to understand as well as to represent. Note that there is no emphasis on skills or competencies mastered but on what the student is able to cognitively demonstrate through language.

The purpose of emphasizing the student's use of language, instead of skills, is to be sure that each student's level of functioning is recognized and respected. In this way, each student is able to work from the point of strength rather than from the teacher's designated skill, which the student may or may not ever perform. Assessing language use of cognition or thinking also tells the teacher where each student begins and where the teacher needs to begin. Most classrooms (K-12) have at least 30% of the students at a preoperational level either socially and/or cognitively for any given task or content area. *Respect* for the whole group comes only when the teacher is able to start at the preoperational level so that all students are respected by being included. (See Chapter Four for more explanation of how to begin events/context at a preoperational level through story telling, "I" stories, etc.) The teacher moves all students to higher order thinking and learning levels. In these example, all students are able to produce work at a higher level as assessed by the topics used.

Exhibit 7.3 – Twelve-year-old functioning at preoperational level socially but capable of functioning at the concrete level cognitively.

The men are going To put the garbage in the garbage can. WOMEN

MEN carrying

Exhibit 7.4 – Twelve-year-old functioning at the concrete level socially, and academically but capable of functioning at the formal level cognitively.

Disneyland

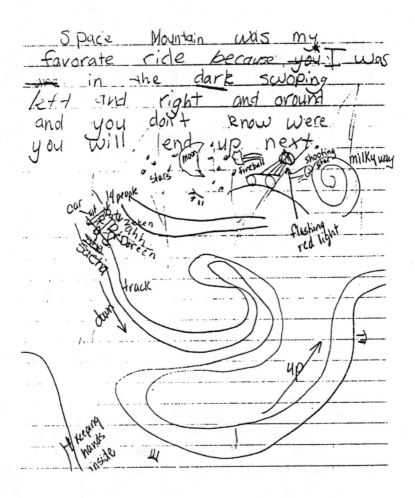

Activity

1. **List the characteristics of preoperational language. Give examples.**
2. **Explain how preoperational thinking limits respectful verbal and nonverbal behavior.**

Concrete Language

1. *The characteristics of language that represent a concrete level of cognition are related to how the speaker or writer relates to others.* For example, "Claire helped me find the library book we needed for the project" or "My mom drove me to school this morning so that I didn't have to walk in the rain." "The principal helped us establish new committees for curriculum review." "The professor offers multiple ways to learn the material." Concrete language goes beyond the individual to include others.

2. *The child or adults feels comfortable with certain levels of knowledge.* The student or learner is able to cooperate with others on an equal basis, share equally in classroom functions, offer to others information, help others when appropriate, and/or organize ideas or materials for others. Language sounds like this. "Sarah, would you like some help with the illustration?" "Mark, thank you for taking the time to help with the references." "Libby is always willing to organize the reading materials for us." "How do you feel about the changes in your position?" There is more of a "shared power" with these types of statements indicating that the speaker thinks about more than his or her own ideas.

3. *The child or adult who uses a concrete level of cognition uses examples to describe ideas or concepts.* These examples are like a list of descriptors or comparisons that allow the learner to connect past experiences with present experiences. For example, the educator might ask a student about what the student does on the weekend. The student

lists the separate events. "I go to volleyball. I eat lunch. My friends come horse around. Then we go to the mall. Then we go home. We eat dinner, that's all." From this list, the educator is unable to know the relationship of some information such as "do all of the students go to the same place for dinner." The assumption is that the student telling the story knows the details but the listener does not. However, from these examples or lists it is apparent that the speaker is thinking about what he does in relationship to being in a group. Unlike preoperational thinking about me, myself and I; concrete thinking is about we, even in list form. Lists may also occur in writing. The student is asked to write an essay about the civil war. The student lists major events of the war. This list of events is, at best, a concrete level of understanding of the civil war. Since the US Civil War may be understood with much more formal depth of conceptualization, the student's work could be refined past the concrete listing.

4. *The concrete level thinker uses language to show that he or she understands his or her identity in relationship to other groups.* Typically these groups are school groups, social groups such as scouts, family groups, or church groups. As long as the student feels a part of a group, then the student will take on the identity of the group. For example, if a classroom is based on teaching splinter skills such as reading separate from content, then the student who can't do the task, feels disenfranchised from the group. In a respectful classroom, splinter skills are products of the process of learning so that students all achieve according to their own learning level. Language sounds like this. "I belong to the Mock Trial Team even though I didn't make varsity this year." "Soccer is my favorite sport because I get to play soccer with my friends on Saturdays." "When I go to my church, I like to listen to the gospel music." "I teach in the Portland District." It is the group or class that is functioning as a whole which allows the person to be part of the group. If the group did not work with rules as a whole, then the person wouldn't talk about their affiliation with the group. For example, "I like Mock Trial" says nothing about being on a team. "I like to play soccer"

says nothing about being with a group of friends. "I go to church," says nothing about being part of a church membership. Or the teacher who says, "I teach third graders," says nothing about being a part of a district, school, etc. All of these latter "I statements" are preoperational whereas the former statements about being connected into a group or agency are concrete because they show that the person is part of being within a group. Obviously, all classrooms would function best if the tone of the individuals were more concrete than preoperational. Sometimes, a classroom that is set up without a "concrete wholeness" operates as a teacher directed center where it is the teacher in relationship to all the individual students. In these cases, the substitute teacher becomes a target for the students to engage in the well-known "sink-the-sub" game. On the other hand, when there is at least a concrete level of group *respect*, then the substitute has an entirely different experience. Substitutes enjoy a concrete level of group participation. In these classes, substitutes ask to come back, leave a business card with a thank you note, personally call the teacher, etc.

5. *Extending language, such as appreciation (between the here-and-now of one's immediate personal needs) to others, is also a concrete form of thinking.* For example, Mr. Young would always write a thank you note to a substitute. Most substitute teachers replied to say that the thank you note was the "first" thank you note ever received for substituting, even when the substitute had been actively involved in the same school with the same teachers for years.

6. *The concrete thinker is capable of shifting the external control or reward system to something that is more internal. This shift is a result of the concrete thinker being able to see the characteristics of the other people, places, and things as they relate to the thinker and/or to others.* When the relationships extend beyond the "thinker," this person has more ways to understand others and their needs. In this way, the concrete thinker begins to use rules or criteria for making decisions, choices, etc. These rules and criteria then become more of the thinker's make up. As a result, the concrete thinker is able to "generalize"

situations, criteria, and experiences through language. For example, the first grade teacher expects students to sit in their seats during a large group experience. When Marie goes to second grade, she expects to sit in her seat during large group experiences. But in fifth grade, the teacher says, "You may move around quietly during large group activities, if you must." Marie will need to have "must' defined, as she has never had choices, just rules. *Rules work as external motivators or punishers if the person has personal meaning for the rule.*

At the concrete level, learners can use language to find out what a rule means to them as well as to others. In this way, the concrete thinker can begin to use language internally as a way to reward oneself. The mental language might go like this: "I don't think that I would like to have someone walking around the room during my presentation because I might think they are not listening or that they don't care about me, as a presenter. So, I will wait to get out of my seat to sharpen my pencil until Claire is through presenting. Also, I really would like to ask her a question about her idea but I can tell that everyone is listening and my question might interrupt the flow so I will write it down and wait to ask the question when there is more of a group pause, etc."

This type of mental head language in spoken words or pictures allows a person to respect the group process (concrete) while attending to personal needs (preoperational). Finally, the concrete thinker uses this head language to self-motivate or reward. The concrete thinker does not need the teacher or presenter to remind the person that he or she is to sit in the chair, etc. Such shift from a preoperational need to be rewarded or controlled to an internal shift in understanding rules is a cognitive change from preoperational thinking to concrete thinking.

7. *At the concrete level of thinking, the learner understands that consequences are also a result of what the learner or others do in the environment. In other words, the concrete thinker begins to take others' perspectives to situations or problems.* For example, Levon, a student functioning at the concrete level, might say that he does not like a task but he will try to do the task anyway. This suggests that Levon will share

in accepting responsibility for his own responses, acts, or behaviors. As a concrete learner, Levon tries to do the task so as to try to see or understand why the other person wants him to do the task…it's another perspective. The teacher gives a class a very difficult assignment. Levon tries the assignment the best way he knows how. The preoperational students don't try the assignment. Levon realizes that even though he may not know everything about the assignment, he realizes that he can always learn something new.

8. *The learner at the concrete level is more likely to understand how his actions affect others in the classroom.* As a concrete learner, the student may ask for clarifications, may try the task and then get help, may explain why he can't do the task, etc. Whereas, the preoperational thinker is able to match with other's behavior and therefore may refuse to do a task that he can't match or understand. The concrete functioning student is able to understand that he has more shared responsibility in the setting. In the case of the aforementioned example, this concrete thinking student, Levon, understands that he has choices in doing a task. His choices could be to refuse, to ask for help, to try the task, etc., and more importantly, that he is responsible for making those choices. In other words, *his behavior is a consequence of his choices…others do not make him behave in a certain way.*

9. *The concrete thinking student is also able to share in the planning of the curriculum because this level student sees how the other students fit into the classroom.* For example, Sharon might suggest that the class have a meeting to discuss other ways of completing a project or she might ask for more time for a project on behalf of the entire class. Language for such a request is at a concrete level. For example, a preoperational need might sound like this. "I need more time. I didn't finish the task." A concrete request might sound like this. "Dr. Arwood, would it be a good time to ask for a class discussion about the projects?" "Why do you want a class discussion?" "Well, I still have a number of things I would like to do on my project but our projects are due by tomorrow. If I do all the things I want to do, I am not sure I will finish in

time. I am wondering if there are other class members in the same situation and I would like a class discussion to see what others are doing to meet the deadline we all agreed upon." Students as young as third grade are capable of this latter type of language. Even children before third grade can engage in this type of request but with simpler ideas and language. Concrete use of language should be underway by the time a child is seven or eight years of age.

10. *Learners at the concrete level also try to gain support from others in a group so as to work comfortably with others and so as to provide success for all students.* Because all students at the concrete level are dependent on the group for the development of self-esteem, these students are dependent on being successful in the group. As a concrete student achieves, the student develops a higher self-esteem. A teacher who sets up the classroom for all students to achieve will typically observe that most of the students function with concrete language.

11. *Concrete learners create a classroom that shares a group identity.* Therefore, individual improvements also are reflected in the whole group. For example, students who enter a respectful, authoritative classroom for the first time are sometimes confused at the expectation to be a contributing member of the group. They are used to following teachers' and parents' directives. Yet, when they realize that their contribution to the running of the classroom is not a joke or a trick, they begin to use the opportunity. "May we have a class meeting about_____?" "Is there time for_____?" "May we set up a field trip to_____?" "I will come in before class to teach you the Korean greeting, if that is a good time for you?" "I think that we should give our visitors the choice of working with us or just observing, what do you think?" "I found a really funny story. Could I read it to the class?" "My dad is a truck driver. He will bring his truck to school, if some of us would like to climb up into the seats and see the gears. The truck's gears are different than the type of gears in our science book." "I brought some pictures of my horse to school since bringing a horse would not be such a good idea. But, my

mom said that we could arrange to come to the farm and then anyone could ride or pet my horse if they wanted."

12. *Concrete thinkers are able to share the language of respect.* For example, the students are constantly praised for being "mature," for helping to design lessons for class, for helping chart the direction of the curriculum, for redesigning the flow of the classroom, for discovering the needs of others, for changing the climate of the classroom into something more positive and fun, for sharing their special talents, etc. As the group becomes more of a respectful classroom with an authoritative-shared power environment (not authoritarian), the group begins to show a more concrete to formal level of expression.

Communication shifts from "I" to "we" and the group is constantly discovering talents. One positive comment can excite a group to new heights. "Randi, I am so impressed by your discovery. I didn't know that there is anything faster than the speed of light. How could we all learn about this finding of yours?" Randi thoughtfully pauses and then says, "My neighbor teaches physics. I will ask him to come talk with our class." The teacher says that is a good idea and then follows up with Randi at recess. Before the class can even think about the possibility, the university physics teacher is in the fourth grade class room eagerly sharing a myriad of hands-on experiments to show light speed and to explain how some scientists think that the speed of light could be faster than originally thought under some conditions. On one hand, the day of physics experiments is more than most students would have wanted to know about photons but on the other hand there are valuable lessons learned. Randi is a leader. She is a contributor. Randi's friends are important to the well being of the group.

Learning to listen and to stretch one's mind to include others' ideas is important. At the end of the day, the teacher validates the students for their willingness to participate. He says to them, "I am so proud at all of your questions, your thoughtfulness. I think Dr. Smith really felt comfortable in our class. He teaches college students, but he was so impressed that our class members were excited to learn. He said to me as we were walking out that he was surprised to see fourth grade students be so mature. I told him that this class of fourth graders is exceptional." The class then has a discussion on how they thought the day had progressed. *The emphasis is always on communicative thoughtfulness as part of respect; surprisingly the emphasis is not on physics.*

Because the social expectations have challenged the students' functioning, the students are quick to talk about their learning. *And, because they have the functional use of language at the concrete level, they are also amazed at how much they have learned about light and physics.* High school at-risk students are especially needy to fit into multiple groups. For example, some street-wise secondary gang students, "required" to attend summer school, showed up on the third week of class with sacks of clothes. The authors were a bit reluctant to ask them where the clothes came from...but the young men changed clothes before class and came into class wearing three piece suits, hair combed, clean shaven, etc. They looked like TV journalists. They had decided to create a videotape of a newscast that showed that they had been learning about news in other countries. They were encouraged to make the tape as professional as possible. They wrote scripts, they sat differently, they critiqued their use of language by playing back the tape, etc. They produced a professional tape that their teachers then encouraged the young men to share with the other classes. These young men gained a lot of praise. Their functioning in class after this experience was very different. However, they did change clothes before they boarded a city bus to their own neighborhood. Their use of gang membership may be seen as preoperational in nature, but they showed that they were able to function as part of a societal group. Given the opportunity to be respected for their ideas, they could function at the concrete level or above. Moving out of the gang depends on how well they may belong to another group.

13. *The concrete-thinking students also share membership in more than one group because concrete thinking represents multiple ways to think about ideas.* The concrete thinker also has more than one group

membership or they will spend a good part of their thinking at a preoperational level. The groups might be school, home, community agencies, church groups, school sponsored extracurricular groups, etc. If a student has several groups with whom to share ideas and belong, then the student is more likely to have several perspectives in a given situation. For example, Enrika does not feel comfortable at home. She doesn't feel she fits into the family expectations. At school, the teachers expect her to be able to do the spelling tests, the reading, and the math like the other students. Enrika is not able to do these tasks like the students, so she thinks that she is alone. By the time she is in high school, she has found that boys like her and that she has only one option in life...to get married and have babies. Once married and now in an abusive situation, she does not think she has other choices. Suicide seems the only option. Somehow she realizes that she can't leave her babies alone or with the abusive father so she decides to start doing things for her babies. By the time she is in her thirties, she realizes that she can do for the babies and for her new, non-abusive husband.

By having two affiliations, Enrika sees that other options such as education exist. Within this process she learns that her way of thinking with mental pictures is okay and that she can spell and do math differently. As a learner she becomes empowered, something that could have happened when she was in elementary school with respectful classrooms. Today she is a fine science teacher. Enrika's ability to extend beyond herself into other affiliations offers changes that go beyond the "here-and-now" into the future, into the family, into the social agencies, into the church group, etc. When individuals progress from the preoperational level to a more concrete way of thinking, then learners are empowered to share with families and communities. Societies change in the same way as the individual. Therefore, *when a classroom allows individuals to grow in their ability to think and use language, these individuals' abilities to respect others extends beyond the present student-teacher experiences.*

14. *When a learner is able to think and use language at a concrete level, then the learner is able to maintain an individual identity that contributes to the overall well-being of the group.* In this way, a student can work at his or her own speed producing different products which show the uniqueness of the student's contribution to the overall classroom projects. Because each student's contribution is being accepted for whatever the student is able to do or not do, then the students can also accept themselves as part of the overall group. In this way, a student who doesn't take notes with words becomes a well-respected member of the group as an illustrator who is able to cartoon, flowchart ideas, and design. Once the student has illustrated his knowledge, then he also learns how to become conventional and use written language.

All students are members of the group or community. The community, in turn, is dependent on all contributions of each student. *Respect is a shared opportunity to honor others' differences as well as similarities based on societal rules.* In other words, the student who is able to contribute his illustrations to a group soon sees his illustrations written and printed for display. Since the student has his own understanding of what he drew and his explanation of a printed form, the student also has the language for reading and writing about that topic. The student soon begins to read and write so as to contribute more about the topic. It is not long before the student is academically functioning at a higher level. Gaining the language about what a student already mentally "knows" is the connection between social awareness of a topic and academic functioning about the topic. Most nonreaders at an older age (third grade and above) already have the mental language about a wide variety of topics and they need to be able to crack the code. By being given opportunities to overlap what the student knows with what the print looks like, the student begins to pick up the coded patterns.

Concrete language allows students to connect with others, to identify with groups, to fit into societal expectation, to depend on the relationships of others for survival, etc. Concrete users of language may function independently in society whereas the preoperational thinker is dependent on society coming to him.

Activity

1. **Describe the characteristics of concrete thinking and language. Give examples.**
2. **Explain how respect is limited at the concrete level to rules. Give examples.**

<u>Formal Language</u>

The highest level of conceptualization is a formal way of thinking. This level of thinking uses symbols in word form to represent real experiences and events. Concepts such as "government," "truth," "Egypt," "chlorophyll," "gravity," and "anger" are ideas that are created from other symbolized forms that result in ideas that can't be seen with the eyes, touched with the hands, or felt with the body. Words such as "gravity" represent abstract concepts that can be understood at the preoperational as well as concrete levels. A formal understanding of a concept like "gravity" requires that the person is able to define in words and/or picture multiple meanings and multiple examples. The language characteristics of formal thinkers use these word definitions in the following ways.

1. *A formal thinker takes responsibility for his or her behavior.* "I forgot to put those questions on the test and I said that I would ask them. Is there anything I can do to rectify the situation?" Educated individuals who understand how they are responsible for their own behaviors often express formal thoughts. "I am sorry I hit your car. I didn't see you. I know that this is a huge inconvenience for you. I will do what I can to make the insurance process as easy as possible." However, seldom do we hear the following, "I was sent to prison because a jury of my peers believed that I had murdered my friend. I understand how they came to

that decision. I am responsible for the way I behaved." Even though members of society want individuals to take responsibility for wrong doings, most responsible people do not deliberately do something wrong, such as murdering a friend. The person's thinking and subsequent language representation would not allow a responsible person to do such an act. However, formal thinkers may use language to play semantic games so as to rationalize behavior. "I really didn't bug the hotel room to catch the Senator. I bugged the hotel room because I thought there was some wrong doing." Such rationalization is really using language at a lower than formal level of cognition. But such verbal acts make the person think that the acts are justifiable. In other words, the person protects himself by using language to "right" his own thinking.

2. *A formal thinker uses a personal code of ethics as well as others' codes of ethics for making decisions.* Here are some examples of language that reflect a use of personal or professional codes of ethics. "There is no rule about whether or not it is okay to use another student's paper for a grade in the English class. But, I don't think I would be learning if I did, and I think that the use of such a paper would cheat others from the same opportunity to compete for grades. Therefore, I will not use that person's paper." "I found the teacher's answers in my book. I would want the answers to the test back if I were that teacher." "Someone keeps ringing the fire bell at school. My friend Jack knows who is doing it. The school has had to post a $1000 reward to find out who is pulling the alarm since no one will tell. But I will ask Jack to tell. If he does not, I will go ahead and tell him that I am giving his name to the Counselor since the ringing of the fire alarm affects all teachers and students, it is not right for one student to have negative effects on everyone else." "The professional code of ethics says that students shall not be restricted from learning. Therefore, I need to learn as much about students' learning systems as possible so I don't ignorantly restrict students learning. Besides, as a student, I would want to learn as much as possible."

3. *A formal thinker* **respects the welfare of the whole group (society) as well as the members of subgroups and the individuals of those groups.** For example, "Recycling is a beginning process that helps all people but we have to provide individuals and groups ways to understand a western culture's need to compensate for waste. Not all cultures understand our wasteful ways and therefore the need to recycle." "The others have decided that we don't need more time for the project, so I will adjust my work accordingly so as to turn the project in with everyone else. Otherwise, I am not contributing with everyone and I might inconvenience students as well as the teacher." "I will ask the teacher if I can have more time. I understand that if I have more time that the teacher will want to extend that option to everyone." "Drama students always leave on Wednesday afternoons to get ready for their matinee. I wonder if any of them need someone to help with the missed material. I will ask them if they would like me to help." "The teacher is moving all of the tables. I think I will help her so that she doesn't have to move everything by herself. I know I would want help."

4. *A formal thinker uses integrity of "self" to separate his or her actions from those of others.* For example, "I understand that Ms. Jones is experiencing personal difficulties but her words are devaluing of others and I personally feel belittled by being called 'incompetent.' Rather than complaining about the situation, I will plan to meet with Ms. Jones to see if we can work out some communication guides." Now, if Ms. Jones refuses to meet or rebukes the attempt to work collegially, then the person with integrity separates his behavior from that of Ms. Jones. In other words, he doesn't begin to act like Ms. Jones by name calling and being disrespectful.

5. *A formal thinker realizes that he or she is not responsible for others' responses or behavior and cannot make another person act rationally, respectfully, or collegially.* The authoritarian notion that "it takes two to tango" is true when both want to dance. But, the reverse logic is not true. If one person doesn't want to dance, the other dancer is not responsible for his partner choosing not to dance. In other words, a student is told to

work amicably in a small group. This student, Laura, is bossed around by another student, is belittled by Josh, and finds herself without the task complete. But the teacher says, "If you would have worked together, the task would be complete." Laura takes the project home and works to complete it. She separates herself from the behavior of the other students. She takes responsibility for the project and for the teacher's lack of understanding of how shared power works. Laura completes the project for the group and comes back the next day. Josh insists on presenting Laura's work. Dan jumps on Laura's spoken words and takes over in front of the class. Much to the surprise of Laura, she receives a "B" grade while Dan and Josh receive an "A." The teacher tells Laura that she does not participate enough in class. Laura is angry and frustrated at the teacher and her peers. She goes home and tells her mom. Mom says, "Laura, I'm proud of you for not letting down your peers, for not belittling them or putting them down. I am glad you are not like them. You need to talk with your teacher about what you did." Laura goes back to school and asks to talk with the teacher. The teacher is open to a conversation. Laura says, "I wrote the presentation that Josh read and I made the poster that Dan shared. I feel like have participated enough to earn an 'A' grade." Laura did not put down the boys or tattle on them or complain about her grade. She separated herself from the behaviors of the teacher and the boys and advocated for herself. In this case, the teacher is supportive and says, "Thank you for telling me. I will give you an 'A.'" Sometimes, the teacher cannot separate out the expected behavior for the group from the individual behavior. In other words, the authors have seen teachers give "B" grades to the whole group since not all three presented equal amounts. Or, the authors have seen unique and outstanding teachers (as requested by parents and as noted by student enthusiasm and test scores) punished for being unique…different from the group.

6. *At the formal level of thinking, uniqueness is diversity and diversity is expected as well as honored. Respect* for oneself as well as for others is formal when the individual works within the rules of the group while

maintaining self-discipline and a positive self-concept. Self-discipline helps the person separate one's behaviors from others' acts and a positive self-concept asserts one's beliefs rather than bullying others or coercing or controlling others into a false sense of obeying or being loyal. These authors have seen children as young as third grade able to advocate for themselves like Laura did. Likewise, there are many educators and their administrators who are threatened by other educators' differences and therefore they feel the need to devalue, belittle, control, retaliate, etc. *The classroom and the educational workplace is most positive and self-satisfying when the individual is respected within a group that functions as a whole.*

7. *Formal thinkers use shared power to create an assertive, win-win, atmosphere that allows all people to feel successful.* Military, heavy handed or controlling bosses and teachers may get results from being aggressive and rule governed (concrete) but the creative juices for learning and for feeling "good" about learning or working comes only from being "unique" and assertive. *Assertive styles of communication necessitate a formal sense of communication between all parties. Only thoughtful, respectful words that assign positive meaning to all acts, allows acceptance of all members.* For example, "Class, I need some understanding about how we will complete the plans for the field trip. Does anyone have an idea?" As ideas are shared, individuals are credited with contributions and negotiations occur. Sincere appreciation is offered as students help to assign the final tasks and organize the work into a functional timetable that meets everyone's needs. Some "pieces" of the plan are negotiated out while others are negotiated into the plan. There is no pre-designed way that the plan has to look…only budgetary, time, and other resource limits.

8. *A formal thinker is principled, not rule governed, in decision-making.* For example, "I don't think it's appropriate for me, as a boss, to engage in any form of intimate personal relationships with my employees. They deserve equal impartiality in their work with me. I don't need the legal system or others to tell me if my conduct is appropriate. I know if I am

being appropriate in my behavior." This person is beyond reproach by the judiciary system. Individuals who are concrete and must use legal definitions and rules to decide behavior may find themselves in compromising situations. Since most schools are designed to be rule governed, the principles for a win-win situation must begin at the classroom level. All parties are in the success journey together. If the teacher allows a student to not be successful, then the teacher also loses. So, it becomes very reinforcing in the classroom to be sure that all parties *see* the progression of the group as well as the individual members. A verbal awareness statement can be so encouraging to a student and to the group. "Anna, I see that you have really spent a lot of time on your paper. Class, I want us to be sure to take a look at Anna's paper. She has spent a lot of time on it." Writing out an awareness statement on a 3 X 5 card is also a dynamic way of sending the message to the student and/or the student's parents. "I saw you help Dan with his poster. Thanks for being so thoughtful to one of your class mates." *Appreciation is part of the principles of respect and therefore is part of being a formal thinker.* The authors have often received letters or notes or have seen letters or notes displayed years after the situation. These letters or notes were simple awareness statements put into an appreciation form. "Thank you for taking the time…for working so hard…for coming to class…for taking time out of a busy schedule…." The principle of appreciation is greater than the simple rule to say thank you. Often learners are "told" to say thank you but the formal understanding of "thank you" occurs when the individual realizes the principles of appreciation.

9. *Respect is a formal concept.* This concept can't be seen, touched, smelled, tasted or heard. It is created by layers of conceptualization (see Chapter Four) through language. Therefore, for students to represent it with their behavior, the adults in their environment must assign meaning to a variety of behaviors, one step at a time. First, the student learners start at a preoperational level of how *"respect"* relates to them, they then develop concrete rules for how to be *respectful*, and finally they engage

in a win-win situation in which they work off principles of *"respect."* These principles are ethical and create a collegial atmosphere of honoring all individuals. A good teacher or a good manager brings along all players or students on this positive journey of respecting oneself as well as others in their successes so that all group members function at their personal best. Exhibit 7.5 shows how a formal thinker uses a flow chart to organize ideas before writing and Exhibit 7.6 shows the written formal thinker's work.

Exhibit 7.5 – Formal thinker

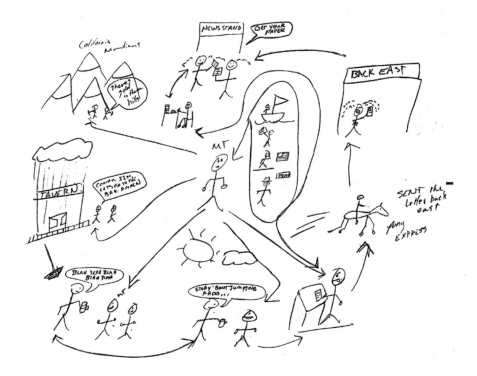

Exhibit 7.6 – Formal thinker

Mark Twain was a River boat capt,
art PRINTER, EDITOR, REPORTER, AND SOLGER. [soldier]
HE WENT TO THE MOUTIANS IN CALIFORNIA
WITH HIS FRIEND JIM TO MINE FOR GOLD
ONE RAINY DAY, HE AND JIM WERE IN
THE BAR AND AN OLDE PROSPECTER NAMED
BILL COON CAME IN AND TOLD ENDLESS
STORIES ABOUT PROSPECTING. BOTH TWAIN +
JIM THOUGHT THEY WERE VERY FUNNY BECAUSE
COON TOLD THEM IN A MONOTONE VOICE WITH
NO FACIAL EXPRESSION. A FEW DAYS LATER,
COON TOLD TWAIN ABOUT A JUMPING
FROG, TWAIN THOUGHT IT WAS SO
FUNNY, HE WROTE IT DOWN AND SENT
IT TO HIS FRIEND BACK EAST, WHO WAS
A PUBLISHER. HIS FRIEND ENDED UP
PUBLISHING HIS STORY AND THE PUBIC
LOVED IT. MARK TWAIN WENT ONTO
WRITE ALOT MORE STORIES SUCH AS
HUCK FINN AND TOM SAYER, WHICH HE
IS FAMOUS FOR.

Activity

1. **Explain the characteristics of formal thinking and language.
   Give examples.**
2. **Describe how *respect* is a formal concept.**

<u>Summary of Pre and Post Cognitive and Social Language Sampling</u>

*There are three thinking stages which show specific observable,
behavioral characteristics corresponding to the use of language at each
of the levels.* These stages are preoperational, concrete, and formal.
Examples of each type of behavior and the corresponding language used
to represent such thinking have been described. Using the characteristics
at each level as criteria allows the teacher to assess each student's level
of functioning within the classroom separate from testing. These criteria
may also be used within assignments. In other words, the teacher may
determine that a student is functioning at a preoperational level of
thinking at the beginning of an activity. For example, "I know about the
Mayas." "What do you know?" "I know their name." Then with the help
of class direction and resourcing the student is able to list all sorts of
pieces of information about the Mayas. Such listing means that the
student now has a concrete understanding of the Maya concept. Finally,
the student is able to write, draw and talk about formal concepts such as
"Mayan Culture" when asked about the Mayas. This shows an increase
of cognitive development in the one area or topic. *Remember that higher
cognitive levels increase overall learning* as described in the learning
principles of Chapter Two. Ideally, teachers would want to facilitate all
students to a higher cognitive level about all topics. One final note to
remember is that most "responder" types of activities such as worksheets
and end-of-chapter, question-answer matches are at a preoperational
level as is any copying or matching task. This level of functioning does
not provide much overall learning and over time will appear to be a level

of disrespect for the student. On the other hand, students who are shown how to "learn" at a concrete or formal level and are therefore successful learners feel good about themselves and about school and therefore *respect* their community as well as themselves. Being able to succeed at a concrete or formal level allows learners to be part of a group (concrete "we") as well as to respect others and the group (formal). Fitting into a group through others' respect as well as being successful as an individual does not allow for product failure or for students to be disenfranchised.

Activity

1. **Describe each cognitive stage and the corresponding language, learning behaviors.**
2. **Describe how these cognitive stages help assess what level a student is using language for functioning in the classroom, academically, socially and behaviorally.**

Using Assessment Data

Even though students have typically been tested for what the student has been taught or has learned, it is acceptable practice today to assess a student's abilities according to how a student functions within a prescribed context. The characteristics of the aforementioned levels of conceptualization provide a guide of knowledge for the teacher to begin to use in assessing students' work (as demonstrated by samples) as well as materials. Figure 7.1 shows a list of ways to assess materials (Arwood and Brown, 1997).

Figure 7.1 – Observer's Checklist (Arwood & Brown, 1997, p. 9-10)

Observer's Checklist
What do I see in the classroom?

1. Are there visual structures?

    ___ Cartoons   ___ teacher made   ___ student made

    ___ Flowcharts   ___ teacher made   ___ student made

    ___ Students' own work displayed   ___ yes   ___ no

    ___ Event based schedules   ___ teacher made   ___ student made

    ___ Event based pictures   ___ teacher made   ___ student made

2. Can I see what the teacher is doing without any words being used to explain what is done?

    ___ yes ___ no   subject area _____ assignment type _____

3. Can I see what the students are to do on a specific task without any words being used to explain the task?

    ___ yes ___ no   subject area _____ assignment type _____

4. Are the students doing an event?   ___ yes   ___ no

    ___ Scientists investigating questions

    ___ Mathematicians solving problems

    ___ Authors writing stories

    ___ Historians investigating social dilemmas or social complexes

5. Are the students resourcing materials for information gathering?   ___ yes ___ no

    ___ Books   ___ Articles/Journals

    ___ Magazines   ___ Computer

    ___ Encyclopedia   ___ Newspaper

6. Are there multiple varieties of resource materials for students to use as an agent within an event?

    ___ Books   ___ Articles/Journals

    ___ Magazines   ___ Computer

    ___ Encyclopedia   ___ Newspaper

7. Are lessons progressing developmentally? ___ yes ___ no

    Preoperational events to multiple concrete examples? ___ yes ___ no

    Examples: _____

    Concrete examples to formal understanding of concepts? ___ yes ___ no

    Examples: _____

8. Is the classroom organized by space? ___ yes ___ no

    Examples: _____

9. Do students have individual strategy checklists to help with study skills?

    ___ yes ___ no   Examples: _____

    _____

10. Are assignments organized by space? ___ yes ___ no

    Examples: _____

    _____

It becomes imperative that educators are able to see the change in a student's conceptualization from the beginning to the end of a project. Exhibit 7.7 shows the refinement steps in a child's work to move the child from a preoperational level to a concrete level of conceptualization. In this way, students are able to see their own progress. When asked what they are learning, the students are quickly able to tell more than just "what" they are doing but also what they have learned. *The data works to help the teacher, student, parents and administrators to see individual progress within the group as well as to help these individuals refine work into a higher level of thinking.*

Exhibit 7.7 -- Refinement steps to move a child's work from a preoperational level to a concrete level of conceptualization.

Exhibit 7.7 -- Continued

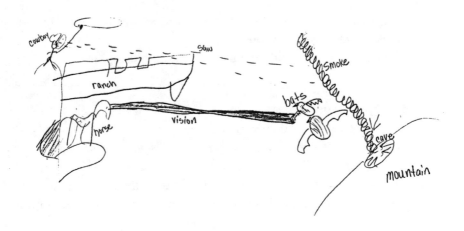

Activity

1. **Explain some ways to use language sampling data in the classroom. Give examples.**
2. **Describe the rationale for using language samples.**

Building Language

As students improve their levels of conceptualization for a particular topic, they must also improve the ways to represent their ideas. It is their use of language that allows for ideas to be stored in long term or semantic memory. If the students don't represent their ideas in a variety of ways, then they will not have the long-term memory storage. In other words, if the students learn at a preoperational level, there will be little learned, that is, little long-term memory storage. If students learn at a concrete level, they will be familiar with the topic and be able to "spit back" facts. If students learn at a formal level, they will be able to show an integrated understanding of the topic—be able to apply it to new settings, etc. To achieve at the formal level, the student must be able to represent the ideas of the topic in a variety of ways. **Various representations are opportunities for use of language at the three cognitive levels.** *In this way, the student is building cognitive stages with small steps of learning.* Such learning shows the student that there is respect for the process as well as the products. Students are building language, which in turn builds cognition. The use of higher levels of cognition is observed in the students' use of language to read, write, and talk about topics.

RESPECT *or the Right of Each Student to Participate in an Environment of Communicative Thoughtfulness* assumes that the student's learning will be honored for diversity as well as for ability. So, all students must be able to build language to feel successful. In an environment of communicative thoughtfulness, higher forms of cognition result in higher forms of thoughtful language. When students are not allowed to learn at their maximum level or cognitive ability, then they feel like they are meeting others' needs, but not necessarily their own needs. The meeting of others' needs is a form of honoring others, unless learners begin to feel like their needs are not being met. Most early elementary students are quick to please and to "do for the teacher." By fifth or sixth grade, the students may be weary but are still developing from others so these students are typically willing to continue to try...to try to meet their needs while satisfying what the school personnel, teachers, and parents want. Finally, in junior high or middle school, students too often realize that their needs are not being honored or respected and they begin to feel devalued or dishonored. As a result of such feelings, school and parents too often become the "enemy." *When in reality, all learners at all developmental levels want to learn. They want to be honored for what they know, can do, and are challenged to do better.*

Assessing students for their learning levels helps the educator provide students with feedback about being nurtured, supported and protected (see Chapter Three) for being a learner. There are many successful programs announced each year. When these programs are evaluated, it is not the methods, the curriculum, nor the students...it is the way the teacher has established a respectful way to interact which appears to be the commonality. Some teachers are naturally better at fostering respect through language than others because of their own past experiences and ability to cognitively assign positive meaning (see Chapter One). Some methods and programs or curricula lend themselves to this type of "best learning." In any case, **RESPECT**, as defined in this text, is what each of the successful programs have in common. Parents, teachers, and schools agree that a variety of programs work, if there exists **RESPECT**.

From the initial assessment to the final assessment, students take baby steps. Each step is built on top of the previous step through refinement of ideas and semantic corrections, connecting what a student knows in one form of representation to another form of representation (previous example was given in Chapter Four). The overall assessment is whether there is a tone of respect within the group (see Chapter Eight).

From an assessment viewpoint, the product is improving as the child's learning shows changes from one cognitive stage for a topic to the next, and so on. For example, a group of fifth graders do not know how to take notes in a variety of ways when reading reference material. So, class time is used to show the students how to take notes like a flowchart or graphic as well as by words. Then these pieces are put onto 3 X 5 reference note cards. The students are then taken through how to use these cards to organize a map or flowchart of what the final project will look like. The student is shown how to write to each of these pieces, comparing the student's content to the map. Any discrepancies in meaning are marked and further refined by resourcing. Some students are shown how to edit the written work by cartooning. Ideas that are not connected are drawn so that students are able to see the missing pieces. Students are given checklists of what to check for corrections and how to correct meaning. Self-assessment and assessment by others is facilitated as previously described, in thoughtful ways to share power.

Building the steps of a project is a series of assessment steps, each step being evaluated for how the individual uses language for learning and for creating products. *The goal is to move all students individually as well as part of a group to the next level of cognitive development.* Since the classroom that fosters respect is also an event of agents functioning as a whole, then the importance of how to build these steps through individual self-assessment is critical. The whole is developed as each individual contributes to the assessment learning process of "Who an I?," "What do I have to contribute?," and "Where will I go next on this journey of learning?" Building language through assessing each step and improving or refining each product creates a learning process with no beginning, middle, or end. All activities are part of the process. All learners individually build through the group process. Assessment of how the child moves through the steps also provides the steps for language to develop concepts.

Activity

1. **Explain the steps for improving language. Give examples.**
2. **Explain how improving cognition and language fit together with learning to *respect*.**

Self-Language Assessment

Self-language assessment is a process of connecting the meaning of one's feelings to one's behavior for the ultimate understanding of "personal best." Teachers and parents often ask children to do their personal best. For many children, "personal best" is a formal term that is abstract in meaning. Personal best is something that the adult likes so that when the adult says, "Did you do your personal best?" The student always says "yes" to have the adult's approval. But, the concept of "personal best" is understood at the child's level of language. For example, a child comes running to the teacher and excitedly says, "Look at my dinosaur." The teacher judges the situation and says, "You did a good job." The child hangs her head and goes back to sit down. She puts her head on her desk and remains in that position for 20 minutes until recess.

The teacher, with good intentions, judged the child's excited voice as being positive and then placed the teacher's value of the drawing onto the child's drawing. But, the child was excited because she had smeared the green crayon onto the blue sky. She was very upset with her product and wanted the teacher to make her feel better. The child's feelings about the project are valid. But the teacher placed emphasis on the product and judged it against other products in the same room or against products for that age child; therefore, the teacher misses finding out the child's self-assessment. In a classroom where individuals' feelings are to be valued, then self-assessment must be part of the set up. The child's or student's evaluation is important.

Assisting the students with self-assessment is part of the overall tone or culture of the classroom. Language is used all day to allow students to give their feelings, their evaluations of their work, their needs, and their resourcing. Each time a child or student is encouraged to give their feelings, then the child is validated, not just the product. The child's own assessment is encouraged. For example, a child showed a picture of an animal and the teacher said, " Wow, what a great horse. I really like your horse." The child frowned, put her head down and said, "It's a dog!" Instead of evaluating the product, the teacher could use complimentary remarks about the process. "I like it. You're quite an artist. Tell me more about your drawing." In this way the students do not hear about artistic interpretations of the product but just appreciations and encouragements.

One of the authors once heard a teacher respond positively to a child's unintelligible utterance with "Oh, that's great, that's nice." As the day went on, the student who had major speech and language difficulties became more anxious and more adamant about hearing his words. Finally, the student's guardian came to pick up the child and the teacher said, "Oh, you must have had a wonderful weekend, John was so insistent on telling us about it all day." The guardian then said, "What do you mean? He cried all weekend as his favorite aunt who takes care of him every day died Friday night." Honesty is part of complimenting which is why "I" statements are so powerful. The teacher needed to say "John, I don't understand. My ears are not working well today. Could you show me or draw for me what you are wanting me to understand?" *The teacher needed to take responsibility for the communication.* Assessing what a child says does not have to be oral or in writing…it can be drawn or shown. To assess adequately, there must be a shared referent…something that both the speaker and the hearer can see or hear. **Respect for each other comes through the shared idea that is used for complimenting one another in the process of communicating respectfully.**

As learners improve in cognitive use of language, they are more able to self-assess. The adult's use of asking for the student's opinions, values, beliefs, and interests continue to provide models for the student to respect his or her own ideas. Group processes that use class time to discuss, negotiate, and design the classroom functioning help students to see that their ideas and contributions are valued. The continued refinement of work helps challenge students to see what "personal best" is about. Finally, the dissemination of students' work goes beyond the limits of the classroom. The shared ideas bridge the student's thoughts about his or her ability to the community. Future goals and plans are fostered through self-language assessment.

Activity

1. **Describe the components to self-language assessment.**
2. **How might a student self-evaluate a level of "personal best?"**

Assessment of Others' Works

Self-assessment at a concrete to formal level does not exist without the assessment of others' works, others' ideas, others' opinions, others' needs, etc. Too many students sit in classrooms where they don't even learn other students' names in nine months or know anything about the people with whom they spend five to seven hours each day, five days a week. Their friendships revolve around the few students with common dress, who sit at the same set of desks, who play the same sports, or walk the same routes. *Such emphasis on the individual over the group creates an exclusive rather than inclusive community. To know the members of that group, all members must be able to compare and contrast each others' self-constituents as well as products.* For example, many times students are asked to present or share something in front of the class. But there are no listeners. The teacher is grading papers. The students may be quiet but their nonverbals are involved with each other, not the speaker. The student finishes. The teacher says "thank you" and the child sits down.

To respect this presenter, there must be some evaluation of what was said. Otherwise, there was no presentation to a group but a monologue that could have been delivered in one's own room with a mirrored reflection as an audience. It is important that the students learn to use each other as sources of information as well as "friends" or colleagues who support and nurture one another. (Chapter Eight considers the group assessment.) One example of how the individuals contribute to the whole group is provided here. The fifth grade class has 45 minutes to work on their questions about an event that has just been introduced. The teacher is monitoring in the classroom. He walks over to Mary's desk. "Mary, you have quite a lot of information on Mayan culture and only 15 minutes have gone by. How did you manage to get two pages of notes so quickly?" Mary replies, "Well, I used the dictionary, our social studies text, and an encyclopedia." The teacher speaks to the whole class, "Class, if you were on Mary's writing team, where else would you think of doing your research?" Hands fly into the air and the students discuss using the Internet, going to the school library, calling the local library, etc. The teacher turns to Mary and says, "Mary, would you mind showing me your paper in 15 minutes? I'm anxious to see what you achieve in that time limit, here in class. I am also looking forward to seeing how many other sources you can incorporate from outside of class." Typically, students begin to want the teacher to see their papers in 15 minutes and they begin to see how many other ways they can bring information into the "whole class." It is not uncommon for Mary to go home and work on this paper even though there is no outside assignment. Mary and her colleagues are learning to respect each other for their ability to contribute to each other's ideas. *Multiple students helping to acquire multiple ideas about a topic provides a formal level of respect for Mary's learning as well as for the others in the classroom.* Mary and her peers are also learning to evaluate what they know and how to assess their own ways to learn by using multiple sources.

Positive critique is part of the classroom process. The students learn through the way the teacher models how to assign positive meaning and through class discussions on how critique provides positive feedback. Rules protect individuals from judging and using devaluation while fostering assertive ways to establish a win-win way to receive feedback. Chapter Eight describes more of this group process.

Activity

1. **Explain why it is important to evaluate others as well as oneself.**
2. **Describe how the evaluation of others' works and products increases learning and therefore improves the development of a formal conceptualization of "respect."**

Summary

Assessment is a form of evaluation that allows the student rather than the products to be respected. *Teachers may use knowledge about development and language to create criteria about assessment.* Even though content standards are necessary to see what concepts are to be targeted, increasing students' conceptual learning also builds skills and represents how the child is learning. The student's personal best begins to develop from what the student is able to understand about his or her work. Language improves through cognitive stages of development therefore increasing the way the students use language to communicate thoughtfully about themselves as well as others. Self-assessment as well as critique of others' works becomes a valuable part of the learning process.

Assessment fits into an authoritative classroom where the student experiences the role of teacher, assessor, evaluator, learner, contributor, etc. Assessment through these roles provides multiple authentic opportunities.

REFERENCES

Arwood, E. & Brown, M. 1997. *Administrative Manual on How to Assess Classroom Materials, Teaching Effectiveness, and Learning.* Portland, OR: APRICOT, Inc.

Chapter Eight
Learner Outcomes

Upon completion of this chapter the reader will be able to do the following:

1. Describe a variety of techniques to set up a responsive classroom.
2. Describe the importance of group identity to the individual's need for respect.
3. Explain the authoritative culture of group respect.
4. Give examples on how to use **the language of RESPECT** for the whole group as well as the individual.
5. Discuss planning a classroom based on **RESPECT**: *the Right of Each Student to Participate in an Environment of Communicative Thoughtfulness.*
6. Explain how the group process is developed through language used in the classroom.
7. Describe how the group is assessed for its identity and communicative thoughtfulness.

CHAPTER EIGHT

Group Respect

How do we use group language to foster respect?

The student sits in the classroom wanting to belong...
The adult knows not how to belong.
The community is a place for both...
Only when each one's "self" develops from within.

The child climbs onto the busy city bus. It's an US American city and so the child sits in the nearest seat. At the next stop, an elderly man slowly enters the bus, but he must stand because there are no seats. For the US student, he has learned the system well...each person has the individual right to be on the bus and to occupy the seat of his choice. Across the globe, a child climbs on a crowded bus and sits down in a nearby seat. An elderly person climbs aboard and surveys the crowd and purposely stands in front of the young child. The young child stands allowing the elderly person to sit. Both smile at each other out of respect for the role each plays in life.

The child in the second scenario feels a sense of pride in being selected to be the person to provide a seat for the elder. The child has gained respect from all around him. The elder feels happy to have given the youth the opportunity to practice respect and honor. Both have gained an important piece of identity that will and already has contributed to the well being of that group. On the other hand, the US child has gained only the personal satisfaction of having a seat. In fact, the US child's gains are self-centered. Such focus on personal needs create more opportunity for the US child to withdraw into his own world to satisfy his needs, at all costs. The US child sees the elder person as being unsuitable to be recognized and considered. The US child finds satisfaction in being a person who is able to not only sit, but to race past all others to sit in the front of the bus. The differences between the US child and the elder increase. The child and elder lose the positive relationship that could exist between the two people, one at the beginning of life and one at the end of life. The US child belongs more to exclusive groups. Membership in an exclusive group means that the US child is seeking to be better than those who don't live up to the US child's expectations. These groups include others who are like the US child, able to obtain a seat first, who are the same age, who have the same interests, etc. The child from another place on this globe becomes more inclusive of grouping. This child expands his relationship to include others who may or may not be just like the child. This child expects to include others from different ages into his life.

The purpose of this chapter is to provide the reader with techniques, insights, and examples of how to create a classroom in which the authoritative system (see Chapter Five) works to develop each person's identity within a group while allowing each person to develop a shared sense of power as being an unique and active member or learner within the group. In this way, the classroom is not a room with 30 unidentified students, but the classroom consists of 30 individual students whose contributions make up the group. The group has its own identity based on trust, respect, and consideration for the individuals who make up the group. When both the individual and the group are honored, then it's a "win-win" situation for all parties making life a "fun," life long adventure of self-discovery. In this type of win-win classroom, the student develops the tools for not just "making it through school," but for "reaching" out into adulthood as a life long learner. The student learns lessons about the community, about how to be *responsive* to others' needs, about how to contribute to the whole, even about how to be a member of a family that might be different from the way the child was raised. *Respect for the group becomes a positive way of assigning meaning for the respect of the individuals within the group. Respect becomes the basis for creating a group atmosphere where all individuals are included.*

Authoritative Development of the Group

As previously defined, **the authoritative environment is one of shared power.** *The individuals within the group are supportive of each other as well as nurturing and protective of each other.* Within this type of win-win classroom, the *individual student is proactive in learning and the group is responsive to the needs of the whole class.* **The purpose of developing a *responsive* classroom is to create a microcosm of society; a group of individuals who reflect the values, beliefs, and behaviors that are an accepted part of the culture.** Chapters Four and Five described the characteristics of the responsive classroom. Examples, insights, and language techniques are offered in this chapter as ways to develop an authoritatively responsive classroom. The responsive classroom is based on the previously described philosophy about **respect** for the individual learner, the way the learner thinks, the learner's social and cognitive development, as well as the learner's self-constituents. A classroom based on learning principles (Chapters One and Two) and an authoritative philosophy becomes *responsive* to individual as well as group needs (see Oldfather, 1994, for another description of the responsive classroom culture).

To establish such a classroom, the teachers and administrators must also have developed an individual self-identity as being unique so as to be authoritative. In other words, the first step is for the teacher and/or administrator to be sure that he or she is ready for respecting the process (see Chapter One). The second step is to see if the teacher's individual values are part of the way the class is set up. Ideally, the more authoritative the classroom, the more balance there is between the power of the individuals and the power of the group. Table 8.1 provides a recap of the characteristics previously described. These characteristics are added to the personal characteristics of the adult learner as described in Chapter One. The relationship between the teacher and the students creates the authoritative type of management and learning system. For **respect** to be the basis of a classroom, the chosen class type is authoritative, not authoritarian, in nature. Remember that the authors are using **RESPECT** as an acronym for the *Right of Each Student to Participate in an Environment of Communication Thoughtfulness*; and, it is through language that such a classroom is established.

TABLE 8.1. What Does The Classroom Look Like?

Authoritative Characteristics	*Authoritarian Characteristics*
• Choices are real: "I chose X."	• Choices are controlled: "I had to..."
• Power is freely shared: All behavior is viewed as a contribution	• Power is controlled: The rules are preset and disciplined by the adult
• Learning is seen as an intrinsic	• Tasks and behaviors are externally rewarded
• Communication is respected and all communication is validated	• There is a time and way to communicate as determined by the adult
• The class members are all equally respected and valued; "Authority doesn't come with size, just because the adult is taller doesn't make the adult more valuable."	• The class is adult directed
• The class has an internal value and attachment for the group.	• The class has no identity but through the individual members.

Each of the aforementioned characteristics will be discussed so that the reader, as a teacher or administrator, may analyze his or her own "self" in terms of current philosophy and beliefs prior to deciding to try to implement a "responsive classroom of individual and group respect." In other words, the teacher might read down the authoritative characteristic list and ask whether or not these characteristics pertain to the teacher's own classroom. If the teacher realizes that there are some areas that are *not* authoritative, then those areas become ones that can be refined. *The more authoritative the classroom, the better the group respect.* As each of these characteristics is discussed, the reader may want to try to apply the discussion to his or her own philosophy and classroom.

Choices are Real

From an authoritative parenting system, a child learns to have choices. By the time the child is 7-11 years of age (see Chapter Three for social development), the child has developed the values of some group. Usually these values belong to a school group, a family unit, a community agency such as athletics, or a religious group. When a child feels successful and supported by one or more of these groups, then the child has a sense of belonging. This belonging to a group is what characterizes the preadolescent's development. If a child does not feel like he or she belongs, then the child moves into adolescence and adulthood trying to fit into some group. The authors estimate that eighty-percent of the US population of adults are still trying to fit. This means that many of the adult educators who are working with students are still looking for an identity that will allow them to feel like they fit into a greater group or culture. This level of psychosocial development as an adult results in feelings of insecurity and inadequacy that promote a lack of respect for oneself as well as for others.

If a person is unsure of being a "competent" human being and being an honored group member, then this person may feel the need to defend actions or position. The teacher's defensive posture may result in internally developed stress from the role confusion between the teacher, as the adult, and the role of the student, as the child or adolescent. For example, the authoritarian teacher may tell the students that the project will have points deducted for any extra work such as adding a cover page or including illustrations. A self-confident teacher will encourage students to make choices that go beyond the immediate minimum requirements. In this way, the student has choices that are real. The student is able to choose a variety of ways to represent more than the expected minimum. Bringing outsiders into the classroom offers more validation as well as more opportunities to use language to assign meaning to the student's competence. Formal concepts such as responsibility, pride, independence, respect are all easier to demonstrate when there are more people, choices, and outside agencies involved.

Using language that represents "real choices" is powerful. For example, "Who has an idea about how to create an experiment to measure density of water?" For this question to be valued, the person asking the question must sincerely want the listeners' ideas to be offered. If the person asking the question wants a specific answer, then the question loses its potential of having individuals contribute ideas that create real choices.

For language to offer real choices, the opportunity to make a choice must really exist. For example, it is not a choice for students to bring weapons to class. Therefore, when a teacher says, "You may bring anything to class to support your project," the statement is not completely accurate. The teacher and students need to have a discussion about appropriate ideas for projects as well what types of objects or props that can be brought to school. Teachers need to monitor more closely those students with preoperational to concrete levels of language to be sure that their choices match societally acceptable behaviors. Remember that a preoperational student is self-centered and thinks only in the here and now. The concrete student may be rule governed but not able to take another person's perspective. Both the preoperational and concrete level thinkers are at risk for engaging in behavior that results in consequences that may harm someone else. *Using language to make choices real also shares power among group members.*

Activity

1. **Define "real choice" as it relates to an authoritative classroom.**
2. **Give examples of real choices.**

Power is Freely Shared

To create an environment where power is freely shared, the classroom must be open to outside influences...parents, teachers, principals, legislators, etc. Examples are provided later in the chapter for how other people might be accepted and incorporated into the classroom. ***Power is knowledge!*** The more knowledge each student has about why he or she is doing what is expected, the more freely shared is the classroom power. The students must know what their roles are within the classroom and freely be able to exchange roles so that all students are able to freely participate. There should be no secrets about how to get information or how to solve a problem or how to learn.

Each person within the classroom is an open book for all others to enjoy! Everyone is a resource! The students and teacher are in the room for nine months together, why not make the experience pleasant? Thirty heads are better at providing more power, knowledge, resourcing, and fun than one head! Sharing solutions, tasks, and situations provide individuals with freedom and cooperation from an environment that nurtures, protects, and encourages one another. Everyone is invited to help each other learn. Language is an open tool for learning!

Language is used to invite others to contribute (Chapters One and Six) and language is also used to share power freely. Authoritarian comments such as "Go look in your book!" is not acceptable. *Free-flowing open communication that provides real choices for everyone to be a source of power is critical to a classroom based on* **the language of RESPECT.** For example, one teacher enthusiastically seeks activities that are new and challenging; free from preconceptions, prior experiences and that, with shared power, allows students to be successful. One activity is diagramming sentences for fourth graders. The students soon discover that few, if anyone, in their families have had successful experiences with diagramming. Students use their stories and projects to identify the language parts of speech. Because the words belong to the students, then simple definitions for parts of speech are easy. "Nouns, for example, are the people, places, and things in your story." Students soon find that they are able to identify the parts of speech from their own use of language. The teacher then begins to randomly give opportunities to students to identify parts of speech on social studies, science or any other written material in class. Students lead these sessions and assist in calling on each other and giving explanations. Examples are voluntarily written on the board for classmates. These sessions are fast paced and videotaping is offered to all volunteers. No one sleeps through the student led sessions!

After students are comfortable in identifying parts of speech in language segments, then students are shown how to take those pieces apart and put them into a graphic called a diagram. These visual structures give students ample opportunity to see written language in a different form. Complex sentences become a game to see who can challenge each other (as a group) as well as the teacher and family members. As students become more confident, more options are added such as gerunds, predicate adjectives, or infinitives. These latter options are offered to those who want the challenge. Students create charts, poster examples to hang in the hallways, and games to take home to families to show their skills. Peers and the teacher offer praise to all.

The smiles of the "new learners" would melt a glacier. These students are "new learners" because they are successful at something new. *By sharing the power of language through activities that are designed to be fun and challenging, students become eager to participate and more relaxed.* Written language is more of a graphic game and less of an auditory task. Students use their mental visual language as graphics to share knowledge about diagramming. Some use colors to code and decode for their peers a particular part of speech. These are rearranged in sentences that are sometimes "hilarious." Even foreign terms are used. The power in these activities is not with diagramming, but with the way to share one's knowledge with others. Students learn that they are powerful with their language!

Activity

1. Describe "shared power."
2. Give examples of ways that classroom knowledge or power is shared outside the classroom.

Learning is Intrinsic

As previously described (Chapter Four), *learning is a process of individuals organizing internal meaning from group members who assign external meaning to behaviors. The external assignment of meaning offers individuals a variety of ways to create, solve, act upon, and respond to material and to situations.* The higher the individuals' cognitive levels of understanding, the greater the learning, and, the better each individual learns within the whole group. For example, all students feeling comfortable with their contributions to the group results in a group pride where all students are included rather than some being excluded. Such responsibility for each person's own learning contributes to the wellness of the group process. Students begin to take ownership for their work. "I don't seem to understand that math concept. I looked in the book but I didn't see an explanation. Would you have time to explain the problem to me?" *The external assignment of meaning shifts to an internal understanding of how to acquire meaning.*

Individuals within the responsive classroom use their multiple opportunities for language representations as ways to shift external assignment of meaning to an intrinsic understanding of concepts. For example, in many classrooms the student is dependent on the teacher telling the student if the student's work meets the teacher's standards, or if the students have expressed the "right" answer. However, when students begin to learn at a higher cognitive level then the students also begin to show that the process of learning is more important. It is not uncommon to find that the intrinsic need to learn more is expressed in a responsive classroom. Examples follow.

Upon turning in a 60 page report (20-30 pages is suggested), the sixth grade student says, "I wished I had had more time to write about ancient Egypt. Just before I finished my paper I found another exciting source." Or, a second grader says, "I have too many ideas to write only 10 pages." Or, a college student says, "I have submitted my paper in a condensed form to be published." These are not exceptions, but how the majority of students in an authoritative classroom *respond* to the challenge of learning. These students view the learning process as more important than the separate requirements in order to receive a grade for the product.

Activity

1. **Define intrinsic learning.**
2. **Give examples of how to foster intrinsic learning.**

All Communication is Respected and Validated

"All communication is respected" means that all forms of communication are accepted…blurting, raising a hand, stomping a foot, etc. Then the communication must be assigned a meaning that fits socially. The child who blurts out is given the opportunity to share his great ideas with others (a more complete example follows in a later section of this chapter) or a child who always has his hand up is given strategies for taking visual notes so as to offer more information to the group in fewer pieces. Even adults are often relieved when someone else asks the question that the adult is "afraid" to ask. *By accepting all forms of behavior as forms of communication, learners feel validated for trying to communicate their ideas or needs with others.*

If all behavior communicates, then it is the adult's responsibility to assign meaning to behavior. So, the teacher or parent assigns meaning to any behavior. By assigning meaning to the behavior, the learner quickly finds out what is expected. For example, a student has his feet draped over the hand railing at the third step into the building. His arms are stretched out to the hand railing on the opposite side. He is truly draped from one side of the steps to the other side of the steps. Not only is such a position a potential fall for the student, but his position also blocks others from using the steps. So, what does his behavior communicate? Using knowledge about cognitive stages, it is apparent that this student is making himself part of the steps, a preoperational grounding. This type of functioning also means that he does not have meaning for the rules about using the steps, and he does not understand that he may fall, or that others may need to use the steps. By recognizing the student's level of functioning, then meaning can be assigned to his behavior so as to give him more knowledge. "Jerome, I see you with your feet and hands on the step rails. I see that you are using your feet and hands to move down the steps. But, when you move down the steps with your feet on the rails, then others can't use the steps. So, you need to put your hands on this rail and your feet on this (pointing) step. (He is helped to his feet). Now, you can use your hands to tell your feet where you are, and, you can use your feet to tell your body where you are. I will walk next to you so you can move down the steps." This student quickly uses other people to help him walk down the stairs. After a couple of tries, he is able to quickly walk down the stairs by himself. If his behavior were punished instead of assigned positive meaning, he probably would still look like a student "goofing around" on the stairs.

Activity

1. **Explain how all behavior is communication.**
2. **Explain how positive meaning is assigned to all behavior. Give examples.**

All Class Members are Equally Respected and Valued

Sometimes, teachers see all students as equal, but the teacher as "unequal." The unequal partner, the teacher, chooses what roles he or she wants to play. The classroom based on respect is designed to allow all activity roles within the classroom to be played by all members...teacher or students or parents or community visitors. However, there is a recognized unequal level of experience, knowledge, and wisdom. The adult sets the boundaries, understands limits, and determines appropriateness of all activities, behaviors, etc. The student is considered unequal in knowledge because of less experience. So, it is the adult's professional role to be like a parent...to nurture, protect, and support all individual student's needs.

In a classroom, based on respect, the adult provides the student with a level of responsiveness to all nurturance, protection, and support. The parenting teacher provides a form of structure that respects the roles of students and teachers. In other words, all human beings are equally valuable; however, their needs, desires, and wants may be different. *Such differences are honored by setting a parenting tone of authoritative discipline through a structure that provides a rationale or explanation for why or why not a task, behavior, or academic activity is acceptable to the whole group.* The students then share the power of the knowledge within the group so the group begins to take on an identity. By honoring differences, the students see the adults as consistent. Consistency is developed by explaining the reasons for behavior. The students then trust the adult expectancy levels. This trust allows learners to experience empowerment, personal growth, self-confidence, and wider comfort zones. The responsive classroom uses the **language of RESPECT** to create spiraling positive growth!

Activity

1. **Explain how all class members are equally valued and respected.**
2. **Describe authoritative parenting as a way to respect individuals within the group.**

Internal Group Attachment

Educators often think of individuals bonding psychologically to a parent or significant other at a very early age of infancy. However, individuals may become attached to a home or classroom in a similar way. Students who feel like they fit begin to talk about what they can do to help the whole group. They talk about the classroom as their group.

They refer to the activities and the students by name and by affirming use of language. "My favorite elementary grade was the fourth grade. We had a great teacher. She taught us all to respect the way we learn. We had fun parties and I learned a lot about pioneers, the solar system..., I really miss my fourth grade classroom." Interestingly, this student had the same classmates, for the most part, in fifth grade but it was an authoritarian classroom, therefore the culture of the classroom was different even though the students were the same.

The aforementioned characteristics are translated into behavior that is represented by the way a person talks or uses language. In other words, unless feelings of honor, respect, charity, thoughtfulness, kindness, etc., are internalized, the outward behaviors can hardly reflect these positive enhancing qualities. As one student so aptly put it, "You can't give what you don't have." The following statements are provided as examples of how the adult communicates authoritarian feelings of insecurity. "The curriculum is responsible for how one chooses to teach." "The supervisor won't let me talk with the students." "I never liked math when I was in school." *In order for the students to be responsive to the curriculum and to the value of school, the communication must be thoughtful.* The teacher's language must shift from being authoritarian to authoritative resulting in statements that are full of possibility. "I like the way you work on your math." "We have some new curricular ideas that I am looking forward to trying." "I always look forward to talking with my students."

In the following section, the statements that shut down thoughtful communication will be given first...followed by how the language can be changed to show respect for the group process. In this way, the language characteristics are authoritarian in nature will be offered first, followed by language that is authoritative in nature. The language represents which characteristics are being valued. *Group attachment comes from language that respects group involvement whereas authoritarian language tends to control the individual separate from the group.* Again, the authoritarian examples are provided first.

<u>*Authoritarian Phrasing*</u>
- *"I had to do that job."*

This statement implies that the person had no choice in deciding whether to perform a task or job. The job controls the person. There is no opportunity for the person making the statement to honor the job or the reason for doing it. Therefore, the situation allows for little growth or learning. "Puppets make very poor philosophers." This statement means the educator lacks self-respect and consideration for the group.

- *"The curriculum tells me what to do and how to do it."*

This statement suggests that the teacher doesn't have the knowledge base or security to separate what he or she does from what the source of knowledge (the curriculum) offers. This person is often "lost" when there is no solution to a child's needs or no solution to a "next step" for a child. It's almost as if the adult hasn't found a way to fit into a professional realm of resourcing. In other words, the teacher hasn't had the authoritative experiences of how to be a unique person in a professional role. This teacher can't walk in the students' shoes and cannot see her or himself as a source of problem resolution or knowledge.

- *"That parent is such a pain...she is always at school."*

This statement suggests that the parent is causing the adult speaker pain. In other words, the adult feels that the parent is responsible for how the adult responds to what the parent does. The adult has no choice in how to respond to the parent. The parent's actions are therefore responsible for how the adult feels. This need to make the parent responsible for the teacher's feelings suggests that the educator can not separate his or her own acts from the other person's actions, the parent. The teacher wants to be able to control the parent in an authoritarian way much like the educator wants to control the students in the classroom. The defensive posture of the teacher suggests that the teacher's controls are "demigods" in that the teacher knows what is best for the parent and the student. This type of control shuts down the communication between the parent and the educators so that potential allies are now enemies. Instead of community welfare, there are community lines of battle. The student learns the battle lines of demarcation. The student knows that the parent and the child are viewed as the same person. The parent is a pain, so the child feels that the teacher sees the child also as a "pain." The educator who establishes these groupings (parents vs. teachers vs. students) is trying to control the teacher's relationship with all parties. Unfortunately, the control of other group members results in the identity of the whole group being eroded. The responsiveness of the group is divided by this educator's need to control the parent, thus lacking the willingness to share the power. The individual parent who is "not a pain" is put into an exclusive group much like the students. The classroom tone becomes "smaller sets of groupings" rather than a whole group of working individuals. There are exclusive rather than inclusive groupings. A student who tries to align with the teacher or parent is put into a position of making choices. To put a student in a position of "choosing" between home and school is immature, negative, and counter-productive. The student needs adults to be consistent, objective, and equally aligned with the learner's group identity. Everyone loses in these tugs-of-war based on selfishness and disrespect.

- *"That mother is a real problem."*
This statement shows how insecure the teacher or administrator feels in attempting to control other people. The teacher has a need to fit and to be right from an authoritarian philosophy. This mother has asked for something and the response has been to "make her the problem" so that the mother's need isn't heard. To hear her would mean that the educator would have to negotiate a position. The mother would have to be validated. If the educator does not feel self-validated as a unique person, then the educator must fit into a group, and the educator cannot validate her. To be unique would mean letting go of control and thus hearing and validating someone else.

By making the mother a problem, then the educator has created an external problem that no longer requires the educator's attention. In this way, the teacher has made a grouping...those who are problems...that exclude the teacher from having to be part. The teacher or administrator can further boost support for this grouping by other phrases such as "Mom undermines my teaching" or "She always discredits my judgments." The teacher wants to reinforce his or her standing in the educational community by devaluing the mother as a problem. The educators who listen and participate with this devaluation also feel the need to align themselves into a group much like the preadolescent who picks only those who students who can kick the ball for the team and then grumbles when the student who can't kick is added to the team. There lacks a respect for others' needs when there is an individual need to validate one's one thinking. The tone of the classroom becomes one where the individual students compete *against* the other class members to become validated individuals.

- *"That parent is never satisfied."*

This statement suggests that the educator can only be satisfied by what the educator believes to be the right way to do things. This belief is very authoritarian and suggests that the educator must be in control of the solutions or resolutions of concerns. Again, the inability of the educator to share in the process results in the teacher being the only expert. The parent is outside the politically correct group. The educators have the child for nine months. The parent has the child for a lifetime. This type of authoritarian statement and underlying belief suggests that the parent's views are not respected and the child will have to choose which group, family or parents, are right. There is no winner in this power struggle between parents and the educators, only a loss of resolution of the concerns and validations for the parents involved. The parents and educators are not afforded the opportunity to grow as equally contributing members of the school community. Respect for the parent and the parent's needs is challenged. The choice splits the classroom into those who are right from those who are wrong.

- *"She (the parent) bothers everyone."*
  This statement suggests that the teacher or educator feels that there is little choice over how to incorporate this parent into the community setting. In fact, the teacher or administrator sees the parent as an outsider...a person who has no business at school or in the activities of the student's affairs. Open door policies are not a choice for this teacher and parent. The faculty, staff, and administration belong to an elitist club in which the door windows are even covered much like an exclusive club, for example, the Ku Klux Klan. The operations of the classroom are "secret" like the family secrets about abuse. This defensive "closed door" attitude suggests that the educators are the only valuable adults in the students' lives. Parents stay away and perpetuate the unhealthy system of trying to not "rock the boat" because someone might be upset. This system of educators creating their room in a way to prevent the gifts of outsiders results in a dysfunctional authoritarian educational system based on deficits, not assets. There is little opportunity for the parents to give to the system--all are losers in this power struggle. Respect for all points of view as well as all others' needs are diminished. The classroom tone or atmosphere is one that fosters a lack of sharing or resourcing. There also exists a lack of trust among all parties in this type of environment.

- *"The kid doesn't fit."*
  Whenever a teacher or educator does not see a child or student as being able to be included, then the teacher creates a greater division among the students. The students quickly learn how to make the same value judgments, which makes each student struggle to fit. Such struggling to feel better about oneself results in "put downs" and the devaluation of others. In other words, if a child fits into the group, then the child must be okay. If the child doesn't fit, then the child is not okay. Similarly, the educator believes that it is his or her

right to decide who fits or who doesn't fit. In the US American way, the group consists of those who fit...the group does not change to allow all to fit. The teacher or educator perpetuates this "fitting" or membership criteria through his or her own need to fit. The teacher is afraid to say, "I don't know how to reach this child." Instead the teacher says, "The child doesn't fit." Otherwise the teacher feels that others may judge the teacher as not being a "good teacher." Respect for the child's diversity is challenged because the teacher does not have the tools to reach the child.

- *"He upsets the whole class."*

The educator who makes this remark has taken upon her or himself to own the feelings for each person in the class. The students haven't said that a particular kid upsets the class. The teacher has not asked the other students if a particular child upsets the whole class. The teacher judges the child's behavior as "upsetting." Furthermore, this statement suggests that the educator feels insecure about meeting a particular child's needs. It is easier for the educator to excuse the child's behavior as a problem than it is to work the child into the class. Valuing a child by providing the child with the opportunity to be a part of the group allows the child to fit into the group. Not allowing the child to fit results in all parties losing as a group. Only those individual members who fit membership criteria gain personal benefits. Respect for how important the group is to the student's individual needs is challenged. The child's behavior must be reassigned a meaning that will allow the child to fit and the group to include him or her into the classroom.

Summary of Authoritarian Language

The language used to separate and to conquer the respect of the group is authoritarian in nature and sounds much like the previous examples. Because the speaker's own needs, values, beliefs are emphasized over the group process, there is a breakdown in the way the group functions as a whole. In addition to the aforementioned examples, the authoritarian language has a sort of a "blame" tone to it. For example, "He takes up too much time." "That kid pushes my button." Sometimes, a teacher might list a string of blame statements about one student. For example, "He takes up too much of my time. He doesn't have the skills. He is just like his brother. That whole family is like that. I'm glad I don't have that kid. That kid doesn't what to learn. That kid is going to be in prison some day. That kid is going to destroy my class. Thank goodness there's only eight more months in the school year with him. His sister was so nice that I enjoyed working with her. The parents are so nice, I don't know what happened to this kid. Oh, wait until that next teacher gets him. This kid should be in the military." *Authoritarian language lacks tolerance for individual differences of the students, their parents, and even colleagues.* Such language statements aimed at students or colleagues sound like this: "I get sick every time I look at that kid." "I can't stand Mrs. Smith." "You are so anti-social; you never eat in the faculty room." These authoritarian types of language limit choices, divide classrooms into subgroups, and devalue individual's needs. *In order to create a responsive classroom that fosters group wellness and individual uniqueness, the communication must be thoughtful for the student and the student's environment. The student must feel like choices are real and the educator must feel like there are real choices. Such shared power for enhanced choice development comes from creating group language that is authoritative. The section provides authoritative choices of language.*

Authoritative Phrasing

The language used to create a group identity sounds very open to all ideas and to all differences. The teacher is secure and comfortable and the language is natural. It sounds like this. "I see Mrs. Key is on her way to the school. She must have something important to say. I will give her 30 seconds or the opportunity to set an appointment." "I really enjoy working with Felix. He has so many interests. Some are like his brothers' interests but I learned that he likes to ride horses and his brothers don't like to ride." "Working with Manuel is a challenge. He always has something new to say." "Did you see Kenny's new drawing?

He brought a drawing of the hospital to school. He is quite artistic."
"Betsy has a new baby brother. She is really disappointed that he is not a
she." "The principal is bringing in a new speaker. I am looking forward
to hearing the speaker. I can always learn something from someone
else." "The new content standards are out. Great! I know I will be able to
use them." "Mr. Richards wants to bring some human hearts to school to
dissect. Great! We will work it into the curriculum." "Amelio brought a
bird to school today. We privately talked about why the school has a rule
about no pets. We then shared with the class why Amelio felt it was
important to bring the bird. The bird is like a baby brother to Amelio. He
even tucks the bird into bed at night by covering the perch. We then had
a class discussion about how we could share important pets with each
other without bringing them to school. Amelio suggested several ideas to
include drawing, photos, and writing a story. Chuck asked if we could do
a project on pets. The class discussed how the unit would fit into the
science projects. We then brainstormed and set up individual
assignments for their projects, etc." The following section will take the
reader through some of the authoritative ways to foster group respect
through communicative thoughtfulness. These language statements
replace the types of statements provided in the previous section.

- *"I see Mrs. Key. She is a very concerned parent."*
  The situation is that Mrs. Key comes very often to school. In an
  authoritarian system, these frequent visits might seem like they
  interrupt the teacher's **control** (see previous section). But, in the
  authoritative classroom of thoughtful communication and respect,
  the visits are viewed as the parent's need to share the power, the
  parent's knowledge about her child's needs, and to express the
  parent's own needs. Therefore, the respectful teacher communicates
  the boundaries and limits. "I see Mrs. Key is on her way into the
  school. She must have something important to say (validates Mrs.
  Key's needs as a person who is important to the child). I will give
  her 30 seconds (sets limits) or the opportunity to set an
  appointment." When the parent walks into the room, the teacher

quickly and enthusiastically says, "It is so good to see you. Your timing is good. I have just 30 seconds to chat or we could set up an appointment?" The educator keeps a mindful eye on the time and when 30 seconds are about up, the teacher says, "We need to set an appointment." The teacher grabs an appointment book and says, "What time is good for you?" Ironically speaking, most parents who frequent the classroom only need 30 seconds when they are approached with openness and encouragement and as the "experts" of their children. Some parents, like teachers, are really insecure and they need encouragement from authority figures, too. This is a win-win situation that allows the parent to grow as well as models respectful language for the students. *Such thoughtful communication allows a bridge to develop between the school and the home so that the child might find more than one group in which to fit.*

- *"I really enjoy working with Felix. He always offers me the opportunity to learn."*

Felix has a school history of being demanding of the teacher's time and energy. In an authoritarian system, Felix would be viewed as "demanding" and a "controller of someone else's time." His demands might even be seen as disruptive to the group process. He may even be referred for a diagnostic label such as Attention Deficit Hyperactive Disorder (ADHD). However, in an authoritative classroom that encourages respect of the whole child and works to incorporate or allow Felix to fit within the group, Felix's needs are viewed as usable strengths. "I really enjoy working with Felix. He has so many interests. Some of his interests are like his brother's interests (the teacher had the brother the year before) but some are unique to Felix. I learned that he likes to ride horses but his brother doesn't." Once the teacher has assessed Felix for his level of learning, has adjusted the classroom to meet the way he learns, and has assigned positive meaning to Felix's strengths, as well as all other students, Felix is no longer demanding. He is part of the group process because the teacher has allowed Felix to be respected.

Reassigning meaning to Felix's behavior as a strength helps Felix fit. The teacher will also need to be mindful of how Felix learns best (see Chapter Two) so that she can communicate the classroom needs the way that Felix will understand the teacher's language. This win-win setting becomes positive for Felix and the class. The classmates turn to Felix as an expert because of Felix's interests rather than trying to exclude him because he is different.

- *"Working with Manuel allows me to help other class members learn better."*

Manuel came to the third grade as a student who always had his hand up during class, blurted out ideas, seemed easily frustrated, and lacked specific skills in math. The authoritarian classroom would want to see Manuel tested for impulsivity, perhaps ADD or ADHD, and remediated for math. In an authoritative classroom that focuses on the individual's needs as well as the group needs, Manuel is viewed as needing some help in learning how to be a part of the group as well as in doing the math the way that Manuel learns, not the way the teacher insists on teaching. "Working with Manuel is a positive challenge for me. He always has something new to say. This gives me the opportunity to learn how to help him the best. The other day he said he needed to see the numbers, but the numbers were already written on the board. So, while the class began the math, I walked over to his desk and asked him what he meant that he needed to see the numbers. He said that he couldn't see the numbers on the board. I began writing the numbers on his paper and he said that he could see the numbers, but he didn't know what they meant. So, I began to use some drawn symbols (picture symbols represent the numerical concept) to match with the numbers. Manuel asked to come in after school and do some more math. I was thrilled at the opportunity to see him grow." Using what a child says and does is an opportunity for everyone to learn to respect the needs of others. When others' needs are respected the group grows as a whole. The group also sees Manuel in a positive light. Even parents begin to see

Manuel for his strengths. It should be noted that Manuel's eyesight is okay. The problem was in processing the language for the meaning of numbers.

- *"Did you see the intricacy of Kenny's drawing?"*

Kenny has been referred for reading and writing help. He is in sixth grade, but he is reading at a pre-primer level. His writing is negligible at best. The teacher in an authoritarian system often becomes frustrated at not being able to control Kenny's learning. Such frustration results in comments of blame about how "Kenny needs to try harder," "the parents need to read to him," etc. He draws beautiful pictures *all* the time. From the earlier chapters, the reader probably recognizes that Kenny has a unique strength...these pictures are meaningful and he can't learn to use sound connected to letters to understand what he reads. Therefore, Kenny thinks in pictures, not sound words. His reading program needs to shift from phonics to one that allows Kenny to picture the idea or concept in relationship to the printed pattern (for example, Arwood and McInroy, 1994; Arwood and Unruh, 1997). Furthermore, the teacher's language can shift from blame to acceptance. "Kenny, I see that you like to draw and I am really impressed with your drawings. Let's use your drawings to figure out how to take the print off the page. You draw what we were talking about in class. Then I will print the ideas that go with the picture you've drawn after you tell me about your drawing..." The focus shifts from blaming Kenny or his parents to accepting Kenny's gifts as opportunities for respecting his learning system and for helping him to feel successful as a reader and writer. Instead of complaining to others about Kenny drawing all of the time and then punishing Kenny for his strength by taking away his drawing avenue, the drawings become a language vehicle for Kenny to learn to read and write. Kenny's elaborate drawings are an asset to the group. Kenny can become the expert illustrator who is assigned the task to help others also learn to draw. When talking to other teachers, instead of authoritarian statements filling the air with

"All that kid does is draw. If he spent half the time reading as drawing he would be okay" there would be positive statements such as "Did you see Kenny's latest drawing that he brought to school? It was of a hospital. He is really artistic." Using thoughtful communication to show respect for Kenny's differences in learning also respects Kenny for what he *can* contribute to the group. The group also learns that Kenny is part of the classroom because Kenny is successful in his own way, just like the others in the group. Even though it is important for the educator to recognize how the child learns and to use methods to match, it is **more** important for the educator to work from the child's needs. The best reading methods for Kenny will fail him, if the educator does not recognize that Kenny can be unique and can learn to read in a way that supports Kenny's learning system. Furthermore, the group of individuals needs to see Kenny as a contributor to the group reading process. His individual success will not feel comfortable to Kenny if the group does not recognize his ability to learn to read as a unique strength.

- *"Betsy has a new baby brother!"*

Often, when teachers do not "know" the students in the classroom, then the opportunities for understanding the individual student's needs is bypassed in the authoritarian system. In a group where communication is open and the others in the group are accessible, then knowing each other forms the group's identity. For example, Betsy is a second grade student. One morning, she does not act like her usual happy self. Something is not the same. In an authoritarian classroom, this difference in Betsy might be viewed as "a bad day" or rationalized for her as "Oh, she is feeling left out since her new brother came." Bad days can actually become months or years. In a classroom where individuals are respected for their gifts and strengths, changes in individuals are also honored or respected. "Betsy, how are you doing today (stated one-on-one)?" She gloomily sighs, "Fine." "Well, I see that your face is not smiling. Why are you not smiling today?" Betsy says, "cuz." The teacher pauses, "Maybe you could draw for me what you are thinking about." "Okay." Betsy draws a picture. The teacher asks her to tell the story about her picture. Betsy says that she has a brother, not a sister. She wanted a sister to share her room and to play with her after school. So, the teacher looks at the picture and says, "Um, I wonder what I could do with a baby brother?!" Betsy begins to talk about all the things that her baby brother does. The teacher says, "Wow, I didn't know baby brothers do so much. Would you like to make a book about your brother to share with the class?" Betsy is smiling and nodding, but still struggling with the loss. The teacher adds, "I know a story book about a baby brother and a girl just like you. I will go to the library and ask the librarian to help me find it. Then, maybe we can read that book at story time." The book is about a girl who is also disappointed about a baby brother not being a sister. This teacher knows that unless time is spent with Betsy's personal needs, then Betsy will not be able to solidly contribute to the group's needs. By using thoughtful communication to bring Betsy back into the group, Betsy's personal needs are also respected. *Time spent on personal needs is an investment into the group as well as the individual. The individuals become responsive to the teacher and to the other individuals. The class sees that the teacher cares and is caring. They learn to show "caring" too.* The group becomes a caring, nurturing, environment for safe learning. Trusting and risking become part of the group process of individuals responding to others' needs.

- *"The principal is bringing in a speaker...."*
In an authoritarian system where the classroom teacher "knows" all about his or her class, there is little thought about how others' contributions might fit. Teachers often use language about speakers, principals, parents, etc., that indicate that anything presented is "already known." This suggests that the educator is really not open to lessons outside the knowledge or content of the curricular material. In other words, the teacher feels that he or she has all the

content and knows how to run the classroom, what else is there? When the presenter begins to talk, the educator must defend his or her own knowledge by making sure that the presenter's ideas either totally fit ("I already do all of that") or don't fit ("I don't know why we had to listen to this garbage"). But there are group lessons to learn with a presenter. Such lessons might include "I wonder how these ideas would affect the students in my class?' "I wonder what the students would think of these ideas." "I wonder if we could get together as a group of teachers and discuss how we will use the presenter's idea. In this way, someone else might have picked up something I missed." Statements that are open and thoughtful show that there is always something to learn. "The principal is bringing in a new speaker. I am looking forward to hearing the speaker. I can always learn something from someone else." Even lessons of validation and support can be part of what others present. In order to set up a classroom where group discussions are honored; individual's ideas that show dissent, self-evaluation, or critique are viewed positively as part of the learning process. *Communicative thoughtfulness comes out of an authoritative viewpoint of shared power and respect for others. This respect for others goes beyond the walls of the classroom.* Examples of ways that others' contributions are used to foster respect in the classroom are offered later in this chapter.

- *"The new content standards are out for me to read."*
Many states, districts, schools, and their teachers and parents are struggling with new content standards or essential skill goals and objectives. An authoritarian position might be one of feeling controlled by others...the district, the committees, the legislature, etc. However, in an environment that promotes respect as part of the process, all individuals are honored and all positions respected. It is each person's responsibility to establish as much of a "win-win" atmosphere as possible. So, even when the teachers feel bypassed or overlooked, they can still exude confidence for themselves as they

work within the system or group. "The new content standards are out. Great! I know I will be able to use them." As educators, parents, and students become more authoritative, there is a group response of respecting the individuals. Teachers are asked for their opinions just like the authoritative classroom where all students are respected. *But, to get to the point of shared power, each individual must use thoughtful communication to try to develop more of a respected environment. This thoughtful communication shows a shared viewpoint for those who set up the standards as well as those who are asked to implement.*

- *"Dr. Allens wants to bring human hearts to school...."*

All of these examples are from real scenarios. This one is no different. A local cardiologist was invited by the students to come and talk about the heart. He brought beef hearts for demonstration. When he found the students armed with thoughtful questions, acts of appreciation for his time and knowledge, and positive interaction, he then arranged to bring human hearts for dissection by the students. The cardiologist brought a team of nurses and technicians to assist the fifth grade students. As the reader knows, the cardiologist had to go through significant effort and paper work to bring human body parts. If the health curriculum were evenly divided among all of the concepts to be taught that year, the class would have spent only one week on the circulatory system. Because of Dr. Allens' generous willingness to contribute, the class spent a little over eight weeks, an entire grading period, on the heart. The teacher assigned positive meaning to the activities so that more of the curriculum was covered. He had the students research all of the ways the cardiovascular system affects other body parts. Students learned about diseases, muscles, bones, the brain, smoking, eating habits, etc. The learning principles previously described (Chapter Two) were maximized in this type of setting where the event is the student dissecting hearts but the knowledge is related to the event in a variety of ways. *Language arts are the tools...the students wrote, read, drew, made posters, gave presentations, etc. The students also learned how special each of their learning efforts was.* The teacher would say, "My daughter is in med school and she hasn't dissected a heart yet. This is very special for all of us. I have never seen a human heart." Or they would learn how to be gracious, "Dr. Allens is a very busy man. He gets up at 4:00 in the morning and has appointments until 9:00 at night. What could we do to show Dr. Allens how much we appreciated his efforts?" or they would learn about ways to learn. "When Dr. Allens comes with the hearts, we need a plan so that we look like fifth graders. Fifth graders know how to organize themselves in new situations. What will our plan be?" Because the class already belongs to the students, the students are quick to decide who will greet Dr. Allens, who will find out what Dr. Allens needs while he is visiting, who will personally assist him while he is there, who will run the videotape or camera to be sure that the event is remembered, etc. Students even suggested that they write or phone Dr. Allens in advance to see if he had any special AV needs or table, water needs. The class also followed through and wrote thank you notes to everyone including the principal. One student contacted the media and a newspaper reporter covered the activity. The students assisted the reporter also as a special guest. In an authoritative classroom, such offerings of support from the community are not only appreciated and welcomed but also encouraged. *The classroom is like the students' homes. Respect is offered to all people who come into the classroom, and for all activities, ideas, and needs.*

Summary of Authoritative Language

Authoritative language sets the ***responsive*** tone of the classroom. The educator brings along the students through using specific language that shows respect of individual needs and honors the diversity of the learners. Without such language, all methods, and activities soon revert back to looking like a classroom that is authoritarian or control-based. Rich language, full of possibility (see Chapter Four), models the value of the excitement of the group. Specific strategies that help to add to this excitement follows in the next section. These strategies follow the authoritative style of parenting, so as to create an atmosphere that respects all members of a group.

Activity

1. **Describe authoritarian examples of language.**
2. **Describe authoritative examples of language.**

Language Strategies for a Responsive Classroom

1. *Begin the first day by getting to know the students* (see Chapters Three, Four, Five, and Six) individually as well as in the group. Record their interests. Share the students' interests with the group by typing out what each student shares as their interests, foods they like, things they like to do, etc. Maintain this atmosphere of wanting to know about the students throughout the year.

2. *Create the classroom* displays, walls, etc., from what the students develop. In other words, begin the classroom with empty walls and only the equipment necessary for the particular age of child (see Chapters Four, Five, and Six). In some of the responsive classrooms, the room is completely void of teacher constructed articles the first day. Ample paper, cardboard, boxes, and recycling materials are available for construction. Students are encouraged to contribute (see Chapter Four).

3. *Use the first day (as the students begin to know each other) to create the tone of the classroom.* For example, the youngest children need to draw what they see around the room to begin to create themselves as they see themselves fit "in" the classroom...how they get to other places...what their behavior is to look like...what the events of the day look like as the teacher goes through them, etc. The early elementary students need to draw, write their names, determine their places in class, what other places in the room are for, the events of

the day, the expected way to work, how to have a class discussion, why rules exist during a group decision, etc. The older elementary, middle and high school students need to engage in a teacher directed facilitation of what their room will look like, what the rules will be, goals, purposes, etc. The tone for all levels is one of shared power— this is our classroom and it is based on **RESPECT.**

4. *Provide opportunities for shared power the first day, the first minute of class.* The teacher doesn't provide all of the information or give all answers. Students give what they know, the teacher assigns meaning, and the teacher validates each student as part of the classroom team. Shared power might come from the teacher asking individual students to do different tasks for the teacher, etc. As each child enters the room, the teacher engages with the child and helps assign tasks for shared power.

5. *Provide assigned expertise to students by the end of the first day.* Each student should have an expertise assigned to either behavior or work. Over time, each student will experience multiple expertise assignments (Chapter Three). A child's expertise might include being able to say "hello" in French, offering a lot of ideas to the group, illustrating, drawing, computing, helping with the chalkboard, etc. Whatever the student can do will become a behavior that is assigned an expertise level of confidence by the teacher.

6. *Model positive functional language day in and day out so that students can see a way to talk to peers that may be different than past teachers or parents.* Any sort of verbal put down, name calling, value judgments, etc., are openly discussed by the students with the purpose of developing different types of language (Chapter Six). The rationale for appropriate or inappropriate behavior is considered in the discussion. Outcomes and consequences are determined.

7. *Model "I" language with feeling statements* for social (Chapter Three) as well as academic reasons (Chapter Four). This also provides the students with a shared power for knowledge...the

teacher doesn't know everything or have all of the answers. The teacher is human, vulnerable to all aspects of being social.

8. *Students are given reasoning behind all tasks and activities related to their needs, desires, and learning skills so that they* find purpose to resource (Chapters One and Five). They also begin to realize that they are the critical, most important, beings when it comes to their learning.

9. *Students are encouraged to do personal best work so as to challenge all students to reach a higher learning, cognitive level* (Chapter Seven). Quantity is not the goal...quality of work is the goal. Students are encouraged to go beyond what they have already accomplished personally as well as academically. Whenever the student presents something, there is always room to show appreciation by wondering aloud with the child on how the child's work might be disseminated or shared with others...creating more need for more personal best work. "Perhaps, the middle school students would like to help us with this project (fifth grade)." Students are told on the first day of class that they are powerful, important, and indispensable players on a championship team. Individual contributions will win important games for everyone. A lack of contribution is hardly considered desirable or productive. Just like a champion relay team cannot depend on reluctant runners, the class activities depend on everyone's contribution.

10. *Personal best work is expected across academic as well as social parameters.* For example, we stand in a classroom to speak so that others can hear, others can see, we can feel positive about what we are presenting, etc. Explanations about sound waves, speech reading by members who see mental pictures, etc., add to the reason for standing, for calling others by their last names, for taking off caps in the room, for not chewing gum while presenting, etc. **Rule of thumb: The classroom is the student's place to learn how to market who the student is, not just what the child can do for the**

teacher. The students are developing and practicing citizenship skills (Chapter Five).

11. *Use an authoritative classroom—language, structure, and attitude to foster the Right of Each Student to Participate in an Environment of Communicative Thoughtfulness* (Chapters Five, Six, and Seven). The previous section of this chapter provided an overview of the authoritative principles. An authoritative classroom offers support, protection, and nurturance through language so as to foster group as well as individual development.

12. *Develop the individual student cognitively while valuing the student's social needs* so that learning carries the student into more mature ways to act and to treat others (Chapters Three and Four). Lots of activities are brought to the classroom for enjoyment, but students will value the classroom more positively when they are learning. Therefore, activities should always be designed to take a student from his or her level of knowledge to a higher level. In this way, the student's learning parallels the student's level of social maturity.

13. *Shift all reinforcers from external rewards to internal, intrinsic rewards by the third month of school* so that learning with friends becomes the reason for coming to school (Chapter Six). To make such a shift, give out as many compliments, written thank yous, chips, tally marks as possible at the beginning of school. It is not uncommon to hand a sixth grade student 30,000 points at a time...soon the student can't keep up with the deluge and doesn't need them. Very young children, for example Kindergarten age, won't even ask for them if their classroom begins with learning being the internal reward. Rule of thumb: Give what the student needs. If the student appears to need an "A" to participate fully, give the grade before any work. One of the authors was recently invited to a celebration for a student who was receiving an award. She had been in the author's classroom six years prior to the celebration and the author had not heard from the student since that time. As part of

the acceptance speech, this student talked about the author's honesty and trust...how the author had trusted the student to do the work even though the student was suffering a family member's death, experiencing chicken pox, and could not physically complete the work until after the grades were due. The student would not graduate without a passing grade. The author doesn't remember the particulars or even the student as being an exception. The student remembers the situation...somehow, this former student feels that this display of trust in meeting her needs by giving a grade "changed how she viewed relationships." She had not been raised in a family of trust nor had she ever experienced such trust in her schooling. Giving what others need is an act of **RESPECT**...it honors the person and takes nothing from anyone else.

14. *Create an atmosphere of joy and fun much like a positive job satisfaction rating as an adult* (Chapter Six). Mr. Young referred to this as the fun factor. Are the students having fun? Is the teacher having fun? Learning is fun because it is an internal neurological "high." A lot of adults do not have a positive feeling about work and they score their job satisfaction as low. They do not enjoy work. Perhaps such job satisfaction begins in school.

15. *Treat the classroom like a pseudo-family.* Expect to know the students, to teach them the joy of learning and to protect, nurture, and support them. Verne Jones, a well-respected, educator once visited Mr. Young's classroom. After his visit, he said, "You have created a pseudo-family in your classroom." If the reader comes from an unhealthy family structure then this may not seem very favorable. On the other hand, Dr. Jones meant that the classroom was a healthy, safe place for learning to take place. The classroom had the positive family dimensions of all individuals being valued for their contributions to the whole, the family or class.

16. *Make all activities event-based learning opportunities.* Each event consists of the agents, actions, and objects engaged within an

authoritative context (see Arwood & Unruh, 2000). This type of planning respects all learner's cognitive level of understanding.

17. *Shift the auditory, authoritarian language to more visual, authoritative language honoring all students ways of thinking in language.*

Summary of Strategies

The aforementioned listed language strategies have been discussed independently in the previous chapters. From these strategies, the classroom tone is developed by the teacher in conjunction with the students. *The group's identity is full of respect as the communication generates events that are thoughtful and purposeful.* Each student in this authoritative type of classroom becomes a powerful agent who is capable of being valued for his or her own "self-constituents" and "respected for individual differences" in products. This type of responsive classroom is open to all who seek it. It is available for all who demand it. It is possible for all who value **RESPECT**...*the Right of Each Student to Participate in an Environment of Communicative Thoughtfulness.* Specific examples of teaching activities are provided in the last section to be used with the philosophy and the strategies.

Suggested Activities

All activities are only used with *respect* when they are made into *authoritative* and *thoughtful* ways to *communicate* the lesson's goals and objectives. If the classroom teacher is intent on creating specific tasks to "control respect," then the tone of the classroom will still be authoritarian because the teacher is controlling the tasks. To have shared power in any activity, the teacher must set the tone of the room for the entire year, independent of specific tasks or activities. **All activities must have at least four components: 1) Allow all students to individually participate at their cognitive and social level; 2) Create ways for students to evaluate and refine products into something that is at a higher level than previously accomplished; 3) Allow for maximum ways to apply learning principles (bridge, network, trough, and building) for all individuals; and 4) Allow for**

dissemination in a variety of ways for students to participate as a group of learners as well as individual learners so that a pseudo-family is co-created in the classroom. Each of these shared power components will be discussed as examples of activities are provided.

1. Students need to individually participate at their cognitive and social level. All activities must offer a variety of ways for students to participate so that each student is able to work off of his or her own learning system. For example, a class of fifth graders created an activity that became a mainstay in later years. The activity was named "Heart Attack Day" and was spawned during a class meeting. A fifth-grade student complained that her parents treated her as a child at times, and then expected her to assume responsibilities on other occasions. Others nodded their heads in agreement. After a few more testimonies, the teacher asked for solutions.

One student suggested that the teacher could write a newsletter home to parents about the problem. The teacher agreed he could do that. Another student wanted the chance to speak to the parents at a meeting. The teacher said that he could call such a meeting, but could not be sure that all parents would be able to attend. A few more comments approached defiance toward parents and with direction from the teacher, the students all felt that that would only create larger and more serious problems with the generalized attitude. Finally, one student put her finger on her chin and looked thoughtfully toward the ceiling. The teacher called on Miss Brown. Miss Brown rose slowly. She said she had the same problem at her home, but felt that things might be better if she just "showed" her parents that she could be adult-like.

The teacher commented, "Great idea!" The idea just hung in the air for a moment. Then the flood of answers came. Homework could be started without seven or eight reminders, pets could be fed or walked without being nagged about it, and the toughie of all toughies---not fighting with brothers and sisters over anything could happen.

The teacher read the enthusiasm in the students who were now challenged to do something more than in the past and at the same time something so personal that the lessons to be learned were huge. He asked for a brief time-out as he raced to boot up his computer. He had the class form groups of three to formulate ideas that could be used as a class to demonstrate maturity at home on a consistent basis. It was a 10 minute, small group meeting.

The class reconvened. Each student dictated his or her own weekend plan of action as the teacher typed. The class picked the upcoming Valentine's Day as their target date. The class agreed that no one would discuss their secret project outside the classroom, but that the teacher would type up each student's plan and share it with the entire class. Any student who preferred not having his or her plan shared with the class could tell the teacher. No one felt that it was necessary to not share with the whole class. For a week, time was allotted to add or delete to individual plans. Here are two examples of plans.

Miss Brown:

1. I will begin my homework each day before 4:30 P.M. for a whole week.
2. I will walk my dog without being told for a week.
3. I will empty the dishwasher each day before my parents come home, for a week.
4. I will fix my bed every day for five days straight.
5. I will vacuum the whole house on Mondays, Wednesdays, and Fridays for two weeks.
6. I will not argue with my younger brother for two days straight.

Mr. Macias:

1. I will wash my father's car on Saturday.
2. I will fix my parent's bed everyday before I go to school for a week.
3. I will fold the clothes every day for a week.
4. I will go to bed at 9:30 P.M. without being told (and I won't read in bed till late).
5. I will clean up after myself in the bathroom for a week.
6. I will eat all of the vegetables my mother gives me at dinnertime for three days.
7. I will pack my backpack before I go to bed for a week.

Many of the students had much longer lists. Many had really emphasized specific things they could do for the Valentine's weekend as well as for the weeks after. On Monday morning, the day after the heart attack weekend, the teacher could barely drive into the parking lot at school, as several of his students were anxiously waiting for his arrival. It should be noted that teachers arrive an hour before students do. As the teacher drove into the lot, several students ran toward his car and he had to "creep" into a parking space in order to avoid possible accidents with the five or six students that were waving and jumping up and down.

Before the teacher had turned off his engine, there were several students all yelling comments at him through his still-closed window. He gathered that they were excited about surprising their parents on the weekend. Giving one of the students the classroom keys, they stuttered and strutted their way into the school building as each student tried to gain the teacher's attention. Even when they arrived at the classroom, he had to put down books, his laptop computer and ask the students to sit down to gain some semblance of order. Finally, they had a single speaker who enthusiastically reported that her parents were shocked when she prepared breakfast-in-bed for her Mom and Dad. She had put a flower in a juice glass as she prepared scrambled eggs, sausages, toast, coffee and half-an-orange for each parent. The teacher congratulated her and asked her what were the parents' reactions? She could only sputter that they loved it and could not believe it. Her mom hugged her three times and her dad could hardly eat his breakfast because he kept shaking his head in disbelief.

A second student reported that it was tough, but she did not fight with her middle school brother whom she described as "an absolute nerd." She said she wanted to pour the whole bowl of mashed potatoes on his head at supper time when he had called her some "bad names." She simply kept quiet and managed to keep up a conversation with her parents. Her father had to tell her brother to "cool it." And...she gave her dog a bath by herself in the bathtub before her parents came home that day.

A third student and then a fourth began to share experiences. Before the teacher could settle down, eight students were sharing their weekend experiences. There were only positive reactions reported. A few students from other classes filtered into this class when they saw so many students circled in desks around the teacher. These other students were on their way to their own classrooms to help their teachers with before school routines. Many of these other students were unsure of what they were hearing, and had so many questions for these reporting students. In general there was a look of disbelief on their faces. Why would students do their homework without reminders? Why would they have cooked dinner (from soup to nuts) on their own? Were these kids sick? After standing around for about three minutes, these other students had heard enough and simply turned and walked out. They could not get enthused about doing jobs that they hated. These students exhibited a clear difference between the classroom which had an authoritative culture of doing their personal best to grow and to learn and how students from an authoritarian classroom viewed doing these activities as not having to be done because it wasn't required. These visiting students only knew to do something if they were told to do it, and if it were part of their "job description."

As might be expected, the class actually began early that morning. As the busses arrived, there was a thundering of feet toward the classroom. More students had tales of wonder to share. One parent asked his son, "How much do you want for all of this work? Nothing? Are you feeling okay?" Everyone wanted to change the usual routine to discuss the weekend. A class vote was taken and the motion carried to change the routine. The energy in the classroom was as if everyone had won a lottery. It was great to see the bright gleams in eyes, to hear their excited speech, to see that each student had so much to share. The 45-minute period took a little over an hour. It was time well spent. Everyone was excited, to say the least.

Several parents called the teacher by the end of that Monday, to verify that the weekend was truly a class-wide project. One parent offered to pay for the class treats, if the teacher would do heart attack weekend again. Another parent felt that the class should do it as a monthly project. The parents did not give a single negative message. One parent did call the teacher at home over the weekend to tell the teacher that he (the teacher) owed the parent a new kitchen broom. Her son had washed the father's car, as well as the sedan. He then swept the kitchen and was at that very second, when the parent called, cleaning the fireplace by standing in the fireplace with his father's hard hat and using his mother's good kitchen broom. She then laughed and complimented the teacher for his magic. She did not expect a new broom, but she would gladly buy a broom for each room of his house if he could keep the enthusiasm up. The teacher could not promise that but assured the parent that much of her son's enthusiasm had been generated at home through support and modeling and that he (the teacher) could *not* take full credit for her son's good works.

The class was more than ready to share the parent reactions. Yet, the class discussed the matter of attitude change among parents. They discussed the effectiveness of just one weekend of "outstanding behavior" to change the attitudes of parents. They discussed their continued activities for the next week(s) since many had written goals that covered more than the weekend. Yet, there was a general agreement that it was a worthwhile project. They then discussed planning their next project within the week. This class had set a precedent. Each class from that year on would have a "Heart Attack Weekend."

This activity is particularly good at crossing both the individual and group needs for social and cognitive development. From a social standpoint, the students had a chance to be viewed by others (concrete level) outside the room as being a competent being. Each student chose his or her own tasks so that the tasks are socially relevant to that student as well as shared among parents, siblings, and other classmates. Bigger concepts such as "responsibility," "respect," "consideration" receive attention from a variety of students who all participate (as a group) within their individual situations to create a better community.

Academically, the students use oral language, written language, refined language, and organizational skills to represent what they are ready to demonstrate to the rest of the world. This type of project provides a win-win situation for each student within a group, within the community, within the larger society of what is expected of people who are responsible, respectful and considerate of others' needs. These young fifth graders are acquiring a formal understanding of such concepts, something that many adults will struggle with their entire lives.

Another example of an activity for younger children which allows the students to individually be successful at their social and cognitive levels has to do with setting the classroom up as an event. A first grade group of students came to school expecting to sit where they were assigned, just like in Kindergarten, and continue to work on specific reading, writing, and math skills. They were in for a treat. The teacher, Ms. Lee, designed her classroom to belong to the students. As the students walked into the classroom, they asked about why there weren't any bulletin board pictures and what they were going to do. This teacher helped each child find a place to sit, did the introductions, and then told the students about her summer. She had photos to share, written scripts with the photos, and lots of props. The students had questions about her son and daughter, about the teacher's husband, about the family pets, etc. As the teacher accepted questions she drew out her home, her family and the events about the family as stick figures on the chalkboard. Students sat glued to their seats as their wide eyes attended to the teacher's drawings and her explanations. Students learned to take turns so all could share, to raise hands so that we all knew who was contributing, etc. The students were then given the option to draw or write about their families, their homes, and their activities. Any student who did not have enough language to initiate ideas could use the teacher's drawings and ideas for drawing something. By the end of the day, one bulletin board was complete with drawings, some writings and a heading about the class...Who are we? These papers could be taken down the next day to add new information. In addition to these papers, the teacher took

Polaroid shots, and the class began another story about what the teacher did with her family the night before, pointing to pictures, etc. The papers were refined and returned to the board with expanded pictures, etc. Each day, the class began looking over what they had completed the day before which led to the next piece of the event for that day.

At the end of the third day, the students brainstormed what they had to do to make their classroom look like a home, the place where most of them lived or would like to live with their families. The students wanted to build a kitchen, a bedroom, a car for getting to school, etc. By the end of the third week, the entire room was taking shape with roads for getting to school, libraries for shelving their own written books, etc. Students had begun to read, write to their drawings from the teacher labeling their stories. Rules of conduct for behavior was based on what was meaningful. For example, one day, one of the six-year-old boys who had been expelled from Kindergarten and whose family had had difficulty finding a classroom for him, decided to leave his area and go to other places in the room. At each place, he would help for a few minutes and then leave again. One of the assigned rules in the classroom was for students to work on their piece of the event. If the student was finished, the student could move to another piece of the event as long as there was space for the student. So, when the students came into the big circle after 30 minutes of working on building different pieces of the room, the teacher said she noticed that the road was incomplete. The six-year-old had decided that a road was needed from the home to the school and he had begun working on the road. Ms. Lee asked the group, "What shall we do to finish the road?" The six-year-old's hand shot up and he blurted out, "I'll fix it." He jumped up. The teacher reached over to him and drew him sitting on the floor with the others with thought bubbles over his head thinking about how to do the road. The six-year-old looked at himself in a sitting posture on the paper and *immediately* sat down. Ms. Lee asked the students if they had any other ideas about finishing the road. A couple of students said they were finished with their piece and would help the young boy with the road. The teacher used a socially appropriate behavior to replace an unwanted behavior, roaming around the room. She used the student's learning system, pictures of what her words looked like to show him what she expected. And, she included him into the classroom so that he could fit. He did return to the road and finished the road when the whole group broke up to work on their pieces of the community. The students were learning how to respect all learners.

Summary

The authors have seen rooms turned into aquariums with written displays, artwork about marine specimens, and research projects that include language arts, science and math as well as many other museums. But, *the strength of any activity is the teacher's language of respect for the students.* **Giving an assigned positive meaning to students' strengths gives opportunities for students to grow and learn not just about the aquarium, but about being a citizen.** *By setting up the classroom with the students, the students learn to appreciate* **RESPECT:** *the Right of Each Student to Participate in an Environment of Communicative Thoughtfulness.* Chapter Nine provides the reader with how to exemplify the language of **RESPECT.**

REFERENCES

Arwood, E, and McInroy, J. 1994. *Reading: It's So Easy to See (RISES) Pictured Language.* Portland, OR: Apricot, Inc.

Arwood, E. and Unruh, I. 1997. *R.I.S.E.S. II: Reading/writing: It's So Easy to See.* Portland, OR: Apricot, Inc.

Arwood, E. and Unruh, I. 2000. *Event-Based Learning Handbook.* Portland, OR: Apricot, Inc.

Oldfather, P. 1994. When Students Do Not Feel Motivated For Literacy Learning: How a Responsive Classroom Culture Helps. *Reading Research Report, No. 8.* Athens, GA: National Reading Research Center, University of Georgia.

Chapter Nine

Learner Outcomes

Upon completion of this chapter, the reader will be able to do the following:

1. Explain how to be responsive to the individual learner's needs.
2. Explain how to set up an activity that meets both the individual and group needs.
3. Plan a classroom that is respectful and then conduct the classroom as a responsive teacher who models **the language of RESPECT**.
4. Describe the outcomes of a classroom based on respect.
5. Describe how the respectful classroom results in better cognitive or academic outcomes, not just social improvement.
6. Explain how to set limits and boundaries within a classroom in order to promote respect.
7. Explain how communicative thoughtfulness through the language of respect promotes learning.
8. Explain responsiveness.

CHAPTER NINE

Becoming Responsive to RESPECT

How do we respond so as to show respect?

The parent whirls around in excitement.
Her hands tremble with the thought…
Maybe her son is okay.
Maybe her son is responsive.
Maybe his teacher is RESPECTFUL.

The college students line up at the School of Education Office at a state university. There are 17 students waiting for an interview to be considered for admission to a teacher education program. As part of the interview, the prospective candidates are asked, "Why do you want to become a teacher?" All of these candidates have an undergraduate degree in some content area. They all believe that education is the solution to many societal problems. They want to be a piece of the solution. They want "to make a difference." They "want to teach." But only a few of them have thought about teaching being an interactive process that *shares* power. Only a few of them have thought about being "in the shoes of a teacher." Only a few of them have the family background that encourages respect for the individual's needs as well as the group process. In other words, as eager as these teacher education candidates might be, and as interested in education as they express, only a few of them are ready personally to become responsive to students. Only a few of them are ready to establish a classroom based on **the language of RESPECT:** *the Right of Each Student to Participate in an Environment of Communicative Thoughtfulness.* The purpose of this chapter is to provide additional support for the teacher to become *responsive* to creating a classroom "environment" based on the **language of RESPECT.**

Responsive to the Language of RESPECT

Previous chapters described the various components of a classroom based on the **language of RESPECT. These components include thoughtful communication, awareness of cognitive and social assignment of meaning to individual students, assessment of the students' cognitive and social needs through language, awareness of differences in student learning needs, and fostering the individual within the group.** Also, suggestions for activities as well as multiple examples of how students and teachers interact were provided. But, knowledge and examples may not be enough to set up a classroom based on the "**language of RESPECT.**" A teacher may still have difficulty setting up the classroom so that the atmosphere is *respectful. To truly create an atmosphere of a functional "pseudo-family," the teacher must be responsive to student differences. Responsiveness involves recognizing individual needs through positive verbal and nonverbal use of language.* In this way, the classroom environment *respects* the process of learning.

Positive Verbal and Nonverbal Language

To be responsive means to be "open" to what the students do in order to "readily react." So, the teacher who sets up an atmosphere of *respect* must also be *the teacher who is able to work from the students' words, the students' verbal and nonverbal behaviors, and the students' personal needs.* The teacher must not only be willing to react positively to what the student says or does, but must be able to be open to the student behavior. For example, the student says, "I hate science!" An empathetic teacher might say, "Yes, I don't care for science either, but we have to study it." The teacher is not being "positive" about the learning environment, only about what the student said. In fact, the teacher has not challenged the student into being more respectful of his or herself or of the subject matter, but has set up an adversarial environment…student versus science. The teacher's comment has "closed" the communication. The child's attitude as well as comment has been affirmed…it is okay for the student to continue to hate science.

A responsive teacher would have heard the student by validating what the student said, "Oh, you hate science?" Now, the teacher "opens" the setting to a challenge of beliefs and values. The student says, "Yeah, I can't do these graphs." The teacher now has an open interaction to engage the student. "So, let's see what I can do to help you with the graphs." The teacher is not solving the student's problem, but opening communication to assist the student in being successful. If the teacher had said, "This is how you do the graphs" then the teacher would have again closed the communication. Solving the graphing problem for the student is not a positive reaction because it "closes" the language necessary for being open to learn. Telling a student what to do and how to do something for the purpose of getting something "complete" closes the *language of respect* for the activity. *Just like tutoring helps to get products accomplished, tutoring does not free a student to the intrinsic challenges of learning. Positive assignment of meaning through language opens the communication for additional learning.* Helping students to use language strategies for learning opens communication whereas tutoring finishes products.

Furthermore, the attitude that a particular subject matter is "hated" does not set a positive tone for further learning in the subject. So, the teacher might step back and try to further open the student's comment. "Hmm, do you know why you can't do the graphs?" "Yeah, they're stupid." *Namecalling is a form of verbal, emotional abuse and is unacceptable in a classroom based on the* **language of RESPECT**. The student has just engaged in calling the graphs a name…stupid. So, the teacher who is standing next to the student and is *not* addressing the whole class says, "Mike, I know you are having difficulty doing the graphs, but we have talked about name calling. Why do we not name call?" The teacher gives the student this information in a calm and quiet way. Based on class discussions and based on having set up the room in a positive, responsive way, the teacher waits for the student to respond. The authors have found that when the teacher's manner is sincere and open to knowing what the student is saying, and, yet, not accepting of the put downs or devaluation, then the student usually responds in a like manner. "I didn't mean to namecall." "Why?" Mike responds, "Well, we talked in class about how namecalling makes people feel bad. I do feel bad when I say that the graphs are stupid." "Do you want to feel different?" "Yeah." The teacher says, "Mike how do you want to feel?" "I want to feel like I can do the graphs." "Oh, that is easy, may I help you with the graphs so that you feel good about doing the graphs?" Mike nods his head. The teacher looks closely at the paper and "responds" to Mike's work, not trying to just solve the graph problems. "Mike, I see that you are putting the numbers on the graph. That's a good strategy so you can remember the numbers, but your writing covers the place to put the dots to connect the lines of the graph. What could we do to put the numbers down on paper so we can remember the number values and still not cover the place to put the dots?" The teacher has responded to the "real issue." Mike has nothing against science as subject matter. He has nothing against doing graphs. Like all learners, he just wants to be successful. The teacher has used language with Mike to give him the necessary learning strategies to be successful. With strategies, Mike has the power to learn. He then becomes *responsive* to the learning process.

Being responsive to Mike's work, to Mike's words, to Mike's behavior is being open to Mike. *The teacher who wants a room that is based on respect must be responsive to* Mike's *learning needs* and to all of the other individual needs in the room while also respecting the learning process. Using the same subject, here's another example of being *responsive.* A second grade student said, "I hate science." Her mother asked her, "Why?" She said, "We have this science lady. She says to make a circuit. I wait and wait and wait for my wires and battery. I raise my hand and wait some more. Then she says that I'm goofing off." "Why did she say you were goofing off?" " 'Cuz', I didn't do the circuit." "Why didn't you do the circuit?" " 'Cuz' she said to raise our hands for the wire and battery. I raised my hand and she never gave me any wire or a battery." "What did you say to the teacher when she said you were goofing off?" "She said it to all of us, not just me. And she is not my teacher." "Who is she?" "She is some special science lady." "Did some of the students build a circuit with wires and a battery?" "Yeah, the boys did." "How did they get their materials?" "They just walked up and took them." "I thought you said the lady told you to raise your hand?" "Yeah, but the boys didn't raise their hands." "So, did all of the boys build a circuit?" "No, just the ones in the front of the room who got out of their seats." "So, now that you couldn't build your circuit, you don't like science?" "No, I don't like science. I already know how to build a circuit." "Where did you learn to build a circuit?" "Remember, we did circuits at the summer school science fair last summer." "Oh, yeah, that's right." "So, explain to me one more time why you don't like science?" "I don't like the science lady." "Oh, you don't like the behavior of the science lady...you don't like what she did!?" "Right!" "Well, not all people do science like this lady, she really has nothing to do with whether you like science are not. You can choose to not like her behavior, but still like science. Sometimes, I don't like something you have done, but I still love you." "Okay, I don't like the science lady's behavior, but I still don't like science. I am going to make some juice." The mother, having been trained in assigning positive meaning to a child's learning and valuing respect for all learning, quickly responded. "Beth, you can't use the water in the sink because you hate science. The water that comes from the pipes in the sink is available to you because of scientists, who have cleaned the water, who have built the pipes..." Beth interrupts, "Okay!" She walks over to the cupboard to get a glass. Her mother says, "Beth, that glass was made by a scientist, a person who works with materials to make a glass. And, you won't want to mix or stir the juice concentrate because that is chemistry...how molecules change properties when mixed." Beth said, "Well, I won't have juice." Her mother said, "Well, you won't be able to have a snack either because the snack will involve science. Everything you do involves science." Beth sighed, "Okay, I don't like the science lady telling me I am goofing off and letting the boys just get up and get the materials, but I **do** like science." If Beth's mother had not been responsive to the situation, Beth may have done poorly in science in later years of school because she had her feelings and her needs mixed up. It's the adult's responsibility to help a student separate personal needs from a particular context.

Being "responsive" means to set an example of being open to all learning so that Mike and Beth learn to separate their feelings from the acts and tasks within the setting. In this way, Mike and Beth are open to learning. *Their attitudes shift from blaming others for their feelings and abilities to being able to separate what others do from their own acts.* As explained in previous chapters, this change from blaming others to separating behavior from feelings is also an increase in cognitive development. In this way, Mike and Beth are learning to be sensitive to others and responsible for their own behavior and reactions. So, both Beth and Mike receive lessons that involve social development, being sensitive to others, and cognitive development, using a higher form of language. **Learning is a social and cognitive process.** Beth and Mike are learning in both areas for maximum growth and development. Their relationship with these adults is also developing trust that allows for a pseudo-family type of interdependence. Interdependent relationships generate a *responsive* tone to the teacher as well as to other members of the group.

Activity

1. **Define responsiveness. Give examples.**
2. **Explain how "the language of RESPECT" helps a teacher to be responsive.**

Teacher and Student Interdependence

Becoming responsive to the **language of RESPECT** *means creating an interdependence among the students and teacher.* **This interdependence is a healthy form of pseudo-family structure that establishes an environment of communicative thoughtfulness.** The environment includes the people, the setting, the topics, and the issues. The tone of the environment is the atmosphere. A positive atmosphere includes all of the individuals' self-constituents. In other words, how the individuals believe, think, desire, want, etc. And, these constituents must be "positive" for the individuals or the tone becomes negative. For example, Beth's and Mike's interpretations of "science" resulted in a negative attitude about something that they are just beginning to learn. In fact, when investigated by the adults, the students did not have a problem with math or science, but with their ability to complete a task in a positive way. If their attitude had been reinforced with empathy or left heard and unchallenged, then all tasks related to science would have resulted in a "negative attitude" by these students. *Negative attitudes, thoughts, beliefs corrode away positive learning. Positive attitudes, thoughts, beliefs create positive atmospheres for better learning.* To create these positive atmospheres for a better environment, the teacher also needs to respond to students so that positive limits and healthy boundaries are established. The following section addresses both boundaries and limits.

Activity

1. **Define interdependence.**
2. **Define the term "a healthy pseudo-family."**

Boundaries and Limits

To create an environment that communicates thoughtfulness and establishes a positive atmosphere, the teacher needs to respond to students with positive limits. These positive limits set boundaries that are healthy, the type of boundaries found in healthy families. **Limits are defined as "what is acceptable." Acceptable behavior is the behavior that the society or culture approves and validates. Boundaries are the overlapping or shared roles of two or more people in a**

relationship. Chapter Five discussed how society influences the development of such limits and boundaries. To establish healthy limits, the teacher needs to *respond* to each student with the **language of RESPECT.** By fostering respect, the teacher is using the limits as a way to establish healthy boundaries. Regardless of grade or level, the teacher is the dispenser of stepladders, mirrors, gold keys, and words of encouragement to each and every student. With these items, students are able to climb to higher advantage points, to see themselves in new views, to open doors to new opportunities, and to hear positive messages of hope, validation, and confirmation.

The teacher must be clear about what he or she expects of the students and what the student to teacher roles involve. If the expectations for the teacher or student are unclear, then the student does not feel the validation or confirmation. For example, a teacher has introduced a Spanish lesson to primary students (grades 1-3). In the lesson, she talks about her adventures living in South America. She asks the students if they have ever seen condors? Most say, "NO." She then says, "See if you can find a picture of a condor and bring it to class tomorrow." One of the second graders who trusts her teachers and has really good language remembers to go home and tell her mom that they need to find a picture of a condor. After an hour of searching, they find a front-page color photo of a condor on a *National Geographic* magazine. The child is thrilled! She goes to class the next day with her magazine. She takes it up to the teacher before class. The teacher snaps, "What do you want?" And before the child could answer, the teacher says, "Sit down!" The child hands her the magazine and returns to her seat, even though class has not yet started. The teacher grabs the magazine and sits it on the counter. At the end of the day, the child goes home without the magazine. Upon inquiry for seeing such a sad face, the parent discovers that the child has been punished for following a teacher's request to resource, to do more than the minimum. The parent asks the child to talk with the teacher and to bring the magazine home. The child brings the magazine home. The condor is never acknowledged by the teacher, shared with classmates, or even discussed further. The child is now grown and doing college work...but to this day, she has never done more than the minimum to get her "A" grade as she might be embarrassed or put down. Second grade Spanish was an elective. This adult is 'gifted' in languages, but it wasn't until languages were offered as part of the regular curriculum that this student would again risk participation. The Spanish teacher was unclear in her perception of what she expected of the students. She told the students to find a picture because that sounded like a good idea for "work." She did not realize how important of a role she played in this student's life. The teacher did not realize that learning is more about how we feel as learners than just doing work.

What does this example about Spanish have to do with limits and boundaries? Well, the teacher had difficulty setting her *own* limits; that is, she did not fully understand the power of her language as an adult. She did not read the behavior of the child to see that the child had something to offer. She did not recognize the child for her positive contribution. In other words, the teacher saw herself as the "controller" and she set the limits. She did not have an understanding that students have personal limits as well. For example, each child has the ability to interact with the teacher based on his or her past experiences. The teacher did not understand that the child's limits are interdependent with the teacher's limits based on the teacher's assignment of meaning. The teacher assigned a negative meaning to "engaging in conversation with an authority figure," the teacher. The assignment of meaning to the child trying to share a picture with the teacher was "What do you want? Sit down!" This meaning suggests that the child has nothing to offer and therefore unless the child behaves in the exact way the adult is thinking, the adult will not assign positive meaning. Without positive meaning, the child has no identity. In other words, the adult overtakes the child's identity. Figure 9.1. represents the different ways that relationships form boundaries. In this case, the Spanish teacher and the child must exist within the same limits and be the same; or, the child doesn't exist.

Figure 9.1 – Relationships form boundaries

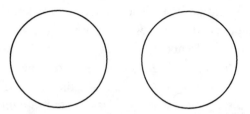

Disengaged; individuals do not know the boundaries and limits.

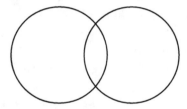

Shared healthy boundaries and limits.

Enmeshed; individuals depend on others being the same.

Here's another example from a high school elective, public speaking class. The fall semester begins with 42 very-diverse students from all high school levels and abilities. The teacher is a veteran. He has taught all sorts of language arts courses and speaking courses. He tells the students that the class is about learning to speak in front of a group, learning to persuade others, to negotiate, to exchange ideas, etc. By the beginning of the second semester, 32 students have dropped the class. There are only 10 students left in the class for the remainder of the year, if they all make it. Why? The students cannot trust the teacher. What he says and what he does do not match logically. For example, when one of the students asked the teacher if it would be possible to change the temperature of the room by closing the windows, he said, "Live with it!" The student persisted by "arguing" that his learning was being affected by being too cold. The teacher said, "You aren't properly dressed." The student said, "I am wearing a long-sleeved shirt, pants, and a jacket. Don't you think this should be suitable for class? I don't get cold in other rooms." The teacher responded with a referral to the counselor for "talking back." The class is not about learning to use speaking as a way to function in society, but about doing tasks in front of the teacher for the teacher to judge. The teacher's limits exist as a duplication of himself. He has no awareness of student needs or limits. The boundaries are for cloning because there are no shared relationships with the students. They imitate him or they don't last in his class. The students are convenient, helpless victims that have given up advocating for themselves. Removing themselves from the situation is the only safe way to participate.

Let's take the same examples in order of their presentation in the text and reconstruct them as having healthy boundaries and limits. All of us forget what we have said to someone else. So, the fact that the Spanish teacher did not remember about asking the students to find a condor photo is disappointing, but understandable. So, let's assume that the teacher forgot about the request. The child remembers. The child comes into class early. She walks toward the teacher. Now observe the child. Is she smiling? Does her body have an open posture (hands out or to the side)? Then the child has something to give…maybe it's a statement, an idea, a request, a package, or a photo. But, she has something to give! *It's the teacher's job to be responsive to the giving. To be responsive, the teacher opens her posture.* Arms are open and she faces in the direction of the child. Perhaps the teacher is busy doing something. The teacher being busy is a limit to the child's approach. So, when will the teacher be approachable? It's the adult's role to assign the limit. If this is not a good time, then the teacher needs to express that information. "Beth, I have a lot of papers to grade before all the students arrive. As soon as the papers are graded, I will let you know and we can talk." So, the next question is "When does this teacher allow students to talk about the previous day, about a previous lesson, about unfinished business, or to allow students to discuss their needs for learning, etc.?" If this is an isolated instance of shutting down communication between the child and the teacher, then addressing the child's needs will happen once class begins. In other words, the teacher will open class with an opportunity for students to share about their learning from the previous lesson. But, this example is really a problem with the entire classroom environment. To change how this teacher relates to students begins to help alleviate the problem. *Starting with open postures and the understanding that students are "giving" of themselves is a way to begin to change the environment so that students feel received and supported and their teachers feel that they are responsive to the needs of the students. As soon as a teacher steps onto school property, the job description of "educator" should be operative, evident, and noticeable to all. By being open to the student's gifts, she becomes a civil engineer who can **build** bridges, channel **troughs,** and establish **networks** (see Chapters One and Two for learning principles).*

Likewise, the high school teacher does not understand the power of his language. He does not see how influential his teaching may be on assisting adolescents into adulthood. It is not his content, but the way he models the content for the student that develops the adolescents for adulthood. In other words, *the gifts in this classroom are twofold…the content is cognitive power, but the teacher is the social adult model!* These young people will be interviewing, speaking before groups, persuading others to believe in what they believe, and so forth. They also will be separating themselves from their families while they are looking for their own unique identities. *If the teacher were responsive to the idea that he has powerful content and he is a model of "adulthood," then the teacher could alter his relationships with the students.* Instead of controlling the environment, the teacher could share in the control of the environment. "So, John is cold. The room by the heaters is hot to me. What do you think (addressing the class)?" The students discuss the problem and the class decides how to resolve it for John. The solution could be anything from moving John, to closing some or all windows with someone in charge of opening them when the room is too hot, to offering John additional clothing. John's need is a class need. If John's need is not responded to in a way that resolves the need, then the class has lost a valuable contribution from John. John can only have healthy limits if he is assigned positive meaning when he self-advocates. And, the teacher does not have the solution or John would not have the need. *The responsive teacher allows the students to assist in meeting John's needs. More importantly, meeting John's needs is a social lesson of how to communicate thoughtfulness. The teacher's social use of language is more powerful than the content in this case.* The students turn away from the content because their personal needs are not met. In this situation, they drop the class, missing out on the power of the content as well as the social respect for the group of individuals.

When there is a positive relationship between the teacher and the students in terms of personal needs being met, then the teacher and the students share self-constituents. The sharing of constituents might be about needs, wants, desires, beliefs, values, or interests. This sharing creates an overlap of people's identities. The teacher becomes a positive adult role model and the students gain insight into becoming unique individuals who make positive contributions as citizens. This connection between the teacher and students creates a pseudo-family based on relationships that are interdependent. *The students depend on the adult to establish limits for their needs to be met while the adult depends on the trust of the students for staying within positive boundaries. In this way, the students look forward to a safe class environment because the students know what to expect from the adult.* The adult nurtures, protects, and supports individuals in a way that allows the students to perform within the set limits because of their ability to have needs met. Best of all, the teacher gains so many insights, unique perspectives, wonderful ideas, rich friendships, and productive learning and teaching systems with a rich and respectful classroom environment in place. The interdependence found in a responsive environment is safe for all!

Setting positive limits comes from what is best for the group. And, *healthy boundaries are developed when all students have a positive identity as a contributor to the whole group.* The tapestry continues to weave trust and interdependence among its constituents creating a positive environment with the language of respect. An environment of communicative thoughtfulness creates an *energy* that parallels the innate need for all people to learn (see Chapter Two about how one learns). *Energy is needed for a classroom of students to be responsive.*

Activity

1. **Define boundaries. Give examples.**
2. **Define limits. Give examples.**

Energy

Creating a classroom environment that has a positive capacity for action or accomplishment comes from the teacher being responsive to the students' needs, interests, desires, and passions (self-constituents are explained in Chapter One). Since the positive capacity for action is one definition of "energy" (American Heritage Dictionary, 1983), then the classroom that has such a capacity is full of energy.

This energy comes from the bonds of the relationships among students and the teacher. Bonds are created through the trust and the development of interdependence. These are not relationships among peers, but student-adult, authority relationships that are established through positive limits that set the boundaries. The expected role is for the teacher or adult to be the authority figure with more wisdom, past experience, and knowledge. The role of the student is to be the child with less experience, knowledge and wisdom. In these roles the teacher shares part of who he or she is and each student shares specific pieces of him or herself. For example, when the teacher assigns expertise (see Chapters Three, Six, Seven, Eight) to a student then that assignment of meaning from the teacher to the student creates a bond or tie between the teacher and the student. *The authority figure has made an investment of trust, confidence, and respect in the student for who the student is. The student has responded with part of who he is. These bonds are unique to each student and the teacher. The relationships form a classroom of webs among the teacher and students. Multiply these bonds of relationships across the number of students in the class and there exists a sense of energy that is different than often found in a classroom. This energy acts as an environmental catalyst for positive action and accomplishment.*

"Energetic participation" is the type of *response* that comes from a student who likes coming to school, who wants to be in the classroom, and who can't wait to share his or her work. Master teachers evoke this type of participation. *Many master teachers share certain commonalties: The ability to create positive opportunities for learning, for helping students to be successful, and for challenging students to grow.* In a classroom filled with energy from these positive bonds, the master teacher becomes the student, learning from the actions and accomplishments of the students. Here are some examples from teachers who were able to create such a *respectful, positive atmosphere.* One high school English teacher was able to reach the different ways students learn and therefore challenge students to grow. She began her first class with a story about herself. She then opened up a class discussion about whether or not students had similar experiences. As she wrote their experiences on the board, students began to bring in different media experiences—books, shows, movies, etc. Finally, the teacher said, "You know, all of these examples help me to understand this other story." She lifted up a heavy book by Shakespeare and opened it to Macbeth. "But," she continued, "I have a problem. I don't know how we should study this story." Hands shot up! The students suggested they read it, tell it, the teacher read it, draw it, watch a movie about it, etc. Students wanted to know why they even had to understand it. The teacher listed all the possibilities for study and even answered the question about "why study it" with an explanation about what educated people were suppose to know and related that information to real world examples. She then asked students for reasons of why they thought the study of Macbeth was in the curriculum. At the end of the class period, they, as a class, had developed a plan. First the teacher would tell the story (she had great story telling gifts) keeping the story line to 15 minutes. While she told the story, Ralph would draw out the story on the board. Ralph was a student who always sat in the back of the room. He typically received "D's" in English and seldom, if ever, volunteered to do anything. He exhibited the body posture of a "dare-ya-to-teach me anything" attitude. But, Ralph was going to illustrate the story because the teacher had asked the class for the best drawer. The classmates knew Ralph could draw. And, he did! He drew realistic castles, elegant robes, and fantastic scenery. As the days evolved into weeks, students were found sneaking into high school before first period to work on projects. The teacher had to get special permission and hall passes for students to use before school, during lunch, and after school. Toward the end of the semester, *all* students had written (including Ralph), read, talked about, and acted out William Shakespeare's Macbeth. The energy was contagious! The atmosphere was positive. Students were engaged with each other about the content and were learning from what each student could do. All parties were included in the activity so that the language of respect existed. Even the "history of Shakespeare" was treated with *respect!* The *shared power* within this classroom created *energy* that allowed for a level of *responsiveness* that fuels *respect*.

A sixth-grade teacher had discovered that the relationship between the students and the teacher could create a special environment when she followed principles of learning as well set up the class for the best cognitive development. She created the classroom with the students, established rules with the students, and began developing positive bonds as students brought in their gifts to share...violin recital music, soccer trophies, books about pets, horse statues, shells from a trip to the beach, etc. She always began lessons with a story about what she understood from the previous lesson and connected the previous event to current lessons. The students' academic skills began to skyrocket. She then began to give them strategies for high school and college. For example, she would ask them how to take notes. Different students would suggest their best way. She would comment on that method and ask the students when would be the best time to take notes that way. In the end, all students could take notes off their mental pictures of what was said or off their mental sound words of what was said. Because this teacher used language strategies for sharing power, all students were speakers for all others, including the teacher. They created science and social studies projects, developed health units, integrated math, and used all of the language arts for representation. Parents stopped by to see why their "kids" wanted to attend school. Teachers asked this teacher why the students' test scores were two years above the rest of the school (by the way, some teachers were upset that the students had excelled...they didn't know what they would be able to teach them since the students were ahead of the other students). By the middle of the second semester, the teacher realized that the *energy* of the classroom drove the activities. She could actually come to class and stand back while the students engaged themselves in learning. At that point, she figured that she had found what teaching was all about. The year ended and she started the next year. But, she had forgotten what was behind the *energy* of last year's class. Instead of turning the power of learning over to the students to be guided by the teacher, she brought in all of the wonderful activities and ideas created by last year's class. The bonds between the teacher and *the new* students did not exist, yet. The classroom belonged to the teacher and her past experiences. She soon noticed that the attitudes were different than the year before. Students were grumbling, "Why do we have to do this?" Students sighed as they came into the classroom and slithered with shoulders drooped as they took their seats. Tardiness and absenteeism increased. This teacher was a good reader of the students. She thought about her relationship with the students and realized that *the energy comes from the process of creating the activity*, not from the activity. She went into class and apologized to the students for controlling the activities. She asked for their ideas and soon the class was back on track. She had momentarily forgotten to *respect* the students for their gifts. *Once she responded to them by giving them the opportunity to plan, develop, and participate in an environment of thoughtful communication, the class developed a different responsive tone.* Students were energized to attend and to learn.

The next example of how to create a positive classroom atmosphere comes from a primary grade teacher. She was assigned to a third grade classroom. The school district administrators were asking teachers to spend at least 45 minutes a day on reading, as many of the students were not reading close to grade level. She decided to "try" to set up the classroom based on *respect* for the students' differing ways to learn. She had recently learned that some students learn to read by seeing the printed ideas matched to the language pictures in their head while others learn to read by connecting the sounds and letters. She also had learned that increased academic performance comes from establishing an event based classroom that parallels students' cognitive (not grade) levels (see Chapter Four). And, she knew that students who write better do a better job of reading. So, she set up an event around reading. She told the students a story about how she went to the city library to pick up some books about one of her interest areas. She drew (stick figures) the language on the board as she told the story. Then she asked the students how they could resource. They gave all sorts of ways to get information including going to the school library. She asked them if it would be helpful to have a library in their classroom. They brainstormed about what they would use the library for, what would be in the library, and then how to set the library up. She accepted all ideas by putting the ideas word-for-word on the board. By the end of several months, the students had developed all sorts of activities related to the event of setting up a library. They had written all sorts of materials and had refined their works so as to be included in the library. The students had interviewed three different librarians (videotaped and wrote out specific questions they created) from different types of libraries found in the community. The students were eager to learn, the language arts skills of reading and writing were improving for all students (standardized test scores also showed increase), the students' behaviors and attitudes were positive. And, the teacher noticed the difference in classroom atmosphere when they were working on students' events. The students' positive attitudes for learning spilled into other subject matters and the class became a positive responsive environment based on the **language of RESPECT:** *the Right of Each Student to Participate in an Environment of Communicative Thoughtfulness.* The energy shared among teacher and students created a positive environment that developed life-long lessons.

In a classroom built on the language of **RESPECT** *the bonds or ties between the teacher are life long lasting because the lessons are social and cultural, not just academic in nature.* Students learn lessons about how to create positive relationships, how to communicate needs, how to learn, and how to resource. The next section will take the reader through each of these life long lessons.

Activity

1. **Define "energetic participation." Give examples.**
2. **Explain how a responsive classroom creates positive energy in the environment.**

Life Long Lessons

When teachers become pseudo-parents and the classroom becomes a pseudo-family, the energy from the bonds and ties go beyond the walls of the classroom. The value of respect or honoring oneself by being a successful learner reaches into the community. The community becomes a benefactor of the student's gifts. Each student *knows* that he or she has something to offer. Each student knows that he or she contributes to the whole group. Each student samples the feeling of belonging, even if it is just for that one class. Each student knows that learning can be fun and a positive venture, even if such an experience occurs in that one classroom only. And, each student knows what positive relationships feel like, even if they come from an abusive family. These are life long lessons about communicating one's needs in an appropriate way, learning how to learn in all situations, and learning to be a source of knowledge (giver) as well as a resourceful person (taker).

Communicating Needs

Basic needs are paramount…safety, hunger, thirst, sleep, and love. The first four needs are usually easily recognized, but the last need, love, is often overlooked. *Being responsive to others develops a form of respect that is generated by many others.* Others return the responsiveness that offers opportunities to give to others. Responding to others is also caring for others…their needs, interests, desires, and passions. It is also caring for oneself in such a way that the need for love is satisfied, but this process is developmental. Before age seven, children depend on others to meet their love needs. Between the ages of seven and 11, children seek out a group that helps to expand on their love needs. The preadolescent looks to develop specific relationships in *addition* to developing a sense of belonging to a group or groups. When looking at a child's needs from a developmental perspective, the importance of school as an agency that could meet certain basic needs, including love, becomes apparent. Learning to respond to the basic needs including love comes from individuals within groups (church, school, social groups like Girl Scouts, sport teams). So, preadolescents are looking to authority figures to provide a sense of loving…a basic caring for the child as a person. Over age 11, adolescents and adults separate their own need for loving individuals from their family needs to love and belong. Unfortunately, learning to communicate "love" to a student is typically not part of a teacher education program.

Communicating to a student that a teacher cares, that the other students care, and that the environment is caring seems to be natural for some teachers, but foreign to other teachers. In other words, education personnel often see teachers as naturally "warm and caring" and as "teachers of content." If a teacher is not *naturally* warm and caring, then the need to provide the teacher with ways to communicate such respect becomes paramount.

Since caring for someone is part of a value system and since public schools are shy to "teach" values, then teaching teachers to "value" students, that is to respect them for who they are, is typically ignored. Unless a teacher is committing gross intolerance to student needs, then this issue is not part of the teacher evaluation process. But, learning to communicate care for someone else is learning to use interpersonal forms of positive communication (Chapter Six provides examples and an explanation of what the language of respect sounds like when it flows and validates students). *Interpersonal forms of communication flow out of the values of the person communicating.* Barriers to caring forms of interpersonal communication include bigotry, opposite values, and a lack of education about communication.

All people have biases or beliefs about who they are, what they believe, and who other people are. Only when these biases are used to discriminate against another person's rights do the biases or prejudices become bigoted. For example, a person might believe that his style of clothing is best for him. But, when that person pokes fun at someone's clothes, then the values show bigotry in the actions. Or, for example, one person might like science class the best. But, when that person says, "All people should like science class the best," then that person is bigoted about science classes. These bigoted verbal actions represent a form of discrimination against another person. The child who doesn't have clean clothes or the child who hasn't learned that science classes can sometimes be fun may be the target of a teacher's bigotry. It is important for teachers to use individual differences in choice of clothing, hair style, shoes, foods, sports, music, movies, and course subject preferences, etc., to show how we can care for all people whatever their differences might be. It only takes one "positive" whole class description to set up examples to show that individual differences are valued.

Educators and parents need to explore within themselves to determine what bigotry lies at the heart of their own actions. Being aware of bigoted actions, allows the parent or educator to decide or make a choice about the action. For example, both authors believe that education is valuable, but we try to treat all people, educated or not, the way we would like to be treated. Both authors usually dress in a professional, conservative manner because we believe that is the image that is most accepting by society. However, many of our students have found that clothing is one way to get attention. For example, a shaved head on a seventh grade female with 1960's "flower child" clothes on does stand out. Both authors have had personal talks with individual students as well as group discussions to help the students decide why they wear certain clothing. For example, "What image do you want to convey when you are presenting to your classmates, to the parents, or to the dinner guests?" The authors are aware of societal values about clothes and try to help students feel comfortable with themselves so that they convey the image that will match their goals in a society that assigns meaning to the way a person dresses. However, both authors are bigoted about certain dress. Exposing any part of the body typically covered by a shirt and shorts is not acceptable in school because of our personal value systems. Some of the situation comedies on TV represent a set of values that are bigoted about certain ideas, people, issues, values. The authors do not value some of these bigoted values so the authors involve the students who attend to these shows, etc., to help decide why tee-shirts or other clothing that sport those shows are not worn in the authors' classrooms. Likewise, school districts have put into place rules for "no gang clothing" marking individual's belief systems that do not represent societal values. Lengthy discussions are needed to assist students in matching their actions with their beliefs or values and possible reactions and interpretations by the general public.

Bigotry can be hidden and extremely hurtful to students' growth and learning. For example, there are numerous gender articles in the research literature that suggest how students are discriminated against by different teachers at different times. Most teachers are not aware that they are showing any preference for boys or girls, for clean or neat dressers, for children with better hygiene, etc. One of the authors recently received an e-mail about a child who was not at age level academically in a private school. The teacher decided to try to get the parents to remove the child, after all, she "had 18 other students to consider." The e-mail expressed pity for the child's drooling, slow movements, etc. After all, he had a terminal illness. The parents begged the teacher not to move the child because he liked being at that private school. The teacher agreed but she tried to "ignore" him and his needs. Ignoring a child means she didn't really accept him. However, it should be noted that ignoring a human being often takes more energy than spending time to get to know the other's gifts. One day, the child said, "I love you Ms. Shannon" in front of the other students. He was taking care of the teacher's emotional needs...he was parenting the teacher who could only feel pity for this child who needed to be with "his kind." The teacher still did not realize that she had not accepted him for who he was and for his gifts. And, she missed a giant teachable moment about "love" and the importance of it to us all. It wasn't until a spring activity when the child showed his understanding of how religion ties into Easter and the teacher realized that the child had gifts...he had some knowledge! Most of the faculty who shared their reactions to this e-mail were able to relate to the religious meaning the child had shared. In other words, most faculty were touched by this e-mail that showed that even this "pitiful" child had gifts. These authors were personally saddened by the content of the e-mail and by the reaction of most recipients. Few recipients noticed that the teacher's words showed a lack of caring for the child. The child's gifts were always there and he, if accepted, always belonged. He was looking for the same *respect* in having his needs met as the other students did. The teacher did not know how to reach him so she could not let him belong. She could not assign positive meaning to him or his needs. In fact, she would rather have had him go away and not even be a part of her classroom. In fact, in the e-mail, the teacher acknowledges that the classmates giggled when he shared his feelings for the teacher. Feelings and expressions from the soul are never funny! They are part of the person's who and being able to express them is important. The teacher did not realize that she was modeling and encouraging discrimination by her own tolerance of the giggles (she needed a class discussion about how to treat each other). The teacher didn't even realize that there was any problem with the giggles. She had *respect* only for his ability to produce knowledge about Easter. She did not show *respect* for the child's person even though the authors are sure she meant well. She was bigoted about the child's looks (slow and drooling), his language (slow), his level of production (several years behind the other students). Her bigotry stemmed from a lack of ignorance about how to assign positive meaning to *all* students so as to include all students. Her bigotry probably also relates to how she expects students to be "like her" in class. *Bigotry slows down the energy in a room and steals from the positive tone of acceptance. Communicating needs is difficult when the listeners can not hear the expression of personal needs as positive. All students have gems to offer and each teacher has a virtual diamond mind.*

Nine "learning disabled" college students sitting on a panel so local educators could learn about these individuals' ways to learn, expressed that "not one of [their] teachers cared." These individuals had not discussed this issue with anyone else. They were surprised that all of their learning disabled peers felt the same "lack of caring" by their teachers. When questioned about why they said their teachers didn't care, the individuals spoke very kindly and warmly about how the teachers were too busy and how the teachers worked very hard to meet their needs, but couldn't.

The college students expressed empathy for their elementary and high school teachers. Six of the nine college students are now very successful master teachers. They learned to value and respect education, but they did not feel their teachers' caring. When asked if the teachers *respected* them, they unanimously said "no." Here is the type of added information they gave..., "How could a teacher *respect* a child who is obnoxious. I was obnoxious. My teachers said I was obnoxious. I was always talking out. I couldn't do spelling even though I tried really hard. I couldn't hear what the teacher said even though I had normal hearing (see Chapter Two about the learner). I was called 'slow,' 'loud mouth,' and I was told I should go home and stay home. I was the class clown because I couldn't pronounce words right. Some of my teachers would call on me to pronounce something so that all of the class could laugh. Some teachers felt pity for me and said I was stupid and couldn't help it. All of my teachers would tell my parents I wasn't trying hard enough. So, I would work really hard and then be in trouble for asking too many questions. I had no friends...." When asked why the teachers called this person "obnoxious," she said that she "really didn't know." She wanted so badly to do well because her parents were educated and her father was "brilliant," but she didn't know what to do to be successful so as to be included. She was just looking for her basic needs to be met. She was looking for the teachers' caring words, the classmates help, and the right to be loved like all of the other students. The behaviors could have been assigned positive meaning so that she would have been seen as a curious, interested, kind person who had lots of energy and who learned differently than the teachers learned. Unfortunately, her needs were communicated through behaviors that the teachers assigned negative meaning..., "an obnoxious, loud mouth, who couldn't spell."

When students are not able to do what other students are able to do, these students *are communicating*. They are saying nonverbally, "I am a human like all the other students. I want to fit and to belong. I want to have my needs met. I want to be loved like the other students. Please help me to be successful." As the students reach middle school and high school, they will have formed their personal beliefs, about whether they are lovable, whether they are stupid or obnoxious, whether they are able to fit into the group, etc. *It is the adult's responsibility, as a parent or educator, to provide the student with the love they deserve and the respect of who they are.* There is no room for bigotry based on who the child is---whether it is for race, religion, sexual orientation, gender, or "ability" to do what the teacher or parent wants. There are resources available to help teachers and parents help students. *Accept nothing less than the* **Right for Each Student to Participate in an Environment of Communicative Thoughtfulness (RESPECT***).*

To communicate needs means that the adults or teachers have roles to play in the development of the **language of RESPECT.** The basic principles are as follows.

- *Empathize with the student as a human.*
- *Assume that all students have gifts.*
- *Assign positive meaning to any behavior and you give gifts to the child* (see Chapter Six).
- *Treat the child in the way that honors the child's needs, not necessarily the way that you were treated as a child.*

Name calling and any other label or devaluation is bullying. Bullying by teachers and peers is not acceptable...it does not respect the child's "who." Values or beliefs that result in bigoted actions are not acceptable ways to treat a child. These actions lack *respect* for the child, the school as an important value, and the family. *Communication must be positive and affirming for all parties to exist in a structure that respects the individual as well as the group.*

In summary, communicating that the teacher cares helps the student learn that the student is a competent learner, a competent person, and a competent citizen. When a child's needs are met, then the child begins to learn how to learn. To acknowledge a skill, a pretty picture, a nice act or a kind deed is a *powerful* way to say "I love you." The one act of recognition may be the key that opens other doors of opportunity for a student to gain access to priceless treasures waiting to be shared and enjoyed. In reality, *it is the responsibility of the respectful parent, teacher, or specialist to seek, identify, and convey the positive attributes of each student and child. The size of a true champion's heart may be the willingness of that grand champion to stoop down and help a child enjoy his or her right to be treated with dignity, respect, love, thoughtfulness, and compassion.*

Activity

1. **Explain the life long lesson of "communicating needs."**
2. **Give examples of barriers that interfere with hearing communicated needs. Be sure to discuss bigotry.**

Learning How to Learn

Communicating with a student about learning is also a gift that works two ways. The student is learning that he or she will always be a successful learner and the educator learns something valuable about the student. Group discussions about learning (see Chapter Two) as well as *individual one-on-one discussions about how to meet "personal best goals" based on a child's particular way to process mental symbols is empowering.* These types of conversations help all parties learn about each other as humans.

Conversations, about how to learn and how to achieve goals, use language that weaves the social and cognitive aspects of learning together. The human language system uniquely functions to merge the human brain to the mind in these situations. Through the use of language, the students and teachers acquire a respect for individual differences while also learning how to learn academically. These discussions lend themselves to unique findings. For example, one student might write the story in her head before she starts to put anything on paper while another student outlines the story on paper before he begins to write. Understanding each other's differences opens the discussion to each other's strengths. Charlie draws beautifully because he can mentally make any situation a two dimensional picture allowing for clean lines to draw, but Leann can't see any pictures in her mind. Judy learns Romance languages (French, Latin, Spanish, etc.) quickly because she can hear the spoken sounds simultaneously matched to the mental sound language, but Kara can't learn foreign languages from reading letters and sounds on a page. Charlie and Leann have different ways to use mental language (see Chapter Two) and therefore different strengths, but they both still have the same basic needs as well as classroom product expectations. Judy and Kara also have different ways to learn and they both want to be successful at taking a foreign language.

Because these students' learning strengths are different, a *classroom based on* **respect** *honors these individuals for their strengths and differences.* Therefore, honoring these students would mean to accept their differences with thoughtful consideration. If they were treated as similar in strength, then a teacher might ask all students to draw like Charlie. But to be like Charlie would be a verbal put down of Leann. Honoring both students would mean to recognize Charlie for his drawing as an expertise, but also at some time honor Leann for her language skills. Leann can also draw but she uses mental spoken language to make her hand do the drawing. The e-mail child (previously described in this chapter) who walked slowly and drooled could have been honored for his humor, his endurance, his strength to work so hard, his ability to show caring values toward the teacher, so forth. Personal strengths are just as valuable, if not more so, than the acknowledgment of skills.

Knowing the strengths of each student adds power to the students themselves, the class as a whole, and certainly the teacher who must orchestrate various activities such as teaching and learning from different levels. Honoring students is basically reporting what already exists! There is no research required, no complex decisions needed, and even more, it is simply the reporting of some wonderful people doing some very nice things. The simple planting of an acorn can produce a mighty oak tree!

If strengths are used for both Kara and Judy who want to learn French, they will need the opportunity to learn the language in different ways. Kara will learn the language by hearing it spoken and then mentally matching the patterns to her English written language whereas Judy will learn the language in most any way it's presented. However, Kara may end up with a better acoustic match to the sounds and therefore better pronunciation. For these students to adjust to the way material is presented, they need to learn how to learn. Most learners don't know how they learn best. They may know how they typically work or study, but that may not refer to how they learn best. For example, Kara takes her French book home every night and tries to study the words in the book. She does not know how the printed "words" sound, based on what the words look like on the page. So, even when she studies, she cannot answer the teacher's spoken French questions the next day. She thinks she learns by seeing the words, but she doesn't have the mental language for the words. In English, she studies off the page, but she creates visual mental pictures when she looks at the English words. These pictures are her language system. She does not have the French learned so as to make mental pictures. So, for her to learn how to learn French, she needs to have access to the tapes that go with the book. If she knows how she really learns language, then she could adjust the way she studies.

To promote students' learning means to recognize more than the cognitive academic skills, but also the social, personal strengths of how students learn. The student who is quiet is learning. The student who is drooling is learning. *Learning is a neurobiological status of being alive. If the student is alive, the student is learning. Assigning meaning to any behavior is a way that communicates caring and, therefore, assigning meaning to what a child does also values learning.* Through this process the child acquires knowledge about learning how to learn. Discussions about the differences in learning also help the student understand how unique he or she is. For example, a second grader is sitting under her desk. She believes she cannot write but the class members are supposed to be "writing." The teacher proudly informs one of the authors that the girl isn't able to do "anything" and that the girl be tested for learning problems. The teacher walks away and one of the authors starts to work with a child who asked for help spelling a word. "Frank, I don't know how to spell 'popcorn,' but it looks like this." The author wrote the word on the page for Frank. The little girl under her desk immediately popped out and looked at the word. "Elise, do you want to write this idea, 'popcorn'?" Elise says, "I don't know how to write." "Okay, Elise. Let's see if we can just put down our ideas on the paper. What was the story about?" Elise immediately began to rattle off the story. Her oral language told about how the class made popcorn. She was asked, "Elise, are you supposed to write that story on the paper?" She nodded. "So, where is your paper?" Elise pulled out her paper and an alphabetized teacher-made dictionary in which she was supposed to be writing new words.

By showing Elise that she could use her mental pictures to remember what words looked like and that she could write those pictured words on her paper, she quickly wrote a paragraph about "making popcorn." The regular classroom teacher was not impressed. Elise had not used her phonics to write the paragraph.

Does it really matter how Elise learns to write? Isn't the goal to have Elise's needs as a reader and writer met so that she is successful? Isn't success important to all learners? Failure does not allow students to learn how to learn. Only if the students are allowed to learn do they acquire the life long lesson of "learning to learn."

Elise learns best by seeing the ideas, not by saying the sounds of the letters to spell ideas. Her writing was grammatical and there were no spelling errors because she is able to see exactly what ideas look like as printed words in her mind. Such a learning process is not typically discovered by taking standardized or formalized tests. *Only by communicating with a student and listening to their needs can a person determine how a student learns best.*

Activity

1. **Explain the life long lesson of learning how to learn.**
2. **Describe how learning to learn is important to the "language of RESPECT."**

Resourceful and Knowledgeable

All humans need to feel competent as learners. To feel such competence, students also need to feel the caring or the love of the teacher for just "existing." The student then becomes resourceful about how to care for others. The student also becomes knowledgeable about more than just the lessons, content, and the skills of academia. But, this takes work! Work inside and outside! The inside work comes from the adults around the child. As previously described, the adult assigns the meaning to the child by having the adult's actions, words, and deeds match the adult's beliefs. For example, the teacher may say, "I know you can do math," but the child's actions or deeds do not match. The child has to be able to show the teacher he can do the math before the teacher can honorably say, "I know you can do math." The teacher may believe that with the right methods and resources that this child will learn to do math, but until the child's actions or behaviors match, the teacher's words are not kind or empathetic. *Kindness comes from not only feeling honest from within, but being honest from the child's viewpoint as well.*

Teachers need to know their feelings, beliefs, and values in order to recognize whether their actions and deeds match the student's needs. Matching such needs requires resources. *Not any one teacher, educator, or parent can be everything to any one child.* Therefore, the child must be given significant opportunities to internally believe that he or she is a competent person, is able to understand how to resource, and is able to relate to others and what they have to offer. From the teacher using **language of RESPECT** with the student, the student learns how to use **language of RESPECT**. By the student's verbal behavior matching with what adults expect, the student learns valuable life long lessons about resourcing and about being knowledgeable. For example, the teacher is leaving school for the day. School has been out for two hours. There are three boys on the black top surface playing with a glass bottle. Since glass bottles are not allowed at school, these boys have brought the bottle to the school grounds. The school grounds are used like a neighborhood park where parents bring preschool children to play on the small equipment while older students gather to meet friends and shoot a few hoops. The teacher sees the boys and continues to walk across the street and climb in her car. On the way home, she thinks about how these boys are not being adequately parented. She believes that "if their parents were positive influences, the boys would not have the glass bottle on the playground." Her viewpoint is valid. But, where are the parents? And, where is the teacher? Why doesn't she stop to use language to explain to the boys where they need to put the bottle and why it is not safe to play with it on a hard surface? Why doesn't she explain about the little ones who would be cut by broken glass and how they would cry and be afraid to come and play? Why doesn't she explain how some people like to shoot baskets and they might fall on the broken glass, if the bottle were to be broken, etc.? Why doesn't this teacher take responsibility for who she is?

This teacher does not take the time to make her beliefs match with her actions. If she made her actions match to what she knows and believes about broken bottles on the playground, the students would learn a valuable lesson that others care enough to stop and talk. If positive meaning were assigned, these boys might become resources for other students who bring bottles as they would have the knowledge. The actual situation happened like this. The teacher stopped because she was working at personally making her beliefs and behaviors match. She did not know the boys and it wasn't even her school. She even thought the boys might hurt her but she stopped anyway. The boys asked her if she was going to drive off. She said, "No. I will stay and help." The boys and the off-duty teacher spent 45 minutes picking up bottles, broken glass, etc. She then sent them a thank you note in care of their school principal. The boys were treated like "philanthropists." Their names were announced in the school news. Parents and teachers went out of their way to thank them. The teacher deliberately drove by the school for a week. At the end of the week, she saw the same boys on their bicycles. They shared their stories and asked her if she wanted to "play" at the school again. She did meet with them one more time to clean the grounds. This time they had help from some friends and she encouraged them to start a "clean up club." These boys were learning to be knowledgeable and to resource from others. They were also learning how such knowledge helps them make better decisions about the needs of others. These boys were learning life long lessons about empathy. Specifically they were learning about how others used the playground and how their actions affected these other people. They were learning to walk in others' shoes.

It should be noted that empathy is the ability to walk in another person's shoes, it is not pity. With pity, the person feels sorry for the individual, but sees so resolution. **In empathy, the person attempts to understand how their fellow human being is feeling and then becomes part of the solution.** The **language of RESPECT** provides students and adults opportunities to allow for empathy. By walking in the shoes of another person, the student learns to take another person's perspective. In this way, student differences are honored and life long lessons about being competent as a learner in relationship to other learners are acquired. The child grows up believing in being able to *resource for knowledge*. Therefore, the child never needs to have all of the information, all the right answers, or all the knowledge. The child understands that as a competent being, he or she can walk in another person's shoes. *In this way, the students are able to give to their community…they are sources of gifts for others.*

Activity

1. **Define resourceful and give examples.**
2. **Define knowledgeable and give examples.**

Responsive Language

Classroom activities and methods work in tandem along with the teacher's personal value system represented through **the language of RESPECT.** *This creates a match between the teacher's external assignment of positive meaning and the students' behaviors.* The teacher's values for **RESPECT** interact between the methods and the activities through language that assigns meaning to the student. *The teacher's ability to set up a classroom based on* **RESPECT** *cannot be taught.* But, the teacher can learn significant knowledge to create a classroom environment of "respect."

Once the teacher sets up the opportunity to assign meaning to the students, then the students' responses create energy that interacts among the methods and activities. How effective the teacher is at establishing the positive values of "respect" will determine how effective the classroom functions. The teacher's knowledge about **RESPECT**, the teacher's values of "respect," and the teacher's ability to assign positive meaning to respectful behavior function together. The teacher uses all of his or her knowledge as a way to align the students' needs with the teacher's beliefs and values.

This delicate balance between student responses to the teacher, and the teacher's responses to the students creates a tension. The teacher guides and coaches, but the student initiates and follows. The teacher encourages and promotes, but the student develops and learns. The teacher is behind the students. Students gradually take command. The classroom members shift the responsiveness to the teacher as the teacher fosters better social and cognitive student learning.

The learner's skills and knowledge come from the teacher's understanding of how personal values interact with the techniques and the methods. Once the teacher is able to assign positive meaning to all students' personal needs from an empathetic viewpoint, the classroom of **RESPECT** comes to life. Cognitive development or learning becomes the product of the interpersonal process between teacher and student. Such an experience for a student lasts a lifetime. Both authors are amazed at the number of times adults walk up to them in public to thank them for their life long lessons...not about just being a great teacher about how much they learned about themselves personally which paid off in later years. *There isn't a greater compliment in teaching than to know you have offered the opportunity for another human being to develop as a person.*

As students change in their personal values so do their behaviors. They become citizens in that they have learned to fit their behavior into what society expects while also being able to feel competent as unique individuals. The balance between being valued as an individual while being *responsive* to others' needs is a key to understanding the paradigm shift in society from an authoritarian communication style (individual needs are based on others' needs) to a more authoritative communication style. The **language of RESPECT** then moves into the community and becomes a more natural way to honor individual differences. Changes that occur at home and in school ripple into the community. *Responsive language is then valued and expected.* Listen to the differences in the following examples. All of these examples are from actual situations.

An angry middle school student who is experiencing academic difficulties raises his right hand in a fist at another boy. A teacher rushes over to his side and gets into the boy's face saying, "Do you want to kill him?" The boy is puzzled. Such mental pictures of killing another boy have never come to the student's mind. The teacher has now put those mental pictures of killing the boy into his head. What does the teacher believe? If the teacher does not believe in violence, then her *language* needs to be of *respect*. Her verbal behavior needs to match her beliefs.

She could have gone over to the boy and asked him what the fist meant and then followed up on his anger by having him draw and write out his needs. If she couldn't follow through, then she could have sent him to someone else to assign positive meaning and to redirect the anger into something more socially acceptable. *Resourcing is crucial to being responsive.*

Although community businesses proudly support all sorts of educational activities, sometimes the merchants use language that gives a different message to learners. For example, as young students eagerly shop for "back-to-school" clothes and supplies, merchants readily express regret at "having to go back to school." They might say, "So, you have to go back to school. Too bad!" "I bet you wish you didn't have to go back to school." "So, it's time for school again…bummer!" Or, if a student has to miss school for an appointment, professionals say, "You got out of school this morning! I bet you liked that!" These are the same merchants and professionals whose education has helped them have their life long careers. Why couldn't these same people value education by using language of respect? "Well, I see you are getting ready for school. You will always be prepared that way. I am impressed!" "I am sorry you had to miss school. I am a medical doctor today because I attended a lot of school. I will hurry so you can get back to school." So, why do these merchants and professionals typically not use this type of positive language of respect? Because most people in the US do not value education as part of character development. Most citizens view education as something that has to be "done" to meet requirements (certifications, diplomas, etc.) set by others. In other countries such as China or Taiwan, educators are highly respected. In Taiwan, on Confucius' birthday, the business community gives educators gifts.

The mixed message between the view that society values education, but that education doesn't promote the person, is difficult to overcome. A shift in paradigm from responding to others' demands to being responsive takes time. Responding to others' demands is authoritarian in nature. "I do what I have to do because I am told what to do. I then expect to be told, so I take no initiative unless told." This authoritarian message acts as a barrier to taking initiative and to being responsive. Being responsive means to accept responsibility to one's own behavior as well as to one's roles as an adult in society. For example, how often do we see children engaged in play that could be harmful to them or could destroy someone else's property such as furniture at a restaurant? The child's guardians say nothing about the behavior and the other observers of this behavior say nothing. In order to be responsive, one's actions and beliefs must match—the adults' behaviors must model what is responsible. Furthermore, the adults must assign meaning to what is socially acceptable. For example, it is not okay for the preschooler to stand on the benches at a fast food restaurant. The child's shoes are getting the seat dirty and someone else might want to sit down. The child's feet could slip and the child will fall and hurt himself. Or, the appropriate behavior of sitting on one's bottom so as to communicate with others at the table in a face-to-face manner could be shared. *Responsive behavior means to be responsible and open to the communication of language that respects individual differences. Being responsive also means to be willing to initiate behavior that explains and describes appropriate social behavior for others with fewer skills.*

When individual parents and teachers change the message of their homes and classrooms to one of **RESPECT, then verbal and nonverbal language also changes.** Individuals are valued for their character and their personal development is responsive to the energy of an environment that respects individual differences in learning and in self-constituents. As these individuals grow up to become merchants and professionals, their actions and behavior match their beliefs because they respect the validity of others' views, beliefs, interests, desires, and passions. Their value in education shifts from a repository of children who are controlled through taught content to a pseudo-family that uses the **language of RESPECT,** so that there exists *the Right of Each Student to Participate in an Environment of Communicative Thoughtfulness.* Schools and homes become valued for institutions that provide life-long learning about how to be a source of energy or a giver as well as how to be part of the group so as to feel the fit.

Summary

The *Right of Each Student to Participate in an Environment of Communicative Thoughtfulness or* **RESPECT** through the **language of RESPECT** is the product of a dynamic process of turning a classroom into a *responsive pseudo-family.* The class provides the basic needs as well as emotional needs of becoming a whole person who functions as a citizen.

Creating an atmosphere that is *energetic* and *communicative* through empathetic and *thoughtful actions,* matched to values and beliefs, creates the *responsive* classroom. This is the kind of classroom that superintendents show up unannounced to observe and where there are more parent and adult helpers than needed. This is the kind of classroom that reaches into the community offering a connection between school and citizenship. This is the kind of classroom described as "unconventional" on teacher evaluations, but parents go to school boards begging for their sons and daughters to have the same teacher for another year, etc. This type of classroom *feels* good to observe. Even observers feel a sense of belonging, a desire to return again and again. The actions in this type of classroom fit the beliefs of US culture: All students have the right to learn; no student's learning shall be restricted (see NEA code of ethics); and all students are society's future. This classroom promotes the value that all students are the sons and daughters and the mothers and fathers of someone loved. The authors challenge the reader to be that someone, to be the caring adult for all students...to be more than a teacher...to be a family support system for learners. Then, as educators, we can say we make a difference, we are valuable, and we are contributing members to society. We do something humanly *unique* that computers, TV, and other equipment can't do. The last scenarios (Scenario One and Two) are about Mr. Smith, the teacher who was introduced in Chapter One. He is teaching in different settings, with different students, but the language is the same. His **language of**

RESPECT assigns positive meaning to all learners and sets the context for all learners to be *responsive* citizens. Again, these are true situations!

Scenario One

A first-year-teacher stands before an inner city classroom of 14 to 16 year-old teens. He is prepared to teach, to plan lessons, to know the curriculum, and to care for his students. Teaching jobs are easy to find here because the students do not *respect* the classroom or the teacher. The year is 1973. The students are from a "different part of town" as they are dressed with chains, unconventional hairdos, gang clothes, leather jackets, and the facial attitude that "school is not for them." Most of the students do not talk as they are greeted. Language usage is minimal. The teacher greets the class with a friendly opener, "Hello, my name is Mr. Smith" and he turns to write his name on the blackboard. As he finishes writing the last letter, a shot rings out. A starter's pistol fires as two students wrestle for its possession. Knees shaking and fears of dying, being terrorized, and losing his job race through this teacher's head. But, he remembers his martial arts training about how the attacker earns *"respect"* by giving the attacker the right to "correct" the setting. So, he turns around and calmly looks in the eyes of each of these students and "asks" for their weapons. He quickly assigns meaning to one student, Jefferson. "I see you are alert and ready. Good! So, please use the wastebasket to collect all guns, knives, steel knuckles, chains, and anything else used as a weapon." As the basket is filled, the teacher passes around any other containers he can find, looking at each student with an affirming look of "I know you and I care." After the containers are full, he thanks them warmly for contributing to the success of the activity. He reminds them that the principal will hold their weapons until parent meetings can be set up. He encourages them to leave their weapons at home, outside his classroom and away from school. He begins a classroom using language based on **RESPECT**: *the Right of Each Student to Participate in an Environment of Communicative Thoughtfulness*. By the end of the year, the gangs had drastically reduced their activities at this school. These at-risk students became involved in the curriculum, learning was generated from these students, and they were meeting academic standards. They often wanted more time to talk, chat, and engage socially with the teacher during lunch, before school, and even after school. In fact, for many students, it was a privilege to spend time with Mr. Smith as he would cook them lunch, teach them to cook, etc.

Activity

1. **Give five examples of the "language of RESPECT."**
2. **Explain how Mr. Smith used "language of RESPECT" to handle a potentially harmful situation.**

Scenario Two

The year is 1994. The classroom is in an "included" urban model summer project. The same teacher is starting the first day of class for 28 students ranging in age from 7 to 11 years of age. The class is quite diverse. Over 40% have identified special needs issues with Individualized Educational Plans. Some students during the regular academic year are in programs for bilingual students or for non-readers, but are not identified for special education. At least two students are later identified as Talented and Gifted. Two parents report that their children have Attention Deficit Disorder...one of these two children is on Ritalin and one is not. And, there is one student, Mr. Clark who is age 11, communicating with only sensory-motor squeals.

Mr. Smith comfortably greets the students at the classroom door. He warmly invites ALL parents, guardians, and family members to stay or to come and visit at any time. He encourages students to find their own seats and to begin to write a nameplate with sir names (Mr. Little, Miss McDonald, Mr. James, Miss Santos, etc.) on folded 4 X 6 file cards. He monitors and shows those who can't write how to write. As the bell rings, he walks to the board to write his name. Mr. Clark begins a self-stimulating action with his hands and high-pitched squeals. Mr. Smith calmly says, "I see that Mr. Clark wants some help so Miss Shaley (local university volunteer) would you please see if you can help Mr. Clark." By the end of the day the students have calmly sat through hours of high pitched loud screams. Mr. Smith quietly thanks the class members for their patience and their desire to help Mr. Clark. He explains that we all learn a bit differently and that we all need support. He asks the class members, "How can we support each other" and the hands dance wildly. The students feel empowered with the *respect* that the teacher might not know everything and that the students have ideas that are useful, effective, and responsible. By the second day, the university volunteer along with Mr. Smith and an outside resource person set up a communication system for Mr. Clark that empowers his learning beyond the sensory motor level of being cortically deaf and blind. By the third week, individual students are observed working closely with Mr. Clark on the computer to assist him in learning. Mr. Clark is beginning to work in the large group as well as small groups and his behavior is more appropriate. The class is on its way to using language to **RESPECT all learners,** to create *the Right of Each Student to Participate in an Environment of Communicative Thoughtfulness.*

Activity

1. **Explain how Mr. Smith demonstrates the use of language to create an atmosphere of RESPECT.**
2. **Define the acronym "RESPECT."**

REFERENCES

American Heritage Dictionary. 1983. Boston, MA: Houghton-Mifflin.

LaVergne, TN USA
09 February 2010
172466LV00004B/74/A